D1644165

KA 0227807 3

ENGLISH RENAISSANCE STUDIES

DAME HELEN GARDNER

ENGLISH RENAISSANCE STUDIES

Presented to
Dame Helen Gardner
in honour of her
Seventieth Birthday

OXFORD
AT THE CLARENDON PRESS
1980

Oxford University Press, Walton Street, Oxford OX2 6DP

OXFORD LONDON GLASGOW
NEW YORK TORONTO MELBOURNE WELLINGTON
KUALA LUMPUR SINGAPORE HONG KONG TOKYO
DELHI BOMBAY CALCUTTA MADRAS KARACHI
NAIROBI DAR ES SALAAM CAPE TOWN

Published in the United States
by Oxford University Press, New York

British Library Cataloguing in Publication Data

English Renaissance studies presented to
Dame Helen Gardner in honour of her
seventieth birthday
1. English literature—Early Modern,
1500–1700—History and criticism—Addresses,
essays, lectures
I. Carey, John II. Gardner, *Dame* Helen *b. 1908*
820'.9'003 PR423 79–40839
ISBN 0–19–812093–1

Printed in Great Britain
at the University Press, Oxford
by Eric Buckley
Printer to the University

Preface

IT is a measure of the range of Dame Helen Gardner's learning that no single collection of tributes could match it without appearing wholly miscellaneous. To forestall this eventuality, it was decided to restrict the topics treated in the present volume to English literature of the late sixteenth and seventeenth centuries. One regrettable result of this is that no proper recognition can be made in these pages of Dame Helen's work on T. S. Eliot, culminating in her recently published *The Composition of 'Four Quartets'*, which has transformed a major area of Eliot scholarship almost as radically as her edition of the *Divine Poems* transformed the study of Donne.

Indeed, the gathering together of scholarly essays, upon whatever subject, is in a sense too parochial a gesture to suit the occasion. For the notion that literature is written merely for scholars is one that Dame Helen has been at pains, throughout her career, to scout, and by means of such anthologies as *The Faber Book of Religious Verse* and *The New Oxford Book of English Verse* she has enriched the lives of thousands of readers quite untainted by academicism.

Yet scholars are only human, and it is natural that those who have worked with and learned from Dame Helen should wish to accord her such honour as they are best qualified to pay. Inevitably, friends and colleagues eager to join in this birthday tribute were far more numerous than could be accommodated within its covers, and the selected contributors must be regarded as no more than a sample of a far larger and equally appreciative band.

The essays which follow are drawn from three continents, they span drama, poetry, and prose, and they exhibit a wide variety of skills, approaching Renaissance literature by way of history, biography, textual scholarship, music, iconography, science, and the visual arts, as well as criticism, and the criticism of criticism. Accordingly they will give some inkling, it is hoped, both of Dame Helen's versatility and of the international esteem in which she is held. Though we offer them to her discriminating eye with due trepidation, we do so, also, with a full measure of affection and regard.

JOHN CAREY

Contents

Dame Helen Gardner *frontispiece*

Sidney and Titian 1
KATHERINE DUNCAN-JONES, *Somerville College, Oxford*

The Morality of Elizabethan Drama: Some Footnotes to Plato 12
HARRIETT HAWKINS, *Vassar College*

Repetition and Echo in Renaissance Poetry and Music 33
FREDERICK W. STERNFELD, *Exeter College, Oxford*

Two Dead Birds: A Note on *The Phoenix and Turtle* 44
JOHN BUXTON, *New College, Oxford*

Shakespeare at Work: The Foul Papers of *All's Well That Ends Well* 56
FREDSON BOWERS, *University of Virginia*

'Look There, Look There!' The Ending of *King Lear* 74
JOSEPH H. SUMMERS, *University of Rochester, New York*

Riddle and Emblem: A Study in the Dramatic Structure of *Cymbeline* 94
GLYNNE WICKHAM, *University of Bristol*

Shakespeare's Humanist Enterprise: *The Winter's Tale* 114
LOUIS MARTZ, *Yale University*

Shakespeare's Inner Stage 132
KATHLEEN M. LEA, *Lady Margaret Hall, Oxford*

The Date of a Donne Elegy, and its Implications 141
I. A. SHAPIRO, *The Shakespeare Institute, University of Birmingham*

Donne and Coins 151
JOHN CAREY, *Merton College, Oxford*

Angels and the Poetic Imagination from Donne to Traherne 164
ROBERT ELLRODT, *Université de Paris III, Sorbonne Nouvelle*

Burton and Cardan 180
J. B. BAMBOROUGH, *Linacre College, Oxford*

The Growth of Plants: A Seventeenth-Century Metaphor 194
ELIZABETH MACKENZIE, *Lady Margaret Hall, Oxford*

George Wither and John Milton 212
CHRISTOPHER HILL, *Balliol College, Oxford*

Lycidas, Daphnis, and Gallus 228
J. MARTIN EVANS, *Stanford University*

Milton's Admirer, Du Moulin of Nîmes 245
E. E. DUNCAN-JONES, *Cambridge University*

The End of the Big Names: Milton's Epic Catalogues 254
BARBARA EVERETT, *Somerville College, Oxford*

'Full of Doubt I Stand': The Final Implications of *Paradise Lost* 271
G. A. WILKES, *University of Sydney*

Dryden's Sigismonda 279
EMRYS JONES, *Magdalen College, Oxford*

A Select List of the Published Writings of Dame Helen Gardner 291
Compiled by HELEN PETERS, *Somerville College, Oxford*

Index 299

Sidney and Titian

KATHERINE DUNCAN-JONES

It was as Helen Gardner's research pupil that I began to study Sidney's use of emblematic and pictorial imagery; and I continue to owe much to her exactitude and warm patience.

What first excited my interest was the apparent paradox in Sidney's attitude to the secular paintings of the High Renaissance. Schizoid responses to Italian culture are common among the Elizabethans, who saw the Italians at once as monsters of ingenious depravity and as paragons of aesthetic taste, good manners, and creativity. In Sidney's case the contrast is most conspicuous. His letters from the Continent reveal indifference or even hostility to the splendours of Venice, for instance; and yet the *Defence of Poetry* and the *Arcadia*s display a richness of pictorial imagery which goes far beyond the literary traditions from which they spring, at many points suggesting a particular interest in mythological paintings, not to be seen in England at the time. In the present essay I hope to harmonize some of this apparently conflicting evidence by looking in particular at possible links between Sidney and Titian.

Undoubtedly it is disappointing that Sidney makes so few references to art and architecture during his three years of European travel, one of them spent largely in Italy. He had opportunities for aesthetic experience denied to the other major Elizabethan writers—Spenser, Marlowe, Shakespeare, Jonson, none of whom is known to have travelled beyond the Alps—and might appear to show little sign of benefiting from them. From his letters we would imagine that Sidney's only interest in painting was in its ability to furnish him with images of himself and his friends. He mentions the outward splendours of Venice only once, obliquely, when he assures his elderly mentor Languet of his joyful anticipation of a visit to Germany in the spring of 1574: 'At that time I shall see you, my dear Languet; and I shall take more delight in one conversation with you than in the magnificent magnificences of all those magnificoes.'[1] In a letter now lost he seems to have expanded at some length on what he disliked about Venice, provoking remonstrances from Languet, who admired the Venetian political system.[2] Although a letter of advice to his younger brother suggests that Sidney came eventually to concede that Venice was the one province in Italy whose government might be admired, he says that England's only trade with Italy can be 'to buye their scilkes and wynes'—conspicuously failing to mention their artefacts.[3] In his letter to Languet of 4 February 1574 he mentions Tintoretto and Veronese as the leading painters in Venice, but only in order to determine which master will best make a portrait of him for Languet to keep as a memento.[4] The only other artist mentioned anywhere in his works is the sculptor Antonio Abondio, retained by the Emperor Maximilian in Vienna, who specialized in portrait medals.[5] F. J. Levy transmits the received opinion among Sidney scholars in saying that he 'went to Veronese only to have his portrait painted, and showed no other interest in Venetian art'.[6] Yet critics from J. J. Jusserand to Michael Levey have observed the 'Titianesque' quality of many scenes in the *Arcadia*.[7] This seeming paradox can be partly dissolved by the possibility that it was in Vienna, rather than in Venice itself, that Sidney had most opportunities for sympathetic study of Venetian paintings. The city of Vienna clearly moved him greatly, especially during his second stay there, from August 1574 to January 1575. There he enjoyed the friendship and tutelage of Languet, the companionship of Edward Wotton, and the entrée into the Imperial Court of Maximilian II. This highly cultivated, comparatively informal, and remarkably tolerant court was clearly a congenial and richly rewarding environment for Sidney, in contrast to Venice, where he was in unsatisfactory lodgings and lacked such congenial society.[8] Two of Sidney's most explicitly intellectual

[1] J. M. Osborn, *Young Philip Sidney: 1572–77* (New Haven and London, 1972), p. 121.

[2] Osborn, op. cit., pp. 116–17.

[3] Sidney, *Prose Works*, ed. A. Feuillerat (Cambridge, 1962), iii. 127.

[4] Osborn, op. cit., p. 143.

[5] Ibid., pp. 101, 121, 135–6, and *passim*.

[6] F. J. Levy, 'Henry Peacham and the Art of Drawing', *J.W.C.I.* xxxvii (1974), 174.

[7] J. J. Jusserand, *The English Novel in the Time of Shakespeare* (1901), p. 244; Michael Levey, *The High Renaissance* (1975), p. 99.

[8] Osborn, op. cit., pp. 235 ff. On the courts of Maximilian and Rudolf, see R. J. W. Evans, *Rudolf II and his World* (Oxford, 1973).

works are associated with this stay: the *Defence of Poetry*, opening with his account of his time in the famous riding school, and the sustained political fable 'As I my little flock on Ister bank', which Philisides claims to have learned from the wise and kindly 'Lanquet' one August on the Danube.[9] Bearing in mind the determination of the Hapsburg Emperors to build up collections of paintings which would match those of their Spanish kinsman Philip (Sidney's godfather), it is possible that an appreciation of painting was one of the things Sidney gained in that fruitful stay, along with horsemanship and moral and political theory.

It is by no means surprising that Sidney did not mention Titian along with Tintoretto and Veronese in his letter to Languet. This concerned only the choice of a painter to portray him, and does not pretend to be a full discussion of the current state of painting in Venice. Even in the late 1560s, let alone 1570s, Titian painted very few portraits. His last ventures in the form seem to have been mainly self-portraits, such as his triple portrait of himself, his son, and a young kinsman, now in the National Gallery.[10] Although there seems to have been no truth in Niccolò Stoppio's statements in 1568–9 that Titian was too old to hold a brush, it is most unlikely that a young and by no means wealthy Englishman would consider commissioning a portrait from so august a master. Titian was at least eighty-four, possibly more, by the time Sidney was in Venice. Yet we need not rule out the possibility that Sidney saw him. Titian, and his palace on the Biri Grande, overlooking the lagoon and with a view of the Ceneda hills, was so prominent among the sights of Venice that Henri III, returning from his coronation as King of Poland, took an hour away from his reception in Venice to visit the old painter.[11] This was in June 1574, only five months after Sidney's first visit to Venice. Sidney was following the French king's movements with intense interest from Padua. Vasari describes Titian's house in later years as a place of constant resort for all the 'princes, men of letters and gentlemen who ever came to Venice'.[12] Though not a prince, Sidney

9 Sidney, *Poems*, ed. W. A. Ringler (Oxford, 1962), pp. 98–103, 412–15.

10 Harold E. Wethey, *The Paintings of Titian: Complete Edition* (1969–75), ii. 49–51, 145–6.

11 Ibid., i. 15–16; J. A. Crowe and G. B. Cavalcaselle, *The Life and Times of Titian* (1881), ii. 401.

12 Crowe and Cavalcaselle, op. cit., ii. 35–9.

was certainly a gentleman and a man of letters. Given such strong external testimony to Sidney's interest in painting as his conversation with Hilliard,[13] and Greville's catalogue of those to whom he was a 'generall Maecenas', which is headed by the 'cunning Painter',[14] it is easy to imagine that Sidney may have visited Titian's house as a tourist, even if not as a patron. Nor, if he did make such a visit, would it be at all surprising if he failed to allude to it. Sidney's correspondents, headed by Languet, were to a man earnest Protestant diplomats and scholars who would have been horrified to learn that the subject of their hopes had been stirred by imagery both Catholic and sensual. Letters at this date were not much used as a medium for aesthetic discussion. Poetry scarcely figures in Sidney's correspondence, either, though his commitment to it is not in doubt. But even if Sidney did not visit Titian's house, he can scarcely have avoided seeing many of his compositions, since the palaces not only of Venice, but of Catholic Europe in general, were filled with originals, studio copies, and imitations of Titian's work.

A single detail, in both versions of the *Arcadia*, establishes Sidney's knowledge of Titian's painting. Since it implies recognition on the part of the reader it may suggest also that the Countess of Pembroke was familiar with copies or engravings. In Book 2 of both versions of the *Arcadia* Pyrocles, disguised as an Amazon, visits the spot where he first saw his beloved Philoclea. He is pursued by the doting Basilius, who overhearing him singing the sonnet 'Loved I am, and yet complain of love', interprets this in his own favour. Whereas Pyrocles complains of being too much loved by Basilius and Gynecia, and too little by Philoclea, Basilius decides to turn the occasion to his own advantage: 'but then, loath to lose the precious fruit of time, he presented himself unto her, falling down upon both his knees, and holding up his hands, as the old governess of Danae is painted, when she suddenly saw the golden shower.'[15] Though the tone of this suggests an easily recognizable reference, the 'old governess' was in fact Titian's unique additon to the

[13] Nicholas Hilliard, 'The Art of Limning', *Walpole Society*, i (1911–12), 27.

[14] Fulke Greville, *Life of Sir Philip Sidney*, ed. N. Smith (1907), pp. 33–4.

[15] Sidney, *The Countess of Pembroke's Arcadia*, ed. J. Robertson (Oxford, 1973), p. 114.

theme of Danäe receiving the shower of gold—a detail derived only from a slight reference in Apollonius of Rhodes.[16] He made the innovation in his second version of the subject, painted for Philip of Spain in 1553–4. Sidney could not have seen the original of this in Madrid, but must have seen a copy. Possibly this version of 'Danäe' was among the seven Ovidian *poesie*, copies of which Titian offered to Maximilian in 1568; Sidney could then have seen it during his happy and fruitful time at the Imperial Court at Vienna.[17] Not only was the 'old governess' Titian's invention, but she is rejected by Tintoretto and Veronese in their versions of the subject. Tintoretto, though otherwise closely imitating Titian, gives Danäe a young and quite comely attendant; Veronese presents her alone. Without a knowledge of Titian's composition, Sidney's image might not be immediately understood. The reader might imagine the gesture of upraised hands to be one of amazement or supplication, rather than misdirected greed—the governess tries to divert some of the shower into her own lap, lifting up her apron.[18] The comparison of the foolishly lascivious duke to an avaricious crone is peculiarly appropriate to the early books of the *Arcadia*, where sex and social station are grotesquely confused by the princes' disguise.

Encouraged by this clear allusion to a pictorial invention of Titian's, we may turn to Sidney's most formal use of visual artefacts in the *New Arcadia*. The account of Kalander's 'dainty garden-house' almost comprises an ecphrasis. It opens with a curious image which certainly seems to belong to the world of Mannerist sculpture, though I know of no specific source for it:

> in one of the thickets was a fine fountaine made thus. A naked *Venus* of white marble, wherein the graver had used such cunning, that the naturall blew veines of the marble were framed in fitte places, to set foorth the beautifull veines of her bodye. At her brest she had her babe *Aeneas*, who seemed (having begun to sucke) to leave that, to looke upon her fayre eyes, which smiled at the babes follie, the meane while the breast running.[19]

[16] Wethey, op. cit., iii. 134.

[17] Ibid. 141; but cf. also p. 145, where it is suggested that the copy now in the Vienna Gallery did not leave Italy until 1600.

[18] A stock gesture of avarice; cf. *Timon of Athens*, IV. iii. 136–7, 'Hold up, you sluts/Your aprons mountant.'

[19] Sidney, *Prose Works*, ed. cit., i. 17–18.

There are many analogies in works probably known to Sidney for the use of natural veins or markings as part of the finished work of art,[20] but Venus suckling Aeneas does not seem to be at all a usual subject, either in literature or visual artefacts. Perhaps the invention here is Sidney's, signalling the extreme antiquity of his Greek setting. Once inside Kalander's gallery, 'a square roome full of delightful pictures, made by the most excellent workeman of Greece', we seem to enter a *camera* in a Renaissance palace: a room such as Alfonso d'Este's *studiolo* in the ducal palace at Ferrara, which contained a series of bacchanalian subjects by Titian, Bellini, and Dosso Dossi.[21] This was a room where a 'last Duchess' might well hang concealed; indeed, Alfonso II is thought to have been Browning's model.[22] In Kalander's room, as in the Duke's, mythological subjects precede the display of family portraits. Their implicit common theme is the destructive power of love. All the goddesses depicted brought their lovers to grief in humiliating ways, and there is probably a suggestion that Philoclea, whose portrait is described immediately after, will equally exercise disastrous power over Pyrocles:

> There was *Diana* when Actæon saw her bathing, in whose cheekes the painter had set such a colour, as was mixt between shame & disdaine: & one of her foolish Nymphes, who weeping, and withal lowring, one might see the workeman meant to set forth teares of anger. In another table was *Atalanta*; the posture of whose lims was so livelie expressed, that if the eyes were the only judges, as they be the onely seers, one would have sworne the very picture had runne. Besides many mo, as of *Helena, Omphale, Iole.*[23]

The first scene seems overwhelmingly reminiscent of Titian's painting of *Diana and Actæon*, originally painted for Philip of Spain, and now hanging in the National Gallery of Scotland. A copy of this was among the seven 'fables' offered to the Emperor Maximilian in 1568, so it may have been in Vienna that Sidney saw this, as well as the 'Danäe'. 'Shame and disdain' well describe Diana's mien, the lower part of her face

[20] Heliodorus, *An Aethiopian History*, trans. Underdowne, *Tudor Translations*, v (1895), 134–5; Sannazaro, *Arcadia*, ed. M. Scherillo (Turin, 1888), p. 250; Jorge de Montemayor *et al.*, *Diana*, trans. B. Yonge (1598), p. 218.

[21] Wethey, op. cit., iii. 29–30 and *passim*.

[22] R. A. King *et al.*, *The Complete Works of Robert Browning* (Ohio, 1971), iii. 371.

[23] Sidney, *Prose Works*, ed. cit., i. 18.

masked by her arm, her eyes downcast and angry. The nymph closest to Actæon has a strange open-mouthed expression which could well be described as 'weeping' and 'louring', hinting in her bleary eyes at 'teares of anger'. As the only figure confronting the spectator, this nymph at once attracts the eye. The scene is partly reflected in the bathing pool, which could provide a covert link with the previous passage in Sidney on the 'perfect mirrour' made by a fair pond in Kalander's garden. Apart from the (now lost) copy of Titian's painting which Sidney may have seen in Vienna, there are a good many copies extant now, including one formerly in Venice and one at Knole; and it is possible that the 'picture of Diana and Actæon' at Leicester House was after Titian.[24] This one would presumably have been known also to the Countess of Pembroke. Titian is not known to have painted Atalanta, Helen, Omphale, or Iole. A painter newly arrived in Vienna when Sidney was there, Bartholomaeus Spranger, did paint a *Hercules and Omphale* which corresponds very well with Sidney's fuller description of the subject in the *Defence of Poetry*:

as in Alexander's picture well set out we delight without laughter, and in twenty mad antics we laugh without delight; so in Hercules, painted with his great beard and furious countenance, spinning at Omphale's commandment, it breedeth both delight and laughter: for the representing of so strange a power in love procureth delight, and the scornfulness of the action stirreth laughter.[25]

Sidney's obsession with Hercules and his humiliation by his mistresses Omphale and Iole, whom he confused with each other, may perhaps have been stimulated by a sight of Spranger's very striking rendering of this subject, possibly when he returned to Vienna as ambassador to condole with the Emperor Rudolf in the spring of 1577. The picture's date is very uncertain, however.

Turning to the *Defence of Poetry*, we find two other pictorial themes which were rendered by Titian: Lucretia stabbing herself, and the Emperor Vespasian. The first is used by Sidney as

[24] Wethey, op. cit., iii. 138–41; W. J. Thoms, 'Pictures of the great Earl of Leicester', *N.Q.* 3rd series, vol. ii (1862), 201–2, 224–5.

[25] Sidney, *Miscellaneous Prose*, ed. K. Duncan-Jones and J. van Dorsten (Oxford, 1973), pp. 115–16. Spranger's painting is reproduced in Fransepp Würtenburger, *Mannerism* (1963), p. 41.

an example of the technique of the true artist, who depicts essential qualities, not physical particularities. He contrasts:

the meaner sort of painters, who counterfeit only such faces as are set before them, and the more excellent, who having no law but wit, bestow that upon you which is fittest for the eye to see: as the constant though lamenting look of Lucretia, when she punished in herself another's fault, wherein he painteth not Lucretia, whom he never saw, but painteth the outward beauty of such a virtue.[26]

Titian painted both Lucretia's rape and her suicide. His *Tarquin and Lucretia*, now in the Fitzwilliam, did not leave Spain until the early nineteenth century. But a close copy of his *Lucretia*, which shows a naked Lucrece shamefacedly veiling her eyes with a flying scarf as she points the dagger to her breast, hangs in Hampton Court. It was among the Mantuan pictures purchased by Charles I in 1626–7. It is not impossible that Sidney may have seen some other copy of this. Certainly it is an idealized rendering, indicating interest in the 'outward beauty' of Lucretia's act, rather than in fictitious portraiture. Indeed, Titian avoids attempting to portray 'Lucretia, whom he never saw', by almost completely veiling her face. Professor Wethey says that this configuration 'appears at first somewhat melodramatic, but on further consideration it impresses as a stroke of imagination on a high creative level'.[27] Lucretia's veiled face, like Danäe's greedy governess, seems to be an innovation distinctive to Titian, not taken up by his followers. Veronese's *Lucretia*, for instance, which could probably have been seen by Sidney in Vienna, though its date is not clear, comes over as a portrait of a distinctive and well-dressed Venetian lady, her face fully visible, making only the most perfunctory display of elegant self-destruction.[28] If there is an underlying suggestion in Sidney's account that the 'more excellent' painter might not presume to portray Lucretia's face at all, it would point fairly firmly to Titian's rendering. The other 'Titian' subject referred to in the *Defence* is a rather odd one, used to illustrate a point about historical veracity versus poetic didacticism: 'if the question were whether it were better to have a particular act truly or falsely set down, there is no

[26] Sidney, *Misc. Prose*, ed. cit., pp. 80–1.
[27] Wethey, op. cit., iii. 26–7, 166. [28] Cf. Levey, *High Renaissance*, p. 100.

doubt which is to be chosen, no more than whether you had rather have Vespasian's picture right as he was, or at the painter's pleasure, nothing resembling'.[29] It is difficult at first to see why Vespasian, noted for his low birth, avarice, and physical ugliness, should have been selected from among the twelve Caesars as Sidney's example. A clue to Sidney's choice may be found, perhaps, in the opening sentence of Suetonius's *Life of Vespasian* (here in Holland's version), on the origin of the Flavii: 'a house I must needs say, of obscure descent and not able to show any pedigree and images of auncestors to commend their race'[30]—in short, without any family portraits. Sidney's interest in the Roman identification of 'maiorum imagines' with established nobility is borne out in his *Defence of Leicester*, where he refers to the first Baron Dudley 'bringing, as the Romans term it, so noble an image into the house'.[31] Sidney may well have selected Vespasian as an Emperor whose accurate depiction one would like to see because he was in his own person an image-maker—a generator of nobility. Titian painted eleven of the twelve Caesars in 1536–7, for Federigo Gonzaga. The original series now survives only in Aegidius Sadeler's engravings. But when Sidney was on the Continent, there were plenty of painted versions about, including a set made by Bernardino Campi for Ferdinand I, on which Sadeler's engravings were based.[32] He could have seen these in Vienna. Professor Wethey comments on Titian's Vespasian (as it survives in Sadeler's version): 'Titian unmistakably felt the degeneracy and coarseness of the last four Emperors, all of whom are essentially repulsive. . . . The *Vespasian* shows a bald, fat and unsympathetic figure, as the antique portrait indicates, but Vespasian's prosperous reign endured (70–79 A.D.) and he did much to reconstruct Rome after devastation under Nero.'[33] It is quite possible that Sidney had in mind a favourable comparison between Titian's coarse but powerful Vespasian, carefully modelled on coins of his reign, and the rather softened and standardized sets of Emperors to be seen in many Elizabethan houses, such as Leicester's, which one suspects had a rather

29 Sidney, *Misc. Prose*, ed. cit., p. 88.

30 Suetonius, *History of Twelve Caesars*, trans. Philemon Holland, *Tudor Translations*, xxii (1899), ii. 203.

31 Sidney, *Misc. Prose*, ed. cit., p. 136.

32 Wethey, op. cit., iii. 43–7, 235–40.

33 Ibid., 46.

assembly-line quality. Titian's *Vespasian* is an image of 'true matters, such as indeed were done', and his *Lucretia* a picture of 'what may be and should be'.[34]

It is a striking coincidence that two of the pictorial examples used in the *Defence of Poetry* can be paralleled in the work of Titian. Speculation can be extended a little further, though it may be felt that we here approach the realms of 'salmons in both'. For instance, a covert literary link with Titian may exist through Sannazaro. Titian's friend Lodovico Dolce recorded that Titian alluded to Sannazaro in certain mythological pictures, a likely one being the early *Pastoral Concert*, now in the Louvre.[35] The setting, title, and literary form of Sidney's *Old Arcadia* also of course originate in Sannazaro's *Arcadia*. Like Titian, Sidney adds a visual dimension wanting in Sannazaro's pastoral. An analogue to Sidney's two Arcadian heroines, Pamela and Philoclea, is provided by Titian's never satisfactorily explained *Sacred and Profane Love*, in the Villa Borghese, Rome.[36] The dignified clothed figure, holding a lamp and looking upwards, would correspond with the stately Pamela, described by Sidney as well clothed in pleated russet, while the naked figure would match the near-naked nymph-like Philoclea, whose virtue, springing from natural innocence and ignorance, is more vulnerable. It is perhaps as difficult with Sidney's heroines as with Titian's figures to determine which is ultimately the more virtuous. In both cases the naked figure appears the more attractive and primal, and yet there are more explicit indications of virtuous knowledge in the clothed figure. One can at least say that Sidney's descriptions belong, like Titian's painting, to the larger tradition of Platonic debate about beauty and love which includes also Botticelli's *Birth of Venus*, Bembo's final speech in *Il Cortegiano*, and Spenser's *Fowre Hymnes*. Another common property used by both Titian and Sidney is the concept of art making a better nature, restoring imperfect matter to its original shapeliness. Titian's personal *impresa* was a she-bear licking her whelp into shape, with the motto *Natura potentior ars*.[37] With his strong interest in *imprese*—for instance, he offered a copy of Ruscelli's *Imprese Illustri* to Languet when he was in Venice in 1574—Sidney may well have

34 Sidney, *Misc. Prose*, ed. cit., pp. 87, 81.
35 Wethey, op. cit., iii. 12.
36 Ibid., 175–9.
37 Ibid., 249.

known Titian's device, printed in Dolce's *Imprese Nobili*, and felt its relevance to the aesthetic theory he was to set out in the *Defence of Poetry*.

The attention Sidney gave to the technicalities of painting, as well as to its ethical basis, can be shown by an extended image in the *New Arcadia*. Amphialus visits the imprisoned Philoclea, who has been separated from her lover Pyrocles:

> whome he found (because her chamber was over-lightsome) sitting of that side of her bedde, which was from the windowe; which did cast such a shadow upon her, as a good Painter would bestow uppon *Venus*, when under the trees she bewayled the murther of *Adonis*: her handes and fingers (as it were) indented one within the other: her shoulder leaning to her beds head, and over her head a scarfe, which did eclipse almost halfe her eyes, which under it fixed their beames upon the wall by, with so steddie a manner, as if in that place they might well change, but not mend their object.[38]

Sidney cannot have been thinking here of Titian's *Venus and Adonis*, though he may well have known about it,[39] since this represents Venus holding Adonis back from the chase. But the technique of suggesting melancholy abstraction by means of a partly veiled face, besides conforming with the conventions of melancholic portraiture, is one Titian quite often used, for instance in his *Lucretia*. The melodramatic effect of showing the main figure almost totally shadowed, together with the detailed attention given to posture, surely indicates (as do many other passages of visual description in the *Arcadias*) that Sidney did not, after all, have his eyes closed when he travelled in Europe. Such detailed attention to effects of chiaroscuro and composition is not to be found in the writing of Sidney's untravelled contemporaries, with the supreme exception of Shakespeare, whose use of pictorial conceits in the narrative poems is startlingly imaginative. The tradition of the reluctant Adonis developed by Shakespeare in *Venus and Adonis* originated with Titian: one longs to know whether he was aware of this.[40] Sidney's debt to Titian, though small, was probably quite conscious.

[38] Sidney, *Prose Works*, ed. cit., i. 367.

[39] It was described in a much reprinted letter from Lodovico Dolce to Alessandro Contarini; Dolce, ed., *Lettere di diversi huomini* (Venice, 1554), pp. 124, 530–3.

[40] Levey, op. cit., p. 93.

The Morality of Elizabethan Drama
Some Footnotes to Plato

HARRIETT HAWKINS

IN Borges's 'Tlön' (a third world created by poets and scientists, artists and philosophers), books 'of a philosophical nature' invariably include 'both the thesis and the antithesis, the rigorous pro and con of a doctrine'. 'A book which does not contain its counterbook is considered incomplete.'[1]

This description of the literature of 'Tlön' may serve to raise, even as it answers, some fundamental questions about much of our own literature and criticism. It certainly gives us an accurate description of many great poems, plays, and novels. For instance, the images of loathed Melancholy and heart-easing Mirth in Milton's 'L'Allegro' are countered by the vain deluding joys of idle Mirth and the sage and holy visage of 'divinest Melancholy' in 'Il Penseroso'. Even the *Paradise Lost* that aspires to 'justify the ways of God to man' would seem to contain a 'counterbook' that gives the Devil his due. For Blake, certain 'contrarieties are equally true' and therefore his *Songs of Innocence* summon forth the *Songs of Experience* wherein the Tiger, burning bright, forever confronts—and completes—his vision of the gentle little lamb. Marvell challenges impressive arguments in favour of the Soul with comparably valid arguments in favour of the Body, and with all his sympathy for Aeneas, Virgil gives a fair share of pity, and a very good case, to Dido. Their own Sancho Panzas travel alongside many of the Don Quixotes of art. Many artists have been eloquent advocates for their very own devils.

The theory that many works represent the confrontation of opposed forces or ideas between which even the author may be torn (or give the appearance of being torn), would explain why intelligent readers have interpreted the identical texts in

[1] See Jorge Luis Borges, 'Tlön, Uqbar, Orbis Tertius', in *Labyrinths*, ed. Donald A. Yates and James E. Irby (Harmondsworth, 1974), p. 37.

diametrically opposite ways. The explanation, in terms of Borges's parable, would be that one interpretation emphasizes the 'book' at the expense of the 'counterbook', while the opposite interpretation emphasizes the 'counterbook' at the expense of the 'book'. Thus, one group of readers can insist (with Marvell) that Milton 'draw[s] the devout, deterring the profane', while another group may argue (with Blake) that Milton was 'of the devil's party' all along. Likewise, critical counter-interpretations have been imposed upon Elizabethan tragedies: 'The plays justify the values of society, showing the hero to be deeply flawed . . . they justify the hero, showing society to be wrong; the hero is wrong, but the playwright had such sympathy for him that he is willing to be of the devil's party.'[2]

Critical controversies of this kind can be seen as re-enactments of conflicts active within the works themselves. For part of the time, for much of the time, and perhaps even all the time, a work of art may encourage us to see how easily, how readily, it is open to more interpretations than one, how close to the way the artist seems to want us to see his action and characters are other ways of seeing them. Sometimes the author may write his own 'counterbook', in order to suggest alternative points of view, to exhibit the truth in all its complexity, or to pose, correctly, the problems faced by his characters. 'You are confusing two concepts', wrote Chekhov to his publisher-critic, '*The solution of a problem* and *the correct posing of a question*. Only the second is obligatory for an artist. Not a single problem is solved in *Anna Karenina* and in *Eugene Onegin*, but you find these works quite satisfactory . . . because all the questions in them are correctly posed.'[3] Because so *many* works posit equally intolerable alternatives for their characters, give valid arguments to opposite sides, or in any number of other ways contain their own contradictions, it would seem sensible to take this for granted and go on to discuss the significant and enduring human and literary problems posed within the individual work. Since one would be 'incomplete' without the other, any critical interpretation based exclusively on the 'book' can—and inevitably will—be confronted by an equally valid (or invalid) interpreta-

[2] See Eugene M. Waith, *The Herculean Hero* (London, 1962), p. 12.

[3] Quotations are from *Letters of Anton Chekhov*, ed. Avrahm Yarmolinsky (London, 1974), p. 86.

tion based on the 'counterbook'—and vice versa. It would, therefore, seem futile to insist that we must choose between them. Yet this insistence has become a characteristic feature of recent discussions of Elizabethan drama. Reading certain modern commentaries on Marlowe, Ford, Middleton, and their contemporaries, one might conclude that the business of criticism is to decide between the 'book' and its 'counterbook' in order to determine, forever, the 'moral' stance of the author. And, given the historical controversy over the moral effect of poetry and drama, there are some significant reasons why this is so.

Precisely because of the contrary opinions and the wide range of emotional responses elicited by Greek poetry, Plato banished poets from his ideal state on moral and political grounds. And the following questions have haunted critical discussions of the moral effect of poetry ever since Plato raised them, in *The Republic*: Ought we to admire, on the stage, characters whom we would be ashamed to resemble? Does poetry breed an undue tolerance of wickedness? Should poets imply that the gods are frequently unjust to men? Should we approve of impertinences against those in authority, in prose or verse? Should we not condemn, rather than acclaim, a poet who wakens and encourages and strengthens the passions to the detriment of reason?

The Elizabethan controversy about the moral effect of poetry and drama can be seen as an effort to come to terms with Plato's charges. And Plato's mighty shadow falls over our twentieth-century efforts to answer, once and for all, the same old questions: Does the author wish us to condemn or approve of his characters? Is his play morally orthodox or heterodox? The Platonic implications of these questions deserve fuller discussion later on. In the meantime, here are some reasons why we ought to stop asking them to the exclusion of other, equally important, questions.

The very process whereby Elizabethan plays are judged to be 'morally orthodox' has, by now, become predictable and boring, sterile and repetitious. It is virtually inevitable that, no matter who the playwright may have been, and no matter what kinds of plays he may have written, there will be at least one twentieth-century discussion of him that sounds like this:

Earlier critics have mistakenly described X as an Elizabethan Byron who launched a daring attack on orthodox morality: 'Glorifying and identifying with characters who dare everything to the limits of imagination, X describes his passionate sinners as if he loved them.' This is nonsense. When they are analysed in terms of the English theatrical tradition, it proves evident that a basic morality-play structure underlies his plays and that his 'passionate sinners' are consistently condemned. Any *thinking* Elizabethan would have realized that instead of 'throwing down the gauntlet to the established moral order', X upholds it.

Here are some examples of the critical formula parodied above: 'Tourneur's plays', writes L. G. Salingar, have too often been described as if Tourneur had written 'Romantic poetry of the decadence'. Quite the contrary, Salingar insists: 'The dramatic influence' working in harmony with Tourneur's 'narrowly traditionalist outlook' is 'that of the Moralities'. Marlowe, writes W. L. Godshalk, 'was not creating protagonists with whom he expected us to identify', he was 'trying to force his audience to perceive the evils resulting from human pride'. Godshalk therefore takes to task those critics who see Marlowe 'as a propagandist for Renaissance aspiration' and 'for whom the playwright is a kind of pre-Romantic, perhaps an Elizabethan Keats'. Hazlitt, says Mark Stavig, was wrong to conclude that Ford 'delighted in melodramatic plots, licentious scenes, and revolt against the established moral order'; Ford's intention obviously was 'to add melodramatic and satiric elements to his basically morality-play structure'. If, says J. R. Mulryne, 'we think of *Women Beware Women* as initially a morality play', we can accept 'the integrity of the play as a whole'. And Nancy Cotton Pearse challenges the idea that Fletcher's 'chastity plays' are 'decadent' and 'lack moral fibre', with arguments based on 'their morality-play structure': 'Ingenious variants of shopworn themes were devised not only to make plays more entertaining . . . but also, and equally importantly, to reinforce the traditional moral lessons.'[4]

[4] Quotations are from L. G. Salingar, ' "The Revenger's Tragedy" and the Morality Tradition', *Scrutiny*, 6 (1938), 402–3; W. L. Godshalk, *The Marlovian World Picture* (The Hague, 1974), pp. 7–8; Mark Stavig, *John Ford and the*

Thus the plays which Romantic critics found heterodox have, by now, been pronounced utterly orthodox. Is there, one wonders, a major Elizabethan playwright whose Romantic critics have *not* been severely reprimanded for their failure to recognize his moral orthodoxy? Be that as it may. The point here is that we have five different scholars (and a dozen others could be cited as well) writing about altogether different plays, yet arriving at identical conclusions. It is as if one were reading a single commentary on a single author. Even the prose shows no significant variation. There is no evidence of uncertainty, of groping, of doubt or strain. There is no sense of any deeply felt personal response to an individual text. There are no wild surmises, no surprises here. Each author is said to have been essentially orthodox in his 'moral' outlook. And all are alleged to have adopted a 'morality-play structure'. What we have here is criticism written by formula. But why *this* formula? Does anyone, nowadays, decide to go, or not to go, to a revival of an Elizabethan play because it was, or was not, morally orthodox? What does a play's orthodoxy have to do with its dramatic merit? The formula seems contrived, primarily, to answer Romantic critics, and, simultaneously, eerily designed in order to defend poetry against Plato's charges. It is as if the value of the plays somehow depended on their conformity to the formula, and as if their morality depended upon their conformity to the theological, political, social, and sexual orthodoxies of an age.

The ubiquitous insistence on a 'morality-play structure' underlying virtually all Elizabethan plays indicates that this approach has become a matter of application—the mechanical application of a fashionable methodology—rather than a matter of discovery. Writing about Jonson's 'moral comedy', Alan Dessen reminds us that 'the morality play . . . has been used successfully as a critical scalpel to lay bare the essential structure of such significant and highly developed plays as *Dr. Faustus*, *1* and *2 Henry IV*, and *Othello*'.[5] But if most Elizabethan plays share the same 'morality-play structure', then a recognition

Traditional Moral Order (Madison, Wisc., 1968), p. xv (page references to this book will hereafter be cited in my text); J. R. Mulryne, 'Introduction' to *Women Beware Women* (London, 1975), p. lvii; and Nancy Cotton Pearse, *John Fletcher's Chastity Plays* (Lewisburg, Pa., 1973), pp. 9, 232.

[5] Alan C Dessen, *Jonson's Moral Comedy* (Evanston, Ill., 1971), p. 9.

of that structure cannot explain much about the blood and tissues, the poetry and characterization, which give individuality and continuing life to the greatest of those plays. To pursue Dessen's medical analogy a bit further, what physician today would be satisfied by the explanation of Addison's disease as the result of an imbalance of the endocrine system? What physiologist would be satisfied by the assurance that solar radiation is responsible for energizing muscular contractions? Neither explanation is false. But both are practically useless because they are so vague and sweeping that they might explain a dozen other phenomena as well.[6] It is obviously true that certain plays (like *The Devil is an Ass*) may explicitly—or playfully, or ironically—remind us of the older drama. But many interpretations based on the 'morality structure' of any given play, can, with equal facility, be applied to a dozen entirely different plays. There is a larger question here. What, finally, is the reason for these attempts to turn every Elizabethan play into a morality play—even those deemed by contemporary witnesses to be blasphemous? Although Willard Farnham, a pioneer in the study of the medieval influence on Elizabethan drama, described *Tamburlaine* as 'a medieval tragedy reversed, a rebellious violation of all that *De Casibus* tragedy had set out to convey',[7] Roy W. Battenhouse, among others, concludes that we can now say 'with some assurance' that the 'morality element in the Tamburlaine story' was what interested '*thinking* men of Marlowe's day'.[8]

Implicit in arguments by Battenhouse and other critics cited above, is a class distinction between 'good' or 'thinking' Elizabethans and wicked or unthinking Elizabethans. Their assumption is that 'thinking' people are necessarily orthodox in their thinking. While watching his tragic rebels, 'a thinking person of Ford's own time', says Mark Stavig, would be most concerned 'with living a truly honorable life under God's moral

[6] See P. B. Medawar's discussion of a cognate form of this problem as it occurs in science, 'Scientific Method in Science and Medicine', *Perspectives in Biology and Medicine,* 18 (Spring 1975), 345–52.

[7] Willard Farnham, *The Medieval Heritage of Elizabethan Tragedy* (reprinted Oxford, 1956), p. 369.

[8] Roy W. Battenhouse, *Marlowe's Tamburlaine: A Study in Renaissance Moral Philosophy* (Nashville, Tenn., 1941), pp. 12, 16 (italics mine); page references to this book will hereafter be cited in the text.

law' (p. 114). As opposed to 'good Elizabethans', Battenhouse tells us about heretical 'folk' who held that there was no cause of the good and evil accidents of this life, but either fortune or the will or man: 'Such folk', says Battenhouse, 'were thought by good Elizabethans to be all too numerous. Against them it was necessary to establish the fact of Providence' (p. 88). Battenhouse here overlooks the facts that certain heretical ideas have been suppressed not because of the possibility that they were wrong, but because of the probability that they were right, that Providential justice might be a fiction, and that the critical view which elevates to the highest authority the conventional wisdom of any age has unacceptable consequences. Given such a view, what are we to do about innovators (like Galileo) who advocated opinions with which few agreed, but which finally won the support of almost everybody? In any case, the moral, intellectual, and rhetorical equations here run something like this: 'good', 'representative' Elizabethans were orthodox. Therefore to call a playwright orthodox is to pronounce him a good, representative Elizabethan. It is deemed a far, far better thing to uphold established values than to question them. Thus it logically follows that to prove a dramatist orthodox is to do him a very great favour. It is to remove him from the devil's party and place him on the side of the angels in his own morality play.

There is no denying that the orthodox assumptions of the playwright's age must, necessarily, provide the backdrop against which his characters act out their dramatic destinies. And many Elizabethan plays, like *The Atheist's Tragedy*, may well be essentially orthodox. Yet the greatest playwrights seldom, if ever, reduce morality to the easy orthodoxies of *The Atheist's Tragedy*. Neither do the best critics. A. C. Bradley and Helen Gardner, to name two, have confronted the great moral issues in Elizabethan drama without reductively equating morality with political, theological, and social orthodoxy. Like poets, critics can be profoundly moral without being moralistic —and without denying plays their individuality.

Mark Stavig acknowledges that if his description of Ford's persistent affirmation of the 'traditional moral order' is correct, a charge that is 'sure to be raised' is that 'his work is lacking in variety': 'The answer must be a qualified admission that the charge is justified. . . . We must be satisfied with a dramatist whose vision is circumscribed by his seventeenth-century context, and not try to force him into a more universal, by which we usually mean a more modern, context' (p. 192). Yet if Ford's plays, in their structure and intent, are virtually interchangeable with each other and if his vision was so rigidly circumscribed by his historical context, then why, now, read more than one of his plays? Why read one? In fact, what is 'lacking in variety' is not Elizabethan drama, but formulaic modern discussions of it. To take Ford's accomplishment in tragedy as an example, *The Broken Heart*, his study of repression—his red-and-white tragedy about the conflict between 'morality' and 'mortality', where characters are emotionally and physically bled white—could not differ more from his examination of an heroic delusion in *Perkin Warbeck*, or from his treatment of an incestuous passion whose agents are also its victims. From the point of view of psychology alone, the problems faced—and posed—by Ford's characters are altogether different. So are the dramatic virtues (and defects) of his plays. Their poetry differs just as markedly. There is 'mystery in mourning' in *The Broken Heart*. People speak softly. These are the silent griefs that cut the heart-strings. Giovanni's lines represent a violent outburst against all that stands in the way of his desire. Perkin Warbeck speaks in the dignified, elevated verse appropriate to one who seems utterly convinced that he is the rightful heir to the throne of England. How, then, can we not be dismayed when Ford's contribution to the exuberant variety of Elizabethan drama is negated in favour of reductive references to his 'morality-play structure' and when everything in his plays that is varied, individual, shocking, or tragic is denied for the sake of drearily predictable references to the orthodox morality of the time?[9]

[9] For instance, Stavig apparently considered himself obliged to instruct Ford's readers that 'from a traditional point of view an incestuous love would by its very nature deteriorate and end in destruction' (pp. 95–6). Why, then, need anyone sit through a long play labouring this obvious point? One might, instead, argue that *'Tis Pity She's a Whore* is flawed by Ford's irritating tendency to hedge his bets. He gives mere lip service to the 'traditional point of view' expressed, as it is throughout the play, by characters whose hypocrisy is manifest. His originally sympathetic portrayal of Giovanni's incestuous passion is undercut by Ford's efforts to have it both ways, and so is the affirmation of the traditional point of view. With all its sensationalism, this play suffers from a failure of nerve.

Why need we ask, over and over again, the same questions? For some time, now, the crucial question in critical discussions of *I Tamburlaine* has been whether Marlowe 'glorifies Machiavellian *virtu*, denigrates it, or asks us to suspend moral judgment; is the play immoral, moral, or amoral? No two *Tamburlaine* productions have pointed the question in the same way.'[10] But why should they? Like Machiavelli, Marlowe set forth openly and sincerely what men are wont to do. Not surprisingly, both writers remind us that some of the courses of action likely to achieve political and military success are rather unlikely to bring moral acclaim as well. For this reason, it might be a good idea to go on from there and examine several questions posed, by Marlowe, within the play itself.

Here is a major question: What qualities must a man have if he is to rise from humble origins and conquer Asia? In *I Tamburlaine* Marlowe seems to conclude that a contender for world conquest will have to manifest, from the outset, the 'aspiring mind', the 'thirst of reign', the vision of his destiny that will spur him on to act out his dreams of power and glory. He must also have that instinctive sense of occasion which is the actor's art. On his way up, he will exploit any powerful allies he can get, and then turn on them should they stand between him and the 'sweet fruition of an earthly crown' (II. vi. 29).[11] He will also need to attract, maintain, and reward the loyalty of a retinue of trusted followers, and he must, therefore, possess the 'high astounding terms' that will win others (including, perhaps, certain members of the audience) over to his side. The speech that converted Theridamas, for instance, combines shrewd psychology and great rhetorical power:

> In thee, thou valiant man of Persia,
> I see the folly of thy emperor.
> Art thou but captain of a thousand horse,
> That by characters graven in thy brows,
> And by thy martial face and stout aspect,
> Deserv'st to have the leading of an host?

[10] Quotations are from Nancy T. Leslie's very useful article, 'Tamburlaine in the Theatre', *Renaissance Drama*, NS 4 (1971), 119.

[11] Quotations are from *The Plays of Christopher Marlowe*, ed. Roma Gill (London, 1971).

Forsake thy king, and do but join with me.
And we will triumph over all the world.
I hold the Fates bound fast in iron chains,
And with my hand turn Fortune's wheel about.
(I. ii. 166–75)

He will, sensibly enough, prefer to win men, women, and kingdoms by his 'working words'. To know when to parley, when to march—that is part of his art (I. ii. 128–37). But if words and warnings 'move not submission', Tamburlaine makes it his custom to fling slaughterous terror from his coal-black tents 'without respect of sex, degree or age' (IV. i. 58–63). He cannot claim, by hereditary rank, the 'hallow'd person of a Prince', and therefore he must persuade friends and foes alike to share his vision of himself as a more-than-human-being—the master of Fortune, the living Mars, the Scourge of God, or, in modern terms, the invincible instrument of the historical process, whose customs are as peremptory as 'wrathful planets, death, or destiny'.

To his followers, Tamburlaine represents a creed designed to overthrow the old order based on hereditary claims to power, and replace it with a new order, based on *virtu*. With only shepherds, and 'in disdain of wrong and tyranny', he dared 'Defend his freedom 'gainst a monarchy' (II. i. 54–5). He effectively overthrows the doctrine of 'degree' both by example and by precepts advocating careers open to talent:

Tamburlaine. Deserve those titles I endow you with
By valour and by magnanimity.
Your births shall be no blemish to your fame,
For virtue is the fount whence honour springs.
(IV. v. 119–23)

In this speech, Tamburlaine sounds rather like Bacon, who recommended to the youthful Sir George Villiers 'that which I think was never done since I was born . . . which is that you countenance and encourage and advance able men, in all kinds of degrees, and professions'. This, as Christopher Hill has observed, was a lesson which the Duke of Buckingham never learned—but Oliver Cromwell did.[12]

[12] See Christopher Hill, *Intellectual Origins of the English Revolution* (London, 1972), p. 112.

Like Machiavelli, Marlowe sees military and political success as stemming from the qualities of the leader.[13] Some of the traits exhibited by Tamburlaine seem admirable; some reprehensible; some are morally neutral. Courage, eloquence, and resolution, a single-minded dedication to a cause, the conviction of a special mission in life, have characterized saints, heroes, and tyrants alike. So far as tyrants are concerned, one might argue that *I Tamburlaine* can still serve as a mirror of political truth, confirmed by the rise to power of some more recent scourges of God and men—Napoleon, Hitler, Stalin. To examine how—through the poetry and action, through the praise and criticism given to him by adoring admirers and mortal enemies alike—Marlowe manages to sum up so much about so many mighty conquerors (or, if one prefers Milton's terms for them, those 'Destroyers, rightlier called, and plagues of men') might bring us closer to understanding the dramatic, psychological, political, and historical importance of what Tamburlaine represents than asking whether Marlowe was being moral or immoral when he created his archetypal 'superman'. That, after all, will get us no further than asking whether Machiavelli was being immoral when he wrote *The Prince*.

Dramaturgical, as well as political problems are posed in *I Tamburlaine*, and Marlowe's hero may serve as a dramatic example of a successful overreacher. From all the historical subjects available to him, Marlowe selected a shepherd who violated all the traditional rules and in doing so achieved all the worldly power and glory possible for mortal man to achieve. Throughout *I Tamburlaine* Marlowe tantalizes his audience with the possibility that this overreacher will get his come-uppance. Various characters predict that Tamburlaine will suffer for his misdeeds. But waiting for God to scourge his 'scourge' in this play is something like waiting for Godot—Tamburlaine rides in triumph over all prophecies, all expectations, to end the play in glory.[14] Is not this dramatic violation of common expectations for retributive justice, for *De Casibus* tragedy, rather interesting, rather exciting? Did people go to see the

[13] In *Edward II* Marlowe suggests some of the qualities and courses of action most likely to result in political failure.

[14] See also Michel Poirier's discussion of Part One in *Christopher Marlowe* (London, 1951), pp. 105–6: Marlowe 'dared to break with the time-honoured tradition of poetic justice', substituting triumph for the expected retribution.

second part hoping Tamburlaine would get a just reward for his misdeeds, or hoping he wouldn't?

His choice of a subject who 'neuer fought with man, but he had the victorye ouer hym, so that he never tasted Fortunes bitternesse'[15] allows Marlowe to confront his audience with some facts about human experience that challenge consolatory fictions about the ways of this world. In the end of the second part, when Tamburlaine finally dies—still undefeated, of natural causes—he dies in peace, praised by everyone on the stage. He might well, at the moment of death, exemplify 'that magnanimity / That nobly must admit necessity' for, whether we like it or not, what has been, has been, and he has had his day—his place in the sun. He most certainly had what Hobbes called 'the felicity of this life'. '*Continuall successe*, in obtaining those things which a man . . . desireth, that is to say, continuall prospering, is that men call FELICITY.'[16] Not every human being enjoys such felicity of life. Any number of Tamburlaine's victims—those who were completely innocent (like the virgins) and those who were, at worst, no worse than Tamburlaine himself—illustrate the injustice of the world, and remind us that innocent and guilty people alike have died without having had what they desired from life, to say nothing of having proved invincible in war and triumphant in love.[17]

For that matter, more virtuous men than Tamburlaine have grieved at the loss of their beloved wives, been disappointed by their sons, or pained by the recognition of their own mortality. It is true that in *II Tamburlaine* we are reminded that mighty conquerors, like lesser mortals, must, in the course of nature, die. Yet we are also reminded that anointed monarchs may be

[15] Shute, quoted by Battenhouse, p. 143.

[16] Hobbes, *Leviathan*, ed. C. B. Macpherson (Harmondsworth, 1968), p. 129. Even in the end, Tamburlaine dreams of worlds still unconquered, for, according to Hobbes at least, 'Felicity consisteth not in the repose of a mind satisfied. . . . Nor can a man any more live, whose desires are at an end, then he, whose Senses and Imaginations are at a stand' (p. 160). For Tamburlaine, as for Hobbes, 'there can be no contentment but in proceeding'. And see also Helen Gardner, 'The Second Part of "Tamburlaine the Great" ', *Modern Language Review*, 37 (1942), 24: 'Marlowe shows little sense that the goods which Tamburlaine pursues are in the end themselves unsatisfying.'

[17] See Paul H. Kocher, *Christopher Marlowe* (Chapel Hill, NC, 1946), p. 81: 'Fully half the number of Tamburlaine's victims are not shown by the drama to be guilty of any vestige of sin or crime.'

overthrown, that overreachers may grab a great deal of power and territory, that a tyrant can slaughter innocents without suffering any more than, and perhaps less than, most ordinary men. A number of these truths are morally repellent. Yet there they are, confirmed by history, by human experience.

Thus there are any number of ways of thinking about *Tamburlaine*, and the career of Marlowe's overreacher is one from which any number of moral, immoral, or amoral conclusions may be, and have been, drawn. 'The court', says Chekhov, 'is obliged to pose the questions correctly, but it's up to the jurors to answer them, each juror according to his own taste' (*Letters*, p. 88). It goes without saying that different jurors, upon viewing the same evidence, may come back with different verdicts:

> For though the nature of that we conceive, be the same; yet the diversity of our reception of it, in respect of different constitutions of body, and prejudices of opinion, gives everything a tincture of our different passions. . . . For one man calleth *Wisdome*, what another calleth *feare*; and one *cruelty*, what another *justice*; one *prodigality*, what another *magnanimity*. . . . From the same it proceedeth, that men give different names, to one and the same thing, from the difference of their own passions: As they that approve a private opinion, call it Opinion; but they that mislike it, Hærisie.[18]

Hobbes's statement holds true whether the evidence be dramatic, as in the case of Tamburlaine, or historical, as in the case of, say, Oliver Cromwell. We tend to see what we most want to see in literature and history alike. And since so many Elizabethan plays involve highly dramatic conflicts between orthodox and heterodox ways of thinking and behaving, those who look for heterodox ideas in them will surely find what they are looking for, just as those who have looked for orthodox assumptions have found them. This was evidently true in the Elizabethan period as well. For all we know, the deposition of Richard II may have been, for Shakespeare, the original sin which led to England's tribulations—yet Essex commissioned a performance of *Richard II* on the eve of his rebellion.

[18] Hobbes, *Leviathan*, pp. 109, 165. It is interesting to compare the adjectives his friends and enemies apply to Tamburlaine within the play and those used to describe him by friendly and hostile critics.

It might be argued that modern critical appeals to the orthodox views allegedly held by Elizabethan audiences (like Stavig's contention that, while watching tragedies, a thinking person would have been primarily concerned with living a truly honourable life under God's moral law) cannot but run aground against the facts of theatrical experience. For there come times in the course of dramatic events when most members of any audience—whether thinking or unthinking, Elizabethan, modern, or Greek—will be forced to join the devil's party. Given the choice—You can watch Doctor Faustus go forward, or you can watch him repent—how many people would choose the latter? Marlowe confronts his audience, as well as his hero, with precisely this choice:

> *Bad Angel.* Go forward, Faustus, in that famous art.
> *Good Angel.* Sweet Faustus, leave that execrable art.
> (I. i. 72, II. i. 15)

Indeed, at crucial moments in many works wherein the protagonist has decided to pursue a course of action known by his audience to be dangerous, evil, or in any case, inevitably tragic in its consequences, he will be offered at least one chance to desist or turn back. He may then decide (in the words of Macbeth) to 'proceed no further in this business'. 'Ask me no more,' pleads Tiresias to Oedipus, 'I mean to spare you, and myself'; then Jocasta herself implores Oedipus to abandon his tragic quest. Yet who, in the audience, wants Oedipus to leave the terrible truth unknown? At the last minute before their final encounter with the White Whale, the virtuous Starbuck almost persuades Captain Ahab to reverse course. But after hundreds of pages of pursuit, after incident after incident leading up to that fatal confrontation, might we not feel, to say the least, let down, if Ahab decided to forget Moby Dick and return to Nantucket? Similarly, had Faustus heeded the Old Man and managed an eleventh-hour repentance, many members of the audience might well storm out of the theatre demanding refunds from the management.

In certain works, the author creates a powerful appetite, on the part of his audience, for climax, not anticlimax—for tragedy wrought to its uttermost. Even with the certain knowledge that the Old Man offers Faustus his last chance for salvation, might we not join forces with Lucifer and Mephostophilis to take him to the midnight hour, to the very heart of darkness? For certain members of the audience, as for many tragic heroes and heroines, there can be 'no contentment but in proceeding'. A tragic hero may thus serve as a kind of scapegoat for one's own desires to 'try the utmost', to go all the way. And it is, perhaps, partly because we ourselves may join with those forces—good or evil—which urge them on to tragedy, that we can so profoundly pity those heroes and heroines, villains and villainesses, who must face the consequences of their (and our) desires for ultimate knowledge or power or passion—for the outer limits of human experience. These facts of dramatic experience seem true regardless of the orthodox assumptions of the poet's age.

Sometimes, to call into question narrowly orthodox assumptions about morality may itself be a moral act. In some plays (like *The Duchess of Malfi*) certain orthodox assumptions are shown to be irrational, unjust, unnatural, or inhumane. In *The Broken Heart* John Ford would seem to concur with Stendhal's conclusions about enforced marriages: 'Where there is no love, woman's faithfulness to the marriage bond is probably against nature . . . it is ridiculous to tell a girl she must be faithful to a husband of her choice, and then marry her against her will to a tedious old dotard.'[19] The cruel 'divorce' between her 'body' and her 'heart' is what destroys Penthea. Because Orgilus was the contracted husband of her choice, she considers herself despoiled—raped, ravished, a faith-breaker—in the bed of the tedious old dotard her brother forced upon her:

> For she that's wife to Orgilus, and lives
> In known adultery with Bassanes,
> Is, at the best, a whore.
>
> (III. ii. 173–5)[20]

The equity 'Of very reason' bids Orgilus to claim Penthea as his own (II. iii. 71–2). Yet she remains faithful to the marriage bond:

Penthea with a supreme effort . . . urges her desperate lover to

[19] Stendhal, *Love*, trans. Gilbert and Suzanne Sale (Harmondsworth, 1975), pp. 194–5. Arguments of this sort were not unheard of even in Ford's own time. See Gataker's Sermon, 'A Good Wife God's Gift', quoted by William and Malleville Haller, 'The Puritan Art of Love', *Huntington Library Quarterly*, 5 (1941–2), 263.

[20] Quotations are from *The Broken Heart*, ed. Brian Morris (London, 1965).

resign himself to the irrevocable, pleading that the true quality of their mutual affection will best show itself in virtuous submission to necessity. Which of the two is right? In Elizabethan times when parents disposed of their children in rather more high-handed fashion than now obtains—when Penelope Devereux was carried, protesting, to the altar to marry Lord Rich—was it not a fair question? To which it may be added that Ford himself in his Prologue declares that his story is founded on fact: 'What may be here thought fiction, when time's youth / Wanted some riper years, was known a truth.'[21]

Thus, having placed *The Broken Heart* in its historical context, G. B. Harrison argues that Ford's tragic questions were—and are—correctly posed. By contrast, reading the play in terms of orthodox 'morality', Mark Stavig decides that whereas Ford's heroines, Penthea and Calantha, can hardly be 'blamed' for their suffering, we must remember that they 'undoubtedly . . . should have followed the mean in their reactions to tragedy' (p. 191). 'We can', Stavig insists, 'assume that the audience would have been aware of the traditional view that the mean should be followed in mourning' (p. 164). Can we, however, assume that any audience wants 'the mean' to be followed in a *tragedy*? One wonders if Stavig would argue that 'undoubtedly' the 'mean should be followed in mourning' in the case of King Lear. The assertion that 'the mean should be followed in mourning' is far too facile a solution for dilemmas which Ford himself describes as tragically insoluble:

Morality applied
To timely practice, keeps the soul in tune,
At whose sweet music all our actions dance.
But this is form of books, and school-tradition:
It physics not the sickness of a mind
Broken with griefs.

(II. ii. 8–13)

The 'school tradition' whereby 'the mean should be followed in mourning' was, of course, established, with specific reference to tragedy, by Plato, who argues that tragic characters arouse emotions, like pity, which ought to be repressed:

The poet gratifies and indulges the instinctive desires of a part of us, which we forcibly restrain in our private misfortunes, with

[21] See G. B. Harrison's introduction to *Webster and Ford: Selected Plays* (London, 1974; first published in 1933), pp. xi–xii.

its hunger for tears and for an uninhibited indulgence in grief. Our better nature, being without adequate intellectual or moral training, relaxes its control over those feelings, on the ground that it is someone else's sufferings it is watching and that there's *nothing to be ashamed of in praising and pitying another man with some claim to goodness who shows excessive grief*. . . . For very few people are capable of realising that what we feel for other people must infect what we feel for ourselves, and that if we let our pity for the misfortunes of others grow too strong it will be difficult to restrain our feelings in our own. . . . *Poetry has the same effect on us when it represents sex and anger, and the other desires and feelings of pleasure and pain which accompany all our actions. It waters them when they ought to be left to wither, and makes them control us when we ought, in the interests of our own greater welfare and happiness, to control them.*[22]

Deploring poetry's power to corrupt even the best of us, Plato dictated the terms of the controversy about the 'morality' of poetry and drama which raged throughout the sixteenth and seventeenth centuries and rages on in twentieth-century discussions of Elizabethan plays.

Reacting against the hierarchy of human priorities whereby rational motives were elevated over emotional and physical needs, certain Romantic poets and critics reversed those priorities. Recent critics of Elizabethan drama have, in turn, reversed them back. Yet the emotional, intellectual, spiritual, rational, and physical needs of the human race all have, have had, and presumably will continue to have, their own special claims. The greatest poets of any age—whether writing in Athens or London—may deliberately challenge the valid claims of one set of motives with the equally powerful, and, sometimes, equally valid claims of another. Obviously, irrational behaviour may be the cause of tragic suffering, but so can the repression of emotional and physical needs. In *The Broken Heart* it is seen as tragic when 'life's fountains are dried up' by the repression of natural affections:

For affections injured
By tyranny or rigour of compulsion,
Like tempest-threatened trees unfirmly rooted,

[22] See *The Republic*, trans. Desmond Lee (Harmondsworth, 1974), x. iii. 606, pp. 436–7; italics mine. Following Plato's line of reasoning, we *ought* to be ashamed of any undue pity for, say, King Lear, who certainly shows 'excessive grief'.

Ne'er spring to timely growth: observe, for instance,
Life-spent Penthea and unhappy Orgilus.
(IV. ii. 205–9)

'I would say to my fellow students at the Art School', wrote Yeats, 'that "Poetry and sculpture exist to keep our passions alive", and somebody would say, "We would be much better without our passions" '[23]—thus summing up the conflict between the Romantic and the Platonic views of art. In his Romantic manifestoes, which are profoundly at odds with Plato's contention that poetry breeds an 'undue tolerance of wickedness' (III. i. 392, p. 148), Shelley argues that the excellence of poetry consists in its 'awakening the sympathy of men':

> The great secret of morals is love: or a going out of our own nature. . . . A man, to be greatly good, must imagine intensely and comprehensively: he must put himself in the place of another and of many others; the pains and pleasures of his species must be his own.[24]

Thus Shelley argues that it is a morally good thing that poetry arouses the responses Plato said it ought not to arouse, and praises poetry for doing precisely what Plato banished poets from the Republic for doing. Yeats and Shelley thus provide us with one kind of answer to Plato's contention that poetry has a terrible power to corrupt us (x. iii, p. 436). Scholarly arguments that the Elizabethan drama upholds orthodoxy, that its characters serve, primarily, as examples of how *not* to behave, represent quite another way to answer Plato's charges.

In fact, modern commentators on Elizabethan drama frequently echo the orthodox (as distinct from and opposed to the 'Romantic') case for the defence of poetry which was passed down from Renaissance criticism into twentieth-century scholarship. To Plato's rhetorical question, 'Can we approve of . . . impertinences of the rank and file against those in authority in prose or verse?' (III. i. 390, p. 145), the orthodox defence answers that poets ought to, and do, impose severe punishments on characters who rebel against established

[23] See *The Autobiography of William Butler Yeats* (London, 1969), p. 57.

[24] Quotations are from 'On the Devil, and Devils' and 'A Defence of Poetry', in *The Complete Works of Percy Bysshe Shelley*, ed. Roger Ingpen and Walter Peck (London, 1930), vii. 101, 118.

authority. Plato also claims that 'poets and story tellers are often in error in matters of the greatest human importance': 'They have said that unjust men are often happy, and just men wretched. . . . We must forbid them to say this sort of thing, and require their poems and stories to have the opposite moral' (III. i. 392, pp. 148–9). The orthodox defence of poets and story-tellers claims that they do provide us with the 'opposite moral'. Unlike the historian, who is tied to the 'mere was', the poet can see that *poetic* justice is done. He can, for instance, devise 'new punishments in hell for tyrants' (phrases here are from Sidney's *Defence of Poetry*). All these assertions regularly appear in twentieth-century discussions of the moral orthodoxy of Elizabethan drama. Yet the standard (as opposed to the Romantic) case for the defence necessarily begs, rather than answers, the questions raised by Plato's more repressive assertions. Might not impertinences against those in authority, in poetry (as in life) sometimes be a good thing? Are poets 'in error' when they say that unjust men are sometimes happy and just men wretched? Or are they simply telling the truth? History has its successful sinners and virtuous victims, and wrongdoing sometimes pays. In this world, as Shakespeare reminds us, 'some rise by sin, and some by virtue fall', and 'to do good' may sometimes be 'counted dangerous folly'. If this be error, in terms of an ideal reality, it is truth in terms of human experience.

The traditional Platonic attack and the orthodox defence of poetry have, historically, welded iron masks of theory—two different, yet equally restrictive, masks of theory—over the face of Elizabethan literature. The 'moral' assumptions of Plato's attack have dictated the 'moral' criteria for the defence, and so forced distortions of the evidence provided by the literature itself. Sidney's simplified account of poetic justice (quoted above) is part of his answer to the Platonic charges levelled at poetry by Gosson. And given the Platonic premisses of his own argument, Sidney did as well as anyone could. Yet reading on through the volumes of Elizabethan and seventeenth-century critical essays compiled by Gregory Smith and Joel Spingarn quickly becomes a bore because the claims made on both sides of the controversy about the moral effect of poetry become so tediously repetitive, because the orthodox attack and the orthodox defence seem so obviously directed at each other rather than at the human and literary problems posed by individual writers and works.

Need we continue to argue about Elizabethan drama in the same terms—in Plato's terms? Need Plato (or his Elizabethan successors) still dictate the criteria by which we judge an Elizabethan play to be moral or immoral? Plato's moral idealism is itself the product of a specific historical context: that context might help explain why, in describing his ideal state, he exalts obedience to authority; requires the repression of pity and other passions of the heart; deplores the fact that poetry sometimes reminds us of the injustice of life; and banishes poets because, by these particular standards, they seemed subversive of social order.[25] But why must the standards of Plato's *Republic* determine the moral co-ordinates of our discussions of Elizabethan drama? What if it is true that poets may arouse the desire to know, the will to act, and the power to feel? What's so bad about that? What if it is true that poets countenance impertinences against those in authority? Such impertinences may, sometimes, be justified. What if it is true that (though their sins be as scarlet) the greatest lines of verse, the pity and the terror, are occasionally given to sinners? What's so bad about mercy, or pity, or tolerance, or understanding, or, for that matter, admiration? Do we not occasionally, and perhaps sometimes rightly, extend them even unto sinners, in real life?

It does seem conspicuously true that poets do, sometimes, confront us with the problem of temporal injustice and the inequality of fate—Marlowe, for instance, devises no new punishments on earth or in Hell for the tyrant Tamburlaine. Shakespeare deliberately departed from his sources and so, at odds with all the dictates of justice, Lear's Cordelia lay dead as earth. Here and elsewhere (as Hazlitt observed) Shakespeare, who is by all odds the most profoundly moral of Elizabethan dramatists, left virtue and vice, folly and wisdom, right and wrong, to fight it out between themselves, just as they do on their 'old prize-fighting stage'—the world. Great poets seldom deny the power of evil, and frequently refuse to impose unreal

[25] A controversy now rages about the morality of *The Republic* itself. For discussion of its context, see Desmond Lee's introduction to his translation of *The Republic* (n. 22 above); K. R. Popper, *The Open Society and its Enemies*, vol. i (London, 1967); Eric A. Havelock, *Preface to Plato* (New York, 1971); and Iris Murdoch, *The Fire and the Sun: Why Plato Banished the Artists* (Oxford, 1977).

solutions on problems inherent in our human condition. Thus, through their very fictions, they may confront us with the built-in deadlocks, the books and counterbooks, of life itself. 'This is true of human experience', certain works remind us. ''Tis true 'tis pity', and 'pity 'tis 'tis true'; this ought not to be—but it is—true: 'that that is is'. Dr Johnson noticed that Shakespeare makes no just distribution of good or evil, and yet from his writings a whole system of moral and social duty may be inferred. Could this be because of—and not in spite of—the obvious fact that he forcibly confronts us with some of the harshest truths of human experience? Is it not possible that when they move us to feel magnanimously, to imagine intensely and comprehensively, to experience all the pains and pleasures of our species, and to think with understanding about things as they really are, the greatest Elizabethan poets (like those in any other age) perform their most significant and enduring acts of moral instruction?

Repetition and Echo in Renaissance Poetry and Music

FREDERICK W. STERNFELD

THE use of repetition to create coherence in poetry or to endow an individual passage with intensity or emphasis is centuries, nay, millennia old. Critics of Western poetry from antiquity to the Renaissance have been aware of a device which adds a rare touch of eloquence in the hands of a master craftsman. Since echo is only a special kind of repetition, I should like to discuss first the qualities of enhancement, emphasis, intensification that are inherent in the general employment of repetition. Aristotle was aware of the effect in his *Rhetoric* (III. xii. 4; or 1414a) when he discussed the manner in which the *Iliad* thrice repeats the name of Nireus, that most handsome man, at the beginning of three successive lines: 'Homer has increased the reputation of Nireus . . . he has perpetuated his memory, although he never speaks of him again . . .'[1] This perpetuation of memory (μνήμη) reminds one of μνημοσύνη in Greek mythology, the mother of the muses, and the importance of recall and repetition in such time-arts as poetry and music. When Aristotle discusses repetition in Homer he rightly emphasizes glorification as a result of poetic repetition. It is, of course, through memory that time is conquered, and that conquest of time is a topic that has preoccupied poets through the ages, as any reader of Shakespeare's sonnets must know. But I should like to leap for a moment from considerations of rhetoric at Athens in the fourth century BC to our own epoch and the devices of repetition employed by T. S. Eliot in *Four Quartets*. Time the spoiler, and time the preserver; the flux of time and timeless remembrance are a main concern of these four poems. In the second of them, *East Coker*, Eliot starts with the phrase

[1] Freese's translation of *Aristotle: The 'Art' of Rhetoric* (Loeb Library, London, 1926), p. 421; see also K. Lea, 'The Poetic Powers of Repetition' (Warton Lecture on English Poetry), *Proceedings of the British Academy*, 55 (1969), 51–76.

'In my beginning is my end', repeats it in line 14, and concludes the poem by appropriately inverting the phrase, 'In my end is my beginning'. By a coincidence Guillaume de Machaut's fourteenth-century setting of his own rondeau text, 'Ma fin est mon commencement et mon commencement ma fin', offers some beautiful illustrations of the additional artistry that musical repetition may bestow on poetic repetition. Whether or not Eliot knew Machaut's rondeau we cannot say with certainty, but he did know the French motto of Mary Stuart, 'En ma fin est mon commencement', which is so close to Machaut.[2]

Another, and a more extensive process of repetition occurs in the first quartet. It is less remarkable for some fifteen repetitions of the word 'time' than for its specific repetitions of such phrases as 'time past', 'time present', and 'time future' and the cumulative impact by which the preceding lines are summarized and intensified by the conclusion:

Only through time time is conquered.

But to do justice to this passage, with its many kinds of repetition, simple and involved, a few excerpts are required. Note in passing the repetition of the term 'echo' (lines 11, 14, 18) and extension by repetition (e.g. lines 40 and 42):

Time present and time past 1
Are both perhaps present in time future,
And time future contained in time past.
If all time is eternally present
All time is unredeemable.
. . .
What might have been and what has been 9
Point to one end, which is always present.
Footfalls echo in the memory . . .
. . .
. . . My words echo 14
Thus, in your mind.
. . .

[2] For the relationship of Eliot's repetition to Mary Stuart's motto see Helen Gardner, *Composition of Four Quartets* (London, 1978), p. 42; for other discussions of repetition, e.g., 'quietly, quietly', ibid., p. 57 *et passim*; for an edition of Machaut's music and comment on the verbal similarity between Machaut and Mary Stuart see F. Ludwig, ed., *Machaut: Musikalische Werke* (3 vols., Leipzig, 1926–9), i. 64.

. . . Other echoes 18
Inhabit the garden. Shall we follow?
Quick, said the bird, find them, find them,
. . .
And the lotos rose, quietly, quietly, 36
. . .
Go, said the bird, . . . 40
. . .
Go, go, go, said the bird . . . 42
. . .
Time past and time future 44
What might have been and what has been
Point to one end, which is always present.
. . .
. . . Time past and time future 82
Allow but a little consciousness.
To be conscious is not to be in time
But only in time can the moment in the rose-garden,
The moment in the arbour, where the rain beat,
The moment in the draughty church at smokefall
Be remembered; involved with past and future.
Only through time time is conquered.

From the Greek antiquity of Euripides and Aristophanes to our own century (Hardy's *Human Shows*, Eliot's *Four Quartets*) three types of repetition appear with particular frequency. One, called 'echo',[3] repeats words or a word or parts of a word at the end of a single line.

Secondly, the repeated word may occur at the beginning of successive lines; here the term 'anaphora' is widely used. Finally, repetition may carry on from the end of one line to the beginning of the next. Following Quadrio's treatise here the term 'palillogia' has been used occasionally as a label. It must be owned, however, that none of these tags is generally accepted by Aristotle or Quintilian, Scaliger or Puttenham, Poliziano or Quadrio. The first type, labelled by the French 'rimes en écho', is of considerable importance, not only in the history of

[3] For a discussion of 'rimes en écho' see W. T. Elwert, *Traité de versification française des origines à nos jours* (Paris, 1965), p. 110; also L. F. Bernstein, 'The "Parisian" Chanson: Problems of . . . Terminology', *Journal of the American Musicological Society*, 31 (1978), 193–240 (particularly 240). For a discussion of such rhetorical terms as 'anaphora', 'palillogia', etc. see H. Lausberg, *Handbuch der . . . Rhetorik* (2 vols., Munich, 1960).

poetry and drama, but even more so in the history of music and opera, which explains its predominance in this discussion.

The best-known example of echo verse in classical literature is probably the story of Echo and Narcissus in Ovid's *Metamorphoses*. This passage was undoubtedly known to Poliziano, a keen student of Ovid and the creator of the first known echo poem in vernacular literature. But the examples of classical Greek echo literature precede Ovid in chronological terms, and in his *Miscellanea* of 1489 Poliziano himself refers to an obscure poem in the *Greek Anthology* by an obscure poet, Gauradas, as a precedent for his own lyric. To sketch here the history of Greek echo poetry from classical Athens to Byzantine literature (Tzetzes, Prodromos, Stilbes) would be both a daunting and unnecessary task. But a word must be said about the earliest known instances by Euripides and Aristophanes, since they established the tradition in subject-matter as well as technique. Technically, the end of a line receives polish and emphasis by repetition. Topically, the repeated words are terms of woe (such as 'bewail', 'alas', 'death') and, indeed, the most prominent genre of the Italian echo lyric from the fifteenth century (Poliziano, Serafino) to the eighteenth century (Calzabigi) has been that of the lament. In Euripides' *Andromeda* the heroine, bound to a rock, laments her fate, softly answered by Echo. Aristophanes parodies this passage in *Thesmophoriazusae* by having Mnesilochus, bound to a plank, tell his tale of woe, with the punctuation of Echo's repetitions at the end of his lines.[4]

The love plaints of such Italian poets as Poliziano, Serafino, Filosseno, and Bembo constitute a Petrarchist repertory which undoubtedly influenced Wyatt and Surrey in England, du Bellay and Ronsard in France. At times the lament is both erudite and playful; at other times it sounds more sincere. But whatever the case, death—whether fictitious or a *double entendre*—is rarely absent from the echo rhymes at the end of the lines. Poliziano's 'amore—Ah, more' at the end of his single-stanza poem and Wyatt's 'I die, I die' at the end of his first stanza (or 'I faint, I faint' in a subsequent stanza) are quite typical.

Apart from Silvio's echo lament in the fourth act of Guarini's

[4] Concerning Euripides and Aristophanes see B. B. Rogers's edition of Aristophanes (Loeb Classical Library), vol. iii (1924), pp. 128 and 224–9.

Pastor fido Poliziano's lyric is probably one of the most influential poems of the entire genre. It appeared in print as early as 1494, was transmitted in an authoritative early manuscript now in Florence at the Biblioteca Riccardiana, and its inclusion in numerous anthologies throughout the centuries testifies to its undiminished popularity.[5] Of Poliziano's eight lines five conclude with either 'amo' or 'amore', except for the last line where the noun 'amore' elicits a punning reply which introduces the verb 'morire':

> Che fai tu, Eco, mentr' io ti chiamo? Amo 1
> . . .
> Che fa quello a chi porti amore? Ah, more 8

His poem places the repetition at the end of the line where, in view of the importance of end-rhyme in vernacular literature, it receives more prominence than in the poetry of Athens and Rome. Echo here functions as an answer to the question posed by the preceding text. This was the technique Poliziano had absorbed from the *Greek Anthology* and Ovid's *Metamorphoses*, which then passed from him, directly or indirectly, to such dramas as Guarini's *Pastor fido* and Webster's *Duchess of Malfi*. Finally, with the pun 'amore—Ah, more' Poliziano contributed to the creation of a vocabulary which has dominated Italian echo poetry to the eighteenth century. This vocabulary is restricted for two reasons: that of linguistics and subject-matter. The structure and accentuation of the Italian language are such that only a few words are suitable for echo effects, of which 'Chiamo—amo', 'Amore—Ah, more' are good examples. In terms of subject matter, the eroticism and lugubriousness of 'amare' and 'morire' was soon supplemented by verbs appropriate to the acoustics of the echo process, such as 'rispondere' and 'raddoppiare'. One must note here that the latter verb, Englished, is encountered in Shakespeare's 'passion redoubled' in a passage from *Venus and Adonis* which not only employs the standard vocabulary of echo poetry (moans, woe) but also explicitly refers to 'verbal repetition' and to 'twenty

[5] Note its inclusion in Poliziano's *Cose vulgare* (Bologna, 1494), and in A. Rubbi's influential *Parnaso Italiano* (56 vols., Venice, 1784–91), vi. 284, where it is one of five of Poliziano's poems there reprinted. For further information see I. Maier, *Les Manuscrits d'Ange Politien* (Geneva, 1965), p. 159; and N. Sapegno, ed., *Poliziano: Rime* (2nd edn., Rome, 1967), p. 225.

echoes twenty times cry so'. But perhaps this is not surprising in this early work of Shakespeare which treats an Ovidian subject in a most Ovidian manner:

> Make verbal repetition of her moans;
> Passion on passion deeply is redoubled:
> 'Ay me!' she cries, and twenty times, 'Woe, woe!'
> And twenty echoes twenty times cry so . . .
> Her heavy anthem still concludes in woe
> And still the choir of echoes answer so.
> (line 831–40)

But before proceeding to a consideration of the Age of Shakespeare the work of Wyatt and Surrey should be examined. It is they who first adapted the techniques and attitudes of Italian Petrarchism to the grain of the English language.

It must be stressed that Petrarch used verbal repetition prominently at times, but not the echo effect at the end of the line, of which the first recorded Italian example is provided by Poliziano in the succeeding century. The best-known instance of verbal repetition in Petrarch is probably encountered in his Canzone (No. 206 in the standard numeration of his poems):

> S'i'l dissi mai, ch'i vegna in odio a quella

where the incipit is repeated twelve times within the first four stanzas. In his *Art of English Poesy* Puttenham speaks of a sonnet by Petrarch 'which Sir Thomas Wyatt Englished excellently well', and whereas he does not specify the lyric, he probably refers to Canzone No. 206. (This lyric was so well known that Italian imitators of Petrarch, like Luigi Groto in the sixteenth century, succinctly state 'questa canzon fu fatto a imitatio [*sic*] di quella di Petrarca' without quoting either a first line or a numeral.) Of Wyatt's poems which give prominence to the repetition of a verbal phrase, 'Perdye I said it not' probably qualifies as an Englishing of Petrarch's Canzone, since it repeats the phrase 'And if I did' five times within the opening twenty-five lines. This is a good instance of the emphatic verbal repetition which Aristotle noted in Homer, and Shakespeare in 'twenty echoes twenty times'. Echo, after all, was never restricted to the end of the line, though after the general acceptance of end-rhyme in vernacular literature it tended to outshine the employment of the device in other parts of the metrical structure.[6]

Various kinds of verbal repetition, including echo at the end of the line, occur in Wyatt's 'Heaven and earth', a poem of nine

stanzas of four lines each. The last line of each stanza employs an echo, usually of two syllables: either two words ('I die', 'I faint', 'for shame') or a single word ('farewell'). This love plaint is reminiscent of Poliziano's immediate successors,

[6] For commentaries on Wyatt's lyrics see either editions of Tottel's *Miscellany* (e.g. by Hyder Rollins) or of Wyatt's works. For the present discussion the annotations of Rollins and two of Muir's editions have been consulted, namely that in the Muses' Library series of 1949 and K. Muir and P. Thomson, eds., *Collected Poems of Wyatt* (Liverpool, 1969). The bibliographical references in the later edition should complement earlier studies of Koeppel (1889) and Hietsch (1960). Hietsch's *Petrarcaübersetzungen . . . Wyatts* deals with 'Perdye I said it not' on pp. 200 ff.

particularly Serafino, both in subject-matter and poetic technique. Serafino d'Aquila was junior to Poliziano by twelve years, and from 1502 on editions of his Petrarchist lyrics poured from the Italian presses with considerable frequency. 'More', 'Mora', and 'Morte' are among his favourite echo rhymes, a device he employs more frequently and less discriminatingly than Poliziano. No single poem, however, can with certainty be called Wyatt's model, though most students agree that either he or Marcello Filosseno (whose *Silve* were first printed at Venice in 1507) are most likely to have provided the source, with a 'mora-mora' echo at the end of the stanza. Here is Wyatt's first stanza, with its echo and its verbal repetition:

> Heaven and earth, and all that hear me plain,
> Do well perceive what care doth cause me cry,
> Save you alone, to whom I cry in vain,
> Mercy, Madame, alas! I die, I die.

In passing, the second half of the second line, 'what care doth cause me cry' seems to have influenced Surrey's 'If care do cause men cry', which contains more than one Wyatt reminiscence.[7]

Several music manuscripts from the sixteenth and seventeenth centuries survive which bear either the rubric or the title 'Heaven and earth'. Between them we are able, with reasonable probability, to establish the traditional setting of the tune.[8] The last strain of the melody makes it clear that the words 'I die' at the end of the stanza (or the corresponding two syllables in subsequent stanzas) are stated three times. In other words, the ratio of repetition in a musical performance is increased as compared with a merely verbal recitation. This conforms to our knowledge of Italian echo poetry and music, where, for instance, ejaculations of woe, such as 'ohimé', are multiplied twofold and even threefold in a musical version.

Of the later instances of echo lyrics in English literature, the lament in Sidney's *Arcadia* has been extensively glossed:

7 See *Wyatt*, ed. Muir, p. 56; eds. Muir and Thomson, pp. 55, 315; *Surrey*, ed. E. Jones, pp. 14, 117.

8 See London, British Library, MS Roy. App. 58, fos. 52, 55; Cambridge, Fitzwilliam Museum, so-called 'Fitzwilliam Virginal Book'; in the standard transcription of this famous MS by J. A. Fuller Maitland and W. Barclay Squire (London and Leipzig, 1899; also reprinted as a Dover Paperback), 'Heaven and earth' will be found at vol. i, p. 415.

Fair rocks, goodly rivers, sweet woods, when shall I see peace?
Peace

. . .

In what state was I then, when I took that deadly disease?
Ease

The *Arcadia* survives in two versions of which the earlier may be dated *c.* 1580. This version, usually called 'The Countess of Pembroke's Arcadia' or 'The Old Arcadia', contains two laments, of which the first uses echo technique. Both laments were retained in the later version, though their position was shifted.[9]

As one would expect, the echo lament stresses appropriate nouns by repetition, such as 'grief' and 'death'. In fact, it is difficult to peruse some fifty echo poems and arias, both in Italian and English, without being impressed by the similarity of a vocabulary which, though it overlaps with the standard rhymes of amorous and pastoral poetry, nevertheless has a profile of its own, and that in spite of its obvious linguistic restrictions. Reference has been made to 'raddoppiare' and 'redouble'; to these 'vano' and 'vain' may be added. The English word provides Sidney with one of his rhyme words that is also prominent in Italian texts, as, for instance, in Cavalieri's sacred opera *Rappresentatione di anima e di corpo* of 1600 ('in vano—vano'). Other instances in English literature would be in an anonymous Narcissus play, presented at St. John's College, Oxford, in 1603 ('I die, farewell, O boy, beloved in vain—O boy beloved in vain'); or in a lyric by Lord Herbert of Cherbury, probably of the 1620s, to an Italian tune by Bartolomeo Barbarino, detto il Pesarino ('saying, I call in vain—All in vain').

Of various uses of echo in English literature quite a few occur in dramatic works, as, for instance, in the Kenilworth Entertainment of 1575, Peele's *Arraignment of Paris* and *Old Wives' Tale* (*c.* 1581 and 1590), the Elvetham Entertainment of 1591, Dekker's *Fortunatus* and Jonson's *Cynthia* (both from the turn of the century), the anonymous *Narcissus* play of 1603, and, last

[9] *Works of Sidney*, ed. A. Feuillerat (4 vols., Cambridge, 1912–26), i. 349, 352; iv. 152, 309; *Sidney: Poems*, ed. W. Ringler (Oxford, 1962), p. 402; *Countess of Pembrokes Arcadia*, ed. J. Robertson (Oxford, 1973), pp. 160, 331. Concerning the intensity of these laments see *Review of English Studies*, 17 (1966), 123; see also the reference to Sidney's echo lament in Fraunce's *Arcadian Rhetorike*, ed. E. Seaton (Luttrell Society, Oxford, 1950), p. 55.

but not least, Webster's *Duchess of Malfi* of 1613/14. Then there are various masques by Jonson, Campion, Browne, and Milton, all before the dissolution of the theatres. Nor are examples wanting from the Restoration period: by Davenant, Settle, Shadwell, and others. The example from Milton's *Comus* of 1634 is curious, as the dramatic tradition and certain lines of the dialogue strongly suggest an echo song, for example

> Compelled me to awake the curteous Echo
> To give me answer.

But no echo is specified in Milton's text of

> Sweet Echo, sweetest nymph that liv'st unseen

nor is any to be found in the contemporary musical setting by Henry Lawes. On the other hand, when *Comus* was revived in the eighteenth century, with music by Thomas Arne, the composer provided echoes. Certain musical settings by Italian composers of the seventeenth century, for example of stanzas from Ariosto, also suggest that some lyrics were treated in echo fashion, although the extant literary text gives no indication of that practice.

However that may be, there is no doubt about the application of the device in the *Duchess of Malfi*, surely the best-known example of echo technique to students of English literature. In spite of its dramatic and even melodramatic power the scene is far from typical, since it foretells death in oracular fashion, rather than invoking death as the sympton and consummation of love. In fact, Webster's scene belongs to the tradition of the Italian 'ombra' rather than that of the 'lamento'. These 'ombra' scenes often employ settings such as graveyards and such dramatic devices as incantations, oracles, ghosts, speaking statues, and so forth. (Probably the example most familiar to the modern student of opera is the *Don Giovanni* of Da Ponte and Mozart.) Certainly, Webster's scene displays traditional echo rhymes with dramatic propriety, adumbrating the topic of death, for example 'like death', 'deadly accent', and, most of all:

> Echo, I will not talk with thee,
> For thou art a dead thing. Thou art a dead thing.

Delia's remarks about the echo (lines 22–4) also suggest music, though no contemporary setting is known:

> I told you, 'twas a pretty one: you may make it
> A huntsman, or a falconer, a musician,
> Or a thing of sorrow.

The dramatic power of the scene, and its obvious connection with a tradition of long standing has inspired extensive commentaries, quoting instances from Euripides to Thomas Hardy. What impresses the reader, though, is not so much the profusion of examples over the centuries, but rather the homogeneous style which they command. It seems that circumstances of literary fashion, of linguistics and acoustics, have assisted in the creation of a genre of individual stamp. Naturally, that genre, like the general practice of repetition of which it is a special instance, tends toward emphatic eloquence at one end and toward sheer boredom at the other. It is remarkable that in lyrical and dramatic literature so much eloquence prevails.[10]

[10] There remains to be made a study of the history of the operatic echo aria from the *Dafne* of Rinuccini and Peri (Florence, 1598) to Boito's and Verdi's *Otello* (Milan, 1887). An excellent and international survey of echo literature is offered in *Webster: Works*, ed. F. L. Lucas (4 vols., 1928), ii. 195. Lucas's commentary should be supplemented by J. R. Brown's edition of Webster's *Duchess* (Revels Series, 1964), pp. xxxv f. and 158 ff. Ringler's commentary on Sidney's echo lament, already quoted, also provides additional data. On Italian echo literature, preceding and following Guarini's *Pastor fido*, see V. Imbriani, 'L'Eco responsiva nelle pastorali italiane' which appeared in two instalments, in the *Giornale napolitano di filosofia e lettere*, the first covering the sixteenth century in vol. ii (1872), 279–314, the second covering the seventeenth century in vol. ix of a new series (1884), 843–65. The important first instalment can be found in Naples but, unfortunately, not in London or Paris or, for that matter, in Rome or Florence.

Two Dead Birds
A Note on *The Phoenix and Turtle*

JOHN BUXTON

ON 21 September 1586 Thomas, the elder of the two sons of John Salusbury of Lleweni in Denbighshire, who had inherited the estate some eight years before, was executed for complicity in the Babington Plot.[1] The fortunes of the house of Salusbury of Lleweni, which was the dominant family in the west of the county,[2] therefore devolved upon Thomas's younger brother, John, who was then twenty years of age. Within three months of Thomas's execution, in December 1586, John Salusbury married Ursula Stanley, an illegitimate but acknowledged daughter of the fourth Earl of Derby, the most powerful man in North Wales, who is said to have 'made liberal provision' for her.[3] The alliance was important for young John Salusbury, to whom and his bride fell the responsibility of giving new life to his name. John was now the sole representative of his branch of the family, and the ancient legend of the Phoenix, the only one of its kind, was apposite to this situation. So, at least, it seemed to Robert Chester, who had somehow contracted the fashionable itch to celebrate an occasion in what he supposed to be poetry. But since the occasion was a marriage the Phoenix could not be praised alone: it must (whatever the consequent disruption of myth) be provided with a mate; and what better than that recognized symbol of marital constancy, the Turtle-Dove?

There are indications that Chester may have been a client of the Stanleys who had been brought to Lleweni by Ursula on her marriage. He seems to have begun his poem without any allegorical intention, and to have thought of the Phoenix (correctly) as sexless. His revisions, which I suggest were made

1 *Poems by Sir John Salusbury and Robert Chester*, ed. Carleton Brown (*E.E.T.S.*, 1914), p. xv.

2 A. H. Dodd, 'North Wales in the Essex Revolt of 1601', *E.H.R.* (1944), 348.

3 *Victoria County History: Lancashire* (1907), iii. 162, n. 10.

when he knew that Ursula Stanley was to be married, are too careless or hurried to allow the older material to fit the new purpose.[4] His primary interest remains with the Phoenix, which, in the circumstances of the marriage, he then makes feminine. (The legendary Phoenix, sole of its kind, had no need of sex.) The image may have been suggested by the heraldic device of the bird and bantling (eagle and child) which the Stanleys derived from the Lathams, for in heraldry the Phoenix is always shown as a demi-eagle issuing from flames of fire.[5] The Stanley eagle with 'wings addorsed, hovering over an infant in its nest'[6] may, through an obvious visual association, have prompted Chester's original allegory, for a Salusbury bantling was much to be desired. Chester made up for a lack of talent or discrimination by an excess of energy, and into his long poem he put not only all he knew of the legends associated with the Phoenix and with the Turtle-Dove but much about King Arthur, a lengthy catalogue of flowers, trees, fishes, beasts, and birds culled from recently published books, together with some confused history and geography, in which the island of Paphos (which is not an island) is translocated to North Wales, and Ferdinand and Isabella become Ferdinando (the name of Lord Derby's heir) and Elizabeth. The one glimmer of imagination in this gallimaufry is Chester's choice of the theme of the Phoenix and Turtle, uniting two incompatible legends to celebrate a marriage which should ensure the continuation of the Salusbury line. And indeed, after Chester had completed the main part of his poem—he wrote 'Finis. R.C.' at the end and characteristically forgot to remove this in the printed text—the birth, in October 1587, of the Salusburys' first child, Jane,[7] prompted some additional stanzas. Jane would have ten siblings in the next thirteen years, but Chester refrained from adding further stanzas for these, though he was still at Lleweni

[4] W. H. Matchett, *The Phoenix and Turtle* (The Hague, 1965), p. 65.

[5] A. C. Fox-Davies, *A Complete Guide to Heraldry* (London and Edinburgh, 1909), p. 240.

[6] *Boutell's Heraldry*, revised C. V. Scott-Giles (London and New York, 1954), p. 60. 'Danielle' in a poem in Christ Church MS 184 refers to Ursula Salusbury as 'of egles brood hatcht in a loftie nest'.

[7] Carleton Brown, ed. cit., p. xvi, prints a transcript from the registers of Bodfari parish in which, under the year 1587, we have: 'Jane Salusbury. Daughter to John Salusbury Esquier and heire of lleweny was baptized the xth daye of October.'

as late as 1604, when he witnessed a deed executed by Sir John Salusbury.[8] (Another witness was Robert Parry, author of *Sinetes Passions*, 1597, a book of poems which he dedicated to Salusbury.) We may conclude that Chester wrote, or revised, his poem for the marriage of John Salusbury and Ursula Stanley late in 1586, and that he made some additions a year later.

The poem remained unpublished for about fourteen years. It had been written for a private occasion and, when at last it appeared in 1601, Chester referred to it in the dedication to Sir John Salusbury as 'my long expected labour'. The delay need cause no surprise. John Salusbury could write much better verses himself, and he had an introduction to the literary circles of London through his membership of the Middle Temple and through his wife's half-brother, Lord Strange, whose company Shakespeare joined in 1589. He would be hesitant about incurring ridicule as the patron of Chester's stuff: it might be acceptable in North Wales, but scarcely in London. Salusbury was a frequent visitor at Knowsley; he named one of his sons Ferdinando in memory of the fifth Earl of Derby, and in 1597 he 'very Royally entertained' at Lleweni the sixth Earl and his Countess.[9] Salusbury certainly knew Ben Jonson, whose early ode to the Earl of Desmond, in Jonson's own hand, is included with Salusbury's and Chester's poems in a manuscript at Christ Church,[10] and early versions of the *Proludium* and *Epode* contributed to *Poetical Essays* are in a Salusbury manuscript now in the National Library of Wales.[11] He may well have known all the contributors to the collection compiled in his honour.

Chester continued to write poems for Christmas and New Year at Lleweni and in compliment to members of the family, Blanch Wynn, the wife of John Salusbury's half-brother, and Dorothy Halsall, sister of Ursula Salusbury, among them. In March 1595, when Salusbury was appointed Esquire of the

[8] I am obliged to Mr Dafydd Ifans of the National Library of Wales for sending me a transcript of this deed, which is dated 28 November 1604.

[9] 'Robert Parry's Diary', *Archaeologia Cambrensis* (1915), p. 121.

[10] MS 184.

[11] *Ben Jonson*, ed. C. H. Herford, P. and E. Simpson (Oxford, 1925–52), viii. 107–9, xi. 41; *N.L.W.*, MS 5390D.

Body to the Queen,[12] Chester wrote a poem entitled 'A Welcome Home', of which the opening lines may be quoted.

Your eares having hard the Nightingall soe long
I feare will blame my hoarse-throat ravens song.
The swanns that lave their blacke feet in the streames,
Have in their sweetnes sang you golden theames;
Court-bewtefying Poets in their verse,
Homerian like sweete Stanzoes did rehearse:
Then blame not my homebred unpolisht witt,
That in the Nightowles cabinet doe sitt
Yf that my lines be blunt, or harsh, or ill,
Seing they proceed from rustick Martins quill,
Yet how I strive to please my still pleasde fremde,
Let my true harty thought my lines commende.

Bould and to bould.[13]

(The last line recalls the inscriptions over the doors in the House of Busyrane, *Faerie Queene*, III. xi. 50, 54.) Chester shows himself aware that his master consorts with better poets at Court: he would have been prepared for the *Poetical Essays* appended to his poem a few years later.

Salusbury's appointment, though not of much importance any longer, at least showed that he had regained the royal favour, and two years later, on the recommendation of the Earl of Pembroke as Lord President of the Council in Wales, he became Lord Lieutenant of Denbighshire. Probably Pembroke was seeking to restore the balance between rival factions in North Wales.[14] Clearly John Salusbury was succeeding, by means other than the indefatigable begetting of a large family, in his efforts to revive the house of Salusbury; and on 14 June 1601 the Queen set the seal on his success by conferring on him the honour of knighthood.[15] The Salusbury Phoenix had assuredly risen again from the ashes of Thomas's disgrace and death.

About that time Sir John may have casually mentioned Chester's earlier poem of celebration, composed at the outset

[12] 'Robert Parry's Diary', p. 120.

[13] Christ Church MS 184.

[14] A. H. Dodd, 'North Wales in the Essex Revolt of 1601', *E.H.R.* (1944), 347–8.

[15] 'Robert Parry's Diary', p. 125; Christ Church MS. 184, fo. 288^{v} (heading of a Welsh poem of congratulation).

of his climb back to reputation,[16] to Jonson or some other of his Court-beautifying poets, who then saw in the theme of the Phoenix and Turtle unrealized possibilities for poetic exploitation. Word went round among the circle of poets to whom Sir John was known, and they decided to celebrate the knighthood, which had completed his restoration of his family's fortunes, by reusing Chester's theme. Hence the group of poems added to Chester's *Loves Martyr* in 1601 which bore the title: *Diverse Poeticall Essaies on the former Subject; viz: The Turtle and Phoenix. Done by the best and chiefest of our moderne writers, with their names subscribed to their particular workes; never before extant. And (now first) consecrated by them all generally, to the love and merite of the true-noble Knight, Sir John Salisburie.*

The poets who contributed these poetical essays—the title had been used two years before by Samuel Daniel for a collection of poems—and who subscribed their names were Shakespeare, Marston, Chapman, and Jonson. There were also contributions from 'Chorus Vatum' (perhaps of composite authorship) and 'Ignoto'. Since Jonson and Marston had recently been engaged in the violent Stage Quarrel we cannot suppose that either would have invited the other to contribute; and Shakespeare and Chapman both seem unlikely editors. The mystery remains. But it is clear that all the poets were writing 'Variations on a Theme by Robert Chester', a theme which he had proposed to celebrate the beginning of Sir John Salusbury's restitution of his house through his marriage to Ursula Stanley fifteen years before, and which might now be appropriately used again to celebrate his completion of that task. (His grandfather, from whom Thomas inherited—for their father died early, in the year of John's birth—had also been Sir John, and Chamberlain of North Wales.[17] The new knighthood therefore had especial significance.) But these poets used the theme of Phoenix and Turtle as myth, not as personal allegory; and some make ironic reference to Chester's poem. It is naïve to assume, as most commentators on these poems have assumed, that an occasional poem must comment on its occasion.

[16] It is perhaps significant that his name often has added 'heir of Lleweni' in manuscript references, as if this was his chief concern.

[17] Carleton Brown, ed. cit., p. xii.

In the sixth book of *The Faerie Queene*, which had been published five years before, Sir Calidore approaches Mount Acidale and comes upon

> An hundred naked maidens lilly white,
> All raunged in a ring, and dauncing in delight.
> (VI. x. 11)

In the midst of their circle are the Three Graces, and again, in their midst, as a fourth Grace,

> Another Damsell, as a precious gemme,
> Amidst a ring most richly well enchaced,
> That with her goodly presence all the
> rest much graced.
> (VI. x. 12)

The music to which they were dancing was provided by Colin Clout, by Spenser himself. For a time Calidore remained unseen amid the surrounding trees, astonished and delighted with what he saw, but not knowing what to make of it. After a while curiosity overcame him, and

> Therefore resolving, what it was, to know,
> Out of the wood he rose, and toward them did go.
> (VI. x. 17)

Immediately the dance ceased, and

> They vanisht all away out of his sight.
> (VI. x. 18)

Colin Clout, in grief at this turn of events, broke his pipes, and he told Sir Calidore that no one could call his dancers back again. So does Spenser instruct his readers how to read poetry: one must not intrude upon the poet's vision and ask, 'What is it all about? Who are these people? What does it *mean*?' Poetry can be appreciated only by those who are willing to submit to the imaginative experience which the poet offers. The kind of question appropriate in a reader of history, who rightly seeks to identify historical characters and to understand historical contexts, can only result, if applied to poetry, in a total loss of the essentials of poetry. Spenser gave similar advice to his readers elsewhere, as in the proem to Book II: it is advice we do well to remember when reading Shakespeare's sonnets or the poems which he contributed to *Poetical Essays*.

Whoever was responsible for bringing together 'the best and chiefest of our modern writers' to do honour to Sir John Salusbury on his knighthood must have suggested that each should contribute a pair of poems to suit the theme proposed, consisting of an introductory poem followed by a second of more serious import. At least, except for Chapman, they all conform to such a plan. A pair of poems by 'Vatum Chorus' is succeeded by a pair by 'Ignoto'. Then come Shakespeare's poems, the first untitled but introductory to the *Threnos* or dirge. Marston follows with a pair of poems, in the first of which he alludes to Shakespeare's *Threnos*:

O 'twas a moving Epicedium.

But he composes his own very different variation on the set theme, defending Platonism against Shakespeare's treatment of it as an intellectual game. He concludes the second poem of the pair with 'Thus close my rhymes', but then adds two more poems. Chapman, with a single poem which breaks the pattern, comes next; and Ben Jonson completes the series with a pair of poems which conform to the design, but then, like Marston (and not to be outdone by him), adds two more. (These added poems are not paired.) The last line of Jonson's *Epode*, the second poem of his concordant pair, had been quoted by Robert Allott in *Englands Parnassus*, 1600, and there attributed to Jonson, who perhaps decided to use something he had by him. But the line quoted is of a sententious kind which needs no context.

The first of Shakespeare's poems, the only one in the collection without a title, is in two parts. In five stanzas whose mood is imperative the poet sets the scene for the traditional self-immolation of the Phoenix on its nest in a tree: in Greek 'phoenix' was the name both of the legendary bird and of a palm-tree. The bird on the sole Arabian tree is the Phoenix.[18] Every five hundred years according to Herodotus (II. 73)—some authorities give other periods—the unique Phoenix built a nest in a palm-tree which proved to be its funeral pyre and also the birthplace of the next Phoenix. Now, in the medieval tradition of the birds attending a Requiem Mass, the Phoenix

[18] John Florio, *A Worlde of Wordes* (1598), defines *Rasin* as 'a tree in Arabia whereof there is but one, and on it the Phoenix sits'.

summons the birds to the ceremony of her death. Skelton had used this tradition with wit and charm in 'Philip Sparrow', where Jane Scrope lists indiscriminately all the birds she can think of. The Phoenix, 'the bird of Araby', is there among more familiar fowl, and pronounces the *Absolutio super tumulum*. Shakespeare is more selective: not all birds are summoned by his Phoenix. The screech-owl, whose property of foreboding death in certain families is well known to this day, was forbidden; so also were the birds of prey, except the eagle which, no doubt, was admitted in compliment to Lady Salusbury. The white swan, which traditionally sang only before its own death (like the Phoenix) is the least unexpected of the attendants at the ceremony; but the long-lived crow, often, like the screech-owl, a bird of ill omen, is here acceptable because of its legendary reputation for chastity. In a chapter entitled *Of unlucky birds, and namely, the Crow, Raven and Screech-Owl* in Philemon Holland's translation of Pliny's *The History of the World*, published in this same year, 1601, we read:

> Ravens for the most part lay five eggs: and the common sort are of opinion, that they conceive and engender at the bill, or lay their eggs by it. . . . Aristotle denieth this and saith, that the ravens conceive by the mouth, no more than the Egyptian ibis: and he affirmeth, that it is nothing else but a wantonness which they have in billing and kissing one another, which we see them to do oftentimes (I. x. 15)

Crows and ravens were thus also symbols of mutual affection. The temptation to see here a further heraldic allusion to the Corbett family of Moreton Corbett in Shropshire should probably be resisted.

When the Phoenix has summoned her chosen birds of chaste wing to participate in her obsequies, the poet marks a change to another section of his poem by inserting a stage direction,

> Here the Anthem doth commence.

The poet has set the scene for the birds to join in singing an anthem in praise of the Phoenix and Turtle, and with the shift of mood from imperative to indicative he now withdraws and leaves the scene to them. The remaining lines of the stanza state the facts which are to be celebrated: Love and Constancy, united by the singular verb into the idea of Constancy-in-Love, suggest the allegorical figures of Phoenix and Turtle, which are now first named in the poem.

The setting, with the priest in surplice white, the requiem, and the black-clad mourners was implicitly Christian; the hymn in praise of Phoenix and Turtle is not, and the language now is neither scriptural (as we should expect in an anthem) nor liturgical, but philosophical, a fusion of scholastic and Platonic terms. 'Essence', 'distinct', 'division', 'property' are all used in scholastic theology. The unity in love of Phoenix and Turtle can be adequately described only by analogy with the unity of the Father and Son, whose Persons were distinct, though they were of one essence. (In the bestiaries the Phoenix is associated with the Resurrection of Christ.) We need not suppose that Shakespeare studied the *Summa Theologiae*: this terminology was current in his day, and not only among recusants. Hooker employs it in *The Laws of Ecclesiastical Polity*,[19] and so do Bacon and Donne. Shakespeare was always avid for words and never hesitated to gather them, when they might serve his need, from learned sources, in the law, medicine, music, astrology. In his most recent play the vocabulary of Wittenberg had never been far from Hamlet's speech, and the use here of a learned diction was in keeping. Shakespeare, writing his variations on the theme initiated by Robert Chester, wished to suggest, by an extravagantly sophisticated diction, an ironic response to the clownish original. The irony of Marston's and Jonson's poems is more obvious, and satirical; but Shakespeare's subtlety should not lead us to disregard the underlying irony in his poems.

The anthem praises Love, not two lovers: it is not 'about' Sir John and Lady Salusbury's marriage, as Robert Chester's poem had been. It was intended, as Chorus Vatum declares, 'to gratulate an honourable friend' who had just been 'worthily honoured' with a knighthood. But above all it is an artefact, to be regarded as such without reference to any occasion. Shakespeare, invited to contribute to a volume in honour of Sir John's elevation to the rank which his grandfather had held, chose to offer an aesthetic variation on a myth which had been used to celebrate the start of his restoration of the family's fortunes. His concern is solely with myth, and the poetic con-

[19] v. lvi. 5 and cf. 2–3.

tent is removed as far as possible from any occasional reference. Whatever his personal response to the occasion, he offered his poems simply as poems. Spenser, even when he offered his bride on her wedding-day the most splendid occasional poem in the language, invited the readers (including the recipient), in the *tornata* that closes the *canzone* form, to stand aside and regard the poem as a poem, as a work of exquisite craftsmanship rather than as the expression of human passion. It was that too, but now Elizabeth Boyle was being presented by the greatest poet in England with a work of art of consummate skill, which love had prompted and which should

> Be unto her a goodly ornament
> And for short time an endlesse moniment.

So, a goldsmith commissioned to design a cup to commemorate Sir John's knighthood would design as handsome a vessel as he could and, though he might incorporate some heraldic emblem, would certainly not attempt to convey any comment on the occasion. Shakespeare chose to do the same in the only occasional poem which, so far as we know,[20] he ever wrote. His poems are not *about* the occasion, they are *for* it; and the kind of questions which have endlessly been asked about them are as irrelevant to our understanding of them as Sir Calidore's questions to Colin Clout. The anthem treats the concept of unity in love as a philosophical proposition, not as a family event, to the inevitable confusion of Reason, whose function is the principle of distinction, of choice, of seeking answers, a principle which Love, no less than Faith, by its very nature must deny. The conflict between Reason and Passion, the subject of so many sonnets of the time, found its resolution in an ideal Love guided (as Pietro Bembo says in *The Courtier*) by Reason. Therefore, in conclusion, Reason itself composes a dirge for the Phoenix and the Dove. This again, like the anthem, is introduced with a stage direction:[21]

> Whereupon it made this Threne.

Both the *Threnos* and the introductory poem are written in trochaic heptasyllabics: in the introductory poem these are

[20] That is, unless we accept Dugdale's attribution to him of another Stanley poem, the epitaph on Sir Thomas Stanley's monument in Tong church, Salop.

[21] These devices emphasize the poet's detached attitude to what he is making.

arranged in quatrains, with occasional octosyllabic lines to accommodate feminine rhyme, but in the *Threnos* the lines are arranged in triplets, without intrusive octosyllabics. The effect there is of the solemn regularity of a dead march. Shakespeare had experimented with this metre some years before, in *Loves Labours Lost*,[22] and the poem had been reprinted in *The Passionate Pilgrim* in 1599, and again in *Englands Helicon*, 1600. He may have composed the lines to fit an already existing air—a common practice at any time—for in *The Passionate Pilgrim* they are in the section entitled 'Sonnets to sundry notes of Music'; and he would have known songs in *Astrophel and Stella* which could have served as models for the quatrains.[23] (There were ancient precedents too, in Alcman and in Aristophanes' *Frogs*, whence it derived its name of *ληκύθιον*.) There is a difference in metrical structure between the two poems in each of the paired poems.

This contrast between quatrains and triplets is reflected in the diction, which is recondite and ambiguous in the introductory poem but simple in the *Threnos*. The first poem has several nonce-words: precurrer, defunctive, distincts; and the contrived ambiguities of the anthem have no place in the dirge of mourning which follows it. Reason, confounded by the mystery of Love, recovers certainty when confronted by the conclusiveness of Death. The Phoenix had lost its unique, sexless quality by taking a mate; therefore, paradoxically, there could be no posterity for the Phoenix. It was the nature of the Phoenix to be sole in its generation, and Constancy in Love, even Love itself, could not be its concern, since both imply duality. By denying its own nature in uniting with the Turtle-Dove the Phoenix had prevented the birth of a successor from the ashes of its nest:

Death is now the *Phoenix* nest.

The intrusion of Love had destroyed the possibility of any successor, and the Phoenix had become extinct,

Leaving no posterity.

This is the paradox which Shakespeare exploited. Crude interpretations of 'infirmity' as 'impotence' or 'sterility' in a sexual

[22] IV. iii. 101–20. [23] Especially the second song.

context that could never relate to the Phoenix only reveal the critics' incapacity for reading poetry as poetry and not as something else. Truth in poetry must be imaginative truth, not factual truth, nor even, here, the truth conveyed by allegorical equivalence. Shakespeare might have repeated Sidney's warning to the readers of *Astrophel and Stella*:

You that with allegory's curious frame,
Of others children changelings use to make,
With me those pains for God's sake do not take.
(Sonnet xxviii)

For, in the end, Shakespeare's poems have not been about Sir John and Lady Salusbury (nor about the Earl of Essex and Queen Elizabeth,[24] nor about the Earl and Countess of Bedford),[25] nor about their marriage, nor about the restitution of the honour of their family. In so far as they are 'about' anything they are about the Phoenix and Turtle which were the subject of Robert Chester's clumsily contrived myth, and which, on the title-page of *Poetical Essays*, had been announced as their subject also. Shakespeare wrote his poems for an occasion and (as he says) about two 'dead birds'—a subject whose triviality had been amply demonstrated by Chester but which, in the hands of a poet of genius, could be shaped to a perfection of form far beyond the range of any poet who merely wished to comment on an occasion. We must take warning from Sir Calidore and, remaining within the wood, be content to wonder at an exhibition of pure poetry.

I am most grateful to Miss Enid Roberts of the Department of Welsh in the University College of North Wales for excellent advice on the history of the Salusbury family.

[24] So Grosart in his edition of *Loves Martyr* (New Shakspere Society, 1878), followed by W. H. Matchett, op. cit.

[25] So B. H. Newdigate in his edition of *The Phoenix and Turtle* (Oxford, 1937).

Shakespeare At Work
The Foul Papers of *All's Well That Ends Well*

FREDSON BOWERS

IN Sir Walter Greg's words, 'There can, of course, be no doubt that behind F [of *All's Well that Ends Well*] lie the author's foul papers',[1] a conclusion that has been reaffirmed by the latest scholar to look into the question.[2] Without further discussion, then, it may be taken that the printer's copy given to Jaggard for this play consisted of Shakespeare's own working papers, traditionally called 'foul papers', which had not been marked in any significant manner by another hand.[3] It follows that an enquiry into the evidence for certain details of the composition of the play can be made in the belief that the Folio print represents substantially what was present in the authorial manuscript copy, faults included, from which it directly derived.

Significant evidence for Shakespeare's revision of the text, as well as for his method of working at this play, may be discerned when the speech-prefixes for a character alter within a scene in the stint of the same compositor; or when a change of compositors occurs but the alteration does not coincide with the shift in workmen. An excellent example appears in I. iii. This was the first scene of the play to be set in the backward progression of pages V3^v and V3^r by Compositor D and then of V2^v by Compositor B.[4] In the initial setting, that on V3^v,

1 *The Shakespeare First Folio* (Oxford, 1955), p. 353.

2 George K. Hunter, New Arden edition (London: Methuen & Co., 1959), pp. xi–xiv.

3 Sir Edmund Chambers in *William Shakespeare* (Oxford, 1955), p. 450, thought that the book-keeper might have 'added the initials G and E. to 1. and 2. by which the author discriminated the brothers Dumain', who could have been the actors Gough and Ecclestone. But G. K. Hunter (pp. xv–xviii) effectively explodes this possibility.

4 In what follows the description of the printing is drawn from C. J. K. Hinman,

D without the benefit of any stage direction must have followed his copy in assigning to the Countess the prefix *Old Cou.* for her first three speeches at TLN 479, 487, and 494. This series contains the discussion whether Helena could or could not be called the Countess's daughter, a passage ending at 512. Then with the Countess's next speech at 514 the prefix changes to *Cou.* and so remains for the rest of the scene, concluding on the same Folio page. Compositor D next turned to V3, which held the middle part of the scene. The first prefix he set was on the fourth line of the page at 349, and it was *Coun.* A number of prefixes in the form *Cou.* follow, ending with 443, the last speech of the Countess before Helena's entrance at 450. Immediately after this entrance, although the Countess's speech continued without interruption other than Helena's entrance direction, the continuation was given a fresh prefix, this time in the form *Old Cou.*, which appears twice more on the page. Finally, Compositor B completed the setting of the scene with its start on V2ᵛ, where on his first acquaintance with this character he three times gives her the prefix *Coun.*

From this evidence we may construct the forms of the prefixes in the order that Shakespeare wrote the scene. The copy-prefix may well have been *Coun.* as in B's work on V2ᵛ at the

The Printing and Proof-Reading of the First Folio of Shakespeare (1963), ii. 457–70, 481–2. However, on the evidence then available, Dr Hinman assigned sigs. V3 and V3ᵛ (pp. 233–4) to Compositor A, whereas it has recently been shown, on more refined evidence, that they belong to Compositor D: see T. Howard-Hill, 'The Compositors of Shakespeare's Folio Comedies', *Studies in Bibliography*, 27 (1973), 61–106. All references are to the TLN (through-line-numbering) as marked in the Norton facsimile of the First Folio edited by Hinman (1968). The bibliographical situation, involving the setting of pages in the first half of a gathering in a general inverse order from $3ᵛ to $1 so that the later text of a scene on a page of $4–6ᵛ may be set before the earlier in the next or even in the same forme, can be difficult to comprehend in description; hence consultation of the Hinman Folio may prove necessary for readers who wish to follow closely each stage of the argument. As an example, quire V was typeset beginning with the inner forme sigs. V3ᵛ: 4 of the innermost sheet, so that the composition of the play actually started with Compositor D setting V3ᵛ (476–602) ending Act I and beginning Act II, while Compositor C simultaneously set V4 (603–733) continuing Act II. Thereafter D worked backward, setting V3 of the outer forme (346–475), C matching him to complete the forme with V4ᵛ (734–863). At this point Compositor B took over the exclusive composition of the rest of the play. He completed the quire by setting the pages in the order of V2 (93–220), V5ᵛ (992–1123), V2ᵛ (221–345), V5 (864–991), V1 (the end of *The Taming of the Shrew*), V1ᵛ (1–92), V6 (1124–249), and V6ᵛ (1250–374). The effect of such discontinuous setting on a compositor's knowledge of the play and its characters is obvious.

start, particularly because this is the form in the first speech on D's page V3 at 349 before he settled down to the short form *Cou.* The speech of the Countess headed *Cou.* at 443 continues at 451, broken only by Helena's entrance, but with a shift of prefix there to *Old Cou.* which is maintained on the next page, also, until the discussion about the mother–daughter relationship is concluded, whereupon the scene ends with a sequence of *Cou.* tags starting at 514. Given the inverse order of typesetting this scene, and the fact that it is the work of two compositors, no case can be made for compositorial variation except between *Coun.* and *Cou.* Instead, only one conclusion can be drawn: the Countess's soliloquy, or aside, on Helena from 451 to 459, followed by the discussion ending on 512 about Helena calling her mother, must have been written at a different time from the material before and after it. Thus if we are not to suppose that the original interview began with the Countess's blunt question at 514 (not very probable in view of the manner it follows on the preceding speech), revision should be present here between 451 and 512, not simple insertion.[5]

Another scene where the speech-prefixes prove to be significant for information about the composition is II. iii, beginning on sig. V5 recto. Although in the opening direction he is named simply as *Lafew*, Lafeu's first speech in the next line (893) is prefixed *Ol. Laf.* and this form follows thirteen more times until the entrance of the King and Helena puts a stop to the strangulated dialogue between Lafeu and Parolles. After their entrance Lafeu makes comments at 933 and again at 937

[5] In the New Cambridge edition (pp. 104–5) Dover Wilson acutely noticed the shift from *Cou.* to *Old Cou.* at 451, coinciding with the end of the prose speeches with the Steward and the start of the verse, but he concluded there had been 'piecing' and that the rhyming verse had probably been pieced on to the prose. He did not pursue the implications of the return of the former prefix *Cou.* and of course he was unable at the time to place the anomaly within the context of the inverse order of typesetting by the two compositors. The fidelity of Compositor B to copy in the speech-prefixes of *Julius Caesar* has been shown in an important article by Professor Brents Stirling, '*Julius Caesar* in Revision', *Shakespeare Quarterly*, 13 (1962), 187–205, to include the setting of Cassius's prefix from different copy in the revised sections as *Cas.* whereas in working from the normal part of the manuscript he invariably set *Cassi.*, a distinction also observed by Compositor A. Hence there is some reason to trust the evidence of the variant speech-prefixes of *All's Well* as reflecting the copy. This is the conclusion reached in the present writer's study, 'Foul Papers, Compositor B, and the Speech-Prefixes of *All's Well*', *Studies in Bibliography*, 32 (1979), 60–81.

prefixed as *Ol. Laf.*; and lower in the same column his four remarks about the young lords' responses to Helena are headed *Old Laf.*, *Ol. Laf.* (twice), and *Old. Laf.* His fifth and last comment on the young lords occurs early in the first column on the next page V5ᵛ, also set by Compositor B, at 997, where the prefix takes the form *Ol. Lord*, which may reasonably be regarded as a misprint.[6] He does not speak again until after the general exeunt at 1088, succeeded by the curious direction, *Parolles and Lafew stay behind, commenting of this wedding.* In the verbal abuse that Lafeu then showers on Parolles, beginning with 1091, his prefixes change to *Laf.* and so continue to the end of the section on V6.

In this example the switch in the form of the prefix occurring at a literary division is suspicious enough; but when the division is headed by so unusual a direction, there can scarcely be a difference of opinion. The only point at issue is whether it was a note about material that Shakespeare was proposing to skip in order to press on with the end of the scene, or with some other scene; or whether (more probably) it was a note made at a point where he was interrupted and wanted to remind himself how the scene was to be continued whenever he was able to return to the play. It seems clear, then, that after some indeterminate interval Shakespeare resumed writing the scene; but instead of the commentary he had noted as the subject of the discourse, he substituted the comic abuse of Parolles, for the only comment on the wedding that in fact occurs is Lafeu's announcement at 1148 on his re-entrance, 'Sirra, your Lord and masters married'. The abuse is then picked up and continued to Lafeu's final exit at 1170. This interlude before Bertram's entrance after his marriage (or indeed the rest of the scene ending at 1208) forms a self-contained unit and it is prefaced by the extraordinary non-direction.[7] When, in addition,

[6] Since V5ᵛ was set before V5, this *Ol. Lord* was B's first acquaintance with Lafeu. What was probably the copy abbreviation *Laf.* he did not seem to have understood as a name and quite naturally set it as *Lord* under the influence of the prefix *4. Lord* in the line immediately above. When he came to set V5 he had the name in the opening stage direction to guide him, but in fact this was not needed since in the second column of preceding V5ᵛ a direction held Lafeu's name and hence the succeeding prefixes in this column followed it correctly.

[7] Generations of critics have remarked the curious nature of this direction. Steevens in the '78 Variorum thought that it was a prompter's note; Dover Wilson was inclined to take the direction as an instruction to Shakespeare's 'collaborator

the change in Lafeu's speech-prefixes at this spot is considered, the plausibility of the hypothesis for a delay in composition may seem to be considerably strengthened.[8]

Lafeu's prefixes cannot be considered in isolation: this same scene contains a mutation of Bertram's prefixes as well. In the early part of the scene on sig. V5, before the break, he is assigned only one brief comment on Lafeu's remarks, which is prefixed by '*Ros.*' (901), the preceding stage direction being merely '*Count*'. When next he speaks, on V5^{v} at 1005 (no direction intervening), his prefix is *Ber.* as he is rejecting Helena and confronting the King, and it so continues until his capitulation at 1081 and the general exeunt except for Lafeu and Parolles. On V6 when he re-enters at 1174 after the Lafeu–Parolles interlude following the comment-on-the-wedding direction, the stage direction calls him '*Count Rossillion*' and his prefixes are '*Ros.*' (once '*Rossill.*') for the rest of the scene. If we conjecture that Compositor B in this scene followed copy faithfully in the matter of the speech-prefixes, it would follow that after his memorandum Shakespeare did not merely skip the Parolles–Lafeu dialogue before the re-entrance of Bertram but instead broke off writing altogether—this last being the cause of the memorandum, not an urgent desire to work at the ending of the scene before he wrote the preceding dialogue. (If the memorandum had been written only to remind himself of the context of a skipped section and he proceeded immediately to the entrance of Bertram, the change in prefixes is difficult to lay to him.) If, instead, he returned on some later occasion to complete the scene starting with 1091, the change from *Ber.* to *Ros.* at 1174 would associate itself with the change from

to fill in the scene (New Cambridge, pp. 109, 151). The New Arden editor, more judiciously, finds it a note by Shakespeare to himself, as assumed here.

[8] This is the strong probability. Otherwise, one would be forced to conjecture that, though the prefixes continued in the manuscript as *Old. Laf.*, the stage direction with *Lafew* (1089) started B off with simple *Laf.* as the tag. It is true that Compositor C on V4 after the entrance *Enter Lafew.* at 661 gave him two speech-prefixes as *L. Laf.* before settling down to simple *Laf.* But this shift is less the influence of the direction than the simplifying of the prefix after its full form had been established. On the other hand, in III. ii after the direction *Enter Countesse and Clowne* (1401) B twice set the prefixes *Count.* (1402, 1406) until at 1411 he reverted to the standard *Lad.* This is his single aberration of such a nature in the play. For instance, on the next page X1^{v} after the direction at 1555 *Enter Countesse & Steward* he immediately set the prefix *La.* in 1556. (Sigs. X1 and X1^{v} were set in that order.)

Ol. Laf. to *Laf.* at 1091 when in both cases Shakespeare had overlooked the forms he had used in the preceding text of the scene.[9] This hypothesis appears to harmonize the evidence in a manner not possible in the several alternative conjectures.[10] Hence it may be suggested that II. iii contains no revision despite the changes in prefixes: the case may be presumed to be one of interruption and the later resumption of writing the scene.

A fairly clear case of revision by expansion is revealed not by speech-prefixes but by a misplaced stage direction. In II. iii when Helena makes her general address to the lords who have been assembled for her choice, at 957 occurs the stage direction '*She addresses her to a Lord*' which is inappropriate at that point although properly placed in connection with her question at 972, 'Sir, wil you heare my suite?' Unless the direction should read that Helena addresses herself to '*the Lords*', it is possible that 958 to 969, her introductory remarks, are an addition that should have been typeset before the stage direction.

Another possibility for revision is worth mentioning, perhaps. The play has three places where the same character speaks a second time without interruption and is given a second speech-prefix for the purpose although no speech by anyone else intervenes. The first occurrence in I. iii involving the Countess has already been considered. Hence it need be remarked only that in this instance because of Helena's entrance the fact of the

[9] After this scene Bertram's prefixes with only one exception are constant as *Ber.* for the rest of quire X regardless of whether the stage directions introduce him as *Bertram* (1269, 2016, 2869), *Rossillion* (1539), *Count Rossillion* (1730, 2189), or *Count Bertram* (2734). Beginning the play in I. i the first direction identifies him as *Count of Rossillion* (2) and assigns him the prefix *Ros*; another direction with *Bertram* (262) is followed by the prefix *Ber.*; and '*Count, Rosse*' (595) is succeeded by the prefix *Rossill.* and *Ros.* On sig. Y1 at 2930 the prefix *Ber.* of quire X changes back to *Ros.*

[10] Various alternatives, with slight differences, are possible, all relying on Compositor B to have varied the prefixes according to the preceding stage directions. But this would not readily account for the form *Ros.* after the direction *Count,* this *Ros.* then followed by *Ber.* with no intervening direction. It is probable that Shakespeare in the first two acts used both *Rossillion* and *Bertram* according to the scenes, just as he varied the name in the stage directions. But when in II. iv at 1272 the steady prefix *Ber.* begins, following the direction naming him as *Bertram* (1269), it is a problem whether Shakespeare or Compositor B settled on the one form. The evidence of the change during V. iii between the prefixes *Ber.* on X6v and *Ros.* on Y1 (for which see below) suggests that Shakespeare could have varied the prefixes in different scenes but B normalized to *Ber.* when he had become thoroughly familiar with the character.

repeated prefix is not the major evidence for a revision but instead the change in the form of the prefix upon repetition. The second and third examples appear to be related and they are troublesome. In the first, in II. iii, a continuous speech by the Countess is prefixed *Lady* by Compositor C at its start in 861 at the foot of V4v, and *La.* (after C's catchword *Lady.*) by Compositor B in 864, the first line of the next page, V5. There may be a mechanical explanation for this anomaly, although one is hard to suggest because the repeated prefix begins with the catchword. Except that it does not occur between signatures, the third case in II. iv on V6 is parallel, whereby the Clown has two consecutive replies to Parolles (1243–7) each prefixed by *Clo.* Editorial opinion has tended to conjecture a lost line or so by Parolles between the Clown's two speeches, but the example of the Countess's two prefixes does not encourage the hypothesis. The better proposition would seem to be to conjecture that both for the Countess and the Clown we have, instead, a marginal addition with prefix. In the Countess's two speeches no crux is present and only an addition can be conjectured. On the other hand, the Clown's two speeches do offer difficulty in continuity and it is barely possible (but only doubtfully probable) that the second was intended to replace the first.

Except for the major question of the two French Lords E and G, still to be considered, other evidence for revision is uncertain. If it is indeed proper in I. i to move Lafeu's 'How understand we that?' from 62 following Bertram's request for his mother's blessing and to place it immediately after the Countess's riddling remark in 59–60, to which it must directly apply,[11] an error of placement is most readily explained by an

[11] The position of Lafeu's speech has given editors some difficulty, placed as it is in the next line (62) to Bertram's speech at 61 and hence seemingly dependent upon it. If one is to accept the Folio placement, any defence of the original is subject to the charge of rationalization. There is not much in Kinnear's suggestion that in some manner the remark is a humorous comment on the fact that the Countess's wishes could scarcely be other than holy; and not much more in the New Arden suggestion that Lafeu may be pointing out to the audience an example of Bertram's 'coltishness'. It would seem to be impossible to justify Lafeu's remark as addressed to Bertram's request instead of to the Countess's comment on grief. One could attempt, however, to make Lafeu's puzzled query an aside and to argue that it illustrates Bertram's impetuousness, and very likely his impatience with the preceding dialogue concerned with Helena, so that he breaks in while

addition of Lafeu's line in the margin, the position misinterpreted by Compositor B. Two identical errors in IV. iii in B's sig. X4 should have a common explanation. At line 2226 the ending 'hush, hush' of Bertram's speech needs to be detached and prefixed to that of Captain G in 2227. Correspondingly, in line 2245 'all's one to him', ending Parolles' speech, must be transferred to begin Bertram's speech in 2246. Ambiguously placed speech-prefixes in the manuscript may not be the answer here, for the wrongly assigned beginning of each speech is too short to fill a line and thus to be mistaken (though the first line of a new speech) as concluding the previous speech. Nor is it likely that in the manuscript the wrongly placed part of each speech had been written for effect as a separate line. Thus an interlined or marginal insertion, the position misunderstood, seems to be the most reasonable explanation for these two errors. The time at which such an insertion was made cannot be determined, of course; but it may not have been current with the general inscription if the repetition of error has any significance.

Two other places in the text have been mentioned in terms that, if true, would make them analogous to the two mistakes at 2226 and 2245. Malone suggested that in V. iii the ending 'but how' of Parolles' speech at 2974, 'Faith sir he did love her, but how.', should be transposed to begin the King's answer in 2975, 'How I pray you?' Later editors have shown no enthusiasm for this proposal, except Dover Wilson who admits that it is a possibility; indeed, little can be found in favour of having the King demand 'But how, how I pray you?' What Malone was trying to do was to rationalize the Folio's punctuation of 'but how' with a full stop, a difficulty readily

Lafeu is ruminating the Countess's riddle. This would make an aside by Lafeu a slightly delayed reaction to the Countess's obscurely phrased speech, such an aside filling the space while she prepares for the formal blessing which she is about to bestow on her son. (Coleridge took essentially this position.) On the other hand, the indication of such a delayed reaction does not seem to be present elsewhere in Shakespeare and there could be some question about the clarity of its staging from the point of view of the audience. Bertram's impatience, which is manifested in his abrupt request, is as well illustrated even if it comes after instead of before Lafeu's query since in one way or another it turns the conversation. Hence the simplest and most forthright emendation, suggested by Walker and approved by Kittredge, is to transpose Lafeu's line to precede instead of to follow Bertram's speech.

mended by the usual substitution of a question mark. On the other hand, various modern editors accept the need for emendation in II. iii. Lafeu is commenting on the King's recovery, with echoing assistance from Parolles. The Folio reads at 902–4:

Ol. Laf. To be relinquisht by the Artists.
Par. So I say both of *Galen* and *Paracelsus.*
Ol. Laf. Of all the learned and authenticke fellowes.
Par. Right so I say.

The Globe, New Cambridge, and Kittredge texts emend to read:

Laf. To be relinquished of the artists,——
Par. So I say.
Laf. Both of Galen and Paracelsus.
Par. So I say.
Laf. Of all the learned and authentic fellows,——
Par. Right; so I say.

However, such an emendation would presuppose different conditions from those in the errors of speech-assignments treated above, for it does not attach 'both *Galen* and *Paracelsus*' directly to the start of Lafeu's 'Of all the learned and authenticke fellowes', as if it had been a marginal inserted speech, and it adds a line not found in the Folio. Disturbed copy might produce this emended result, but not a simple case of addition as in the misassignments in IV. iii, for instance. If Galen and Paracelsus seem inappropriate in Parolles' mouth, editors might be better advised not to add Parolles' echoing line but to read:

Par. So I say.
Laf. Both of *Galen* and *Paracelsus*; of all the learned and authentic fellows——
Par. Right, so I say.

This would at least bring the situation into conformity with an addition of 'Both of *Galen* and *Paracelsus*' (with or without the intention to delete what followed), although in the present writer's opinion tampering with the Folio text is by no means necessary here. Indeed, Lafeu's 'Of all the learned and authenticke fellowes' represents a form of paraphrase of Parolles' parading of Galen and Paracelsus (not usually found linked together in their medical theories although joined in fame).

The familiar case of Violenta needs only a mention here in connection with revision. She appears at 1603 in the direction for III. v but has no speeches assigned, and on the evidence of 1724–5 (which should refer to Mariana and Diana) she was not intended to be a character in the scene as we find it at present.[12] In IV. iii at 2181 the direction reads *Enter a Messenger*, but this is Bertam's servant who had accompanied him from Paris to Florence (1491–2 and the prefix here at 2183) and he has no function as a messenger. Inadvertence in a change of plan not corrected appears to be as good an explanation as possible revision, although revision can certainly not be ruled out. Nor, very possibly, need revision be required in V. iii (2876) where Parolles is listed in the entrance direction with the Widow and Diana but in fact does not appear until he is called for and makes his properly noted entrance at 2960. Since Shakespeare does not seem to have been in the habit of writing multiple entries in the French style as favoured by Jonson and the scribe Ralph Crane, a change of plan seems to offer a simpler explanation. This change of plan may have resulted when Shakespeare returned to the play after a break and cast the continuation of the scene starting with 2877 in a different manner from his first intention. Such a hypothesis satisfactorily explains why in seemingly continuous text the speech-prefixes change from *Ber.* and *Old La.* on sig. X6^{v} to *Ros.* and *Coun.* on Y1 when, after the lapse of a considerable time spent in setting quires in the Histories, Compositor B returned to finish the play by setting sigs. Y1 and Y1^{v} and literally followed the copy-prefixes in

[12] The stage direction opening III. v (1603–5) reads, '*Enter old Widdow of Florence, her daughter, Violenta and Mariana, with other Citizens*'. Literally, this should mean that, in addition to the daughter Diana and also Mariana, a girl called Violenta was intended to have a speaking part like Mariana but that Shakespeare either never used her as he developed the scene or else that he cut her dialogue and possibly added some to Mariana. It is perhaps a little odd that in the direction the daughter is not named. There are also the inexplicable and indeed, unless they refer to an omitted scene, pointless opening lines of IV. ii (2019–20): '*Ber.* They told me that your name was *Fontybell.* | *Dia.* No my good Lord, *Diana.*', these following the scene's stage direction, *Enter Bertram, and the Maide called Diana*, which seems to reflect some earlier uncertainty. This slight evidence could lead to the alternative conjecture that Violenta is not a ghost character but instead the original but abandoned name for the Widow's daughter Diana, and that the comma should have come after 'Violenta' instead of after 'daughter', A similar mistake, although made by another compositor, comes in the direction opening II. i (595) in which the abbreviation in the manuscript for *Rossillion* was misunderstood and two characters were made out of Bertram by '*Count, Rosse*'.

what by that time to him was strange text and unidentified characters. The intricacies of this hypothesis are worked out in 'Foul Papers, Compositor B, and the Speech-Prefixes of *All's Well*' referred to above in note 5. In this hypothesis the shift from *Old La.* to *Coun.* is especially significant, since it is necessary to suppose that in setting the various *Ber.* prefixes after the entrance of the Widow and Diana at 2876 on X6ᵛ Compositor B was following the form he had established from preceding copy in this scene even though in his subsequent copy after the direction the prefixes had shifted to *Ross*. This is not a strained assumption since the text is continuous (as was the setting on X6ᵛ) and the character is obviously the same.

Two interesting problems about names occur in connection with Helena and then with the two French lords, the brothers Dumain. It is an anomaly that Helena is named as *Helena* only four times in the play, thrice in early stage directions but only once in the text and then in prose. The name *Helena* in the opening stage direction for the play at I. i (3) is on sig. V1ᵛ, as is the unique use of *Helena* in the text (53). In this case the inner forme of sheet V1. 6 had been completed before the outer, so that the opening direction for I. i on V1ᵛ was the first page set with the name, including the text in line 53. This was followed by the direction for *Helena* in II. iv (1225) on V6 and concluded by the direction within II. v (1325) on V6ᵛ. For what it is worth, therefore, all occurrences of Helena as a name occur in the same sheet. However, when B set these names in V1ᵛ: 6 and V6ᵛ he had previously encountered Helena as a character in sigs. V2, V5ᵛ, and V5, in that order. In V5 alone did he have a stage direction to guide him as to the name of the character abbreviated in the speech-prefixes—this was *Hellen* at 930, followed by the prefixes in the form of *Hel.* On preceding V2 (93–220) her speech-prefixes are *Hel.*; on V5ᵛ the first prefix is, in error, *La.* (994) but the two remaining tags are *Hel.* (1000, 1050). No reason exists to doubt B's fidelity to copy, therefore, when after these pages he set three stage directions with *Helena* and included this form in prose text.

Shakespeare's intentions come in question, however. Even if we admit that *Helena* and *Helen* were in a sense interchangeable,[13] it is slightly odd that the *Helena* form occurs only once

[13] Metrically, *Helen* may have seemed more pliable than *Helena*, just as in

in the text, in prose, and then in the opening scene of the play, and also that the form does not occur in any stage direction after II. v. It might be thought to constitute an open question, hence, whether Shakespeare had not come to think of her name as Helen, not Helena, even before II. v, but certainly thereafter. Yet the case is by no means so plausible as might at first appear. Compositors D and C started to print this play with sheet V3: 4. D's first page was V3^{v}, which has no direction for Helen, and thus his prefixes *Hell.* (for *Hellen*, not *Helena*) seem to reflect the copy-spelling, interestingly the same in 478, 480, and 488, conjectured to be in revised text, as well as in the continuation with original text from 513 on. D's next page V3 contains the direction *Enter Hellen* (450) and two *Hell.* prefixes. The situation with Compositor C is only partly similar. His first page V4 holds the direction *Enter Hellen* at 699, but this is followed on the same page by two prefixes in the form *Hel.* His next page V4^{v} begins with *Hell.* (734) which is repeated in 743, but then *Hel.* resumes for the rest of the scene at 757 except for a single *Hell.* tag at 781. The inference to be drawn is that C favoured the short form *Hel.* (as he did for other prefixes) but was sometimes affected by copy (reproduced faithfully by D) to insert an occasional *Hell.* form.

Compositor B's practice is odd. He first encounters the name, as remarked, on sig. V2, where in conformity with his penchant for choosing short forms the prefix is invariably *Hel.*, as it is twice on the paired page V5^{v} after the odd lapse into *La.* at the start.[14] His next page containing her name is V1^{v}, which holds the opening scene of the play. Here it is odd that after setting *Helena* in the formal opening direction for I. i and in the text at 53, he prefixes her speech at 56 with *Hell.*, repeated on the same page at 83. Why B should follow copy, presumably, for this prefix after previously setting his favourite short form

Measure for Measure Isabella varies between *Isabel* and *Isabella* and Julietta between *Julietta* and the more common *Juliet.* The long and the short forms seem to have been interchangeable in Shakespeare's view, and the same may be true of *Helena–Helen* although some doubt may always remain.

14 On neither page is there a stage direction containing her name. On V2 in the second column B set her name in the text for the only time in this forme, but this *Hellen* in 194 comes only after he had set ten tags as *Hel.* on this page. After the name in the text he continued the page to its end with six more *Hel.* prefixes,

can be subject only to speculation.[15] What is interesting, however, is that on this evidence we are forced to take it that at least in the first two acts the manuscript read *Hell.* (for *Hellen*) in the prefixes, even in the opening scene where Helena for the only time in the play is named *Helena* in the text and is so identified in the important opening stage direction to the play.[16] In short, although writing her name as the formal *Helena* in this scene, Shakespeare seems to have thought of her simultaneously as *Hellen.* Under these circumstances it would be difficult to argue for a drift away from Helena to Helen in Shakespeare's mind if such an argument were to presuppose that at the start she was Helena to him and thereafter he shifted to thinking of her as Helen. From the opening scene the two forms were simultaneously present, and if the Helen form (which Shakespeare seems to have spelled *Hellen* invariably in this play) is constant after II. v it may well be that he ceased to consider the more formal version of her name.

We come, finally, to the complex and textually important problem of the two French lords, the brothers Dumain. These two characters lead a varied existence: they may be *Lord G* and *Lord E*, *1. Lord G* and *2. Lord E*, *French G* and *French E*, as well as *Captain G* and *Captain E.* Although it probably stands for *1. Gentleman* (on the analogy of *1. Lord* at 1378), the prefix *1. G.* at 1466 could be a misprint for *F. G.*, although its position in the scene after the prefix forms *F. G.* and *F. E.* have been established makes this explanation less likely. The prefix *1. Lord* (1378) stands for G, and *Cap.* (2233) is clearly intended for *Cap. G.* (in error for E starting with 2227). In the directions they are variously *the two Frenchmen* (III. i), *two Gentlemen* (III. ii), *the Frenchmen* (III. vi), *one of the Frenchmen* (IV. i), *the two French*

[15] One may only offer the guess—and it can be no more—that when B came to the opening scene of the play he felt an obligation to start off with fuller copy forms of prefixes for the first page, even though he had previously (later in the scene) set his characteristic short forms. If so, it suggests that in setting the prefix *Mo.* on this page for the Countess he was following the manuscript and not taking over the form from the opening stage direction.

[16] As for B's later typesetting, after the *Helena* in the direction at 1325 on $V5^v$ followed by the prefixes *Hel.*, she is named *Hellen* in all subsequent directions—at 1446 (on sig. X1), again at 1640, 1855, 2439, 2592, and 3039—but the prefixes are always *Hel.* Thus B seems to have followed the copy-spelling *Hellen* in his stage directions but to have adopted his own short form for the prefixes, and this short prefix can have no connection with the Helena form of the name.

Captaines (IV. iii), and finally *the two French Lords* (V. iii). These extreme irregularities must go back to the manuscript, especially since the prefixes such as Lord G, French G, and Captain G could not have been derived by the compositors from the stage directions specifying them merely as Frenchmen.

In the present writer's view the speech-prefixes for these two characters correctly distinguish them from each other, with one exception, up to the entrance of Parolles at 2224 in IV. iii, and all editorial attempts to tinker with their assignments (except for making the tags uniform) before this point introduce error into the text. That Lord G is the First and Lord E the Second Lord is well established in I. ii and II. i and is not to be upset by the simple error *1. Lord E.* in IV. i. 1 (1913) or the mistake *L. G.* for *L. E.* in II. i (615). When they enter in III. ii at 1446 with Helena it is of no consequence that *French E* speaks the opening words even though he is the Second Lord. Nor is the presence of the aberrant prefix *1. G.* at 1466 any reason to suppose that it is anything other than a notation for First Gentleman, who would be G. Perfect symmetry results if the speech by *1. G.* is retained by French G and is not given to French E by the usual editorial sophistication.[17]

Correspondingly, in an admittedly difficult passage in III. vi, which may well bear the marks of rough and ready revision of the prefixes, and perhaps of text, *Cap. E.*—who is the moving spirit in the capture and interrogation of Parolles—remarks (1841–2) that he must leave in order to make his preparations, whereupon Bertram says, 'Your brother he shall go along with me.' One would have expected Bertram to accept E's departure

[17] The F1–4 reading *1. G.* is taken by editors from the Globe to the New Penguin to represent 'First Gentleman' and is thereupon translated into their prevailing form of speech-prefixes. For Kittredge, Alexander, and the Pelican he is (correctly in the present writer's opinion) Lord G, but for the Globe and the rest he becomes Lord E and at 1447 the Folio *French E* is necessarily emended to *1. Gent.* or its equivalent in terms of G. It may be doubtful whether this much weight can be placed on the variant, for *1. G.* might just possibly be a slip for *F. G.*, and in any event G is the First Lord elsewhere. It is true that the minority assignment of the speech by *1. G.* at 1446 to Lord G breaks a symmetrical alternation of speeches between Lord G at 1454 and Lord E at 1466; moreover, it gives to Lord G five consecutive speeches. Nevertheless, once Lord G has had his say at 1475–7, Lord E himself has five consecutive speeches before the return of Lord G at 1504. This balance is tempting to maintain. But the really important point is that G is elsewhere the First Lord, and if either the number or the initial is correct at 1466 the speech must be his.

to arrange the plot and thus to request G to accompany him; but it is *Cap. G.* who agrees to leave his brother with Bertram, and himself departs, after which Captain E and Bertram discuss visiting Diana. Editors have assigned an exit (missing in the Folio) to Captain E instead of to G and have given E's concluding speeches to G. But this reassignment must be wrong, for it is E who in IV. iii begins the scene by telling G of Bertram's proposed corruption of Diana that night. Later, G's remark that E is not so much in Bertram's confidence as he had thought (2149–50) refers back, also, to E's visitation of Diana with Bertram. It may seem likely that Shakespeare had originally sent G off with Bertram but at some point recognized his mistake and clumsily repaired the error. At IV. i it is E who, as proposed in III. vi (1754–65), engineers the capture of Parolles and issues orders as the general (1995). Thus when in IV. iii E, in 2209–23, takes charge of the plans for the exposure of Parolles, no question holds but that the speech-prefixes for E and G are there correctly assigned. It is only at the entrance of Parolles at 2224 that the prefixes become reversed and it is G, wrongly assigned as the general who had ambushed Parolles, who in the Folio conducts the interrogation until the unhooding of Parolles begins a new sequence in which the prefixes are correct. This reversal at 2224 is accompanied by two irregularities: the assignment of part of G's speech to Bertram at 2226, and a speech at 2233 assigned only to *Cap.* Neither error, in fact, has any demonstrable bearing on the confusion of prefixes, for this difficulty had begun with Lord G's prefix at 2227, before which 'hush, hush' was taken from him to end Bertram's speech.

The point of major importance, of course, is whether the reversal of the prefixes was compositorial or authorial. The answer is quite clearly that it must be an authorial error and that the Folio prefixes derive from the manuscript. In the first place, the switch begins at a literary division, the entrance of Parolles on sig. X4 (perhaps marking a pause and then a resumption at a later time of Shakespeare's writing the scene), and continues through X4^{v}. When on X5 at 2413 the correct assignment is resumed, the return switch comes also at a literary division (although perhaps a fortuitous one), the farewell after the unhooding, and it is accompanied by two oddities:

first, the unique assignment to Bertram of the speech-prefix *Count* (2412), after he had been invariably *Ber.* from his entrance in II. iv with Lafeu (1269); and, second, the shift from the prefix *Cap. E.* to *Lo. E.* (2413, 2415) although *Cap. G.* is retained (2414, 2417). That revision and perhaps expansion or contraction could have taken place here is perhaps arguable. The problem would be whether the ending on X5 represents the correct original and the interrogation the revision (with its faulty prefixes), or whether the ending alone was revised and in the process given correct prefixes. If there was indeed revision, and not another pause in the writing, or else compositorial intervention, then the second alternative might seem preferable, especially given the mixed forms of prefixes between *Lo.* and *Cap.*

The confusion in the prefixes of the Captains in IV. iii starts at a literary division, as remarked, and is not bibliographically explicable; hence if it does not mark revision, at the least it suggests an interval between writing the preparation for the gulling and the actual interrogation, after which when Shakespeare returned to complete the scene he mistook the order of his prefixes. That the mistake did indeed lie in the copy is strongly indicated, though not demonstrated, by an irregularity in the printing. After the typesetting and printing of the inner forme X3^{v}: 4, a delay occurred while B set some non-Folio matter before returning to set the outer forme X3: 4^{v}, with sig. X4^{v} first. The error starts on X4 and continues on X4^{v}, thus bridging the delay in setting and suggesting that it did not originate in any memorial confusion by B, who under the circumstances of continuous composition might have perpetuated on the next page his initial confusion. Instead, when B returned to setting the Folio with X4^{v} it would appear that he continued to follow the faulty manuscript prefixes[18] until these were corrected on X5 toward the end of the scene.

The difficulty comes in evaluating the evidence for the agent who performed the correction after Parolles' unhooding. If it were Shakespeare, it would be a more reasonable hypothesis

18 That B would consult the already printed inner forme of the sheet and decide to continue his error against copy is a proposition one would not wish to defend. If on returning to set X4^{v} after a delay he had wanted to assure himself of the continuity of the text and prefix forms, the manuscript was the natural document to consult.

to suppose that in revising the conclusion of the scene he discovered and corrected his error than that he originated the error while revising the interrogation section.[19] But if the correction were made during revision, two oddities persist. It is anomalous that in reversing the two prefixes Shakespeare should have retained *Captain* for G while altering E to *Lord.* It is even odder that in reversing the two prefixes at this point he did not then go back into the preceding dialogue to correct his mistake there, as he may have done with the prefixes in 1844–54 at the end of III. vi.

These difficulties in assigning Shakespeare as the corrector should lead us to look at the bibliographical situation, for it is true that the correction comes between the setting of X4^v and that of X5. As a matter of fact, the order of printing quire X could have given B the opportunity to recognize the reversed prefixes he had set on X4 and X4^v and to alter them on X5. This is the hypothesis advanced by the present writer.

Compositor B started to set quire X with X3^v containing the start of IV. iii, the prefixes correctly assigned in the form of *Cap. G.* and *Cap. E.* He then turned to X4, which continues the correct prefixes up to Parolles' entrance at 2224, after which they are reversed in error, conjecturally as in the manuscript. Some non-Folio setting then occupied B, from which he returned to set X4^v, still with the reversed prefixes. The next page was X3, which if B had paid attention to the contents would have shown him that from the start of IV. i it was Lord E who had engineered the plot, captured Parolles, and talked the strange gibberish with the Interpreter found later on X4–4^v already set. Sig. X3 was followed by X2^v, on which—if speculation is correct—B would have seen in the copy Shakespeare's

[19] From one point of view the two anomalies in the conclusion of the scene after the unhooding—the assignment to Bertram of the prefix *Count* and the change from *Cap. E* (or rather *Cap. G*) to *Lo. E* although the form *Cap. G* is retained for correctly assigned G—would strongly suggest that, if a choice had to be made, this was the revised section. That in revising the interrogation Shakespeare forgot the respective roles of these two characters is not a very good hypothesis, for if he had consulted his draft when he started to revise (as would be only natural) there would have been little opportunity to mistake the prefixes. It is much more probable that he stopped writing the scene just before Parolles' entrance and when he returned to it his memory deceived him, just as the awkwardness in III. vi of G's exit and E's remaining with Bertram suggests that Shakespeare had originally got the two mixed up.

own alteration of the prefixes for G and E between lines 1844 and 1854. After X2^{v} he came to X5, which exhibits the correct prefixes. One anomaly, the unique assignment of *Count* as the tag for Bertram, is probably authorial and cannot be explained by anything in X2^{v} or X3. The other anomaly—the change of the form of *Cap. E.* to *Lo. E.* although the form *Cap. G.* is retained in the correction of the prefixes—can be at least speculatively explained. If, as conjectured, it was the example of the opening of IV. i on sig. X3 and also the identification of E as the speaker of the gibberish (not G as in X4 and X4^{v}), plus the possibility of the authorially altered tags in the manuscript copy for X2^{v}, that showed B he had followed his copy-prefixes in error on X4^{r-v}, it may seem significant (*a*) that the form of the prefix for E on X3 is *L. E.*, not *Cap. E.*; and (*b*) that Lord G or Captain G does not appear on this page. Thus if memory of the scene, or reference back to its manuscript sheets, had led Compositor B to correct the prefixes at the very next opportunity, which would have been on X5, it could follow that he adopted the form for E that he had found in the copy for X3 but that he retained on X5 what was surely the manuscript form *Cap.* for the character who now had to be changed to G.

This possible explanation for the association of the correction of the prefixes on X5 with the odd alteration of *Cap.* to *Lo.* for E may weigh in any consideration of the bibliographical hypothesis of compositorial correction on X5 instead of authorial revision, especially in view of the logical difficulties posed by the latter in the brevity of the section concerned, and also of the fact of the coincidence that suspicious revision should occur in connection with a bibliographical unit, the continuation of the text from X4^{v} to X5.

As a coda one may remark that in the odd stage direction at III. vi (1730–1), *Enter Count Rossillion and the Frenchmen, as at first,* Shakespeare's intention seems to have been to refer back to the scene of Bertram and the French Lords at II. i with the opening direction *Enter the King with divers yong Lords, taking leave for the Florentine warre: Count, Rosse, and Parolles.* (594–6); even though the two French Lords are included among the *divers*, they alone have speaking parts. No need exists to suppose that this direction in III. vi was intended to cancel or to modify that calling them *Gentlemen* at 1446.

'Look there, look there!' The Ending of *King Lear*

JOSEPH H. SUMMERS

A. C. BRADLEY suggested that, rather than emphasizing 'those sufferings [in *King Lear*] which make us doubt whether life were not simply evil, and men like the flies which wanton boys torture for their sport, . . . should we not be at least as near the truth if we called the poem *The Redemption of King Lear*?'[1] and he remarked that Lear dies overcome by joy at his belief that Cordelia is alive. If Barbara Everett was correct in 1960 when she wrote that Bradley's interpretation of Lear's death 'is now accepted almost universally',[2] she was not correct for long. Hers was among the first of a rash of essays which took a firmly anti-Bradleyan stance. She concluded, 'there is little evidence in Lear's last lines for anything but his supreme tragic horror at the corpse of what had been intensely alive',[3] and in the same year J. K. Walton argued that Lear must know the 'truth' of Cordelia's death: 'There is in fact nothing in his speech . . . which indicates a transition from grief to joy.'[4] Some years later Carol Marks made the point even more emphatically: 'he dies in broken-hearted knowledge that she has "no breath at all." . . . What Lear sees is the finality of Cordelia's death, which takes from him his last motive for

[1] *Shakespearean Tragedy: Lectures on Hamlet, Othello, King Lear, Macbeth* (London, Longman's, 1904), p. 245. I am grateful to The Folger Shakespeare Library for a fellowship which made work on my essay possible and pleasant.

[2] 'The New *King Lear*', *Critical Quarterly*, 2 (1960), 329. In 'The Catharsis of *King Lear*', *Shakespeare Survey 13* (1960), p. 1, J. Stampfer noted that Bradley's reading was accepted by Granville-Barker, R. W. Chambers, William Empson, and Kenneth Muir. Among many others who agreed in general with Bradley, including most of those who emphasized the possibilities of Christian allegory, one might note L. C. Knights, *Some Shakespearean Themes* (London, Chatto & Windus, 1959), p. 118, and Harold S. Wilson, *On the Design of Shakespearian Tragedy* (Toronto, University of Toronto Press, 1957), p. 204. For accounts of the varying interpretations of Lear's final lines I am indebted to manuscript essays by R. A. Foakes and David Samuelson.

[3] 'The Figure in Professor Knights's Carpet', *Critical Quarterly*, 2 (1960), 175.

[4] 'Lear's Last Speech', *Shakespeare Survey 13*, p. 17.

living.'[5] In a recent collection of essays on the play, W. F. Blissett argues that 'Look there, look there!' means primarily, 'look upon death', while Thomas Van Laan judges that in the final speeches, 'Lear has completely lost contact with external reality . . . the speeches themselves seem no more than noises forced from him, no more than additional "howls".'[6]

Another group in the past two decades has agreed that Lear's last words may indicate some sort of joy, but hardly a redemptive one. Also in 1960, J. Stampfer remarked, 'The tension here . . . lies between an absolute knowledge that Cordelia is dead, and an absolute inability to accept it. . . . Thus he struggles simultaneously for sanity and for the belief that Cordelia lives. Under the strain of these two irreconcilable psychic needs, his mind simply slips and relaxes into temporary madness.' In contrast to Gloucester, Lear dies 'between extremes of illusion and truth, ecstasy and the blackest despair, at the knowledge that his daughter was needlessly butchered'.[7] Nicholas Brooke thought Cordelia's 'death kills all life'. The end of the play, with Lear's 'final retreat to madness . . . makes it impossible to retain *any* concept of an ordered universe'.[8] John D. Rosenburg saw 'Lear's dying in the deluded hope that

5 ' "Speak What We Feel": The End of *Lear*', *English Language Notes*, 5 (1968), 166.

6 *Some Facets of 'King Lear'; Essays in Prismatic Criticism*, ed. Rosalie L. Colie and F. T. Flahiff (Toronto, University of Toronto Press, 1974), pp. 115, 73–4. Other recent readers have left the question of Lear's final emotion uncertain: Rosalie Colie asked, in the volume cited (p. 192), 'does Lear die thinking Cordelia dead or alive—can we tell, or should we try to tell?'; Helen Gardner remarked, 'if Bradley is right in thinking that Lear dies in excess of joy because he thinks that breath has stirred on Cordelia's lips, he dies, as he has lived, refusing to accept what all the bystanders know: that Cordelia is dead, and "all's cheerless, dark, and deadly" ', *King Lear* (London, British Academy, 1967), p. 22; and Northrop Frye, 'Perhaps he thinks that she is coming back to life again, and dies of an unbearable joy. But we do not see this: all we see is an old man dying of an unbearable pain', *Fools of Time: Studies in Shakespearean Tragedy* (Toronto, University of Toronto Press, 1967), p. 115. Maynard Mack cautiously remarked, 'these lines . . . probably mean that Lear dies in the joy of believing that Cordelia lives', *'King Lear' in Our Time* (Berkeley, University of California Press, 1965), p. 114.

7 *Shakespeare Survey 13*, pp. 2–3. 'Relaxes' seems an odd word in relation to Lear's final exclamations, and one wonders whether a human being could be 'needfully butchered'. In *'King Lear' and the Gods* (San Marino: The Huntington Library, 1966), p. 277, William R. Elton echoed Stampfer's judgement and language.

8 'The Ending of *King Lear*', *Shakespeare: 1564–1964*, ed. Edward A. Bloom (Providence, Brown University Press, 1964), pp. 84–5.

Cordelia lives' as 'the last and cruelest of the play's mockeries'.[9] Most of this group, like most of those who reject any notion that the dying Lear feels momentary joy, censured the failings of their predecessors. 'The record', Nicholas Brooke remarked, apparently of nearly all the readings of the play since Dr Johnson's, 'is of a long series of strenuous efforts to circumvent the pain' (p. 77). Rosenburg thought most post-Bradleyan commentary an attempt to 'escape', to 'convert horror into purgation . . . mutilation and murder into salvation' (p. 135). The tone was almost evangelical as the young condemned the old for their failure of nerve, their inability to face 'reality'—the meaningless desolation and despair that are truly 'there'. These critics did not usually consider whether the 'reality' they saw so clearly in the final lines of the play might be conditioned by their own presuppositions and beliefs—although *King Lear* may go further than any of Shakespeare's plays except *The Tempest* to suggest that ordinarily we see only the 'reality' that we make and share.

I am reluctant, however, to accept the notion that the final lines of *Lear* provide only a mirror for our preconceptions, and I resist the assumption that one reading of *Lear* is as good as another. Some accounts include more of the possibilities of any play than do others; when they do so without obvious distortions or eccentricities, they are usually better than the others. The suggestion that there is nothing in the text which allows us to know what Lear 'sees' limits for the worse the very notion of the 'text'. It may well be that we can 'determine', in a manner so as to command universal agreement, little or nothing of particular interest concerning either a play of Shakespeare's or a human life; but at least we can make some shrewd guesses concerning probabilities on the basis of the evidence. A 'text' does not imply simply words arranged according to syntactical patterns or patterns of sounds and rhythms. In a dramatic text these and other patterns are related to the emotions and thoughts of individual speakers: they characterize 'persons' and their changing or repetitious responses to experiences, and they suggest relationships between those persons. To 'read the text' is, of course, what we all try to do. The

[9] 'King Lear and His Comforters', *Essays in Criticism*, 16 (1966), 144.

difficulties in reading Shakespeare's texts often derive from the fact that they provide so many and such various possibilities.

To return to Bradley: if we wish to consider his interpretation of the final lines of Lear, we must go back to what he wrote rather than to unsympathetic summaries:

If to the reader, as to the bystander, that scene brings one unbroken pain, it is not so with Lear himself. His shattered mind passes from the first transports of hope and despair, as he bends over Cordelia's body and holds the feather to her lips, into an absolute forgetfulness of the causes of these transports. This continues so long as he can converse with Kent; becomes an almost complete vacancy; and is disturbed only to yield, as his eyes suddenly fall again on his child's corpse, to agony which at once breaks his heart. And, finally, though he is killed by an agony of pain, the agony in which he actually dies is one not of pain but of ecstasy. Suddenly, with a cry represented in the oldest text by a four-time repeated 'O', he exclaims:

Do you see this? Look on her, look, her lips,
Look there, look there!

These are the last words of Lear. He is sure, at last, that she *lives*: and what had he said when he was still in doubt?

She lives! if it be so,
It is a chance which does redeem all sorrows
That ever I have felt!

To us, perhaps, the knowledge that he is deceived may bring a culmination of pain: but, if it brings *only* that, I believe we are false to Shakespeare, and it seems almost beyond question that any actor is false to the text who does not attempt to express, in Lear's last accents and gestures and look, an unbearable *joy*. (p. 191)

Bradley was reading carefully and imagining a possible performance. He did not, moreover, leave his observation of 'unbearable *joy*' simply as a wayward impression, but supported it with a brief note on the patterning of the last speeches:

This idea may be condemned as fantastic, but the text, it appears to me, will bear no other interpretation. This is the whole speech (in the Globe text):

And my poor fool is hang'd! No, no, no life!
Why should a dog, a horse, a rat, have life,
And thou no breath at all? Thou'lt come no more,
Never, never, never, never, never!
Pray you, undo this button: thank you sir.

Do you see this? Look on her, look, her lips,
Look there, look there!

The transition at 'Do you see this?' from despair to something more than hope is exactly the same as in the preceding passage at the word 'Ha!':

A plague upon you, murderers, traitors all!
I might have saved her; now she's gone for ever!
Cordelia, Cordelia, stay a little.
Ha!
What is't thou say'st? Her voice was ever soft,
Gentle, and low, an excellent thing in woman.
(pp. 291–2)

In the spacious days of 1904, when he could quote the Globe edition without either line numbers or apology and when he was not particularly concerned with the scholarship or commentary of others, Bradley assumed that the note provided sufficient support or 'proof' of his major point for an intelligent reader. In his perception of the pattern of reversal in Lear's last speeches, he touched on one important kind of evidence which any reader must take into account in trying to determine the meaning or meanings of Shakespeare's texts. He could have cited, had he thought it important or necessary, a number of other passages in support of his interpretation.

The sequence of despairing 'knowledge' of Cordelia's death followed by joyful 'knowledge' of her life actually occurs three times in these final lines.[10] When Lear enters with Cordelia in his arms, he has no doubt of her death and its horror:

She's gone for ever.
I know when one is dead and when one lives;
She's dead as earth. (v. iii. 259–61)

But his lamentation is interrupted by the possibility of life and breath:

Lend me a looking-glass;
If that her breath will mist or stain the stone,
Why, then she lives. (261–3)

The scene which seems to Kent and Edgar and Albany the end of the world or an image of its horror is transformed for Lear by a new conviction: 'This feather stirs; she lives.'

[10] Carol Marks exactly reverses the sequence: 'three times Lear tests his illusory hope that she lives, and three times hope dies'—*English Language Notes*, 5 (1968), 166.

The second sequence begins when Lear violently dismisses Kent and Edgar as if their attempt to get his attention had, by interrupting his efforts to revive her, caused Cordelia's death; then immediately changes the tense of completed action for the present as he addresses Cordelia directly: 'Cordelia, Cordelia! stay a little' and 'Ha! / What is't thou say'st?' as he thinks she speaks to him. It seems inconceivable that Shakespeare would have used the pattern twice within sixteen lines had he not intended his audience to understand that in his final lines Lear has again, after full recognition of her death and his own desolation, come to certainty that he sees life in Cordelia's face: 'Do you see this? Look on her. Look, her lips. / Look there, look there!'

Bradley's observation that the word 'Ha' marks the transition 'from despair to something more than hope' might also be supported by noting that on the six previous occasions Lear has used that exclamation, 'Ha!' seems always to indicate his astonished recognition of an unexpected or unconfirmed 'truth'.[11] Even when he is maddest, 'Ha' indicates, in addition to pain or surprise or questioning, a degree of satisfaction in what he believes that he has learned.

If Lear sees Cordelia as alive in the final lines, what does it 'mean'? What is the effect—or the possible effects—when Lear's 'sight' is communicated to an audience in the theatre? L. C. Knights spoke for some of the most sensitive commentators when he remarked, 'The scene of Lear's final anguish is so painful that criticism hesitates to fumble with it'.[12] It is easy to go wrong—to push for a kind of clarity and finality that Shakespeare could have provided but surely did not; and the results of such interpretations can be fairly disastrous in attempts to produce the play on the stage or screen: final concentration on the group of survivors watching the soul of Lear ascend to heaven may be even more distracting than a final lingering on a landscape full of corpses and burning desolation —the world as hell. Clearly, some critics would prefer to the figure in the final lines what they think of as a more 'heroic' Lear: one who died utterly lucid, recognizing all the quotidian reality that the spectators do, and perhaps even cursing the

[11] See I. iv. 62, 228, 304; II. iv. 5–6; III. iv. 106–8; IV. vi. 96.

[12] *Some Shakespearean Themes*, p. 117.

heavens and the gods for the meaningless and cruel universe over which they preside—or fail to preside. Whatever our desires, if we wish to understand Shakespeare's play, we must consider the final lines in relation both to the character of Lear as it has been developed from the beginning and to the play as a whole.

From the opening scene, when his intended bestowal of the 'third more opulent than your sisters' (I. i. 85) upon Cordelia is suddenly transformed by Cordelia's repeated 'Nothing' into his awful disowning of her, Lear's most terrible and poignant moments are marked by sudden reversals of beliefs and emotions and determinations. In the opening scene Lear assumes knowledge. When his assumptions, beliefs, 'certainties' are suddenly opposed or shattered, he responds first with incredulity and then with rage and a pronouncement of banishment or a curse. That pattern, continually repeated, becomes more and more painful as it is crossed by other patterns of emotional response in which Lear attempts to conquer sorrow and tears by 'manliness' and noble anger by 'patience', only to have all dissolve in rage, the desire to kill and destroy, and, finally, madness. One of the things that makes these changes so painful is that Lear's responses are open, exclamatory, and repetitious, and that he early comes to recognize his own guilt and folly:

O Lear, Lear, Lear!
Beat at this gate, that let thy folly in, [*Striking his head*
And thy dear judgment out! (I. iv. 270–2)

His pleas for patience and attempts at control are not mere efforts to retain dignity or propriety or even clarity of judgement, but desperate attempts to forestall the madness that he feels approach in the waves of his overwhelming emotions:

O, let me not be mad, not mad, sweet heaven!
Keep me in temper; I would not be mad! (I. v. 43–4)

These conflicting patterns become particularly oppressive in Act II, scene iv, from the moment when Lear insists that the reasons Kent gives for being in the stocks could not be true:

Lear. What's he that hath so much thy place mistook
To set thee here?
Kent. It is both he and she,
Your son and daughter.

Lear. No.
Kent. Yes.
Lear. No, I say.
Kent. I say, yea.
Lear. No, no; they would not.
Kent. Yes, they have.
Lear. By Jupiter, I swear, no.
Kent. By Juno, I swear, ay.
Lear. They durst not do't;
They could not, would not do't; 'tis worse then murder
To do upon respect such violent outrage. (11–23)

After hearing Kent's account, Lear has a moment when, almost overcome by his emotion, he attempts to control it just before he exits:

O, how this mother swells up toward my heart!
Hysterica passio—down, thou climbing sorrow,
Thy element's below. Where is this daughter? (55–7)

On his return, Lear is incensed by Gloucester's remark about the 'fiery quality' of Cornwall: in his repeated exclamations rage begins to predominate over incredulity:

Lear. Vengeance! plague! death! confusion!
Fiery? What quality? Why Gloucester, Gloucester,
I'd speak with the Duke of Cornwall and his wife.
Glo. Well, my good lord, I have inform'd them so.
Lear. Inform'd them! Dost thou understand me, man?
Glo. Ay, my good lord. (93–8)

In the next speech, Lear, beginning with outrage, makes an enormous effort at control, imaginative sympathy with Regan and Cornwall, and even critical judgement on himself; but it is all swept away by the renewed sight of Kent, his messenger, still sitting in the stocks. It is after Goneril and Regan's public competition to show least love ('What need one?') that the struggles between contradictory emotions become literally unbearable, and Lear comes to the certainty that madness lies ahead.

In the storm the Gentleman tells Kent that Lear is 'Contending with the fretful elements':

Bids the wind blow the earth into the sea,
Or swell the curled waters 'bove the main,
That things might change or cease. . . . (III. i. 5–7)

When we see Lear, however, his commands and invocations entertain more limited alternatives: he bids things to cease, to be made manifest, and to be judged; and in the first storm scene Lear uses none of those doubled words and phrases which have characterized his excited speech of discovery until then. It is in III. iv, with 'Poor Tom's' 'Fathom and half, fathom and half!' (III. iv. 37), that the emotional repetitions are introduced again as Edgar, the Fool, and Lear exchange the language and cries of madness:

Fool. Help me, help me! (40)
Fool. A spirit, a spirit. (42)
Edg. O, do de, do de, do de. (58–9)
Edg. There could I have him now—and there—and there again—and there. (61–2)
Edg. Alow, alow, loo, loo! (76)
Edg. Dolphin my boy, boy. . . . (99)
Lear. Off, off, you lendings! (107)
Edg. And aroint thee, witch, aroint thee! (122)
Edg. Peace, Smulkin; peace, thou fiend! (137)

In III. vi, the repetitions resume with Lear's answer to the Fool's riddle about whether a madman is a gentleman or a yeoman:

Lear. A king, a king! (11)
Lear. Arms, arms, sword, fire! (54)
Edg. Do de, de, de. (73)
Lear. So, so. (83)
Edg. Lurk, lurk. (115)

Lear's maddened, repeated cries reach a climax in Act IV, scene vi, the scene where he meets the blinded Gloucester:

O, well flown, bird! i' the clout, i' the clout—hewgh! (91–2)
Fie, fie, fie! pah, pah! (130)
None does offend, none—I say none; I'll able 'em.
Take that of me, my friend, who have the power
To seal th' accuser's lips. Get thee glass eyes,
And, like a scurvy politician, seem
To see the things thou dost not. Now, now, now, now!
Pull off my boots. Harder, harder—so. (168–73)

After 'preaching' to Gloucester of the necessity for patience (here, seemingly, merely endurance), Lear's effort to give a despairing universal pardon to all offenders dissolves into the desire to kill:

> It were a delicate stratagem to shoe
> A troop of horse with felt; I'll put't in proof;
> And when I have stol'n upon these son-in-laws,
> Then kill, kill, kill, kill, kill, kill! (185–8)

Anne Barton has remarked, 'Not, I think, by accident, are repeated words so characteristic of this tragedy. The last two acts are filled with frenzied repetitions, some of them hammered upon as many as six times in the course of a single line: "Kill," "Now," "Howl," "Never," the monosyllabic "No." One comes to feel that these words are being broken on the anvil in an effort to determine whether or not there is anything inside.' Barton relates these repetitions to the broken syntax and the general inadequacy of language: 'There is no vocabulary for what [Lear] feels.' 'Words define the gap between individuals; they do not bridge it.'[13] Although her formulations are attractive and moving, I think they are also overstated and partial. Not unless we limit 'language' to the clearly denotative or to rational or conceptual propositions or to standard and conventional speech patterns can we maintain that the language of *King Lear* is in any sense 'inadequate'. Those impassioned repetitions are related to Shakespeare's 'unprecedented insistence' in *Lear* 'that the audience actively participate in the emotional experience of his characters'.[14] If at times we feel the enormous gaps between individuals, at other times the language creates, as it explores the limits of human experience, remarkable 'bridges', both between the characters on the stage and between them and the members of the audience.

[13] 'Shakespeare and the Limits of Language', *Shakespeare Survey 24* (1971), pp. 25–7. Winifred M. T. Nowottny had earlier made a similar point: 'Shakespeare concentrates upon Lear the style that gives a felt experience of the incommensurateness of human nature to what it must endure. . . . The play is deeply concerned with the inadequacy of language to do justice to feeling or to afford any handhold against abysses of iniquity and suffering. . . . [Lear] must use language not as the adequate register of experience, but as evidence that his experience is beyond language's scope', 'Some Aspects of the Style of *King Lear*', *Shakespeare Survey 13* (1960), pp. 51–3. In ' "More Pregnantly than Words": Some Uses and Limitations of Visual Symbolism', which appeared in the volume with Anne Barton's essay, Inga-Stina Ewbank remarked of the play, 'Apparently we are faced with a reality so overpowering that language is utterly defeated' (p. 18).

[14] Nancy R. Lindheim, '*King Lear* as Pastoral Tragedy', *Some Facets of 'King Lear'*, pp. 174–5.

We can understand and respond to Lear's incredulous, exclamatory, and mad repetitions partly because the speeches of the other characters create a fabric of analogous and contrasting meanings, a 'language' we learn within the course of the play. Beginning with 'Let's see, let's see' as he starts to peruse Edmund's forged letter (I. ii. 42), Gloucester's early repeated exclamations—simple-minded, a bit self-important, turning to the histrionic in sentimental self-pity—are pale foreshadowings of Lear's later anguish:

O villain, villain! His very opinion in the letter! Abhorred villain! Unnatural, detested, brutish villain! Worse than brutish! Go, sirrah, seek him; I'll apprehend him. Abominable villain! (I. ii. 72–5)

O, madam, my old heart is crack'd, it's crack'd!
(II. i. 90)
O lady, lady, shame would have it hid! (II. i. 93)
I know not, madam. 'Tis too bad, too bad. (II. i. 96)

Edmund parodies his father's melodramatic urgency when he stage-manages his pretended struggle with Edgar: 'Torches! torches! . . . Father, father! / Stop, stop! No help?' (II. I. 32–6). But we have heard Edmund's more natural mode of thought and speech in his first soliloquy in which, with cool and playful malevolence, he contemplated the doubleness of language and value. It is Edmund who tests, to see 'whether or not there is anything inside', the words which ordinarily indicate familial relationships, legal judgements, and moral values:

Why brand they us
With base? with baseness? bastardy? base, base?
Who, in the lusty stealth of nature, take
More composition and fierce quality
Than doth, within a dull, stale, tired bed,
Go to th' creating a whole tribe of fops
Got 'tween asleep and wake? Well then,
Legitimate Edgar, I must have you land.
Our father's love is to the bastard Edmund
As to th' legitimate. Fine word, 'legitimate'!
Well, my legitimate, if this letter speed,
And my invention thrive, Edmund the base
Shall top th' legitimate. I grow; I prosper.
Now, gods, stand up for bastards. (I. ii. 9–22)

In Regan's and Cornwall's repetitions, anger and absolute insistence on their own power and purposes leave little room for any other emotion; impulses toward 'playfulness' are lost in the ingenuities of cruelty:

Corn. Fetch forth the stocks. As I have life and honour,
There shall he sit till noon.
Reg. Till noon! Till night, my lord; and all night too.
(II. ii. 128–30)
Corn. Bind him, I say.
Reg. Hard, hard. O filthy traitor!
(III. vii. 31)
Corn. Where hast thou sent the King?
Glo. To Dover.
Corn. Wherefore to Dover? Wast thou not charg'd at peril—
Reg. Wherefore to Dover? Let him first answer that.
Glo. I am tied to th' stake, and I must stand the course.
Reg. Wherefore to Dover? (III. vii. 50–4)

To these and the following horrible repetitions of 'see', Edgar's cry, 'World, world, O world!' (IV. I. 10) may seem the inevitable response of astonishment and defeat.

It is, of course, Cordelia whose language is able to still Lear's anguished repetitions and to end the storm within him. We learn from the Gentleman's conversation with Kent that, when she heard of Lear's sufferings, Cordelia also experienced inner conflict, but a conflict that differed from her father's. Cordelia shared some of the elements of Lear's trauma (shock, incredulity, grief, attempts at patience), but she was remarkably free from his rage, guilt, and attempts at 'noble anger', as well as his despair, desire to kill, and madness. All of her emotions were compatible with the love which created a novel sort of beauty from the elements in strife within her face. When she finally uttered a language beyond smiles and tears and glances, her repeated exclamations contained no doubleness or ironies, no anger or self-assertion or self-pity, only shock and grief and pity for her father:

Kent. Made she no verbal question?
Gent. Faith, once or twice she heav'd the name of father
Pantingly forth, as if it press'd her heart;
Cried 'Sisters! sisters! Shame of ladies! Sisters!
Kent! father! sisters! What i' th' storm! i' th' night?
Let pity not be believ'd!' (IV. iii. 24–9)

When we hear Cordelia directly in the next scene, her manner and language are precisely as the Gentleman described them. She ends the scene with an apostrophe:

> O dear father!
> It is thy business that I go about;
> Therefore great France
> My mourning and importun'd tears hath pitied.
> No blown ambition doth our arms incite,
> But love, dear love, and our ag'd father's right.
> Soon may I hear and see him! (IV. iv. 23–9)

The final half-line, coming surprisingly after the 'conclusive' couplet, is very moving; one reason may be that we have heard a similar cadence, coupled with love and the desire to aid and a prayer, at the end of an earlier scene, when the Third Servant moved to comfort the blind Gloucester:

> Go thou. I'll fetch some flax and whites of eggs
> To apply to his bleeding face. Now heaven help him!
> (III. vii. 105–6)

It is important that we hear Cordelia's cadences when we do,[15] but Lear does not hear the voice that ends his nausea and madness until Act IV, scene vii, when he wakes to music and a kiss, and discovers his royal robes restored and a daughter who weeps and kneels. He thought he had come to know the truth of life—his life—that it was a hell of torment; Cordelia's face (which he had sworn he would never see again), her kiss, and her words ('How does my royal lord? How fares your Majesty?') convince him that she cannot be living in his realm. Lear's struggle to discover where he is, whether he is asleep, whether he can trust his senses (his questions concern always not what he can 'believe' but what he can 'know'—the difference is that between speculative commitment in a realm that leaves room for contemplative mental distance and total imaginative certainty within the present moment of a life of suffering[16]), is interrupted when Cordelia kneels to ask his blessing. After his immediate attempt to kneel to her, he confesses his foolishness,

[15] A production which follows the Folio in omitting Act IV, scene iii, with its unusually rhetorical Gentleman, seriously weakens the role of Cordelia.

[16] William R. Elton, by contrast, thinks that '*King Lear*'s ultimate question' is 'What can man believe?' ('*King Lear*' *and the Gods*, p. 62). He reads the play as primarily concerned with questioning religious belief.

age, doubtful sanity, and ignorance, and he ventures the *thought* that 'this lady' is Cordelia. Cordelia's repeated assurance ('And so I am, I am') does not go all the way to convince Lear that his former hard-earned knowledge of the world's reality was incomplete. He had thought that, while daughters might speak the language of love when they had none in their hearts and while one might well be recompensed for the gift of a kingdom with hatred and attempts on one's life, good, at least, must be significantly related to, if not identical with, justice: a recognition of, and either reward or punishment for, remarkable 'deservings'. He assumes that Cordelia's tears are marks of remorse for the 'just' punishment which she must, since she is good, intend to inflict upon him for his wrongs to her:

> Be your tears wet? Yes, faith. I pray weep not;
> If you have poison for me I will drink it.
> I know you do not love me; for your sisters
> Have, as I do remember, done me wrong:
> You have some cause, they have not. (71–5)

From Cordelia's 'No cause, no cause' Lear makes a discovery more astonishing than any of the earlier ones: love is as gratuitous as evil; it has nothing to do with 'deservings'; it is long suffering and 'kind', returns good for evil, and perceives 'no cause' for hatred or revenge.

When we next see Lear, he has fully understood. He is utterly unconcerned with the military defeat, utterly indifferent to being king. His exclamatory repetitions are now reserved to ward off Cordelia's suggestion that they should see 'these daughters and these sisters': 'No, no, no, no! Come, let's away to prison. / We two alone will sing like birds i' th' cage' (v. iii. 8–9). Lear's joy is absolute. He is so sure that he and Cordelia are above and beyond the times and tides that govern the powers of this world that he can imagine them only as pastimes for their amused conversation and contemplation.

Bradley remarked, 'I might almost say that the "moral" of *King Lear* is presented in the irony of this collocation:

> *Albany.* The gods defend her!
> *Enter Lear with Cordelia dead in his arms.*

The "gods", it seems do *not* show their approval by "defending" their own from adversity or death, or by giving them power and prosperity.'[17] As excruciating as it is, I think one can imagine more horrible endings than the one Shakespeare gives us—a view of Goneril triumphant, say, perhaps subjecting Cordelia and Lear to slow torture, looking forward to a long rule with her consort Edmund. It would be even more terrible if Cordelia changed and lived to scorn Lear—or even if Lear in his madness thought she did. But such changes would require a change of the principal emphasis of the play from the fate of Lear or inconsistent shifts in the natures of the major characters. One can hardly believe that any of the predators could live long in each other's presence, and what we have heard and seen of Cordelia will not allow us to imagine that her love could change. Granted that the ending must give a sense of completion to the tragedy of *Lear*, Shakespeare's ending seems as painful as one can imagine.

Bradley remarked that, with the ending, 'It is as if Shakespeare said to us: "Did you think weakness and innocence have any chance here? Were you beginning to dream that? I will show you it is not so." '[18] Paul Jorgenson has remarked that Lear's ultimate question 'will no longer be, Who loves me most? but rather, Of what final reassurance is even true love? or, more urgently, What am I if Cordelia is nothing?';[19] and we are drawn into personally anguished involvement with those questions, too. Our attempts to preserve some comfortable distance from the characters, particularly the usual tendency to resist the threats of tragic suffering by clinging to the sense of our spectator's or reader's superior moral perceptions, or imaginations, or knowledge, or at least alertness, have been subtly undermined, I believe, by what has happened to our

[17] *Shakespearean Tragedy*, p. 136. Winifred M. T. Nowottny noted meanings which 'this collocation' suggests beyond Bradley's 'moral': 'Along the receding planes keyed into this tableau we see in an instant of time Lear's sin and its retribution, the wider evil that has struck them both, the full fatherhood of Lear bearing his child in his arms whilst at the same time the natural course of life is seen reversed (Lear senile, so lately cared for by Cordelia), the world's destruction of the love and forgiveness that had transcended it—for the reverberation of the reunion is still strong and the language of that scene has opened the way to those suggestions of a saviour's death which now make it inescapable that Cordelia dead in her father's arms and displayed to the world, should strike deeply into responses that lie midway between religion and art', *Shakespeare Survey 13* (1960), p. 56.

[18] *Shakespearean Tragedy*, p. 271.

[19] *Lear's Self-Discovery* (Berkeley and Los Angeles, University of California Press, 1967), p. 99.

attention in the long and intricate final scene. We in the audience are immediately concerned with the fates of Cordelia and Lear when the Officer who will do 'man's work' exits at line 40; but we do not hear the details of Edmund's written orders, and during the crowded sequence of events which follows (the confrontations between Albany, Edmund, and Regan, the challenge and the herald's trumpet, the appearance of the armed and helmeted Edgar and the duel, the mortal wounding of Edmund, the 'discovery' of Edgar and his narration of the death of Gloucester and the near-death of Kent, the messenger's announcement of the deaths of Goneril and Regan), we are largely concerned with other things. I believe most members of the audience are doubly moved by Albany's conscience-stricken response to Kent's enquiry for Lear, 'Great thing of us forgot!' (236): we too had momentarily forgotten, and we can hardly believe it possible that we should have done so. We have shared to some degree in the awful carelessness or distraction among the well-intentioned which causes or allows or at least ignores disaster, and with weakened defences we share with the other survivors the ultimate question of the play: what if, after wrongs and loss and agony, recognition and the acquisition of knowledge and the discovery of love, one found murdered the one who embodied all that one had come to know and love? Could anything make us feel at such a moment that life was worth living?

If at the end we respond to Lear's death as heroic rather than merely pathetic, it is, I believe, because his final powerful fluctuating responses cast doubt on the 'realities' which we often assume as 'objective' or 'self-evident'—even on the question of what we mean by 'life'. What Lear wills or desires is less important than what he perceives and 'knows'. Those repeated 'howls' at his entrance express his immediate response to his *knowledge* that Cordelia is dead:

> Howl, howl, howl, howl! O, you are men of stones!
> Had I your tongues and eyes, I'd use them so
> That heaven's vault should crack. She's gone for ever.
> I know when one is dead and when one lives;
> She's dead as earth. (257–61)

His request for the looking-glass, which directly follows, indicates his inability to believe that the face on which he gazes is without life. It is neither weak nor mad, but a fairly common experience in the first moments or hours after death—particularly when there are neither physicians nor machines to give assurance of what the eyes alone cannot determine—for the survivors who gaze on the faces of those they have loved to believe that they can see signs of life within them. 'This feather stirs' almost certainly reports what the feather does do when it is held tightly in a trembling hand and observed closely. Lear takes the 'stirring' as evidence of a redeeming possibility.

> This feather stirs; she lives. If it be so,
> It is a chance which does redeem all sorrows
> That ever I have felt. (265–7)

Lear brushes Kent and the others roughly aside when Kent kneels and seeks for recognition, acknowledgement, and a farewell:

> A plague upon you, murderers, traitors all!
> I might have sav'd her; now she's gone for ever.
> Cordelia, Cordelia! stay a little. Ha!
> What is't thou say'st? Her voice was ever soft,
> Gentle, and low—an excellent thing in woman.
> I kill'd the slave that was a-hanging thee. (269–74)

The shifts of tense and address are both astonishing and moving. After line 270, with its assumption that Cordelia is already dead ('she's gone for ever'), Lear addresses Cordelia with the plea, 'stay a little', as if only a slight delay in her departure would be enough, anticipating Kent's later assuredness in 'I have a journey, sir, shortly to go': for these two, as for Hamlet after his return from England, the knowledge that the interval will be brief makes the precise time of death relatively unimportant. Lear's 'Ha!' marks the moment of a new 'discovery', when he thinks that Cordelia is speaking to him. He has learned that he can no longer trust his senses for a full or accurate account of external reality. At the beginning of the play he had heard and believed the words of Goneril and Regan and he had heard and failed to understand those of Cordelia. These and later 'crosses' have provided Lear with an experiential basis for profound scepticism concerning his perceptions. So now he believes that she *is* speaking to him and that it is only her 'soft, / Gentle, and low' voice that prevents him from hearing precisely words, of the emotional import of which he is sure—since they come from Cordelia. The question, 'What is't thou say'st?' is addressed directly to Cordelia; the description of her voice, to those surrounding figures who were just before dismissed (with all the world) as murderers and traitors. With the last sentence, 'I kill'd the slave that was a-hanging thee', he addresses Cordelia once again, telling her of the one recent event she may not have known.[20]

When the Officer confirms his statement, Lear for the first time truly notices those around him. He hesitantly recognizes Kent, but he cannot follow the news that Kent and his 'servant Caius' were the same man, and he agrees without interest or knowledge that his eldest daughters 'have foredone themselves / And desperately are dead' (291–2). From line 274, he seems distracted from the reality of Cordelia's body, but he cannot be much interested in those other persons and events. It is during Albany's speech (295–304) that Lear must again become conscious of the dead Cordelia, and with some sort of paroxysm that elicits Albany's 'O, see, see!' Lear is once again sure of her death:

> And my poor fool is hang'd! No, no, no life!
> Why should a dog, a horse, a rat have life,
> And thou no breath at all? Thou'lt come no more,
> Never, never, never, never, never! (305–8)

Lear's former convictions that 'she lives' and that she spoke to him, are rejected either as illusions or as possibilities now past. With that conviction, 'Pray you undo this button' seems to indicate that, once again, 'this mother' swells up towards his heart and that he is almost suffocated by his emotion and the attendant rush of blood.

But after the touchingly ceremonial 'Thank you, sir' to the character who has helped him undo the button, Lear turns

20 In his effort to demonstrate that Lear has learned nothing and that there is no consolation of any kind at the end of the play, W. B. Elton argues that Lear not only fails in the *ars moriendi* but also ends with 'defiance of the heavens, commission of a confirmed murder . . . and a final heroic vaunt', *'King Lear' and the Gods*, p. 259. I know of no generally accepted usage of the word 'murder', legal or moral, past or present, that would justify its application to Lear's killing of the 'slave that was a-hanging' Cordelia. It is difficult to imagine an ethical standard (except a totally pacifist one hardly envisaged in the play) by which the action could be censured.

back to Cordelia with, once again, a new and opposite conviction, this time an overwhelming and final one:

> Do you see this? Look on her. Look, her lips,
> Look there, look there! (310–11)

If one insists, hard-headedly, that it is sheer delusion, one may still consider it a consummation devoutly to be wished: to die in the conviction that one's dearest loved one is not, as one had thought, dead, but alive. But beyond this, Lear's final convictions that Cordelia is alive and that her lips move are overwhelming recognition of the reality that he has come to know: that the things he has learned from Cordelia about the nature of love (what he has come to perceive as Cordelia's astonishing essence) are more truly alive than anything else in his world. Cordelia's lips speak at this moment more than any other human lips he could ever imagine.[21] Lear had earlier asked Cordelia, 'Have I caught thee?' His last lines indicate that he has indeed, in a sense he had hardly anticipated, by the depth of his unbearably joyful knowledge of a reality and truth that triumph over death and fate and time.

That, I think, is what Lear 'sees', but not what we non-heroic survivors see—except in glimpses of his vision. The monsters may be dead and Lear's sufferings ended, but we may almost envy Lear his passionate certainty. We are left, as often in tragedy, with our eyes directed towards the mortal remains of a figure or figures whose heroic stature is beyond us. We are, moreover, denied even the relative consolation of the usual gestures towards the re-establishment of order. No more than Albany or Kent or Edgar can we care much about promises of continuity and renewal of the state or social fabric. Albany, not wishing to rule, attempts to give the kingdom to Kent and Edgar. When Kent refuses, with the simple reminder that he must shortly follow his master on his last journey, Edgar (if we accept the Folio reading) concludes the play. We may, if we wish, assume that he will accede to Albany's request—that he is the new king, but he does not clearly state this decision. He only remarks that at this moment noble characters no

[21] Sigurd Burckhardt wrote, 'He ends, it might seem, where Gloster, with his "Let's see," began. But he dies believing that he has seen living breath, not letters—words, not signs', *Shakespearean Meanings* (Princeton, Princeton University Press, 1968), p. 258.

longer speak according to their social and political, or even moral responsibilities, and he acknowledges that 'we who are young' will not (by implication *could* not) survive such suffering —or such joys—as those we have witnessed.

Riddle and Emblem: A Study in the Dramatic Structure of *Cymbeline*

GLYNNE WICKHAM

> I know not by what fortune the dicton of *Pacificus* was added to my title at my coming to England, that of lion, expressing true fortitude, having been my dicton before. But I am not ashamed of this addition. For King Solomon was a figure of Christ in that he was a king of peace. The greatest gift that our Saviour gave his apostles immediately before His ascension was that he left His peace with them.[1]

IT will be my contention in this essay that the sentiment lying at the heart of this pronouncement by King James VI of Scotland and I of England provided William Shakespeare and the King's Men with both the riddle and the icon upon which to graft the tragicomedy of *Cymbeline* for presentation at Court in the autumn of 1609.

Although the misfortunes of British Imogen in her love for the Roman Leonatus Posthumus supply the driving force of the play's story-line, the title role is that of Cymbeline, King of Britain: Britain, we must note, not England. It is with this King that Augustus Caesar's envoy, Lucius, negotiates for the resumption of neglected tribute: and it is this King who, on refusing to pay it, receives from Lucius the declaration of war that, without some intervening miracle, can only serve to precipitate his daughter Imogen's predicament towards a tragic conclusion.

Lucius. I am sorry, Cymbeline,
That I am to pronounce Augustus Caesar—
Caesar, that hath moe kings his servants than

[1] See D. H. Willson, *King James VI and I* (1959, reprint 1962), ch. XV, pp. 271–87, and especially p. 272. See also n. 9 below. This statement is represented pictorially in the frontispiece to the first edition of King James's *Workes* (1616). This engraving by Simon van de Passe depicts the King seated on a throne, the arm-rests of which are supported by lions rampant, and under a Cloth of Estate on which are embroidered the words *Beati Pacifici*.

Thyself domestic officers—thine enemy.
Receive it from me, then. War and confusion
In Caesar's name pronounce I 'gainst thee. Look
For fury not to be resisted. Thus defied,
I thank thee for myself.
(III. i. 59–66)[2]

At the start of Act IV Britain has been invaded, though not, as we might expect, at Dover nor at Hastings; instead the landing has been effected at Milford Haven where, in 1485, Henry, Duke of Richmond, had landed to claim the throne of England for the House of Tudor. Lucius is at the head of the Roman legions and consults a soothsayer about his army's prospects. He is answered with a riddle.

Soothsayer. I saw Jove's bird, the Roman eagle, winged
From the spongy south to this part of the west,
There vanished in sunbeams.
(IV. ii. 349–51)

This vision he interprets, not unreasonably, as signifying Roman victory. The battle itself is spread over the next four scenes; but, contrary to the southsayer's prediction, it concludes with a British victory and the capture and imprisonment of Leonatus Posthumus. At this point Shakespeare interpolates an extended, masque-like intermezzo seemingly to effect, with the aid of a *deus ex machina*, a reversal in the otherwise inevitably tragic outcome to the romantic story of Imogen's true-love for Posthumus. While Posthumus sleeps, the ghosts of his dead father, mother, and brothers all plead to Jove to save him: whereupon Jupiter 'descends in thunder and lightning, sitting upon an eagle' and causes a tablet, bearing an inscription, to be placed on Posthumus's breast. On waking, he reads it; but he can make no sense of it.

'Tis still a dream; or else such stuff as madmen
Tongue, and brain not; either both, or nothing:
Or senseless speaking, or a speaking such
As sense cannot untie.
(V. iv. 144–7)

It is another riddle. This one concerns lions conjoined with peace, interlaced with a strange medley of tender air, a stately cedar, and lopped branches: yet, strikingly, *Leonatus* appears

[2] This and all other quotations from *Cymbeline* are taken from *The London Shakespeare*, ed. John Munro (1958), ii. 1169–1291.

here to be deliberately linked with *Pacificus*, since it is predicted that not only will Posthumus's miseries end, but Britain will 'flourish in peace and plenty'.

With this much achieved, and with the way thus open to a happy ending, Shakespeare has seemed to most of his critics to have been singularly inept in electing to revive in his audience's mind at this point in the play the vexed question of tribute. Cymbeline has won. He says to Lucius, now his prisoner,

> Thou com'st not, Caius, now for tribute; that
> The Britons have razed out, though with the loss
> Of many a bold one.
>
> (v. v. 69–71)

Indeed, not only will Augustus not be receiving tribute, but all Cymbeline's Roman prisoners (as is the case in *Titus Andronicus*) are to be sacrificed to appease the kinsmen of the 'good souls' who died at their hands. Yet by the end of this scene, and without any external pressure upon him to do so, Cymbeline stages a complete volte-face: the prisoners are spared, and the King volunteers

> To pay our wonted tribute, from the which
> We were dissuaded by our wicked Queen;
> Whom heavens in justice both on her and hers
> Have laid most heavy hand.
>
> (v. v. 460–3)

In between these two contradictory stances, however, lies the double reunion of Imogen with Posthumus and that of Cymbeline with his three children, together with the unravelling of the two riddles posed earlier by the soothsayer and by Jove: and the play then ends with the couplet,

> Set on there! Never was a war did cease,
> Ere bloody hands were washed, with such a peace.

It is my case that these riddles and the emblems they contain supply the key to the cipher that explains the play's construction and removes the contradictions implicit in what for earlier critics appeared to be spurious passages in the text,[3] and in

[3] Pope rejected v. iv as spurious; Coleridge remarked that 'it is not easy to conjecture why Shakespeare should have introduced this ludicrous scroll which answers no one purpose, either propulsive or explicatory, unless as a joke on etymology'. *Variorum*, p. 384.

what for actors and critics alike today still appear to be the play's most awkward scenes, even if they have come to be regarded as Shakespeare's own.

Since I have already documented elsewhere the climate of opinion that was fostered at all levels in society by poets, play-makers, and pageanteers concerning King James's accession, I do not feel obliged to devote space here to more than a brief résumé of those earlier findings.[4] The names matter: Samuel Daniel, as author of the *Panegyrike Congratulatorie* and provider of the first masque of the new reign; Ben Jonson, who together with Inigo Jones devised most of the other early masques; Thomas Dekker and Thomas Middleton who, together with Jonson devised 'The Magnificent Entertainment' that welcomed the new King into his new capital on the way to his Coronation in 1604; Anthony Munday, as author of the first Jacobean Lord Mayor's Show in 1605—*The Triumphs of Re-united Britannia*; Thomas Campion, the poet and musician commissioned by James I, together with Inigo Jones, to devise the wedding masque for Lord Hay and Lady Honora Denny on Twelfth Night, 1607. Themes matter too: phoenix and turtle; union; peace and plenty; youth and the springtime of the year; old and new Troy; the first and second Brutus; Roman and British imperial power; forgiveness and revenge.

Between 1603 when Daniel published his *Panegyrike Congratulatorie* in Edinburgh and London,[5] and 1611 when Jonson and Jones staged their *Masque of Oberon* at Court, many authors picked up these themes and related them to the new King and his family in one variation after another: and in doing this they were aided and abetted by the King himself every time he elected to address his Lords and Commons assembled in Parliament.[6] What then was the attraction of these themes at this point in time? Why were they projected so frequently and

[4] See 'From Tragedy to Tragi-Comedy: *King Lear* as Prologue', *Shakespeare Survey 26* (1973), pp. 33–48; 'Romance and Emblem: A Study in the Dramatic Structure of *The Winter's Tale*', *Elizabethan Theatre III*, ed. David Galloway (1973), pp. 82–99; and 'Masque and Anti-Masque in *The Tempest*', *Essays and Studies, 1975*, ed. R. Ellrodt, pp. 1–14.

[5] The best modern edition is the Scolar Press Facsimile (Menston, Yorks., 1969; reprint 1970). It is also to be found in *The Complete Works in Verse and Prose*, ed. A. B. Grosart, 5 vols. (London, 1885–96; reprint New York, 1963), i. 139–67.

[6] These speeches are printed in sequence in *The Workes of James I* (London, 1616), pp. 485–548.

so forcefully, both verbally and visually, to Londoners in every walk of life?

The simplest answer—and in my view the correct one—is that it was politic to do so: it was expected. In other words, both singly and collectively, these themes offered analogues, figures, and mirror images of the new King's picture of himself and of how he wished his approach to domestic and foreign policy to be viewed. Although such emblems might be regarded as 'Court hieroglyphics' and thus as 'caviare to the general', poets and painters, and the devisers of plays, masques, pageants, and entertainments, swiftly made it their business to translate them into public property whenever an occasion for doing so presented itself and attracted a commission.

James himself viewed the union of the Scottish and the English Crowns as a major step forward in securing both countries from the threat of foreign invasion, itself the prime requirement for the future commercial prosperity of the nation. He told his subjects as much when he met his Parliament for the first time in 1604, and his speech was immediately made available in print.[7] Just as, a century earlier, English prestige and strength had stemmed from the ending of the Wars of the Roses which Henry VII had effected by uniting the rival houses of Lancaster and York in his marriage to Elizabeth of York, so in James's view the future prosperity of Great Britain depended on ending the crippling war with the Catholic League.[8] A Peace Treaty with Spain was duly signed in 1604. Peace as the bride of Union, and Prosperity as the child begotten of that marriage, thus figured among the first of these potent images to become established in the poetic and visual iconography of the new reign.

7 See *The Kings Maiesties Speech, on Monday the 19. day of March 1603*, printed in quarto by Robert Barker, 1604.

8 The Duc de Guise and Philip II of Spain signed a secret treaty in January 1585 to exclude Henry of Navarre from the French throne; but as English involvement with the Dutch provinces increased so this alliance came, with the Pope's blessing, to direct its attention towards the invasion of England and the deposition (or assassination) of Queen Elizabeth I. In May, Philip seized all English ships in Spanish waters, an act of aggression that was effectively regarded in London as a declaration of war.

James I's Peace Treaty of 1604 contained concessions that were hateful to English pride, not the least being the agreement that English ships would surrender all right to traffic in the Indies and allow any of their sailors caught there to face trial before the Inquisition.

This was accompanied by another theme that could only serve to reinforce it: the idea that this metaphoric marriage and its progeny was both a fulfilment of prophecy and a direct expression of the will of Heaven. The vision thus came to possess a messianic quality that required an active quickening of faith if it was to attain fulfilment. To this end the poets returned to the legend of British descent from Troy; to Merlin's prophecy that Arthur was not dead but sleeping and would return to reclaim his inheritance in the fullness of time; to the belief that a second Brutus would eventually reunite the three severed members of the former single Kingdom which the first Brutus (son of Ascanius, son of Aeneas) had seized from the Giants. And to these myths they added a new one of their own coining: that just as the mantle of Troy's greatness had fallen on Rome, so the fame and prosperity of imperial Rome was destined in the hands of Divine Providence to pass to that Protestant and Elect nation which had challenged the whole of Catholic Europe and survived. For not only had the much vaunted 'invincible Armada' been scattered by the conjoined efforts of the English fleet and the winds of heaven, but civil war had been avoided in the phoenix-like arrival in London of the Protestant James within days of Elizabeth's death. In the euphoric and inflated thinking of the times, one major issue alone remained unresolved: whether to pursue this advantage by trying to wipe the Roman Catholic Church from off the face of the known world, or to attempt instead to heal the rift within divided Christendom in a truly Christian spirit by substituting forgiveness for revenge of past wrongs. King James himself opted for the latter course of action, a policy in line with the teachings of Solomon and Christ: 'blessed are the peacemakers: for they shall be called the children of God'.[9] Yet this was a policy that could not be entertained with any realistic expectation of success without the readiness of both parties to the quarrel to accept compromise and concessions; in a word, tribute. This James himself was ready to do by following Henry VII's example in taking recourse to dynastic marriages for his own children (the eldest two of whom had significantly been christened Henry and Elizabeth), provided Catholic Kings were prepared to acknowledge the legitimacy of Britain's

[9] Matthew 5: 9. See also 1 Kings 2: 25, and John 14: 27.

Protestant allegiance: he also urged his Protestant subjects to marry Roman Catholics and vice versa. This policy, however, was not one that could escape strenuous opposition from the militant Puritan and anti-Spanish factions both at Court and in Parliament, more especially after the scare of the Gunpowder Treason in November 1605.

Against this background, the verbal and stage images of *Cymbeline* begin to make sense, not only in the form of occasional isolated allusions, but comprehensively as formal elements of the device upon which I believe the entire text to have been erected.

The most important of these images, if only because they are reiterated on more than one occasion, are the eagle—more especially an eagle which in its flight from south to west is diminished by the beams of the sun, yet phoenix-like renews itself—the cedar, tribute, and Jove himself. Both the eagle and the cedar are emblems of Jupiter, and Jupiter, as *deus ex machina* within the play, signifies the will of Divine Providence. Divine Providence, moreover, elects to favour the King of Britain at the expense of his 'wicked Queen', her churlish son, Cloten, and Augustus Caesar, who are the explicit losers in this tragicomedy. The winners are Cymbeline, his two sons, his daughter, and her Roman fiancé: for them the play ends happily. 'A Roman and a British ensign' are henceforward to 'wave friendly together'.

If we now take the step which I believe Shakespeare intended his own patron and the Court audience to take and temporarily equate Cymbeline with James, then all the emblems that Shakespeare uses within his riddles hold. James, like Cymbeline, spoke to the ambassadors of continental Europe with the voice of 'the Empire of Great Britain'; and James, like Cymbeline, was in a position to refuse or sanction the marriage of his children to the heirs to Europe's crowns. Thus James, in real life, could aspire, like Cymbeline in the play, to be thought of and discussed in the familiar imperial imagery of Renaissance iconography: and Shakespeare in *Cymbeline* responds as his fellow poets had done in masques, pageants, and entertainments, and were continuing to do. Ben Jonson was the first to speak literally of James as a new Augustus Caesar. Describing the Temple of Janus erected at Temple Bar to greet James on his way through London to his Coronation, Jonson states that the gate, when shut, carried this inscription:

IMP. JACOBUS MAX.
CAESAR AUG. P. P.
PACE POPULO BRITANNICO
TERRA MARIQUE PARTA
JANUM CLUSIT. S.C.[10]

The Pageant of London itself was erected in Fenchurch Street and presided over by *Genius Urbis*, who hailed James with these lines:

How well doth he become the royal side
Of this erected and broad-spreading tree,
Under whose shade may Britain ever be!
And from this branch may thousand branches more
Shoot o'er the main, and knit with every shore
In bonds of marriage, kindred and increase;
And style this land the navel of their peace.

This figure closely resembles that in which Cymbeline's relationship with his three children is depicted in the words inscribed on the tablet placed by Jupiter on Posthumus's breast.

Thomas Dekker in his part of the same Entertainment devised a Pageant of 'Arabia Britannica' presided over by Circumspection, who addressed James as

Great Monarch of the West, whose glorious Stem,
Doth now support a triple Diadem,
Weying more than that of thy grand Grandsire *Brute*,
Thou that maist make a King thy substitute,
And doest besides the Red-rose and the white,
With the rich flower of *France* thy garland dight,
Wearing aboue Kings now, or those of olde,
A double Crowne of Lawrell and of gold,
O let my voyce passe through thy royall eare,
And whisper thus much, that we figure here,
A new *Arabia*, in whose spiced nest
A *Phoenix* liu'd and died in the Sunnes brest,
Her losse, made Sight, in teares to drowne her eyes,
The Eare grew deafe, Taste like a sick-man lyes,

[10] The complete text is given in *Works*, ed. Herford and Simpson, vol. vii, pp. 65–109: also in *Masques and Entertainments by Ben Jonson*, ed. H. Morley (1890), pp. 377–402.

Finding no rellish: euery other *Sence*,
Forgat his office, worth and excellence,
Whereby this Fount of *Vertue* gan to freeze,
Threatned to be drunke vp by two enemies,
Snakie *Detraction*, and *Obliuion*,
But at thy glorious presence, both are gone,
Thou being that sacred *Phoenix*, that doest rise,
From th'ashes of the first: Beames from thine eyes
So vertually shining, that they bring,
To *Englands* new *Arabia*, a new Spring:
For ioy whereof, *Nimphes*, *Scences*, *Houres*, and *Fame*,
Eccho loud Hymnes to his imperiall name.[11]

This speech was delivered by one of the Choristers of St. Paul's. It was immediately followed by a song equating London with New Troy, sung by two other choristers: '*Troynovant* is now no more a Citie'. The second verse explains why.

Troynovant is now a Sommer Arbour,
  or the nest wherein doth harbour,
The Eagle, of all birds that flie,
The Souveraigne . . .
. . .
  or else it is a wedding Hall,
Where foure great Kingdomes holde a Festivall.

The song ended with the lines,

Brittaine till now nere kept a Holiday:
  for *Jove* dwels heere: And tis no pittie,
If *Troynovant* be now no more a Cittie.[12]

The moral is plain: Jupiter, mounted on his Roman eagle, has flown westwards to London and has there undergone an Ovidian metamorphosis in this

New *Arabia*, in whose spiced nest
A *Phoenix* liv'd and died in the Sunnes brest.

This is precisely the figure in which the soothsayer in *Cymbeline* chooses to describe his dream to Lucius before the battle begins.

[11] The full text of 'The Magnificent Entertainment' is printed by Fredson Bowers in *The Dramatic Works of Thomas Dekker*, 4 vols. (1955), ii. 253–303. The description of the Pageant of *Nova Felix Arabia* is given between pp. 275 and 281.
[12] Ibid., pp. 280–1.

Six years later, when Jonson was called on to supply his 'Speeches at Prince Henry's Barriers' (Twelfth Night, 1610), he cast the heir apparent as Meliadus, Lord of all the Isles. Merlin, addressing him, declares:

His fate here draws
An empire with it, and describes each state
Preceding there that he should imitate.
First, fair Meliadus, hath she wrought an isle,
The happiest of the earth (which to your style
In time must add) and in it placèd high
Britain, the only name made Caesar fly.[13]

The Barriers over, Merlin turns to the King and Queen and, after praising Henry's virtues, adds:

Nor shall less joy your royal hopes pursue
In that most princely maid, whose form might call
The world to war, and make it hazard all
His valor for her beauty; she shall be
Mother of nations, and her princes see
Rivals almost to these. Whilst you sit high,
And led by them(,) behold your Britain fly
Beyond the line, when what the seas before
Did bound, shall to the sky then stretch his shore.
(lines 418–26)

If, as seems probable, *Cymbeline* received its first performance in the autumn of 1609, then these lines of Jonson's were spoken directly at the King and his family and before the whole Court, within a few months of the first night.

Here then are clues enough to explain the images in *Cymbeline* of the imperial eagle winging westward only to be diminished in the sunset which the soothsayer at first mistakes as betokening a Roman victory, but comes later (he is now, significantly, named Philharmonus) to reinterpret as promising 'Britain peace and plenty'. They also go some way to explain the presence in the play's riddles of the lofty tree with lopped branches 'which, being dead many years, shall after revive, be jointed to the old stock and freshly grow'; for, as Merlin observes

[13] For this text see *The Yale Ben Jonson: The Complete Masques*, ed. Stephen Orgel (1969), pp. 142–58 from which my quotations are taken: also *Works*, ed. Herford and Simpson, vii. 321–36; Morley, ed. cit., pp. 130–42.

in the Barriers, although Knighthood has seemed dead in Britain for a century, it lives again in Meliadus.

> Aye, now the spheres are in their tunes again!

Chivalry then appears and adds:

> Were it from death, that name would wake me. Say
> Which is the knight? O, I could gaze a day
> Upon his armor that hath so revived
> My spirits, and tells me that I am long-lived
> In his appearance.
>
> (lines 129 and 381–5)

In *Cymbeline* it is the majestic cedar's branches, Polydore (Guiderius) and Cadwal (Arviragus), who with old Belarius will rid the Kingdom of the vicious Cloten and rescue the King, their father, from capture by the Romans: and it is as the cedar that Shakespeare elects to figure James explicitly in *Henry VIII.*[14] Merlin's concluding lines in the Barriers about the 'princely maid' even throw light on what strikes us as a strangely forced derivation of 'tender air' from *mulier* via *mollis*

[14] The passage occurs in Cranmer's prophetic speech at the christening of Elizabeth I when he foresees the accession of James I.

> Nor shall this peace sleep with her; but, as when
> The bird of wonder dies, the maiden phoenix,
> Her ashes new create another heir
>
> . . .
>
> Who from the sacred ashes of her honour
> Shall starlike rise, as great in fame as she was,
> And so stand fixed. Peace, plenty, love, truth, terror,
> That were servants to this chosen infant,
> Shall then be his, and like a vine grow to him.
> Wherever the bright sun of heaven shall shine,
> His honour and the greatness of his name
> Shall be, and make new nations. He shall flourish,
> And, like a mountain cedar, reach his branches
> To all the plains about him. Our children's children
> Shall see this, and bless heaven.
>
> (v. v. 39–54)

The source of the image of the vine and the fig-tree as emblems of peace and plenty is 1 Kings 4: 25, an image which James himself had used in his 'speech to both the Houses of Parliament' at Whitehall, 31 March 1607 (*Workes*, 1616, pp. 517–18), to depict the transformed quality of life in the Border counties between Scotland and England since his Coronation. Less certain is the source of the image of the mountain cedar: the most probable is Ezekiel 17: 22–4, to which my attention was first drawn by my colleague John Northam.

aer, thus making it legitimate to link Imogen with Polydore-Guiderius, alias Meliadus, as well as with Leonatus Posthumus. Tender air, moreover, in the form of the south wind, Zephirus, is a role in which Samuel Daniel elects a few months later to cast Prince Charles (alias Cadwal-Aviragus) in the masque of *Tethys Festival* commissioned to mark Prince Henry's investiture as Prince of Wales on 5 June 1610, when Queen Anne appeared before the Court as Tethys, and the Princess Elizabeth as the river Thames, and where James and Prince Henry are figured respectively as Oceanus and Meliades.[15] Tethys and her rivers, we are told, have assembled

within the goodly spacious Bay
Of manifold inharboring *Milford* meete;
The happy Port of Union. . . .
(lines 147–9)

The object of their meeting is to give Zephirus a trident to take to London as a present to 'the great Monarch Oceanus', and a scarf with a map of the British Isles embroidered on it, together with a sword,

to greete the Lord
And Prince of th' Isles. (lines 158–9)

Once *Cymbeline* is viewed, therefore, in the precise context of Jonson's and Daniel's Masques and of the earlier civic Entertainments that I have referred to, instead of in the usual and much vaguer context of certain masque-like elements within the play, a strong case emerges for supposing that Shakespeare was deliberately manipulating his source material when constructing his play in order to be able to comment indirectly on his patron's own aspirations for his children and for Europe by emblematic means in the same way that Daniel and Jonson were doing at this same time in their respective masques. Shakespeare, however, was writing a play and not a masque: he was therefore obliged to use a different frame; and this, I submit, he found in his reiterated images of union. These are the siting of the Roman invasion at Milford Haven; the lopped branches freshly jointed to the majestic cedar; the reunion of Imogen with Posthumus and with her brothers; the Roman and

[15] The full text of this masque is printed in *The Complete Works in Verse and Prose*, ed. A. B. Grosart, iii. 301–23.

the British ensign waving friendly together; and last, but far from least, 'Th'imperial Caesar' reuniting his favour with 'the radiant Cymbeline'. It is these unions that bring war to an end and substitute peace for war in the play's closing lines. The price that has been paid to achieve it is a double one. The Roman eagle on the one hand 'from south to west on wing soaring aloft' has 'lessened herself and in the beams o' the sun/So vanished'; and in so doing has yielded precedence to the British Phoenix. On the other hand, the King of Britain has agreed to restore 'the wonted tribute'; he has thereby agreed to sanction the marriage of his daughter to a Roman instead of a native Briton. Heaven has played its part in this, not only inscrutably eliminating 'in justice' the wicked Queen and her doltish son who refused to compromise and in doing so provoked the war in the first place, but visibly in Jove's own person by placing the tablet on Posthumus's breast which revealed the divine purpose controlling and ordering these events to the mortals most concerned. Revelation is thus achieved through the transfiguring techniques of masque; and by these means James's own *impresa* of '*Leonatus* impaled with *Pacificus*' is expounded by the dramatic poet to all present with ears to hear and eyes to see in the art form of the stage-play.

Let us then review the sequence of events as they unfold within the play in these emblematic terms of reference. The play starts stormily—

1st Gentleman. You do not meet a man but frowns

—and builds swiftly, like the first scene of *King Lear*, to Cymbeline's angry pronouncement of banishment on Posthumus and placement of his daughter, Imogen, under house arrest. Her offence is to have married a foreigner (no matter how virtuous) instead of a Briton (no matter how vicious). If we think the King's attitude harsh and unreasonable, we should remember that even in this century, where the heir apparent is concerned, passions can still be aroused when personal interests appear to have been placed before national ones. Through the rest of Act I and the whole of Act II the romantic plot unfolds as a simple story uncomplicated by allegorical devices. The only hint that the play may yet operate also on an emblematic level is provided in the oscillation of the stage action between London and Rome.

This aspect of the play's construction does in fact come sharply into focus with the opening of Act III, scene i, in the form of an abrupt confrontation between the King of Britain and the Roman Emperor.

Cymbeline. Now say, what would Augustus Caesar with us?

This question is answered with a reminder from Caesar's Ambassador that Britain owes Rome a tribute of three thousand pounds. Tame as this exchange may seem to us today, for Jacobeans it held reverberations of an acutely topical kind that were bound to stir strong emotional responses touching both religious sentiment and national pride. The Caesar in question is Augustus, first Emperor, to whom James, as I have already demonstrated, had been directly and publicly compared by Jonson, Dekker, and others on his arrival in the capital city of the newly established 'Empire of Great Britain'. Nor could Jacobeans hear the word 'tribute' demanded in such a context without recalling the odious Peter's Pence which England had successfully denied to Rome ever since Henry VIII defied the Pope and, in doing so, launched the Reformation.[16] Indeed, James owed his English crown as much to the fact that he was a Protestant and not a Roman Catholic as to the fact that he was a great-grandson of Henry VII; and it was largely for these reasons that a dreaded civil war had not broken out following the death of Queen Elizabeth I. Even allowing, then, that Cymbeline's initial question in this scene and Lucius's answer may not have recalled memories of these events immediately,

16 Parliament acted in this matter in January 1534. The principal instrument for cutting off the jurisdiction of Rome in England was the transfer of papal authority over the religious houses to the crown. See F. A. Gasquet, *Henry VIII and the English Monasteries*, 2 vols. (1895), i. 151 *et seq.*: cf. Shakespeare's *King John*, III. i, where the King says to the Papal Legate, Cardinal Pandolphus:

> What earthly name to interrogatories
> Can task the free breath of a sacred king?
> Thou canst not, Cardinal, devise a name
> So slight, unworthy and ridiculous,
> To charge me to an answer, as the Pope.
> Tell him this tale; and from the mouth of England
> Add thus much more, that no Italian priest
> Shall tithe or toll in our dominions.
>
> (lines 147–54)

Shakespeare takes pains to stir them up and to blow embers into flames. Lucius's reminder to Cymbeline that the tribute 'by thee lately / Is left untendered' provokes from the Queen the riposte, 'And, to kill the marvel, / Shall ever be so'. Her son Cloten backs her up.

> Britain is
> A world by itself, and we will nothing pay
> For wearing our own noses.

The Queen, using nautical images that vividly recalled the defeated Armada, supports her son with twenty lines of verse that echo the jingoistic language of the war-party at Court who wished to see the war with Spain resumed. Cloten sounds the call to arms:

> Come, there's no more tribute to be paid. . . . Why tribute? Why should we pay tribute? If Caesar can hide the sun from us in a blanket, or put the moon in his pocket, we will pay him tribute for light; else, sir, no more tribute, pray you now.

The provocative and sharply sarcastic quality of these lines is unmistakable.

Cloten's rhetoric wins the day and leads directly to Cymbeline's sturdy defiance of Augustus Caesar and to Lucius's declaration of war. The whole scene is as ominously violent (and should be made to appear so in performance) as it is important to an understanding of the play's construction. For Shakespeare is here not only presenting us with a portrait, in human and kingly terms, of the heraldic lion rampant, but is deliberately inviting us to compare it in the formal setting of a royal audience accorded to an Ambassador with the image he has already created of Cymbeline for us in the domestic environment of Act I, scene i. Yet it is fortitude instead of anger that now informs the King's conduct; and the wrath engendered by Posthumus's impertinent presumption and Imogen's ingenuous folly in abetting it without her father's leave in I. i is here subtly switched away from Cymbeline himself towards the Queen and his stepson, Cloten.

With war now inevitable, Shakespeare carries the action in the next scene westward to Wales, where the banished Posthumus has landed at Milford Haven. Imogen, learning this from a letter, asks Pisanio 'how far it is / To this same blessèd Milford?' and then expostulates upon it in two seemingly superfluous lines:

> And by th' way
> Tell me how Wales was made so happy as
> T'inherit such a haven. (III. ii. 58–60)

Since every Englishman in the audience could have given her the answer to that question, the presence of the lines must be justified in terms of their emblematic significance. This Shakespeare knew; and he used the device to signpost the direction in which his love story was developing at its more serious and topical emblematic level.[17] Everything is now set for us to meet the two boys who 'know little they are sons to the King', and who will later be figured in Jove's riddle as branches lopped from a stately cedar.

The fighting starts; Cloten is eliminated; Lucius arrives with reinforcements; the 'two striplings' turn the tide of battle in Britain's favour; Cymbeline is captured, then rescued by these striplings; Lucius and Posthumus are taken prisoner. All this is accomplished in alternating scenes of exceptional melodramatic sensation and great lyrical beauty. At the centre of them is set Lucius's soothsayer's vision of 'Jove's bird, the Roman eagle', winging from 'the spongy south' to 'this part of the west' and vanishing 'in the sunbeams'. Coming at this point in the narrative (Act IV, scene ii) the ambiguity of this vision is as appropriate as it is accurate. However, as with the two emblematic scenes of the heraldic lion rampant (I. i and III. i) about which I have already remarked, Shakespeare elects to parallel and extend this vision in a second and more visibly realistic treatment: this occurs in V. iv when Jove appears in person mounted on his eagle to the Roman Posthumus asleep in a British prison. This painstakingly literal restatement is presented to the audience in masque-like terms: a dream in

[17] In the manner of Tudor Moral Interludes, Imogen changes both her name and her costume. Emblematically the choice of Fidele for the former is as appropriate as that of Perdita in *The Winter's Tale*, since, just as Perdita represents both herself (the little girl lost of the romance) and also the united kingdom of Great Britain, so the name Fidele expresses not only Imogen's own faith in Posthumus, but that much greater faith that must be quickened if the newly reunited Protestant Empire of Great Britain is to fulfil heaven's will and prosper in peace with the Catholic powers of continental Europe.

which the ghosts of Posthumus's dead father, mother, and two brothers appear in an elaborately orchestrated incantation to Jupiter, and ask for his help in reconciling Posthumus with Imogen, Rome with Britain. Jove then 'descends in thunder and lightning sitting upon an eagle: he throws a thunderbolt'. We have reached the most spectacular moment within an exceptionally theatrical play. Jupiter speaks. What these ghosts have craved is granted; *not* because *they* asked, but because it accords with Divine purpose. It is predestined.

> No care of yours it is: you know 'tis ours.

To prove the point, Jove then lays the enigmatic tablet he is carrying on the sleeping Posthumus's chest; it prophesies that Britain will be 'fortunate and flourish in peace and plenty' as a result of this royal marriage.

However, prophecy is one thing; fulfilment another; and if heaven's will is to be accomplished in this instance the lion-hearted and victorious King of Britain must first become as gentle as the lamb. Cymbeline, blessed by Jove with victory in the war with Rome, must serve as heaven's agent by voluntarily forgoing revenge and seeking peace. This Cymbeline does, thereby transfiguring himself, literally and emblematically, by adding the diction *Pacificus* to that of *Leonatus* which he inherited.

As Cymbeline is physically reunited with his lost children in the closing scene, so Scotland and Wales are mystically reunited with England under James VI and I to become known henceforward as Great Britain: the cedar, thus new jointed to its lopped branches ('which being dead many years, shall after revive... and freshly grow' as Merlin had prophesied it would), now assumes a 'stately', 'lofty', and 'majestic' stature, comparable with that of imperial Rome and a fit nesting place for Jove's eagle.[18] Heaven's will has been accomplished as mercy, forgiveness, and pity mingle to erase the memory of old wrongs and thus to admit a new era of friendship, peace, and plenty.

> Pardon's the word to all.
> My peace we will begin.

[18] See n. 14 above. It is perhaps worth noting in the context of this interpretation of the play's structure that Augustus Caesar was Emperor at the time that Christ was born. See Emrys Jones, 'Stuart *Cymbeline*', *Essays in Criticism*, 11 (1961), 84–99.

Rome's eagle dissolves in the sunbeams of the West as Posthumus and Imogen receive Cymbeline's final blessing on their marriage; and, phoenix-like, it immediately renews itself in 'radiant Cymbeline'. Tribute, too—no longer reckoned in vulgar pence or pounds, but rather in terms of regenerative self-sacrifice, and love in the next generation—has become a renewable commodity. The *Pax Britannica* can begin.

One further point, although seemingly only a corollary, in fact bears importantly upon the date of the play's composition. In Act V, scene iii at line 50 Posthumus is given almost forty lines in which to describe the battle, two of which the Lord to whom he is speaking selects to comment on:

> This was strange chance:
> A narrow lane, an old man, and two boys!

Posthumus finds cause to repeat the image for a third time, and within a rhymed couplet at that.

> Two boys, an old man twice a boy, a lane,
> Preserved the Britons, was the Romans' bane!
> (lines 57–8)

The whole passage reads like Imogen's earlier expostulation on the Romans' choice of Milford Haven for the invasion and is so artificially contrived as strongly to suggest that it contains another riddle, another emblem. As Geoffrey Bullough has remarked,[19] Shakespeare took this incident from Holinshed's *The Description & History of Scotland* (ed. 1587) which he had already used for *Macbeth*. There, the story is related in terms of a battle for the town of Perth between the Scots and the Danes, and concerns 'an husbandman, with two sons busie about his worke, named Haie'. This patriot turned the tide of battle in the Scots' favour.

> There was neere to the place of battell, a long lane fensed on the sides with ditches and walles made of turfe, through the which the Scots which fled were beaten downe by the enimies on heapes. Here Haie with his sonnes, supposing they might best staie the flight, placed themselves overthwart the lane, beat them back whome they met fleeing, and spared neither friend nor fo.

Haie received a peerage for his services, and the incident that thus brought the family land, wealth, and status was preserved

[19] *Narrative and Dramatic Sources of Shakespeare*, viii (1975), 11–12, 46–50.

pictorially in their coat of arms.[20] Haie's seventeenth-century descendant, Sir John Hay, came south to England with King James in 1603, was created a life Baron of the Scottish peerage in 1606, and married Honora, daughter of the English peer, Lord Denny, on Twelfth Night, 1607. This wedding, between a Scottish peer and the heiress of an English peer, was regarded at Court as itself so important an emblem of James's unifying and pacifying policies (to be matched where possible by similar marriages between Protestants and Catholics) as to warrant celebration with a nuptual Masque. This was commissioned from Thomas Campion and Inigo Jones, and printed in 1607.

Campion ends his dedicatory poem to James with the significant lines,

> who can wonder then
> If he that marries kingdomes, marries men?

This suggests to me that Shakespeare, by deliberately making the battle in *Cymbeline* correspond in one key respect to that associated with Lord Hay's ancestors, wished the Imogen–Posthumus story to do double duty in the play, and to reflect this wedding of recent memory, *en passant*, as it were. No less significant is one of Campion's Songs for this Masque.

> Shewes and nightly revels, signes of joy and peace,
> Fill royall Britaines court while cruell warre farre off doth rage,
> for ever hence exiled.
> Faire and princely branches with strong arms encrease
> From that deepe rooted tree whose sacred strength and glory
> forren malice hath beguiled.
> Our devided kingdomes now in frendly kindred meet
> And old debate to love and kindnes turns, our power with
> double force uniting;
> Truth reconciled, griefe appeares at last more sweet
> Both to our selves and faithful friends, our under mining foes
> affrighting.

This song virtually provides a précis in itself of the last Act of *Cymbeline*, and serves further to reinforce the connection between Posthumus's description of the battle and Lord Hay's wedding and its place in James I's hopes for Britain's future. Bullough thinks the battle incident may have been intended to reflect

[20] *Narrative and Dramatic Sources of Shakespeare*, viii (1975), 50, n. 2.

Lord Hay's investiture as a Knight of the Bath in 1610, and thus relates the play to Henry Stuart's investiture as Prince of Wales. He appears, however, to ignore the actual text of Campion's Masque which I find to provide a much more convincing explanation of the related passages in *Cymbeline*, and thus to make the autumn of 1608, or 1609 at the latest, the more likely date of composition. This clears 1610 for the composition of *The Winter's Tale* and restores legitimacy to its claim to being the Investiture play.

Shakespeare's Humanist Enterprise
The Winter's Tale

LOUIS L. MARTZ

The Winter's Tale begins to move within the context of Renaissance humanism through the striking process of 'Atticizing' that Shakespeare performed in adapting material from Greene's *Pandosto*.[1] First of all, he reverses the geographical location of the scenes, thus giving greater prominence to Sicilia, as opposed to Bohemia; in Greene's romance King Pandosto (Leontes) is King of Bohemia, not Sicily. Having chosen to anchor his action in ancient Sicilia, that prosperous Greek colony, Shakespeare is not content to use Greene's curious conglomeration of names for his characters—some sounding Italian, some Latin, one Gothic, only a few really Greek. Instead, he seems to have recalled from North's Plutarch certain appropriate Greek (or Greek-like) names for his characters: Leontes, Antigonus, Cleomenes, Dion, Polyxemus (Polixenes?), Archidamus, Autolycus, Hermione, and Aemylia are all there.[2] Two courtiers in Greene's romance named Franion and Capnio are merged into the figure of Camillo, the Italianate version of Camillus, name of a legendary hero in Plutarch. Garinter, the young son, becomes Mamillius. Greene's maiden, Fawnia, has a name that may suggest a Greek faun—but with overtones of lust hardly appropriate to the Perdita we know.

[1] The substance of this essay, under the present title, was prepared for a lecture at the University of Western Ontario in 1975, as part of a symposium honouring Arthur Barker. Since then, unexpected support for the view that Shakespeare knew the Greek drama has appeared in the important book by Emrys Jones, *The Origins of Shakespeare* (Oxford, 1977), which demonstrates the significance of Erasmian humanism in Shakespeare's education and early career, and argues strongly for Shakespeare's knowledge of Euripides, especially the *Hecuba*.

[2] See the Arden edition of *The Winter's Tale*, ed. J. H. P. Pafford (London, 1963), pp. xxviii–xxix, 163–5; my quotations from the play are taken from this text. In view of Emrys Jones's book, it seems possible that the name Polixenes has some relation to Polyxena, the slain daughter of Hecuba. Such a name, of course, is significant only for evoking a legendary or tragic atmosphere, not for specific relation to individual characters.

One might wonder why the perfectly good Greek name Egistus has been changed to the unusual name Polixenes, but it seems likely that the name Egistus is much too reminiscent of the villain of the Agamemnon story. Likewise the name Dorastus might seem to be more appropriate to the classical setting than the name Florizel, but this name is spoken very seldom in the play itself: throughout the pastoral scene in Bohemia the young prince is called by the splendid Greek name Doricles. At the same time Shakespeare increases the Greek atmosphere by adding two characters with striking Greek names, Cleomenes and Dion, as his two ambassadors to Apollo's oracle on 'Delphos', replacing the six anonymous noblemen dispatched on this mission by Pandosto.

Then Shakespeare proceeds to introduce a scene (III. i) for which there is no exact precedent in Greene: the brief but beautiful glimpse of Cleomenes and Dion returning from the isle of 'Delphos', with their awe-stricken and exalted memories of the island and its ceremonies sacred to 'Great Apollo'. Shakespeare is following Greene in naming the isle Delphos, a conception that seems to fuse Delphi and Delos. But there is nothing unlearned or ignorant about Shakespeare's usage of that name: it was common in Shakespeare's day.[3] The fusion of names indeed works to very good effect, for more and more we come to realize that Apollo is the presiding deity of this play. Thus it is appropriate to have this allusion to the oracle visited by Aeneas at Apollo's chief sanctuary and birthplace, Delos, where Apollo was for centuries honoured by songs, dances, and games in a great festival where people gathered from all the Aegean isles and shores, as we know from the Homeric Hymn to Delian Apollo:

in Delos do you most delight your heart; for there the long robed Ionians gather in your honour with their children and shy wives: mindful they delight you with boxing and dancing and song, so often as they hold their gathering. A man would say that they were deathless and unageing if he should then come upon the Ionians so met together. For he would see the graces of them all . . .[4]

[3] See Terrence Spencer, 'Shakespeare's Isle of Delphos', *Modern Language Review*, 47 (1952), 199–202. Milton twice refers in his poetry to Delphi as 'Delphos': *Paradise Regained*, i. 458; 'On the Morning of Christ's Nativity', line 178.

[4] *Hesiod: the Homeric Hymns and Homerica*, trans. Hugh G. Evelyn-White, Loeb Library, pp. 335–6.

Does this suggest, perhaps, some relation to Shakespeare's pastoral in Bohemia?

In any case, in Shakespeare's play the Greek decorum comes to a climax in the reading of the oracle, when many of these names converge:

Off. You here shall swear upon this sword of justice,
That you, Cleomenes and Dion, have
Been both at Delphos, and from thence have brought
This seal'd up Oracle, by the hand deliver'd
Of great Apollo's priest; and that since then
You have not dared to break the holy seal,
Nor read the secrets in 't.
Cleo. Dion. All this we swear.
Leon. Break up the seals and read.
Off. Hermione is chaste; Polixenes blameless; Camillo a true subject; Leontes a jealous tyrant; his innocent babe truly begotten; and the king shall live without an heir, if that which is lost be not found.
Lords. Now blessed be the great Apollo!
Her. Praised!
Leon. Hast thou read truth?
Off. Ay, my lord, even so
As it is here set down.
Leon. There is no truth at all i' th' Oracle:
The sessions shall proceed: this is mere falsehood.
(III. ii. 124–41)

Leontes has committed blasphemy against the god, a point that Shakespeare has added to the story, for in Greene's romance Pandosto at once admits his folly, in an utterly limp scene, almost totally lacking in Greek atmosphere:

Bellaria had no sooner said but the king commanded that one of his dukes should read the contents of the scroll, which after the commons had heard they gave a great shout, rejoicing and clapping their hands that the queen was clear of that false accusation. But the king, whose conscience was a witness against him of his witless fury and false suspected jealousy, was so ashamed of his rash folly that he entreated his nobles to persuade Bellaria to forgive and forget these injuries; promising not only to shew himself a loyal and loving husband, but also to reconcile himself to Egistus and Franion; revealing then before them all the cause of their secret flight, and how treacherously he thought to have practised death, if the good mind of his cupbearer had not prevented his purpose. As thus he was relating the whole matter, there was word brought him that his young son Garinter was suddenly dead, which news so soon as Bellaria heard, surcharged before with extreme joy and now suppressed with heavy sorrow, her vital spirits were so stopped that she fell down presently dead, and could be never revived.[5]

And she is really dead. Her restoration is all Shakespeare's work. In this way the death of Mamillius becomes the punishment for blasphemy, as Leontes admits: 'Apollo's angry, and the heavens themselves / Do strike at my injustice.' And more than this. Leontes goes on to admit that he has committed all three of the chief crimes against the Greek conception of piety, those crimes for which the Furies punished men: blasphemy against the gods has been preceded by crime against a guest, the attempt to kill Polixenes, and this has been followed by crimes against the family, the attempts to kill his wife and his daughter. All this we realize when Leontes cries, 'Apollo, pardon / My great profaneness 'gainst thine Oracle!' and goes on to repent of the 'bloody thoughts' that he has practised against his 'kingly guest'. The 'piety' of Camillo, he says, 'does my deeds make the blacker!'

Such crimes form the essence of Greek tragedy. Is it then a fantasy, or an irrelevant association, if one should be led by all these Grecian effects to recall that Sicily was also a place which Aeschylus visited several times, a place where he produced at least two of his tragedies?[6] Aeschylus died in Gela, Sicily, leaving behind the famous epitaph thought to have been written by himself and known to every humanist of the Renaissance:

> Under this monument lies Aeschylus the Athenian,
> Euphorion's son, who died in the wheatlands of Gela. The grove
> of Marathon with its glories can speak of his valor in battle.
> The long-haired Persian remembers and can speak of it too.[7]

[5] From *Pandosto* as included in the Arden edition of *The Winter's Tale*, pp. 197–8.

[6] For a thorough treatment of Aeschylus' relation to Sicily, see C. J. Herington's valuable article, 'Aeschylus in Sicily', *Journal of Hellenic Studies*, 87 (1967), 74–85.

[7] From Richmond Lattimore's introduction to his translation of the *Oresteia* in *The Complete Greek Tragedies: Aeschylus I*, ed. David Grene and Richmond Lattimore (Chicago, 1953), p. 1.

Only Aeschylus himself, it seems, would have neglected to speak of his own dramatic achievements. The association of Aeschylus with Sicily was strengthened in the Renaissance by the tradition that he left Athens for Sicily because he had been defeated by Simonides in a competition for the elegy on those killed at Marathon, or, in another tradition, because Sophocles had beaten him in a contest of tragedies. Whatever the truth may be, these traditions firmly attached Aeschylus to the Sicilian soil, so that a Renaissance man might well think of Sicily as one of the ancient homes of tragic drama. Most of this was known to anyone who could read Latin or even talk to someone who could read Latin, for this information is contained in short biographies prefixed to Renaissance editions of Aeschylus.[8] The Latin translation of Aeschylus by Sanravius, published at Basle in 1555, is exactly the sort of edition that Shakespeare might well have read, with the quite considerable Latin that he must have learned at the Stratford Grammar School. Or perhaps Ben Jonson told him all about it.

If the Greek setting in Sicily evokes the spirit of Greek tragedy, one might go on to consider the much debated jealousy of Leontes after the manner suggested by Tillyard. 'Leontes's obsession of jealousy', says Tillyard, 'is terrifying in its intensity. It reminds us not of other Shakespearean tragic errors, but rather of the god-sent lunacies of Greek drama, the lunacies of Ajax and Heracles.'[9] Or, one might add, the terrible fury of the jealous Medea. From this standpoint one might develop an approach that Tillyard does not make, for he goes on to say that the jealousy is 'scantily motivated' and that 'indeed, it is as much a surprise to the characters in the play as it is to the reader'. But if we are reading the play in the mode of Greek tragedy, we know the story already, as indeed Shakespeare's audience might have known at least the outlines of the story, when we consider the popularity of Greene's *Pandosto* and of other stories of this type.[10]

[8] Both Robortellus' Greek edition of Aeschylus (Venice, 1552) and Sanravius' Latin translation (Basle, 1555) include a short *vita* of Aeschylus. Plutarch, in 'The Life of Cimon', also mentions Aeschylus and his reasons for travelling to Sicily: *The Lives of the Noble Grecians and Romans*, trans. Sir Thomas North (New York, 1941), iv. 221.

[9] E. M. W. Tillyard, *Shakespeare's Last Plays* (London, 1938), p. 41.

[10] On the stock elements of the Greek romances, see Carol Gesner, *Shakespeare and the Greek Romance* (Lexington, Kentucky, 1970), pp. 116–43.

Such an approach might solve the problem that many readers have found in what they regard as the sudden onset of Leontes' jealousy.[11] It is possible to interpret the opening of the play so as to indicate that Leontes' jealousy is of long standing (as it is in Greene's romance), and that what we see is the final, uncontrollable outburst of a long-gathering disease —a sort of festering, incipient madness. Certainly such an interpretation can be validly and effectively presented on the stage, as the director has done in one production that I have seen, in the summer of 1975 at Stratford-on-the-Housatonic. Every word that Leontes speaks before his outburst can be spoken in a manner of taut, extreme nervous tension. And then, with increasing signs of unease, Leontes can listen to the long and very affectionate conversation between Polixenes and Hermione, and near the end can hear her say:

> Of this make no conclusion, lest you say
> Your queen and I are devils. Yet go on;
> Th' offences we have made you do, we'll answer,
> If you first sinn'd with us, and that with us
> You did continue fault, and that you slipp'd not
> With any but with us.
>
> (I. ii. 81–6)

At this point Leontes breaks in with his abrupt question, for which Polixenes has given the answer thirty lines before: 'Is he won yet?' When Hermione says, 'He'll stay, my lord', Leontes answers with the pointed remark, 'At my request he would not' and then adds, 'Hermione, my dearest, thou never spok'st / To better purpose.' Is this equivalent to saying that she has at last made clear her guilt? Then she flies off into a heady set of questions to which Leontes seems unable to give the answer:

[11] For interpretations of Leontes' jealousy as long-standing, see Nevill Coghill's 'Six Points of Stage Craft in *The Winter's Tale*', *Shakespeare Survey 11* (1958), pp. 31–41; and Dover Wilson's notes to his edition of *The Winter's Tale* (Cambridge, 1931), pp. 131–3. For the opposite view—Leontes' jealousy as sudden—see S. L. Bethell, *The Winter's Tale: A Study* (London, 1946), pp. 78–9; Northrop Frye, *A Natural Perspective: the Development of Shakespearean Comedy and Romance* (New York, 1965), p. 26; Fitzroy Pyle, *The Winter's Tale; A Commentary on the Structure* (London, 1969), pp. 15–17; Ernest Schanzer, 'The Structural Pattern of *The Winter's Tale*', *Review of English Literature*, 5 (1964), 76; also Schanzer's edition of *The Winter's Tale* (New Penguin Shakespeare, 1969), pp. 21–4. For a summary of the arguments on both sides, see Pafford's introduction to the Arden edition, p. lvii n.

What! have I twice said well? when was't before?
I prithee tell me: cram's with praise, and make's
As fat as tame things: one good deed, dying tongueless,
Slaughters a thousand, waiting upon that.
Our praises are our wages. You may ride 's
With one soft kiss a thousand furlongs ere
With spur we heat an acre.

(I. ii. 90–6)

These are indeed hot words for a jealous man to hear, yet she goes on:

But to th' goal:
My last good deed was to entreat his stay:
What was my first? It has an elder sister,
Or I mistake you: O, would her name were Grace!
But once before I spoke to th' purpose? when?
Nay, let me have't: I long!

(I. ii. 96–101)

But the more she gaily prods him, the less Leontes seems able to speak: he appears choked with passion, as the hidden undercurrent of his thought at last breaks forth to the audience and to himself:

Too hot, too hot!
To mingle friendship far, is mingling bloods.
I have *tremor cordis* on me: my heart dances,
But not for joy—not joy.

(I. ii. 108–11)

I would argue, then, that there is everything in the text to warrant the assumption that Leontes has been in the grip of jealousy before the play has opened, and that the play is best presented when he is shown to be so gripped by this disease, the madness that he rightly calls *tremor cordis*. A shaking of the heart is indeed his trouble, destroying his deepest affections and turning all to hate, as with Clytemnestra or Medea.

Assuming, then, that we know the tale, we may find a Greek dramatic irony even in the bland opening speeches of courtly compliment, as Archidamus says: 'If you shall chance, Camillo, to visit Bohemia, on the like occasion whereon my services are now on foot, you shall see, as I have said, great difference betwixt our Bohemia and your Sicilia' (I. i. 1–4). He is of course speaking of the countries, but in the following lines the meaning shifts to apply to the two kings: 'Sicilia cannot show himself over-kind to Bohemia. They were trained together in their childhoods, and there rooted betwixt them such an affection which cannot choose but branch now' (I. i. 24). But the word 'branch' is ambiguous: it may simply mean 'grow' or it may mean 'grow apart'.[12]

Likewise, the opening of the next scene presents a speech by Polixenes that may have ominous undertones:

> Nine changes of the watery star hath been
> The shepherd's note since we have left our throne
> Without a burden. Time as long again
> Would be fill'd up, my brother, with our thanks;
> And yet we should, for perpetuity,
> Go hence in debt: and therefore, like a cipher
> (Yet standing in rich place) I multiply
> With one 'We thank you' many thousands moe
> That go before it.
>
> (I. ii. 1–8)

With the obviously pregnant Hermione standing before us, we can guess the impact this might have upon the jealous Leontes, for Hermione bears a nine-months' *burden*—'that which is borne in the womb' (*OED*). And there are innuendoes that a jealous man might find in the words 'fill'd up', 'standing in rich place', and 'multiply'. No wonder then that Leontes' first speech may well be spoken in a dry and abrupt manner: 'Stay your thanks a while / And pay them when you part' (I. ii. 9–10).[13] His following speeches may be spoken in a similar tone of constraint and taciturnity. I submit that the full impact of this opening is lost if we do not assume that Leontes is already, like a Greek protagonist, in the grip of a furious jealousy, as in the *Agamemnon*, despite her protestations of love and her flattery, Clytemnestra bears in her heart a murderous hatred and a murderous plan, as everyone in the audience

[12] In *Shakespeare's Wordplay* (London, 1957), pp. 147–8, M. M. Mahood analyses the ambiguity of these opening speeches. See also Derek A. Traversi, *Approach to Shakespeare*, third edition (Garden City, New York, 1969), ii. 298.

[13] Cf. Dover Wilson: 'Though very gracious on the surface, this remark, Leontes' first, is ominous . . . "Praise in departing," [is] a proverbial expression, meaning "wait till the end before praising" ' (*The Winter's Tale*, Cambridge edition, p. 131). See also Coghill, 'Six Points of Stage Craft', p. 33.

knew. Shakespeare too is telling an 'old tale', as the title and the text itself near the close (three times) remind us.[14]

We may then read the play as an ancient legend dealing with the problem that Polixenes sets forth near the beginning:

> We were as twinn'd lambs that did frisk i' th' sun,
> And bleat the one at th' other: what we chang'd
> Was innocence for innocence: we knew not
> The doctrine of ill-doing, nor dream'd
> That any did. Had we pursu'd that life,
> And our weak spirits ne'er been higher rear'd
> With stronger blood, we should have answer'd heaven
> Boldly 'not guilty', the imposition clear'd
> Hereditary ours.
>
> (I. ii. 67–74)

Shakespeare, in keeping with his Greek decorum, avoids the phrase 'original sin', and speaks instead of 'the doctrine of ill-doing', and 'the imposition . . . Hereditary ours'. These are phrases that might describe the curse of the house of Atreus, the sort of hereditary curse that lies behind so much Greek tragedy. (Can we forget that Hermione, in Greek tradition, was the daughter of Menelaus and Helen and the wife of Orestes? And that in Euripides' *Andromache* she is the desperate, unhappy wife of Neoptolemus, caught in a marital tangle, before going off with Orestes?) Though Hermione goes on to speak of 'devils' and 'grace', the Christian implications are so muted that they do not invade the Greek decorum.[15] Similarly the words of Polixenes a little later refer to Judas in a veiled and guarded way: 'my name / Be yoked with his that did betray the Best.' The rhythm would lend itself to the phrase, 'Be yoked with his that did betray our Lord', but Shakespeare chooses a term that might be suited to Greek religion and philosophy. Indeed throughout this entire first action in Sicily (Acts I, II, and III. i. ii) there is, I believe, only one overt anachronism: Hermione's line, 'The Emperor of Russia was my father'. But the ancient Greeks were involved in the

[14] *WT* v. ii. 28, 62; v. iii. 117. Also Mamillius' line, 'a sad tale's best for winter', II. i. 25.

[15] Bethell, on the other hand, regards the religious atmosphere of the play, including the passages here cited, as 'emphatically Christian' (*The Winter's Tale: A Study*, pp. 37–8).

manufacture of Scythian gold, and Russia in any case is a close neighbour to Greece.

This first action in Sicily, then, may be said to form a Greek tragedy, like the *Agamemnon*. But the *Agamemnon* is only the first part of that trilogy in which the hereditary imposition derived from ill-doing is redeemed by a doctrine of forgiveness and by the establishment of a court of justice at the word of Athene, under the auspices of Apollo. Orestes, in the third play of that trilogy, is lying at the foot of the great statue of Athene in Athens. Then the goddess herself enters, a living presence, to redeem Orestes from his hereditary curse. Should we add this reminiscence to the other allusions to Greek tragedy and myth that have long been felt in the statue-scene of *The Winter's Tale*—the reminiscence of the *Alcestis* and the story of Pygmalion? I think we might if we could be persuaded to regard *The Winter's Tale* as a trilogy, a sort of *Leonteia*—a trilogy of redemption on the Aeschylean model,[16] in which, as the middle part, Shakespeare has daringly chosen to present a lyric festival celebrating the powers of 'great creating nature'.

I am not prepared to press this idea very hard: but it may turn out to be a useful analogy that will guide us toward the play's essential design. At the very least, such an analogy may help to counteract a current tendency to see *The Winter's Tale* as a play in two parts,[17] whereas it seems to me essential to see the play as a three-part action performed in three different literary modes: Part I, tragedy; Part II, pastoral; Part III, miracle.[18]

[16] Neither Robortellus nor Sanravius presents the trilogy in its entirety. In an epistle to Marianus Savellus which precedes the text, Robortellus complains about the corrupted state of the Aeschylean manuscripts and, at the end of the *Agamemnon*, he notes, 'Multa desunt in fine huius Tragoediae', going on to explain that the beginning of the *Choephori* is also missing. In Sanravius' Latin translation, however, the *Agamemnon* and *Choephori* appear as one play. The Vicorius edition printed by Henry Stephen in 1557 (Paris) was the first complete edition of the plays.

[17] See, for example, Richard Proudfoot, 'Verbal Reminiscence and the Two-Part Structure of "The Winter's Tale" ', *Shakespeare Survey 29* (1976), pp. 67–78. Also Inga-Stina Ewbank, 'The Triumph of Time in *The Winter's Tale*', *Review of English Literature*, 5 (1964), 83–100, reprinted in Kenneth Muir's *The Winter's Tale; A Casebook* (London, 1968), pp. 98–115; Northrop Frye, *A Natural Perspective*, especially p. 113; Schanzer, 'The Structural Pattern of *The Winter's Tale*', pp. 72–82 (reprinted in Muir, pp. 87–97); and Schanzer's edition of the play, pp. 30–8.

[18] For views of *The Winter's Tale* as a tripartite dramatic structure, see the Arden edition, pp. liv–lv; G. Wilson Knight, *The Crown of Life*, second edition (London, 1948), pp. 76–128; and Pyle's study, especially pp. 152–3.

Part II of this 'trilogy' does not, I think, begin with the entry of Time the Chorus, which the folio marks as the opening of Act IV—often regarded as the opening of the second part of the play conceived as a 'diptych'. But these act and scene divisions may have no Shakespearean authority. Let us ignore them for a time in order to explore the possibility that the second part (or second play) begins with the change of scene from Sicilia to Bohemia (III. iii). It may be wrong to present the opening scenes in Bohemia as they are usually performed, without any intermission, immediately after the tragic departure of Leontes from the stage: 'Come, and lead me / To these sorrows.' A decent interval might be allowed here, to permit the tragic possibilities to linger in the mind. Then, after the interval, the second play (or second part) might begin—on the seacoast of Bohemia—wherever that might be!

But what can one make, then, of the three scenes—really four short episodes—that precede the entrance of Autolycus (at IV. iii) and the beginning of the central pastoral action? These episodes may all be regarded as prologues or preludes, all serving together to shift the place, the time, and the mood: the long speech of Antigonus, recounting his dream of Hermione, is a far better formal prologue to the new action than the familiar, almost jocular, couplets of old father Time. The episodes work by a rapid shifting through four different modes of speech: blank verse in the conversation between Antigonus and the Mariner and in the soliloquy of Antigonus; low, comical prose as Shepherd and Clown converse; familiar speech in loose couplets from old Time; and courtly prose in the conversation between Polixenes and Camillo. These shifting modes of speech, breaking the tragic decorum, accord with the shifting of place, time, and mood and prepare us to receive a new dramatic mode, another genre from antiquity—but here blended with modern English elements to form a timeless pastoral. We have moved into a never-never land, a world that is at once primitive and idyllic, a world where the sinking of a ship with all hands and the rending of a body by a bear may be turned to comedy. It is, above all, a world where the doctrine of ill-doing and the imposition hereditary ours can be suspended, a world where 'things dying' can be removed from sight, so that 'things new-born' can be allowed to flourish.

The central action then begins with the entrance of Autolycus, singing a song of nature's renewal:[19]

When daffodils begin to peer,
  With heigh! the doxy over the dale,
Why then comes in the sweet o' the year,
  For the red blood reigns in the winter's pale . . .

The lark, that tirra-lirra chants,
  With heigh! with heigh! the thrush and the jay,
Are summer songs for me and my aunts,
  While we lie tumbling in the hay. (IV. iii. 1–12)

Then he identifies himself: 'My father named me Autolycus; who, being as I am, littered under Mercury, was likewise a snapper-up of unconsidered trifles' (IV. iii. 24–6). Autolycus was the name of the grandfather of the wily Odysseus; the son of the god Hermes by Chione, in an incident closely related to Apollo and Delphi in Ovid's version of the tale:

Daedalion had a daughter, Chione, a girl of fourteen who, being ripe for marriage and endowed with rare beauty, had a thousand suitors. Now Phoebus and Maia's son, Mercury, chanced to be returning, the one from his beloved Delphi, and the other from the summit of Cyllene. They both saw the girl at the same moment and both, at the same moment, fell in love. Apollo deferred his hopes of enjoying her love till night-time, but Mercury, impatient of delay, touched the girl's face with his rod that brings slumber. At that potent touch, she lay still, and suffered the god's violent embrace. Then, when night had scattered the heavens with stars, Phoebus, disguised as an old woman, enjoyed the pleasure which another had had before him. In the fullness of time, Chione bore twins: to the wing-footed god an artful child, Autolycus, who was up to all manner of tricks, accustomed to turn black to white and white to black, a true son of his crafty father, and to Phoebus, a son Philammon, renowned for his singing and his playing of the lyre.[20]

[19] For Autolycus as the incarnation of spring, see Knight, *The Crown of Life*, p. 100. J. M. Nosworthy, in 'Music and its Function in Shakespeare's Romances' (*Shakespeare Survey 11*, 1958, pp. 60–9), points out that Shakespeare first introduces music at the moment when 'the process of winning order out of chaos is begun, when the winter of the tale looks toward the spring'. According to Nosworthy, 'Autolycus is concordant with the play's meaning less for what he is, "a snapper up of unconsidered trifles," than for what his music symbolizes—the reawakening of Nature.' Traversi presents a similar idea in *Shakespeare: The Last Phase* (Stanford, 1965), pp. 138–9.

[20] *Metamorphoses*, xi. 301–17, in the translation by Mary M. Innes, Penguin Books, 1955.

Shakespeare's Autolycus appears to be a blending of the qualities of this twin birth, his thievery being derived from Hermes, his gift of song from Apollo.

The allusion is important to this second part, for Autolycus serves as a benevolent presence over the whole festival scene, enriching it (and himself) with his tricks and ballads. I say a beneficent presence, for along with his petty thievery he brings joy and song to the shepherds' feast. He sells them what they want, and his cutting of purses while they are entranced with singing his ballads seems rather an appropriate reward for the pleasure that he has brought to them. He prances throughout this second part like a good-humoured satyr; his amorality is harmless, and his singing, if well-performed, could suggest powers beyond his beggarly tatters. In spite of his roguery he brings health, sanity, play, and happiness to the scene. Furthermore, he concludes the second part of the 'trilogy' with services of aid to the escape of the young couple, providing (perforce) the garments of disguise; he knows all, he overhears all, and thus he helps the prince by being true, as he says, to his own principles of knavery, when he deflects the shepherds, father and son, from going to the King with their story. He dominates the last 250 lines of the second part with his ingenious and voluble prose.[21] What the shepherds say at the close turns out to be true:

Clo. We are blest in this man, as I may say, even blest.
Shep. Let's before, as he bids us: he was provided to do us good.
(IV. iv. 829–30)

Thus Autolycus presides over the Bohemian scene, concluding with aid and hope, just as he has brought at his entrance the summer songs that dominate the festival. Summer songs: it is essential to get the season right, for there has been some puzzlement about it, because of a misunderstanding of Perdita's account of autumnal flowers. Perdita first takes Polixenes and Camillo at the surface level of their disguise, as old men with grey beards, and welcomes them accordingly:

[21] For a discussion of Autolycus' development and gradual loss of dramatic dignity in the course of the second and third parts of the play, see Knight, pp. 111–13. One should note that as Autolycus wins less and less approval in the eyes of the audience on account of his striving for courtly advancement, music disappears from the play.

Reverend sirs,
For you, there's rosemary, and rue; these keep
Seeming and savour all the winter long:
Grace and remembrance be to you both,
And welcome to our shearing!

(IV. iv. 73–7)

Polixenes then answers, saying,

Shepherdess—
A fair one are you—well you fit our ages
With flowers of winter.

(IV. iv. 77–9)

Perdita then apologizes by saying that she has to give herbs of winter because she has no autumnal flowers available, and she explains why this is so:

Sir, the year growing ancient,
Not yet on summer's death nor on the birth
Of trembling winter, the fairest flowers o' th' season
Are our carnations and streak'd gillyvors,
Which some call nature's bastards: of that kind
Our rustic garden's barren; and I care not
To get slips of them.

(IV. iv. 79–85)

She is not saying that the year is 'growing ancient' at this moment. She is saying that these flowers which, because of their hardiness, last far on into the autumn, might be growing now, but she has chosen not to plant them, and therefore she has none of them to give.[22] As she goes on to converse with Polixenes she appears to sense from his talking that he is much younger than his disguise indicates and so she offers them midsummer flowers:

Here's flowers for you:
Hot lavender, mints, savory, marjoram,
The marigold, that goes to bed wi' th' sun
And with him rises, weeping: these are flowers
Of middle summer, and I think they are given
To men of middle age. Y'are very welcome.

(IV. iv. 103–8)

[22] Schanzer gives the right explanation of these lines in his Penguin edition, p. 206. Cf. Pafford's confusion about the season, Arden edition, p. lxix.

Midsummer Day, 24 June, was a time of ancient festival (coming at about the time of sheep-shearing)—the 'Midsummer Ale', it was called, just as the Whitsuntide festival was known as the 'Whitsun Ale'[23] (the celebration that Perdita mentions a little later as 'Whitsun pastorals' bedecked with flowers). Shakespeare is here recalling three great English summer festivals of fertility: the sheep-shearing, the Midsummer Day, the Whitsun Ale. In this context little Christian connotation can remain in the word Whitsun, and there is no exclusively Christian connotation in the old shepherd's fear that he will have 'no priest' to 'shovel in dust' on his corpse.[24] Fear of lying unburied was a deep aspect of Greek religious feeling, as the *Antigone* demonstrates.

Then, as Perdita turns to 'Doricles', Shakespeare creates his delicate blending of English flowers and Grecian myths:

O Proserpina,
For the flowers now that, frighted, thou let'st fall
From Dis's waggon! daffodils,
That come before the swallow dares, and take
The winds of March with beauty; violets, dim,
But sweeter than the lids of Juno's eyes
Or Cytherea's breath; pale primroses,
That die unmarried, ere they can behold
Bright Phoebus in his strength.
(IV. iv. 116–24)

The mention of Phoebus takes us back to the opening of this scene, where the prince uses the Greek myths of metamorphosis to tell Perdita that it is quite proper for her to be attired in a manner that suggests the goddess Flora, and for him to be disguised as the shepherd Doricles:

The gods themselves,
Humbling their deities to love, have taken
The shapes of beasts upon them: Jupiter
Became a bull, and bellow'd; the green Neptune
A ram, and bleated; and the fire-rob'd god,
Golden Apollo, a poor humble swain,
As I seem now. (IV. iv. 25–31)

[23] See *OED*, 'Midsummer' 2, 3; 'Whitsun' 1.

[24] For differing views see Traversi, *Approach to Shakespeare*, ii. 313; and Bethell's study, pp. 84, 92.

Thus Greek mythology blends with English country ways and wares, and so, instead of a morris dance, the festival concludes when 'three carters, three shepherds, three neat-herds, and three swine-herds' make themselves 'all men of hair' and present a dance of twelve satyrs. It is a suitable finale for a world without time or place—just before that world is shattered by the re-emergence of the tragic element, as the King unmasks.

Another intermission is desirable before the third part of the 'trilogy' begins with a return to the Sicilian scene, where a strong new note emerges in the opening lines, as Cleomenes says to Leontes:

> Sir, you have done enough, and have perform'd
> A *saint-like* sorrow: no *fault* could you make,
> Which you have not *redeem'd*; indeed, paid down
> More *penitence* than done *trespass*: at the last,
> Do as the heavens have done, forget your *evil*;
> With them, *forgive* yourself.
>
> (v. i. 1–6)

I have italicized the words that set the theme, words that provide a much stronger tinge of Christian reference than anything found earlier in the play. They begin to shift the balance away from things Greek or pagan toward things Christian, things contemporary with Shakespeare. Apollo still is mentioned, but now we begin to feel some special reason for that Christian name, Paulina. She is a bitter reminder of the evil that Leontes has done; she is his conscience, and her words lead toward a scene that may be called a restoration by faith. I cannot, however, agree with those who would attempt to make the whole 'trilogy' into a fable of Christian fall and salvation.[25] *The Winter's Tale* moves from ancient Greek, to timeless pagan, to something very close to contemporary Christian. The triumph of time runs through the ages of human history, not only in one family. Now, in Part III, the language throughout becomes more explicitly Christian. Hermione is spoken of as a 'sainted spirit' and the servant, praising Perdita's beauty, asserts, in strongly contemporary terms,

25 Notably Bethell in his study of *The Winter's Tale* and, to a lesser extent, Traversi in *An Approach to Shakespeare*. I am greatly indebted to Andrea Snell for valuable assistance in the preparation of the footnotes to this essay.

This is a creature,
Would she begin a *sect*, might quench the *zeal*
Of all *professors* else; make *proselytes*
Of who she but bid follow.
(v. i. 106–9)

In this context the word 'professors' is bound to recall such sixteenth-century phrases as 'professors of Christ's name and doctrine', or 'the professors of God's truth in England'.

More and more, within the classical colouring, the Christian note seems struggling to be born, as when Leontes cries out to Florizel:

The *blessed* gods
Purge all infection from our air whilst you
Do climate here! You have a *holy father*,
A *graceful* gentleman; against whose person
(So *sacred* as it is) I have done *sin*,
For which, the heavens (taking angry note)
Have left me issueless: and your father's *blest*
(As he from *heaven* merits it) with you,
Worthy his *goodness*.
(v. i. 167–75)

The plural 'gods' and plural 'heavens' become in the parenthesis a singular 'heaven'.

Then in the penultimate scene, although the recognition of Perdita offstage is narrated after the fashion of a Greek messenger, the effect nevertheless becomes contemporary with 1611, as Autolycus hears the three anonymous gentlemen narrate in courtly prose the miracle of this recovery: 'they looked as they had heard of a world ransomed, or one destroyed.' Bonfires have been lit, ballad-makers cannot express the wonder, and best of all, we have word now of Hermione's statue: 'a piece many years in doing and now newly performed by that rare Italian master, Julio Romano . . .' (v. ii. 94–5). Here at last, with this allusion to the art of Raphael's partner, we have the one great undeniable anachronism in Sicilia, but it is carefully placed, carefully designed, to bring us fully into the world of Shakespeare's humanism. Appropriately, the director of the 1975 production in Connecticut placed Hermione as statue in the garb and posture of a Renaissance madonna.

The effect was breath-taking, and properly foreshadowed the restoration soon to be revealed, as Paulina says first to Leontes, 'It is requir'd / You do awake your faith', and then says to Hermione:

> 'Tis time; descend; be stone no more; approach;
> Strike all that look upon with marvel. Come!
> I'll fill your grave up: stir, nay, come away:
> Bequeath to death your numbness; for from him
> Dear life redeems you.
>
> (v. iii. 99–103)

We have moved from the ancient tragedy of blood through the cyclical, pagan world of great creating nature, and on now to the present time when, in humanist terms, faith, nourished by art and grace, may witness a triumphant restoration of the world to goodness. Yet Mamillius and Antigonus are dead, and Hermione's wrinkles remain, the finest touch of Shakespeare's realism.

Shakespeare's Inner Stage

KATHLEEN M. LEA

Do not anticipate from the title something 'keen and critical' about the non-existent alcove at the back of the *Swan* or any fresh theory as to how the bed was thrust forth. The purpose of this essay is more modest and quite different. The inner stage to be considered is one less actual yet more real, it comprises scenes, events, and figures that we are encouraged to see not with the bodily, but with the mind's eye; its traffic is with the significant shadows that gather round Shakespeare's characters inviting manipulations upon which subtle effects may depend. It is upon the inward eye, the eye of the imagination, that they register.

In this inner world there are Places, Times, and Persons. Time and place need but scant attention; they are only touched on here as reminders of the extension of the subject. The Places are those we suppose belong to the play until we see it staged, and when there is no sign of them we realize that what we seem to have seen has come to us by hearing only. The surge of the sea off Cyprus; Egypt's swarming life, even to the 'cisterns of scaled snakes'; the crow making way to the rooky wood; these are inner-sighted as through the slit windows of a tower. Wider views are more obvious: Ophelia floating under the willows; the night sky above Jessica and Lorenzo with stars reminding them of gold inlay on a palace ceiling; Vernon's description of young Harry,

> with his beaver on,
> His cushes on his thighs, gallantly arm'd,
> [Rising] from the ground like feather'd Mercury;

the sight of Richard disgraced riding through London as York reports it; Falstaff's death-bed, not to be shown except in a film and not improved thereby! These few instances will suffice, none need tax the producer; the scenes live only in the mind's eye.

For undisplayed Times consider the retrospect of Queen Margaret; the immediate past in Buckingham's ironic account of the misfiring of his address to the citizens; Edward IV remembering the cold night air after the battle of Tewkesbury when Clarence gave him his own cloak: the forewarning of Richard to Anne:

> In winter's tedious nights sit by the fire
> With good old folks, and let them tell thee tales
> Of woeful ages, long ago betid;
> And ere thou bid good night, to quit their griefs
> Tell thou the lamentable tale of me,
> And send the hearers weeping to their beds.

This is merely to open doors and whisk by. It is worth looking more closely at some of the Persons who never appear on the open stage. These are not, for the most part, real people, they are abstractions made palpable by personification after the fashion perfectly familiar in the morality drama of Shakespeare's childhood and in the developing cult of masque in his prime. All this is obvious enough. What merits sharper attention is the effectiveness of the occasional conjunction of personification and *persona*. It is an experience of seeing double, or, by skilled contrivance, of perfect stereoscopic vision. In *Twelfth Night* the Duke faced with Viola and Sebastian exclaims

> One face, one voice, one habit, and two persons!
> A natural perspective, that is and is not.

The trick of Elizabethan perspectives may give us a clue in reverse. When it is a case of reconciling the impression of an individual with a sudden insight into the general significance given by his moral abstract at that moment we see two faces to one person. Such focusing occurs when Timon says outright,

> I am Misanthropos;

or when Lear shouts at Goneril,

> Ingratitude, thou marble-hearted fiend,
> More hideous when thou show'st thee in a child
> Than the sea-monster!

or again when Albany looking at the same face and finding

the supernatural horror dominant has to reach out after the human being with an effort:

> Thou changed and self-cover'd thing, for shame!
> Be-monster not thy feature . . .
> Howe'er thou art a fiend,
> A woman's shape doth shield thee.

It is what injects a sense of possessive evil as Othello looks down towards Iago's feet expecting to see hooves in spite of the dismissive 'but that's a fable'. More simply, and most movingly, it is the instantaneous pathos of the Bastard's comment as he sees Hubert lift Arthur's limp body:

> How easy dost thou take all England up!

Watching Buckingham follow Somerset out in the opening scene of *2 Henry VI* Salisbury remarks:

> Pride went before, ambition follows him.

It is as though the real names were written on their backs as in some of the cruder Interludes. We gasp when an incognito is dropped, man facing man; here the shock is perhaps greater as human discovers its moral counterpart.

To borrow a phrase from *Comus*, where Milton himself is borrowing freely, albeit discreetly, from Shakespeare, these personifications are 'calling shapes and beckoning shadows dire'. Milton's *Maske* is full of them though not all are dire. A production of *Comus* does not present a 'blue meagre hag' or a Dian, a Circe, or a Cottyto and yet we are persuaded that we have seen them. No one was ever cast for Queen Mab. Who is most horrifying to the imagination: Macbeth trembling, withered Murder and his sentinel wolf, or Tarquin striding to ravish?

By the frequency and force of his personifications Shakespeare folds in the older style to the new so that the abstract dramatis personae make the receding Morality consciousness play upon the modern realism to provide shrewd glosses. Once in a while to note in slow motion what is happening does no harm, although in the pace of playing the images come more like 'the lightning which doth cease to be / Ere one can say it lightens'.

Through Helena's eyes we can see 'Virtue's steely bones / Looks bleak in the cold wind'; or 'Cold wisdom waiting on superfluous folly'. Richard sees himself as 'sworn brother . . . / To grim necessity; and he and I / Will keep a league till death.' Hermione summarizes her situation in terms that parallel Drayton's dramatic sonnet:

if powers divine
Behold our human actions, as they do,
I doubt not then but innocence shall make
False accusation blush, and tyranny
Tremble at patience.

Alcibiades is coarse but vivid:

now breathless wrong
Shall sit and pant in your great chairs of ease,
And pursy insolence shall break his wind
With fear and horrid flight.

Such examples occur like marginal grotesques and are variously related to the texts they adorn. Others are more closely connected. The economy can best be demonstrated by a contrast. In *Apius and Virginia*, by R. B., 1575 (1567), Apius is torn by indecision as the Vice offers to help him to the crime that is to get him what he wants. The stage direction reads: 'Here let him make as [though] he went out and let Conscience hold in his hande a lampe burning and let Justice have a sworde and hold it before Apius' brest.' Shakespeare found a neater way to represent such a state of mind; words suffice for Angelo's anguish:

O cunning enemy, that, to catch a saint
With saints would bait thy hook . . .

proceeding to the second highly metaphorical invocation, which ends with the cryptic but sufficiently suggestive

Blood, thou art blood.
Let's write 'good angel' on the devil's horn;
'Tis not the devil's crest.

If we were to meet most of these personifications in a narrative context we might say—how dramatic these are, they present tiny scenes. As they appear in drama proper we regard them as poetic accretions. Their true nature and function are to be the places and persons of an inner drama worked into the fabric of the play itself.

Some more elaborate instances are rhetorical; for these the main play stands still while we are invited to listen—even with eyes shut. This is when Berowne gets going on the senior-junior giant-dwarf Dan Cupid; or when the Bastard dilates over 'That smooth-faced gentleman, tickling Commodity'; and when Constance admits:

> Grief fills the room up of my absent child,
> Lies in his bed, walks up and down with me.

It is most memorable in Ulysses' image of Time:

> like a fashionable host,
> That slightly shakes his parting guest by the hand;
> And with his arms outstretched as he would fly,
> Grasps in the comer.

Virginity, thanks to Parolles, has her set piece. Richard musing alone in the dungeon begets a generation of still-breeding thoughts—'In humours like the people of this world'. Most fully developed of all in this kind are Gobbo's comic exchanges between the fiend and his conscience which might be a parody of the temptation of the second murderer as he hesitates before drowning Clarence. Henry V is granted twenty-one lines for the description of an infernal scene applied with relish to the wretched Lord Scroop:

> Treason and murder ever kept together,
> As two yoke-devils sworn to either's purpose,
> Working so grossly in a natural cause
> That admiration did not whoop at them:
> But thou, 'gainst all proportion, didst bring in
> Wonder to wait on treason and on murder:
> And whatsoever cunning fiend it was
> That wrought upon thee so preposterously
> Hath got the voice in hell for excellence;
> And other devils that suggest by treasons
> Do botch and bungle up damnation
> With patches, colours, and with forms, being fetch'd
> From glistr'ing semblances of piety;

But he that temper'd thee bade thee stand up,
Gave thee no instance why thou shouldst do treason,
Unless to dub thee with the name of traitor.
If that same demon that hath gull'd thee thus
Should with his lion gait walk the whole world,
He might return to vasty Tartar back,
And tell the legions, 'I can never win
A soul so easy as that Englishman's'.

Lastly there are occasions when the play is not halted, when the construction is tighter, when it is not a case of interrelation or succession, hardly even of juxtaposition, but so far as our understanding can take it of simultaneity of apprehension. We may not bring into sharp focus Hermione's morality inset quoted above—Innocence shall make / False accusation blush—but we would not be fully with the play if we missed the moment of revelation when Perdita with her hands full of flowers calls for those she lacks:

O Proserpina;
For the flowers now that, frighted thou let'st fall
From Dis's waggon:—daffodils . . .

There is no response from the underworld, nor need there be. She *is* the goddess herself in that instant and the hint is confirmed when later Leontes greets her:

Welcome hither,
As is the spring to the earth.

On the hinge of another hint Shakespeare opens a different door. The young Princes are asking about the Tower and aside from an innocuous remark Gloucester is heard to say:

So wise so young, they say, do never live long.

What say you, Uncle?

I say, without characters, fame lives long.
Thus, like the formal vice Iniquity,
I moralise two meanings in one word.

A Tudor audience would take this at once, though probably without the specific reference that a modern editor can provide. For a moment the mask is lifted and we grasp a fuller meaning to the conventional Richard/devil gibes strewn over the play. The reference makes a more precise identification. Richard's role is more kin to Vice than Devil, albeit a Vice in his most devilish guise. Nor would Shakespeare's first audiences miss the comparison that Escalus makes when Pompey has teased his patience:

Which is the wiser here? Justice, or Iniquity?

Dr Johnson guessed that this harked back to the 'old moralities'. It does: it catches up the final scene of the *Nice Wanton.*

We have been taught to feel the force of Henry's 'Up Vanity' with Falstaff in mind. When Autolycus laughs, 'What a fool Honesty is! and Trust, his sworn brother, a very simple gentleman', Shakespeare might be condensing Wilson's late morality *The Three Ladies of London* to his ribald purpose.

It is in *King Lear* above all that the dramatic effect of combining abstract and concrete is apparent.

Dost thou know me, fellow?
Kent. No, sir; but you have that in your countenance which I would fain call master.
What's that?
Kent. Authority.

Who is it that can tell me who I am?
Fool. Lear's shadow.

There are instances that may have caught our attention earlier, as when Lear says of Cordelia:

Let pride, which she calls plainness marry her,

a fleeting personification echoed by Kent:

To plainness honour's bound
When majesty falls to folly.

There is no evading it when Lear turns on Goneril and the personification of ingratitude begets a litter of animal identifications, wolves, tigers, serpents. Once Lear has seen that monster aspect of her vice we too are called upon to exercise the faculty that allegorical drama trains, and we become aware of the play as full of shadowy presences: Nature—great Goddess; Man, reduced to the thing itself; Age—viewed as 'these fathers'; Youth—as these children; unnaturalness, madness, blindness, rashness, pride, patience are invoked so that they hover and count. Such is the potency of the language in the context of the appalling situations that we seem to feel their reality like the viewless winds. A hint of what is happening may be found in Edgar's greeting to Gloucester as he comes into the hovel with a torch. 'Look,' cries the Fool, 'here comes a walking fire.' 'This is the foul fiend Flibbertigibbet,' says Edgar, 'he begins at curfew, and walks till the first cock . . .' The feigned beggar imposes his interpretation of the sight upon the Fool and does not leave us unaffected. Such a double vision is effected in the mock trial scene where, looking with Lear's eyes, we are almost persuaded that 'this joint-stool' *is* one of 'these daughters'. We realize if we pause at this that the barriers are down; we have been so much in the company of the fey and the feigned fey, of distress, distraction, and incipient madness, of the tumult without and within that we seem to share their consciousness. Yet herein lies a difference from consorting with actual insanity; the poet convinces us that through this crazed state comes vision beyond the ken of common sense. We are persuaded to believe that at last we see true in that it must be on the farther side of such suffering that sanity is to be recovered. The culmination is in the reconciliation when Lear tells Cordelia who he thinks she is and what is his own condition:

> Thou art a soul in bliss; but I am bound
> Upon a wheel of fire . . .

The power to believe in what we cannot at the time see, that is, against the evidence of our senses, holds to the end of the play so that we believe (or perhaps I should say, I believe) in some kind of life even when we see Lear die, bending over Cordelia's mouth, deluded that some breath has come to stir the feather. This is the supreme ambiguity upon which that extra, gratuitous scene is poised, poised perfectly, as I think, to the imagination but with a balance so delicate that it is all but impossible not to upset it by the rational pressure of an explanation.

For the manipulation of outer and inner worlds at its height a scientist writing in a different context provides an analogy, as he explains the phenomenon of stereoscopic vision:

> We gain the sense of perspective and solidity and distance just because our eyes see slightly differently and we accept the two

accounts. We do not super-impose them—for that would make nonsense of what we see—but in some sense we do hold them together. . . . The act of reflection [this synoptic exercise] is akin to the gaining of 'insight', a very different matter from gaining knowledge.[1]

It seems that when the mind's eye is brought into focus with the bodily eye; when inner and outer stages converge, the reward is insight.

[1] C. A. Coulson, *Science and Christian Belief* (1955), pp. 84–5.

The Date of a Donne Elegy, and its Implications

I. A. SHAPIRO

If it has to be dated only by style and versification, Donne's funeral elegy which begins:

> Sorrow, who to this house scarce knew the way,

must be judged an early work, but that is all its editors and commentators have agreed on. In the first edition of Donne's poems (*1633*) it was printed among the Love Elegies, with the heading 'Elegie VI'. In the second edition (*1635*) it was placed at the end of the Funeral Elegies and given the heading 'Elegie on the L.C.'. I believe its title in *1635* derives from an authoritative source, because the content of this elegy prompts a hypothesis about its occasion that explains the occurrence of 'L.C.' in its title.

Grierson's commentary on the poem begins by noting that 'Whoever may be the subject of this *Elegie*, Donne speaks as though he were a member of his household'.[1] This is undoubtedly so. Grierson then proceeds to refute the obvious improbability that the poem mourns the death of Thomas Egerton, Lord Chancellor Ellesmere (d. 1617), but without considering that it might refer to the death of his son, Sir Thomas Egerton, although he mentions the latter in the same paragraph.

Sir Thomas Egerton, elder son of the Sir Thomas Egerton who became Lord Keeper of the Great Seal in 1596 (and in 1603 Lord Chancellor and Baron Ellesmere), was killed in Ireland in August 1599. Donne was then one of the Lord Keeper's secretaries, and a member of his household. 'His Lordship', says Izaak Walton '. . . did always use him with much courtesy, appointing him a place at his own Table, to

[1] H. J. C. Grierson, *Poems of John Donne*, 2 vols. (Oxford, 1912), ii. 216.

[2] Izaak Walton, *Lives* (World's Classics reprint of 1675 edn.), p. 27.

which he esteemed his Company and Discourse to be a great Ornament.'[2] It had been through friendship with the Lord Keeper's son Thomas that Donne came to this secretaryship. 'By the favour which your good son's love to me obtained, I was four years your Lordship's secretary', he wrote to the Lord Keeper on 1 March 1601/2.[3] Thomas Egerton the younger and Donne had both been on the 'Islands Voyage', a naval expedition led by the Earl of Essex in 1597. During that expedition young Egerton was knighted, at the Azores, by Essex.[4] When Essex, as Lord Lieutenant of Ireland in the spring of 1599, gathered an army to suppress Tyrone's rebellion, young Sir Thomas Egerton captained a company in it. He embarked for Ireland towards the end of April.[5] In the middle of August he declined an office that would have taken him back to England, temporarily at least, and 'by his importunity . . . obtained leave to stay'.[6] A few days later he was wounded in the fighting and taken to Dublin Castle, where he died on 23 August.[7] An uncertain rumour of his death had reached the Lord Keeper by 4 September, and was confirmed the following day.[8] His body was brought over to England[9] and a solemn funeral service was held in Chester Cathedral on 27 September. A detailed description of the proceedings has survived,[10] from which we learn that Donne was given the distinction of bearing the deceased's sword and consequently a place of honour in the elaborate funeral procession.

What is recorded above shows that Donne and the younger Thomas Egerton must have been close friends by the beginning of 1598, the latest date for the commencement of Donne's

[3] Edmund Gosse, *Life and Letters of John Donne*, 2 vols. (1899), i. 114. I cite Gosse's texts of Donne's letters because they are widely accessible; although many letters are misdated and some texts imperfectly reproduced, they are quite satisfactory for the purpose of this discussion.

[4] Wm. A. Shaw, *The Knights of England*, 2 vols. (1905–6), ii. 94.

[5] Hist. MSS Comm., *Salisbury MSS.* ix. 113, 141.

[6] Ibid. 298.

[7] Francis H. Egerton, *Life of Thomas Egerton Lord Chancellor* (pr. pr., 1801), pp. 17–18, where the inscription on the younger Thomas's tombstone is transcribed, as in other issues of Egerton's *Life*.

[8] *Salisbury MSS.* ix. 346.

[9] The body had been brought over to Chester by or before 8 Sept.; Arthur Collins, *Sidney Papers*, 2 vols. (1746), ii. 120.

[10] First printed in *The Topographer*, ed. Sam. E. Brydges and Seb. Shaw (1789), i. 126; printed also in R. C. Bald's *John Donne* (1970), pp. 105–6.

secretaryship to the Lord Keeper. Their acquaintanceship, if not friendship, must be dated back to the summer of 1597 at latest, when both were on the 'Islands Voyage', but it is quite probable that it went back much further, to the time when they were contemporaries at Lincoln's Inn.

It would be surprising if Donne, in these circumstances, had not composed a verse tribute to his dead friend, and I believe that this is what we have in the 'Elegie on the L.C.'. Fortunately we do not have to content ourselves with a conjecture based on circumstantial evidence. The allusions in the poem are all consistent with, and confirm, the conjecture. That Donne writes as a member of the bereaved household is by itself almost conclusive, for what we know of other households in which Donne lived before he left Pyrford in 1605 (the style of the poem precludes its dating later) is inconsistent with the poem's allusions. Its first line:

> Sorrow, who to this house scarce knew the way,

would be inappropriate to any such household other than the Lord Keeper's, which until the death of his elder son seems to have been particularly happy. In 1599 Lord Keeper Egerton's wife (his second), was still alive. She was a sister of Sir George More of Loseley and aunt of his daughter Ann, whom Donne was to marry clandestinely two years later. There is ample evidence that domestic harmony reigned while the Lord Keeper's second wife lived.[11] Unhappily she became ill towards the end of 1599 and died on 20 January 1599/1600. The Lord Keeper's grief was great, so much so that it drew unfavourable comment from several observers, and even induced a mild rebuke from Queen Elizabeth.[12] How much happiness he had then lost is apparent in a memorandum of 1610 about his troubles with his third wife, the famous widow, Alice, Countess of Derby, whom he married in October 1600. Before this last marriage, he recorded, he 'was never acquainted with such tempests and storms' as he had endured from Alice's 'cursed railing and bitter tongue'.[13]

[11] Louis A. Knafla, *Law and Politics in Jacobean England* (Cambridge, 1977), pp. 30–1; W. J. Jones, *The Elizabethan Court of Chancery* (Oxford, 1967), p. 94 n. 3.

[12] Collins, op. cit. ii. 164; cf. also John Davies's verse-letter to Lord Keeper Egerton on the same occasion (Robt. Krueger, *Poems of Sir John Davies* (Oxford, 1975), p. 202).

[13] Jones, op. cit., p. 95.

The second line of the elegy contains a further clue to the occasion of the poem:

> Sorrow, who to this house scarce knew the way,
> Is, oh, heir of it, our all is his prey.

The use of 'heir' here is forced and a straining of sense. However, it was the Lord Keeper's heir who had died; this must have been prominent in the thoughts of the whole household, and also in Donne's as he wrote, and responsible for this awkward introduction of 'heir' in the elegy's second line. The closing lines, characteristic of Donne's proneness to exaggeration in funeral elegies, support this identification of the poem's subject:

> His children are his pictures, Oh they be
> Pictures of him dead, senseless, cold as he.
> Here needs no marble tomb; since he is gone,
> He, and about him, his, are turn'd to stone.

The dead man had three daughters: Elizabeth, Mary, and Vere. All were very young at his death.[14]

The heading given to the poem in *1635*, 'Elegie on the L.C.', is easily explicable. If the manuscript or other authority consulted by the editors of *1635* had described the poem as 'Elegy on Sir Thomas Egerton' it would have been understandable for this to be mistaken as referring to the Lord Chancellor of the same name. He had died nearly twenty years earlier, but his memory was still green and venerated. His elder son, dead nearly forty years earlier, seems to have been forgotten, and was not connected with the poem even in the Egerton family. The Bridgewater MS of Donne's poems contains the autograph signature of John Egerton, first Earl of Bridgewater, younger brother of Sir Thomas who died in 1599, and has the Earl's inscription 'Dr. Donne' on its title-page. The manuscript, 'probably put together in the twenties' of the seventeenth century,[15] includes the elegy 'Sorrow, who to this house . . .',

[14] Elizabeth in 1606 had the misfortune to become the 'Wife, widow and maid' celebrated in seventeenth-century verse miscellanies. On her and her sisters see *The Duttons of Dutton* (pr. pr., London and Chester, 1901), pp. 30–4.

[15] Grierson, ii. xcix.

but without any title or identification of the poem's subject. Yet the Earl, when a young man of about twenty, had been in Ireland when his brother died there, had been chief mourner at his funeral, and must have seen Donne's elegy when it was first circulated.

One might have expected that the occasion for this elegy, the milieu in which Donne was writing it, and the fact that its readers would include the Lord Keeper, known for his high standards in intellectual and academic matters, as well as in speech and writing, would combine to draw from Donne a poem in quality above the average of his verse. But the 'Elegy on Sir Thomas Egerton' lacks distinction, either in thought or expression. It is another reminder of a truth too often ignored by students of literature: that we must not assume a writer's works will all be in a line of continual development and technical progress. Dating by stylistic criteria alone is never trustworthy. Were there no other clue to the date of this elegy, its style would suggest it is as early as Donne's first Satires, and certainly earlier than 'The Storm' and 'The Calm' of 1597. In fact its earliest possible date is 6 September 1599, and its latest must be about the end of the same month.

It is thus one of the few early poems by Donne that we can date very closely. It acquires particular interest when we come to consider its placing in manuscript collections of his poems.

As far as is known, Donne wrote no other funeral elegy until 1609. In the earliest manuscripts of his verse the elegy beginning 'Sorrow, who to this house . . .' must have been grouped with his Love Elegies, for we find it so in many of the extant manuscript collections of his poems, as well as in *1633*. If any of these number the Love Elegies in order of composition, as they number the Satires, the 'Elegy on Sir Thomas Egerton', 'Sorrow, who to this house . . .', would mark a *terminus ad quem* for some Love Elegies and a *terminus a quo* for others.

When the projected first edition of Donne's poems was registered at Stationers' Hall, on 13 September 1632, its publisher, John Marriot, was required to omit 'the five Satires, the first, second, tenth, eleventh and thirteenth Elegies . . . and these before excepted to be his when he brings lawfull authority'. The indications are that printing started soon after this entry was made, for a sequence of eight Elegies, including that on Sir Thomas Egerton, occupies pp. 40–55 of *1633*. On 31 October Marriot registered 'The five Satires . . . excepted in his last entrance', and these were duly printed, but at the end of *1633*'s verse section, on pp. 325–49, followed only by the 'Hymn to God the Father'. There is no reference in the Stationers' Registers to the Elegies 'before excepted', and no reason to suppose that Marriot printed them. He had printed three other Elegies in the middle of the verse, on pp. 149–53: 'The Comparison', 'The Autumnal', and 'The Dream' (i.e. Elegies VIII, IX, and X as numbered in *1635* and in Grierson's edition), and, towards the end of the verse, on pp. 300–2, a further Elegy: 'The Expostulation' (no. XVII in *1635* and in Grierson's edition). However, it is difficult to imagine what objections could have been made to the printing of any of these. We must therefore look to those unprinted in *1633* to identify the five Elegies 'excepted' in the entry of 13 September. These include the following, first printed in *1635*, *1650*, or *1669*:

'The Bracelet' (Elegy XI in Grierson's edn.)
'His parting from her' (,, XII ,, ,,)
'Julia' (,, XIII ,, ,,)
'Tale of a Citizen and Wife' (,, XIV ,, ,,)
'On his Mistress' (,, XVI ,, ,,)
'Variety' (,, XVII ,, ,,)
'Love's Progress' (,, XVIII ,, ,,)
'Going to Bed' (,, XIX ,, ,,)
'Come, Fates; I fear you not' (Elegy XIII in *1635*; in Grierson's Appendix B).

The above list includes five elegies attributed to Donne in the manuscript collections as well as in the printed editions, but rejected, or classed as doubtfully his, by one or other modern editor. Another elegy that may have been 'excepted' from *1633* is

'Love's War' (Elegy XX in Grierson's edn.).

This, inexplicably absent from all the early editions, is found in very many of the early manuscript collections. It was first printed in 1802, by F. G. Waldron. Its attribution to Donne has not been questioned.

Conjectural identification of the five 'excepted' Elegies is clearly worthless, even though one might plausibly argue that

Elegies XVII–XIX were probably among them.[16] But since we could not guess at the ordering even of these in relation to those that were printed, we depend solely on the latter for clues to the order of the Love Elegies in the copy for *1633* and the position within that sequence of the 'Elegy on Sir Thomas Egerton'. If we take account of the numbering of those 'excepted', the sequence of Elegies in the copy for *1633* must have been as follows:

1. Unknown
2. Unknown
3. 'Jealousy' (I; Fond woman, which would have . . .)
4. 'The Anagram' (II; Marry, and love thy Flavia . . .)
5. 'Change' (III; Although thy hand and faith . . .)
6. 'The Perfume' (IV; Once and but once . . .)
7. 'His Picture' (V; Here take my picture . . .)
8. Elegy on Sir Thos. Egerton (Sorrow, who to this house . . .)
9. Oh, let me not serve so . . . (VI)
10. Unknown
11. Unknown
12. Nature's lay Idiot, I taught thee . . . (VII)
13. Unknown.

Any of the extant manuscript collections of Donne's verse which contains these Elegies in this order must be related to the copy for the Elegies printed on pp. 40–55 of *1633*. It might even be its source. Of the manuscripts whose contents' sequence I know, only Dowden, C57, Harley 49, and Leconfield[17] contain a group of thirteen Elegies in which the eight printed on pp. 40–55 of *1633* appear in that same sequence, but as the third to the ninth, and the twelfth. These manuscripts are regarded by the most authoritative editors of Donne's poems, Sir Herbert Grierson and Dame Helen Gardner, as of prime authority for the text and canon of his verse. The same editors also agree that these manuscripts must be closely related to the copy for *1633*.[18] Thus there can be little doubt about the

[16] Here and subsequently Grierson's numbering of the Elegies is cited to facilitate reference. Dame Helen Gardner's edition of the *Elegies and Songs and Sonnets* (Oxford, 1965) gives Grierson's numbering in her apparatus to each Elegy.

[17] I use the sigla introduced by Grierson and Gardner. C57 was discovered only in 1916, and therefore is not mentioned by Grierson; his descriptions of the other three manuscripts are in ii. lxxxiii, cviii. C57 is described with the others by Gardner in *John Donne, The Divine Poems* (Oxford, 1952), pp. lvii ff.

[18] Cf. Gardner, *Divine Poems*, pp. lxxxii–lxxxv.

sequence of the thirteen Elegies in the copy for that edition, or about which were 'excepted' from it. These must be as follows:

1.	'The Bracelet'	(XI; Not that in colour it was . . .)
2.	'Going to Bed'	(XIX; Come, Madam, come . . .)
10.	'Love's War'	(XX; Till I have peace with thee . . .)
11.	'On his Mistress'	(XVI; By our first strange and fatal . . .)
13.	'Love's Progress'	(XVIII; Who ever loves, if he do not . . .)

We have now to consider whether the sequence of these thirteen Elegies in the four manuscripts mentioned above is likely to be also the order in which they were composed.

In an often-quoted passage from a letter written in December 1614, Donne repeats a request to his intimate friend Sir Henry Goodere to send him 'that old book of you[rs]', explaining that he needs it to prepare a private printing of his poems.[19] Donne comments that collecting material for this 'will cost me more diligence, to seek them [his poems], than it did to make them'. This comment has sometimes been adduced to justify a picture of Donne carelessly sending poetic effusions to friends without keeping copies himself, and therefore occasionally becoming responsible for variants when relying on memory to provide a second copy of a poem. But Donne's comment, like certain others in his letters, must not be taken too seriously. Even if there is no modish exaggeration here, and some there very probably is, the comment can apply only to a few of Donne's poems, and probably only to some composed during his residence at Mitcham and later at Drury House. It certainly cannot apply to the Love Elegies, for in a letter to an unidentified correspondent, written probably in 1600 or later,[20] and sent with a copy of his Paradoxes, Donne promised 'to acquaint you with all mine [compositions]' provided that 'I receive by your next letter an assurance upon the religion of your friendship that no copy shall be taken, for any respect, of these or any other of my compositions sent to you . . . to my Satires there belongs some fear, and to some Elegies and these [Paradoxes] perhaps shame'. Clearly Donne had retained a copy of his Love Elegies. Equally clear is the evidence that

[19] Gosse, ii. 68; the relevant passage is printed also in Gardner, *Divine Poems*, p. lxiv.

[20] Printed in Evelyn M. Simpson's *Study of the Prose Works of John Donne*, 2nd edn. (Oxford, 1948), p. 316.

even at this date, soon after the Elegies were written, he was preventing copies from being taken and circulated. There is no reason to suppose that his attitude changed later. He is indeed most likely to have become increasingly unwilling to permit the whole of his Love Elegies to be copied or circulated, although no doubt one or two, such as V ('His Picture') or VI ('Oh, let me not serve so, as . . .') might circulate without discredit to their author. His Satires, after King James's succession to the English throne, could be shown without 'fear', but he would be more anxious than ever to avoid what 'shame' he might incur from wider reading of his Love Elegies, especially because of the notoriety of his clandestine marriage at the end of 1601, which he himself ruefully described, seven years later, as 'my disorderly proceedings in my nonage'.[21] Moreover, one consequence of his marriage was his fruitless search, protracted over a decade, for employment. This called for a more serious and respectable attitude than was presented in his Love Elegies. His efforts to suppress knowledge of his secular poems increased after he entered into Holy Orders in 1615. In 1619 Ben Jonson reported that 'since he was made Doctor [Donne] repenteth highly, and seeketh to destroy all his poems'.[22] We may, however, confidently assume that Donne retained his copy of his Love Elegies, though perhaps with the same intention as made him preserve his manuscript of *Biathanatos*: 'if I die, I only forbid it the Press, and the Fire: publish it not, but yet burn it not; and between those, do what you will with it.'[23]

When Donne died an authoritative collection of his Elegies composed before his marriage can have been extant in very few manuscripts and, on existing evidence, possibly only in two. One must have been Donne's own copy, which may have been the original from which the Dowden, C57, H49, and Leconfield manuscripts derive their text of the thirteen Elegies under discussion, and which may also have constituted the copy for the eight Elegies not 'excepted' from *1633*. Rowland Woodward's copy of twelve Love Elegies in the Westmoreland manuscript (*W*)[24] was taken from another source. It has eleven

[21] Gosse, i. 201.

[22] C. H. Herford and P. Simpson, *Ben Jonson, The Man and his Work*, 2 vols. (Oxford, 1925), i. 136.

[23] Gosse, ii. 124.

[24] Described by Gardner in *Divine Poems*, p. lxxviii, and in *Elegies*, p. lxxii.

of the twelve Love Elegies found in the Dowden and related manuscripts, but in an entirely different sequence. It also differs in omitting 'Love's Progress' (XVIII), in adding 'The Comparison' (VIII), and in placing last of all the 'Elegy on Sir Thomas Egerton'. This final difference, separating Love Elegies from the Funeral Elegy, suggests that *W*, or its original, was compiled when a collector of Donne's poems was arranging them by kinds, and that it must therefore date later than the source for Dowden and its related manuscripts. The latter seem to me likely to present their thirteen Elegies in order of composition and thus to provide closer indications of composition date than we have hitherto had for the Love Elegies they contain.

Donne and Coins

JOHN CAREY

DONNE's interest in coins has often been noticed, and that is hardly surprising, for it would be virtually impossible to read through either his poems or his sermons without becoming aware of it. But no one seems to have tried to account for it in anything but the most perfunctory way, or to show how it links up with Donne's other habitual concerns. M. A. Rugoff, in his book on Donne's imagery, observes that the preoccupation with coins and coinage 'assumed the proportions of a mild obsession', and he suggests, in explanation, that the use of an image-source so 'prosaic and even crass' may be 'considered another facet of Donne's rejection of Petrarchian and Spenserian conventions'.[1] There may be some truth in this. The dominant part played by money in 'The Bracelet' seems motivated in part by Donne's wish to advertise his hard-up, hard-headed approach to erotic matters, and to distinguish himself sardonically from lovers of a more sentimental and affluent type. But Rugoff's notion is plainly inadequate as an elucidation of the hold which coins had over Donne's mind. For one thing, coins come frequently into his thought in the sermons and devotional writings, where there can be no question of rejecting 'Petrarchian and Spenserian conventions'. For another, Donne's intention when alluding to coins does not seem, generally, to be to stress their 'prosaic' or 'crass' side.

On the contrary, when he is investigating a theological question he will grant himself and his hearers a moment of lyricism by letting his imagination revert to its loved contemplation of coins. Man falls into sin, he tells us, 'as a piece of money falls into a river; we heare it fall, and we see it sink, and by and by we see it deeper, and at last we see it not at all'.[2]

[1] M. A. Rugoff, *Donne's Imagery: A Study in Creative Sources* (Russell and Russell Inc., New York, 1962), pp. 144–7.

[2] *The Sermons of John Donne*, ed. Evelyn M. Simpson and George R. Potter (University of California Press, Berkeley and Los Angeles, 1953–62), ii. 191.

The liquid lapse of that disappearing coin naturally reminds us of the more famous coins in 'A Valediction: of Weeping', which also fall and disappear, leaving only water. Water, falling coins, and tears again converge in Donne's imagination when he surveys Christ's passion: 'his water was his white money, and his blood was his gold, and he poured out both together in his agony, and . . . in his weeping.'[3] These resemblances serve to show how the customary patterns of Donne's imagination survived or adapted themselves to his change from secular to religious subject-matter, and they also suggest that money, far from being used by Donne as a coarse, anti-Spenserian joke, prompted him to intrigued, reverent, and delicate perceptions.

Even in 'The Bracelet' we are struck by Donne's alertness to the shape, weight, and individuality of different coins. He compares his English angels to French crowns, 'so leane, so pale, so lame, so ruinous', which are 'circumcis'd most Jewishly', and to Spanish écus, 'negligently left unrounded'. When he considers hiring a crier to announce the bracelet's loss through the London streets, the coin he will reward him with is evoked with similar care—'one leane thred-bare groate'. So this coin, like the others in the elegy, takes on personal traits and incites us to regard it as a diminutive human being. Of course, coins were much more human in Donne's day than they are now. Coins circulating in the capital were, as this poem makes clear, extremely varied in type and nationality, thus mimicking the rich cosmopolitan mix of the city population. But, quite apart from that, Elizabethan and Jacobean coins managed to be individuals, as modern coins do not, because they were produced by a haphazard and inefficient method, as people are. Most European currency in the late sixteenth and early seventeenth centuries was struck by the traditional method of hammering.[4] Discs were stamped out of thin bars of precious

[3] *Sermons*, iii. 84.

[4] On the coinage in Donne's day see Sir John Craig, *The Mint* (Cambridge University Press, Cambridge, 1953), pp. 119–31, and Charles Webster, *The Great Instauration: Science, Medicine and Reform, 1626–1660* (Duckworth, London, 1975), pp. 404–10. Craig notes that a brief experiment with machined coinage was made in England in 1561 when Eloi Mestrell, an employee of the Paris mint, brought over machines of a screw type and operated them on a small scale for eleven years. He was hanged for counterfeiting in 1578.

metal, placed between two dies, and hammered, so that the image on the dies was transferred to the coin. So primitive a technique produced irregular results. The bars were not of uniform thickness; the image imparted varied in depth and precision; the imprint was often off-centre. Fat, thin, lop-sided, or vague-looking coins resulted. They were almost as various in their expressions as people, and their precise physiognomy was as worth studying, if not more so. For fat coins could be and generally were culled out by the astute, leaving only inferior coins in circulation. Alternatively they could be clipped, or hollowed and filled with solder—practices Donne's poem mentions. The bullion extracted went towards counterfeiting further inferior coinage. Scrutinizing the physique of the coins he met was, then, a poetic trait bred in Donne by contemporary conditions. Only under the Commonwealth, when the production of machined coins, manufactured by a screw press, was experimentally introduced into England from France, did coins advance towards the characterless counters familiar to us today, and so oust the misshapen humanoids which pass for currency in 'The Bracelet'.

But close attention would, of course, be paid to coins by any sensible citizen, not just by Donne. If we are to explain what made his interest peculiarly intense, we cannot do so by appealing to the alertingly ramshackle state of contemporary money. Rather, we must ask what was singular about his view of coins, and about the work he gave them to do in poetic images. One answer seems to be that, as in 'The Bracelet', he always assimilates coins to human beings and human activities. When Shakespeare's Cleopatra says of her bounteous Antony 'Realms and islands were / As plates dropp'd from his pocket', we could never mistake the image for one of Donne's, because Shakespeare's fantasy-transformation of a coin to a sprouting tract of greenery spirits the coin away both from itself and from the narrowly human referents Donne always concentrates on. Besides, and this brings us to a second distinctive feature of Donne's money images, the word 'plate' in the sense 'coin' would never have recommended itself to Donne, because it suggests a smooth, unmarked surface, whereas for Donne the process of imprinting the coin and the imprint itself were the vital points of focus. A coin for him was not a 'plate' but a 'stamp'. Curiously, however, though the stamp intrigued Donne, he was not much concerned with the most obvious aspect of it, namely the figure or pattern stamped. Since this determined the designation and value of the coin, it would naturally be the most important consideration for most coin-handlers. Yet Donne, in his many references to coins, pays almost no attention to the actual picture or device portrayed, and never describes it. 'The Bracelet' is unique among his poems in even distinguishing between different categories of coin. Usually, any coin will do; for a coin, to Donne, was not an object but a relationship, and any coin would serve as an exemplar of that relationship. It was the correlation between metal and imprint that fascinated him.

That is typical. Donne's poetry is always about relationships, not objects. It is typical, too, that the relationship between the metal of the coin and the imprint should shift and vary as Donne contemplates it. This is true of all the other relationships he concentrates upon: the interplay between faith and reason, for instance, or the relative nature of light and shadow. With coins, we find Donne implying diverse and almost contradictory estimates of the priority of the two partners in the relationship, of the effect of one upon the other, and of the consequence for the whole of the alteration of either. Here, for a start, is a letter Donne wrote to Sir Edward Herbert on the day he took orders, 23 January 1614:

> Your power and jurisdiction, which is entirely over mee, is somewhat enlardged. For, as if I should put any other stampe upon a peece of your gold, the gold were not the lesse yours, so (if there be not too much taken by mee, in that comparison) by havinge, by the orders of our churche, receyved a new character, I ame not departed from your title, and possession of mee.[5]

Clearly there is a strain of courtier-like flattery here, but that does not make the extract less apt for my purposes, because it is precisely the extent to which Donne found the relationship between coin and stamp a pliant, adaptable medium for approaching different sorts of situation that I wish to illustrate. In his assurances to Sir Edward, Donne implies that a coin is essentially to be equated with the bullion from which it is made.

[5] John Donne, *Complete Poetry and Selected Prose*, ed. John Hayward (The Nonesuch Press, Bloomsbury, 1929), pp. 465–6.

That bullion (i.e. Donne himself) still belongs to Sir Edward, he affirms, even though it has received a new 'stampe' (Christ's). In 'To Mr Tilman after he had taken orders', the same image is used with rather different emphasis:

> Art thou the same materials, as before,
> Onely the stampe is changed; but no more?
> And as new crowned Kings alter the face,
> But not the monies substance; so hath grace
> Chang'd onely Gods old Image by Creation,
> To Christs new stampe, at this thy Coronation?[6]

Donne's assumption, in the letter to Sir Edward, that he is indeed the same 'gold' after ordination as before, is here put as a question. Are the 'materials' changed? Or only the 'stampe'? Further, the notion that 'Christ's new stampe' could be imprinted, and yet leave the gold belonging to someone else (someone like Sir Edward) is wholly alien to the spirit of Donne's poem to Tilman. The implication, by the end of the poem, is that though, in a sense, Tilman's 'materials' do remain the same, they also do not; for the 'new stampe' makes them, indissolubly, part of a new mixed whole—a 'blest Hermaphrodite', joining earth and heaven. In the Herbert letter, the coin's stamp is regarded as an incidental, and the lump of gold, in which Herbert has a proprietary interest, is paramount. But in the Tilman poem, Tilman's 'materials' are merely human, while his 'stampe', whether God's old one or Christ's new one, is divine and imparts the value.

Needless to say, the Tilman poem takes it for granted that to replace 'God's old Image' with 'Christ's new stampe' is an improvement. The depiction of Tilman as a coin being restamped is employable, in a poem congratulating him upon taking holy orders, only because the process will unquestionably leave him better than before. But in his musings upon the relationship between stamp and coin, Donne was capable of coming to a precisely opposite conclusion about restamping. 'You shall seldom see a Coyne', he wrote to Sir Henry Goodyer, 'upon which the stamp were removed, though to imprint it

[6] John Donne, *The Divine Poems*, ed. Helen Gardner (Clarendon Press, Oxford, 1952), p. 32.

better, but it looks awry and squint.'[7] It is apparent from the rest of the letter that he is here warning Goodyer against any inclination to change his religion. Goodyer had, it appears, been receiving attention from some Roman Catholic proselytizers. Restamped coins look wrong, Donne cautions, 'And so, for the most part, do mindes which have received divers impressions'. Was Donne speaking from rueful personal experience? He was himself a restamped coin, having abandoned the Catholic Church for the Anglican. He must have been aware of the continuing hold over him of Roman Catholic habits of devotion, evident in the divine poems—habits like the adoration of the Virgin, which most Protestants would have regarded with suspicion. Do these sideways, or backward, glances of his soul account for that image of the crooked looking coin? At all events, the lack of accord, on the satisfactoriness of restamped coins, between the Goodyer letter and the Tilman poem cannot be missed. Nor, for that matter, can the swift brilliance with which Donne's two adjectives, 'awry and squint', personalize the Goodyer coin, giving it a human expression suggestive both of shiftiness and of disarray.

The vexed question of the Virgin, and her place in man's redemption, is itself one which Donne uses his coin image to help him think about. He had called her, in 'A Litanie', 'That she-Cherubin, / Which unlock'd Paradise'. Later, as Helen Gardner remarks in her notes to the *Divine Poems*, he came to deprecate such language: 'nothing that she did', he protested, 'entred into that treasure, that ransom that redeemed us'.[8] The notion of Christ as coin, nascent in the word 'treasure' here, is more fully developed in a sermon preached on Christmas Day 1622. To redeem man, Donne argues, God had to make Christ able to pay man's debt:

First, he must pay it in such money as was lent; in the nature and flesh of man; for man had sinned, and man must pay. And then it was lent in such money as was coyned even with the Image of God; man was made according to his Image: That Image being defaced, in a new Mint, in the wombe of the Blessed Virgin, there was new

[7] *Letters to Severall Persons of Honour: Written by John Donne Sometime Deane of St Pauls London* (London, 1651), pp. 101–2.

[8] *Sermons*, i. 201.

money coyned; The Image of the invisible God, the second person in the Trinity, was imprinted into the humane nature.[9]

So God, Donne concludes, 'sent downe the Bullion, and the stamp', and He also 'provided the Mint'. By transferring the Nativity into these images Donne is able to see Mary's role as vital but not intrinsic. Neither the mint, nor its activities, become any part of the coin: 'nothing that she did entred into that treasure'. As for Donne's attitude towards defaced and re-minted coins, that is here quite different, it will be noted, from the pessimism of the Goodyer letter. The greatest of Christian mysteries, God-in-man, is now just such a coin. The switch-round, like the other mutations of the coin image we have been looking at, is characteristic of Donne's restless, experimental nature. Once a relationship intrigues him, he feels impelled to probe it, modify it, reverse it, and try it out in different concentrations and in various matrices. His mind advances not forward but sideways, spreading out through parallels which are never quite parallel, and analogies which alter what they illustrate. The bewildering range of attitudes towards love and women in the 'Songs and Sonnets' arises from a similarly tentative and self-modifying understanding of the relationship between the sexes.

Since coins, like sex, result from the junction of two elements, Donne naturally enough makes coins and sex converge complicatingly upon each other in the love poems. The poem which Helen Gardner entitles 'Image and Dream' provides an instance:

> Image of her whom I love, more then she
>   Whose faire impression in my faithfull heart,
> Makes mee her Medall, and makes her love mee,
>   As Kings do coynes, to which their stamps impart
> The value: goe, and take my heart from hence,
>   Which now is growne too great and good for me.[10]

Here the lovers do not love—or do not essentially love—each other: they love a coin, which is the outcome of their relationship, and which consists of an image of the girl stamped on the

[9] *Sermons*, iv. 288.

[10] *John Donne, The Elegies and the Songs and Sonnets*, ed. Helen Gardner (Clarendon Press, Oxford, 1965), p. 58.

lover's heart. Donne loves the girl's image on the coin more than he loves the girl. She loves him only because he has the image-stamped coin inside him. The elements of self-love, and of self-deception, indivisible from love, are implied by Donne through his manipulation of the coin image. For the girl values Donne's heart only because her image is stamped on it: that ensures her ownership. Yet ironically it also does the opposite, for it is her image rather than her that Donne loves: the living, breathing girl is superseded. The two lovers do not really love the same coin. Helen Gardner has shown how fond the neo-Platonists were of the idea that the lover might fashion, in his imagination, an image of the girl more beautiful than that which his (or her) senses perceived. It was almost inevitable, given the teasing potentialities of his coin image, that Donne should apply it to this situation.

The assumption in 'Image and Dream' that the stamp, not the bullion, imparts the value to the coin is, of course, intriguingly questionable. Coins, as we have noted, were often clipped and hollowed. The bullion removed was valuable, though unstamped. The coin which remained, though stamped, had in a quite practical sense lost value. Dubiety about where, in the conjunction of metal and stamp, the value inhered, made coins more attractive to Donne, because it made them more adjustable and insoluble as images. Writing of his own poem in 'The Second Anniversary', he seems to place the value wholly in the stamp, assuring Elizabeth Drury:

> nor wouldst thou be content,
> To take this, for my second yeeres true Rent,
> Did this Coine beare any'other stampe, then his,
> That gave thee power to doe, me, to say this.[11]

Donne has just been considering, in the poem, whether to invoke Elizabeth as a saint, and has rejected the idea, for that would be to place her 'stampe' on the coin. He decides that it is worthy to belong to her only because it does not belong to her but to God. The stamp, so conceived, is a proprietary and value-conferring mark. But in one of his sermons Donne proposes rather a different application of the coin image to the

[11] John Donne, *The Epithalamions, Anniversaries, and Epicedes*, ed. W. Milgate (Clarendon Press, Oxford, 1978), p. 56.

writing of poetry. 'It is easie to observe', he claims, 'that in all Metricall compositions . . . the force of the whole piece, is for the most part left to the shutting up; the whole frame of the Poem is a beating out of a piece of gold, but the last clause is as the impression of the stamp, and that is it that makes it currant.'[12]

Donne's theory of poetic structure here highlights endings, and it's odd that it has not been more influential in diverting attention from the 'explosive openings' so often admired in his poems. For Donne's point is that the openings can be seen properly only from the end. Everything in a poem modifies what went before: the ending modifies everything. The notorious ending of 'Aire and Angels', for example, asserting the superior purity of man's love to woman's, disappoints readers who have been entranced by the sanctified awe of the opening. But if we attend to Donne's poetic theory as the sermon outlines it, we must realize that what we are registering disappointment at is the shape and point of the poem, not some lapse of taste tagged on at the end. Donne's emphasis is on the reading of a poem as an unstable, unfolding experience, only truly known when it is over. But (to return to Donne's modification of the coin image in the passage) to say that you cannot appreciate the 'force' of a poem until the 'last clause' is not to say that the last clause is what gives the poem its value. The last clause imparts currency, because once it has been written the completed poem can go into circulation, and in that sense it is equivalent to a coin's 'stamp'. But by likening the whole poem to a lump of gold hammered out, Donne implies that the poem contains value in every particle of itself. Value and stamp are no longer synonymous, as they appeared to be in 'The Second Anniversary'. In other words, Donne has yet again shifted the bearing of his coin image and rethought its internal relationship.

When he envisages—and there is no subject that he envisages more raptly—the resurrection of the body, the value of the coin resides wholly, it seems, in the material it is made out of, and the stamp is unmentioned:

Though I die, I do not die; but as that piece of money which was but the money of a poor man, being given in Subsidy, becomes a

[12] *Sermons*, vi. 41.

part of the Royal Exchequer: So this body, which is but the body of a sinful man, being given in Subsidy, as a Contribution to the Glory of my God, in the grave, becomes a part of Gods Exchequer; and when he opens it, he shall issue out this money, that is, manifest it again cloth'd in his Glory: that body which in me was but a piece of Copper money, he shall make a Talent of Gold.[13]

Donne is always adamant that we shall arise from death with precisely the same bodies as we have possessed on earth, and the gathering and compacting of the constituent grains of dust on the last day is a favourite resort of his imagination. But although it will be the same body, it will also not be the same: 'it is the *same* body, and yet not *such* as it selfe', as Donne explains. This, he admits, is a 'mysterious consideration', and he offers the transfiguration of Christ as an analogy of the change that will come upon our resurrected bodies. This 'glorification' will purge the human body's 'Corruptiblenesse'. Herein lies the aptness of the image Donne uses—the transmutation of a copper coin to a gold one—to represent the resurrection; for the property of gold which made it particularly fascinating to Donne was that it was unsusceptible to corruption (a doctrine that he derived from alchemy).[14]

By mentioning copper money Donne focuses attention on the coin's material sharply, for copper coins were a rare curiosity in his day. Elizabeth had refused to allow a base metal for royal coin in England, though she authorized the city of Bristol to issue copper tokens. The Irish mint struck pence, halfpence, and farthings in copper for the first time in 1601; and James I caused farthing tokens of brass and copper to be struck, but at a value so much inferior to the rate at which they were issued that it was not thought fit to recognize them as legitimate coins, and they soon sunk into contempt and disuse.[15]

Donne, in the passage quoted above, is concentrating simply upon the body as it is put into and taken out of the grave, and for that purpose he places the whole emphasis on the metal from which the coin is fashioned. The stamp receives no

[13] *Sermons*. v. 230.

[14] Mary Paton Ramsay, *Les Doctrines médiévales chez Donne*, 2nd edn. (Oxford University Press, London, 1924), pp. 254–5.

[15] See Craig, *The Mint*, pp. 128–9, and B. Ruding, *Annals of the Coinage of Great Britain*, 3rd edn. (John Hearne, London, 1840), i. 7.

mention. This may help us to understand why the coin image itself fascinated him so much, for it suggests that the relationship between bullion and stamp presented itself to his mind as an equivalent to the relationship which preoccupied him above all others—that between the body and the soul. The bullion represents the body; the stamp, the soul.

To judge from the way Donne depicts his unfortunate angels in 'The Bracelet' this potential of the coin image was one of the earliest aspects of it to appeal to him. The angels who fell with Satan, Donne argues, are at least still angels, though corrupted. But his angels, once melted down to make a chain, will not be angels at all: 'For forme gives being, and their forme is gone.'[16] Donne is playing here on the word 'form', which could mean, on the one hand, simply 'shape', but which also had a metaphysical sense expounded by St. Thomas in the *Summa Theologica* (I. lxxvi. 4). St. Thomas argues that the intellectual soul is the substantial form in man, and that 'the substantial form gives simple existence'. 'Forme gives being' is really a quotation from St. Thomas, then, and it makes explicit Donne's equation of the coin's stamp with the soul, for it is the stamp, not the bullion, which melting will destroy.

The attempt to imagine the relationship between soul and body, which was endlessly alluring to Donne, entails certain crucial preliminary decisions. It has to be decided, for instance, whether the soul is separable from the body, and whether it is joined to it by any intervening body. Aristotle, in the *De Anima*, insists that the soul is not separable, pointing out that if it were it might conceivably leave the body and re-enter it again, which would involve the absurd consequence that dead creatures might rise from death. To illustrate the union of soul and body, Aristotle refers to a physical process virtually identical with Donne's image of the imprinting of a stamp on a coin, and which may, indeed, have first alerted Donne to the metaphysical potential of coins. The process Aristotle selects is sealing. 'There is no need to inquire whether soul and body are one', he stipulates, 'any more than whether the wax and the imprint are one.'[17] Donne, as we know from Helen Gardner's

16 Gardner, *Elegies etc.*, p. 3, line 76.

17 Aristotle, *De Anima*, ed. R. D. Hicks (Cambridge University Press, Cambridge, 1907), p. 51.

perceptive reading of the 'Holy Sonnets', felt, for a time, drawn towards the unorthodox belief that the soul was not separable: that it remained with the body at death, and slept with it until the last day. This was Christianized Aristotelianism, and the coin, regarded as a union of body-bullion with soul-stamp, was admirably adapted to express it. For the stamp, isolated from the coin, was inconceivable.

Later, however, Donne came to agree with St. Thomas, and to believe that the soul did separate from the body at death, though it remained imperfect until reunited with the body at the resurrection. He found that he could modify his coin image (as in the passage about copper and gold money) to fit this belief. St. Thomas naturally disagreed with Aristotle about the absurdity of the body rising from death, but he found Aristotle's sealing-wax image useful when refuting the belief that the soul was united to the animal body by means of another body—a belief apparently encouraged by St. Augustine, who suggested that the soul administered the body by means of fire and air, which are bodies. Countering this, St. Thomas quotes Aristotle's sentence about sealing-wax, and comments: 'the shape is united to the wax without a body intervening. Therefore also the soul is thus united to the body.' This conveniently overlooks the impossibility of the wax's shape existing apart from the wax, as St. Thomas believed souls could exist apart from bodies. Typically dissatisfied with any single view of a relationship, Donne uses his coins in 'The Bracelet' to imply an unmediated union between soul ('forme') and body, but he can also be found subscribing to the common Elizabethan view that spirits, arising from the blood, mediated between soul and body—'Because such fingers need to knit / That subtile knot, which makes us man'.

Perhaps Donne's response to coins was conditioned, then, by Aristotle's seal, and in some respects seal and coin remained interchangeable ideas for him. Winfried Schleiner has shown how fond Donne is, in the sermons, of alluding to the imprint in a seal when expounding conjunctions of the divine and human—as, for instance, the image of God in man. In these sealing metaphors Donne was following the practice of the Church Fathers, particularly Augustine; and the Church Fathers, influenced by Christ's question about the stamp of the coin in Matthew 22: 20, frequently convey the image of God in man through the simile of a coin, bearing the emperor's face, as well as through the simile of a seal.[18] The poem to Mr Tilman shows Donne doing the same. As Donne, in 'The Bracelet' or 'A Valediction: of Weeping', imaginatively involves his coins with fire and water, so he enjoys subjecting his God-stamped human coins to the same elements. St. Bernard's sentence about the damned burning in Hell—*imago Dei uri potest in gehenna, non exuri*—was a favourite with Donne,[19] and he uses the drowned coin to evoke the same indelibility: 'How long will a Medall, a piece of Coine lie in the water, before the stampe be washed off?'[20]

But seals and coins are not precisely interchangeable. For the coin gains from its imprint a property which the seal does not possess, namely currency value. Once stamped, the coin becomes a working model, not like the seal a simple physical illustration, of the union of spirit and matter. The coin unites tangible with intangible, physical with metaphysical. It has two beings, as object and as token. It was, I think, this *discordia concors* within coins which made them pre-eminently absorbing to Donne—made them, indeed, emblems of his poetic method. His sense that the coin's value belonged to a different sphere of reality from its physical qualities, and linked it with the soul, seems to have been an early apprehension, for it is already implied in the elegy 'Loves Progress':

> I, when I value gold, may thinke upon
> The ductillness, the application,
> The wholesomeness, the ingenuity,
> From rust, from soyle, from fyre ever free,
> But if I love it, 'tis because 'tis made
> By our new Nature, use, the soule of trade.[21]

Donne's 'mild obsession' with coins, then, is a clue which leads us to his most deeply ingrained imaginative habits and, consequently, to those problematic relationships which, as poet and theologian, most enthralled him.

[18] Winfried Schleiner, *The Imagery of John Donne's Sermons* (Brown University Press, Providence, 1970), pp. 108–9, 113; also G. H. Lampe, *The Seal of the Spirit*, 2nd edn. (S.P.C.K., London, 1967), p. 254.

[19] See, for example, *Sermons*, i. 160; ii. 247.

[20] Ibid. ix. 332.

[21] Gardner, *Elegies etc.*, pp. 16–17.

Angels and the Poetic Imagination from Donne to Traherne

ROBERT ELLRODT

A PRECARIOUS balance between faith and reason, curiosity and doubt, the spirit of wonder and the critical faculty is a distinctive feature in Donne's conception and handling of miracles, or fables drawn from the 'unnatural natural history' of his age.[1] In a three-volume study of the Metaphysical poets I have tried to demonstrate that there is a network of correspondences between the individual modes of perception, sensibility, thought, and expression of each writer.[2] Analogies between several authors are therefore bound to be superficial unless they extend to the whole frame of mind: two poets can never be alike at one point if they thoroughly differ at another. Donne's approach to angelology should therefore reveal the kind of balance observed in other subjects, and a variety of responses may be expected from the other Metaphysicals.

If angels were no more than rhetorical figures in Donne's poems, his subtler conceits would be a scholastic way of refining upon the simpler praise of the lady's angelic beauty or purity in courtly or neo-Platonic literature.[3] But the angels haunt his meditative poems, his theological essays, his sermons, and his letters.[4] Their persistent presence is only explained when we

[1] As argued in two previous essays, 'The notion of miracle from Saint Augustine to Traherne', *English Studies Today* 5 (I.A.U.P.E., Istanbul, 1973), expanded in 'Miracle et nature de Saint Augustin à la poésie métaphysique anglaise', *Réseaux*, 24–5 (1975), 3–36, and 'Le Fabuleux et l'imagination poétique dans l'œuvre de John Donne', in *De Shakespeare à T.S. Eliot*, Mélanges Fluchère (Didier, 1976).

[2] *Les poètes métaphysiques anglais* (Corti, Paris, 1960; 2nd edn. 1973): see synoptic tables in 'Conclusion' of vol. ii.

[3] e.g. Petrarch's description: 'Non era l'andar suo cosa mortale, / ma d'angelica forma' (*Canzoniere*, 90; cf. 123).

[4] See the *Concordance* of H. C. Combs and Z. R. Sullens (Chicago, 1948) for the poems, and Ch. III of M. P. Ramsay's *Les Doctrines médiévales chez Donne* (O.U.P., 1917) for the prose. This pioneer work still offers the fullest study of Donne's angelology from a theological point of view.

discover that the poet's allusions to their nature, ministry, and faculties are closely related to his impassioned questionings about natures 'of middle condition', sin, time and place, and the limitations of human knowledge.

Even in his youthful impertinences Donne played with angels as objects of intellectual speculation. With rare exceptions he had no eye for their 'beauteous files' (Vaughan's phrase) and no ear for their singing, though their trumpets could startle the sinner at the crack of doom.[5] Spenser, a staunch Protestant, might have shared Calvin's scepticism, yet his contemplative imagination delighted in 'the celestial hierarchy of that supposed Dionysius' (Bacon's wary words).[6] No such aesthetic delight, not unknown to Milton, prompted Donne's search for angels, but a desire to know.

In an age when man was defined as 'a little world made cunningly / of Elements, and an Angelike spright'[7] no one denied the angels a place in the great Chain of Being, and the Dean of St. Paul's was hardly original in claiming, 'They are super-elementary meteors, they hang between the nature of God, and the nature of man, and are of middle Condition.'[8]

The Reformers, however, did not allow them to be 'Mediators betweene God and us, in such sort that they doe darken the power of God'.[9] Jack Donne's opinion cannot be inferred from a sarcastic pun in 'Satyre V' or a metaphorical hyperbole in 'Aire and Angels'.[10] Both the bereaved husband and the preacher abide by the reformed faith in refusing their love or worship to angels not to offend God's 'tender jealousy', yet

5 'Holy Sonnet 4' (Gardner, *Divine Poems*, p. 8). Singing: 'Prince Henry', 98; 'Valediction: of the Booke', 27, etc. Apart from the fire and light imagery of 'Aire and Angels' the only visual image is the libertine conceit on 'white robes' in 'To his Mistris Going to Bed'.

6 Spenser, 'An Hymne of Heavenly Beautie', 35–100. Bacon, *Advancement of Learning*, Bk. I: *Philosophical Works* (Routledge, London, 1905), p. 61; cf. Calvin on Dionysius in *Institutes*, I. xiv. 4.

7 'Holy Sonnet 2', in Gardner, *Divine Poems*, p. 13.

8 *Sermons*, ed. Potter-Simpson, viii. 106. St. Thomas supplied the idea, though not the metaphor: *Summa*, Ia, q. 50, art. 1, ad. 1.

9 *The Holy Gospel . . . according to John, with the Commentary of M. John Calvin* (London, 1584) on 5: 4, quoted by R. N. West in *Milton and the Angels* (Univ. of Georgia Press, Athens, 1955), p. 14.

10 'Judges are Gods' but men should not 'be forc'd to them to goe, / By meanes of Angels' (58–9); 'So in a voice, so in a shapeless flame, / *Angells* affect us oft, and worship'd bee' (3–4).

angels are allowed to 'present our prayers' and 'poure out their owne'.[11] Together with the emphasis on the 'middle condition', the role assigned to angels in the spiritual communication between man and God begins to enlighten us as to Donne's personal response.

The Metaphysical poet further reveals his own bent when he alludes to the Fall of the Angels. His imagination is not fired by the myth (fit for epic poetry): his mind is fascinated by the idea that 'in best understandings, sinne beganne, / Angels sinn'd first, then Devills, and then man'.[12] Which means that the dissolution of the world, now felt to be imminent, began with the Creation: for an imagination which grasps only the significant instants of time,[13] 'then first of all / The world did in her cradle take a fall'.[14] Though Donne usually follows Aquinas in his angelology, he departs from him when he ascribes that fall not only to spiritual pride but to 'a certain fleshlinesse'.[15] And when he suggests that the angels fell for 'reflecting upon themselves', he seems to be aware of the spiritual dangers lurking in the intense self-consciousness of which he had so vivid an experience.[16] His own sense of inconstancy, of the 'fitfulness' of his devotion may also have heightened his interest, whether playful or serious, in the 'confirmation' which made the good Angels 'by Gods preservation safe', though not 'safe in themselves'.[17] On the other hand, the claim that earthly bodies at the Resurrection 'more celestiall / Shall be, then Angels were' ('The Second Anniversary', 493–4), though not contradicting the teaching of St. Thomas,[18] has the distinct Donnean flavour, reminding us of his insistence on the conjunction of body and soul.[19]

Speculations on the nature and proprieties of angels had an even better chance of being oriented by individual preference

[11] 'Holy Sonnet': 'Since, she whom I lovd . . .'; *Sermons*, ix. 218.

[12] 'To Sir Henry Wotton', 39–40; Milgate, *Satires, Epigrams and Verse Letters*, p. 72.

[13] See *Poètes métaphysiques anglais*, i. 82 ff.

[14] 'First Anniversary', 195–6: Grierson, *Poetical Works*, i. 237.

[15] *Summa*, Ia, q. 62, art. 8; *Sermons*, viii. 361.

[16] Ibid. x. 180. Cf. *Poètes métaphysiques anglais*, i. 117 ff.

[17] *Sermons*, viii. 368.

[18] *Summa*, Ia, q. 20, art. 4, ad. 2; q. 89, art. 8.

[19] *Poètes métaphysiques anglais*, i. 216–18. Donne's obsession with death may also be traced in his emphasis on 'an impossibility of dying [in angels], as in the soul of man': *Sermons*, viii. 362.

since they did not concern points of faith, but were, in Bacon's words, 'an appendix of theology both divine and natural . . . neither inscrutable nor interdicted'.[20] Theologians, indeed, claimed in their treatises on angels that this part of Divinity was 'most facill and pleasant: and [had] most connexion with natural Philosophy and Philosophicall Principles'.[21]

In the controversy on the nature of angels Donne was faithful to the Scholastic tradition when he described them as 'pure abstract incorporeal substances devoid of vital union with matter'.[22] That they could assume a body of air was widely acknowledged. Donne's source in 'Aire and Angels' may be Aquinas, but Salkeld's explanation is more picturesque with its 'Shakespearean' cloud metaphor:

The manner therefore of these so strange apparitions and effects is, by the forming a body of ayre, so condensing and tempering both the quantitie, qualities and substance, that it may be apt to receive all manner of colours, formes and figures, like as in the clouds by the divers raritie and densitie of them, doe often appeare divers kindes of colours; yea, most strange representations of men and beasts; yea, of whole armies once fighting against another.[23]

Knowing Donne's interest in the conjunction of soul and body one might have expected him to side with the neo-Platonists, the various Church Fathers, and the many Protestants[24] who believed, as Cudworth later put it, that angels are 'substances, not naked and abstract, but clothed with certaine subtle bodies, or animals compounded and made up of soul and body together'.[25] The reason why Donne unhesitatingly conceived of angels as incorporeal is not to be sought only in his Catholic upbringing. Each man's choice on this point, when it is not dictated by the prevailing theological opinion, reflects

20 *Advancement of Learning*, ii. 58: p. 92 in *Philosophical Works*.

21 *A Treatise of Angels*, by John Salkeld (London, 1613), sig. A2^{r}. Otho Casmannus had answered positively the question 'An Angelographia sit physica doctrina, seu pertineat ad naturarum & creaturarum explicationem': *Angelographia* (Frankfurt, 1597), pp. 18–45.

22 Cudworth's phrasing in *The True Intellectual System of the Universe*, v. iii: *Works*, ed. T. Birch (London, 1939), iv. 26. See St. Thomas, *Summa*, Ia, q. 51, art. 1.

23 Salkeld, op. cit., Ch. VIII, 'How Angels doe really appeare', sig. D4^{v}.

24 See West, op. cit., p. 53.

25 *True Intellectual System*, v. iii: *Works*, iv. 31.

a fundamental opposition between monistic and dualistic modes of thought. This is the Great Divide in the metaphysical vision of reality. To describe an angel as 'made up of soul and body together' inevitably blurs the very distinction this phrasing seems to preserve, for this 'subtile body' evades our senses. Neo-Platonism implies the kind of continuity between matter and spirit plainly asserted in *Paradise Lost* (v. 469–500), and one is not surprised to find Donne and Milton poles apart. To the Metaphysical poet the conjunction of matter and mind is achieved as contraries are united in a paradox: without confusion or interpenetration.[26]

Whenever the poet or the preacher described the motions of angels or their intellectual operations, he had to choose between dissenting opinions, and the choice again disclosed the way in which his own mind worked.

How angels moved from one place to another had long exercised the ingenuity of the Schoolmen. Donne departs from St. Thomas when he asserts that 'God denyed even to Angells the ability of arriving from one Extreme to another without passing the mean way between'.[27] He may have been influenced by the then prevailing opinion,[28] but he must have been

[26] See *Poètes métaphysiques anglais*, Part I, Bk. I, viii. 2 (particularly, pp. 230–1).

[27] *Essayes in Divinity*, ed. E. M. Simpson (Clarendon Press, Oxford, 1952), p. 37. Cf. *Sermons*, viii. 324. The opinion of St. Thomas (*Summa*, Ia, q. 53, art. 2, resp.) is recorded by Salkeld, but deemed improbable: an angel could move at will 'eyther by changing his substance by little and little, as bodies doe, from one place to another . . . or secondly, not by succession, but by transporting himselfe wholy from place to place, which though divers Divines hold, may be alwayes as it pleaseth the Angell, eyther in time, or in one onely instant, and indivisible moment of time; yet it seemeth farre more probable that . . . he never doth or can passe in an indivisible moment of time from one whole place, wherein he was before, unto another; neyther can hee . . . passe from one of the said places to another whole place . . . unlesse he passe (as bodies also must doe) by all that space which is interjacent, or lyeth betwixt . . .' (op. cit., Ch. XVI, pp. 60–77). Donne never leaves the angel any choice nor does he ever suggest the purely 'virtual' contact claimed by St. Thomas (*Summa*, Ia, q. 53, art. 1, resp.). M. P. Ramsay reads the doctrine into lines 69–71 of his 'Eclogue', but the lines simply mean that angels, 'though on earth employd they bee, / Are still in heav'n', i.e. still enjoy the beatific vision, as all theologians agreed (cf. *Summa*, Ia, q. 112, art. 1, ad. 3m).

[28] It had become 'the common current of the Schooles', according to Salkeld: *Treatise of Angels*, pp. 75–7. Yet Thomas Heywood in *The Hierarchie of the Blessed Angells* (London, 1635) still affirmed that the angel 'Is not contain'd in place, as Brutes and we, / But Place it selfe he in Himselfe containes, / Bee'ng said to be still where his Pow'r remaines', which implies that he 'without passing places, can with ease / Or go or come at all times when he please' (pp. 438–9).

confirmed in this opinion by his own empirical sense of reality. Yet, unlike Scotus and his followers, the poet never describes the motions of angels, however swift, as continuous in time,[29] for his imagination always apprehended movement as instantaneous or made up of a succession of instants.[30] For St. Thomas too, movement was discontinuous and always realized *in instanti*, 'through the succession of sundry places'.[31] We find, as it were, an original conflation of Thomistic and Scotist views in 'Obsequies to the Lord Harrington' (81–6):

> As when an Angell down from heav'n doth flye,
> Our quick thought cannot keepe him company,
> Wee cannot thinke, now hee is at the Sunne,
> Now through the Moon, now he through th'aire doth run,
> Yet when he's come, we know he did repaire
> To all twixt Heav'n and Earth, Sunne, Moon, and Aire. . . .

Such conceits should not be pressed too far for theological significance. Our concern, however, is not with Donne's theology but with the structures of his mind and, like the description of the soul's flight to Heaven in the 'Second Anniversary' (181–213), these lines again suggest that his imagination was apt to focus on a point or take a leap rather than follow a progression or expand in space and time.[32] The flashing forth of his conceits reflects the same inclination. In description and dialectics alike each mental representation seems to stand out against a background of emptiness—not the vacant space in which the imagination of Milton and Traherne will move as in a continuous element, but a kind of ontological vacuity, as if successive epiphanies of being were so many projections out of nothingness. The poet's mode of imagination—instantaneous and pointillistic—did not invite a more spacious vision, like Thomas Heywood's or Sir Thomas Browne's, of angelic substance 'without circumscription, unconfin'd' or diffused 'in the

[29] *Opus Oxoniense*, II, d., q. 9, a. 2, n. 8. Cf. E. Gilson, *Duns Scot*, p. 413, and B. Landry, *Duns Scot* (Paris, 1922), p. 276.

[30] See *Poètes métaphysiques anglais*, I. 85–8.

[31] *Summa*, Ia, q. 53, art. 2, ad. 3m; art. 3, ad. 3m. On Scotus see Gilson, op. cit., p. 420 n. 3.

[32] One could object that the decomposition of movement gives a sense of discontinuity in any description: hence the Eleatic aporias. But what is most characteristic is Donne's tendency to describe movement as a sudden and instantaneous propulsion along a trajectory studded with landmarks.

ubiquitary and omnipresent Essence of God'.[33] Yet Donne's curious insistence on the necessity for angels—and departed souls[34]—to touch 'upon the way betweene' when they 'passe from extreame to extreame' may also remind us that this paradoxical poet was a man who early proclaimed that 'meanes blesse' ('Satyre II', 107), declared 'I hate extreames' ('The Autumnall', 45), and truly sought the *via media*.[35]

Donne again steered his own way between conflicting doctrines concerning the angelic mode of intellection. Extreme opinions on this controversial question are summarized in the *Angelographia* of Casmannus, published in 1597: 'An Angeli hominum instar, per discursum, compositionem & divisionem, autem, Dei instar, uno intuitu, & intelligendi actu intelligant, quae intelligunt?' (I. xi). Aquinas had argued that a higher nature required a higher mode of intellection, different from man's discursive reason.[36] Scotus assumed that the angelic mind worked like the human understanding, receiving from things the particular forms or species associated in the processes of reasoning.[37] In 'Obsequies to the Lord Harrington' (lines 87–98) Donne's angel has 'sodaine knowledge', yet it 'growes'

> By quick amassing severall formes of things,
> Which he successively to order brings:
> Just as a perfect reader doth not dwell,
> On every syllable, nor stay to spell,
> Yet without doubt, hee doth distinctly see
> And lay together every A, and B.

This description may be reconciled with the timeless yet orderly 'succession' of concepts admitted by St. Thomas,[38] yet it still suggests a kind of discourse with 'composition' if not 'division'. No undue significance, of course, should be attached

[33] *Hierarchie of the Blessed Angells*, p. 439. *Religio Medici*, ii. 35, ed. Denonain (Cambridge, 1953), p. 54.

[34] Cf. 'Second Anniversary', 189–213, and *Sermons*, vii. 383.

[35] 'And whereas an Angel it selfe cannot passe from East to West, from extreame to extreame, without touching upon the way betweene, the people will passe from extreame to extreame; without any middle opinion': Ibid., viii. 324. On Donne's rejection of extremes see *Poètes métaphysiques anglais*, iii. 69.

[36] *Summa*, Ia, q. 58, art. 3 and 4. Cf. q. 84, art. 2, resp.

[37] *Opera Omnia* (Lyons, 1639), II, d. 1, q. 6, n. 3; cf. Landry, *Scot*, pp. 270, 278.

[38] *Summa*, Ia, q. 57, art. 3, ad. 2 m.

to a poetic simile, but in his sermons Donne insisted on what the minds of men and angels have in common.[39] The simultaneous apprehension of concatenated ideas ascribed to the angelic mind could reflect the poet's own dialectical eagerness: an emotional longing to know all things 'in an instant' is combined with a persistent rationality and sturdy common sense. Unlike the Platonists Donne never spoke in mystical terms of the 'intuitive knowledge' that would allow angels to see things 'in their true reall Essence'.[40] In a sermon preached in 1622 he refused angels a knowledge '*per essentiam*, for whosoever knows so, as the Essence of the thing flows from him, knows all things, and that's a knowledge proper to God only'. Yet he added: 'Neither doe the Angels know *per species* . . . which rise from the Object, and pass through the Sense to the Understanding, for that's a deceivable way'. But how angels know by the unclouded light of their 'Nature', by 'Creation', 'Confirmation', and 'Revelation', we are not told exactly, for only in Heaven shall we 'know how the Angels know, by knowing as they know'.[41]

The poet who wrote 'To Schoolemen I bequeath my doubtfulnesse' ('The Will', 30) was unlikely to commit himself firmly to any opinion on the modes of Angelic knowledge. A hyperbolical conceit in 'The Dreame' rests on the assumption that his mistress could read his thought, which was 'beyond an Angels art'. Most theologians agreed that 'the closet of man's heart is locked up from them; as reserved solely to their Maker'.[42] This tenet is alluded to in the *Sermons* and even used as a warning to sinners.[43] Yet, when the conflicting views of Aquinas and Scotus are seriously confronted, no conclusion is reached and the controversy is declared useless for Christian faith.[44] In one of the 'Holy Sonnets' the poet does not choose between two hypotheses: our hearts may be known to angels (hence to blessed souls) either intuitively or only through

39 *Sermons*, x. 41: 'But Man and Angels have one thing common to them both . . . that is, Reason, understanding, knowledge, discourse.'

40 Heywood, *Hierarchie*, p. 442. Cf. Browne, *Religio*, i. 33: ed. cit., p. 51. The mystic note may also be heard in Puritan writings, but chiefly among the Independents, e.g. when Sir Henry Vane speaks of 'senses meerly spiritual and inward' in *The Retired Man's Meditation* (London, 1655), p. 45.

41 *Sermons*, iv. 127–8.

42 Joseph Hall, *The Invisible World Discovered* (1652): *Works* (1863), viii. 362.

43 *Sermons*, iv. 315; v. 154; x. 58.

44 Ibid. x. 82; The text is quoted by Grierson, ii. 34–5.

appearances.[45] The *practical* conclusion is that God 'knowes best', that is, knows *better* than angels the sincerity of the poet's repentance, *not* that it is known to Him alone. The stanza devoted to the angels in the 'Litanie' (VI) was a profession of ignorance: 'So let me study, that mine actions bee / Worthy their sight, though blinde in how they see.' Yet the 'Litanie' was written before 'Obsequies to the Lord Harrington'. This oscillation between subtle speculation and a kind of *docta ignorantia* cannot be ascribed to a religious evolution, even if we agree that Donne expressed his deeper conviction when he confessed his uncertainty. That we cannot know how an angel knows before knowing as they know is a recurrent idea, expressed again in 1627. Yet even the reiteration of the words 'we know not' betrays no acquiescence in 'unknowing'. Angels are '*aenigmata divina*, The Riddles of Heaven, and the perplexities of speculation', but this is acknowledged by a man whose mind is obviously eager to unriddle mysteries, and therefore longs for the day of Resurrection, when 'we shall be like them, and know them by that assimilation'.[46] What characterizes Donne's attitude is this very tension: on the one hand a Christian readiness to admit that speculative knowledge is unattainable and anyway superfluous for salvation; on the other hand a persistent intellectual curiosity, an irritability of the mind.[47]

Metaphysics and theology in the verse and prose of Donne are seldom divorced from concrete human problems, moral or

[45] 'Holy Sonnet 4', in Gardner, *Divine Poems*, p. 14: see Commentary, p. 77. I discern three steps in the argument: 1 (1–4): a supposition based on the assumption that angels and blessed souls alike can know the minds of men intuitively, i.e. what Donne, following St. Thomas, habitually denied (see *Sermons*, iv. 316; x. 58); 2 (5–8): another supposition obviously derived from St. Thomas, who granted angels some knowledge of men's thoughts when manifested through outward signs in the body (*Summa*, Ia, q. 57, art. 4), hence the fear of misinterpretation (9–12); 3 (12–14): the problem is dismissed by the poet since the essential thing is that God should know his thoughts.

[46] *Sermons*, viii. 105–6. Cf. iv. 128.

[47] Donne is not more dogmatic on other nice points of angelology. When he writes, 'if every severall Angell bee / A *kind* alone . . .', he only frames a hypothesis ('An Hymne to the Saints', 6–7). He reminds us in a sermon that the Angels 'in the Schoole are conceived to be more in number, then, not only the Species, but all the individualls of this lower world' (*Sermons*, ix. 136), but this statement does not necessarily imply that he is siding with St. Thomas (*Summa*, Ia, q. 50, art. 3, resp.) against Scotus, who thought angels could be multiplied even though several angels belonged to the same 'kind' (see Gilson, *Scot*, p. 398).

even social issues. This is best illustrated by his views on guardian angels. As Salkeld noted, '*Calvine* propounding this question; *An singulis hominibus singuli Angeli attributi sunt: answereth, pro certo affirmare non ausim*'. Most Protestants, however, were more affirmative, 'out of the common consent of both the ancient Greeke and Latine Church . . .'[48] That there were guardian angels for Provinces, Communities, and Churches also remained a fairly widespread belief.[49] Donne voices the current opinion in the Seventh Expostulation of his *Devotions* and an outrageous hyperbole in 'The Second Anniversary' is based on it.[50] But a letter, probably written in 1612, reveals the deeper significance he attached to a doctrine described as 'imperfect':

It is not perfectly true which a very subtle, yet very deep wit, Averroes, says, that all mankind hath but one soul, which informs and rules us all, as one intelligence doth the firmament and all the stars in it; as though a particular body were too little an organ for a soul to play upon. And it is as imperfect which is taught by that religion which is most accommodate to sense (I dare not say to reason, thought it have appearance of that too, because none may doubt but that that religion is certainly best which is reasonablest). That all mankind hath one protecting angel; all Christians one other, all English one other, all of one corporation and every civil coagulation or society one other; and every man one other. Though both these opinions express a truth, which is that mankind hath very strong bounds to cohabit and concur in other than mountains and hills during his life. First, common and mutual necessity of one another; and therefore naturally in our defence and subventions we first fly to ourselves; next, to that which is likest other men. Then, natural and inborn charity, beginning at home, which persuades us to give that we may receive: and legal charity, which makes us also forgive. Then an ingraffing in one another, and growing together by a custom of society; and last of all, strict friendship . . .[51]

48 *Treatise of Angels*, Ch. XLIII, pp. 251–2.

49 Still mentioned in 1646 by Henry Lawrence in *Of our Communion and Warre with Angels*, p. 30. The treatise, first printed in Amsterdam, had run to a fourth edition in London by 1652 under the title of *Militia Spiritualis*.

50 *Devotions*, ed. Sparrow, p. 39: 'Second Anniversary', 235–40. The 'hyperbole', however, becomes appropriate if Elizabeth Drury represents either the body of Christ or the truly universal Church (see *Poètes métaphysiques anglais*, i. 453–4): 'every limbe' or member may then be assigned a Tutelar Angel!

51 *Letters* (London, 1651), p. 43. Gosse, *Life and Letters* (1889), ii. 8. The religion 'most accommodate to sense' must be Roman Catholicism. Averroes, earlier

This is a splendid parallel to the famous image in the *Devotions* (xvii): 'No man is an *Iland*, intire of it selfe . . .' Donne's speculations about angels were not scholastic cobwebs: they were related to the problems of life. Theological opinions may be 'imperfect' and yet express a 'truth': the truest needs of human nature. In a similar way the poet's conceits do not require our full assent to be meaningful. In this interpretation of religious myth we have moved away from the allegorical modes of the Middle Ages and the Renaissance. Instead of erecting a superstructure of topological or anagogical meaning over plain historical facts, the inquiring mind of Donne presses through the tight-woven fantasies of 'subtle yet very deep' wits to discover truths of nature and experience. This turn of mind allies him not with the neo-Platonists but with Bacon reading an ancient myth as an invitation not to seek 'things useful for life and civilisation from abstract philosophies' but 'only from Pan, that is from sagacious experience and the universal knowledge of nature'.[52] Unlike the modern euhemerists, however, the Anglican poet, when investing angelology with a new significance, did not discard the doctrines on which Christians of different persuasion were agreed.

Donne's interest in scholastic angelology was singular in an age when Calvinists, Platonists, and the 'new philosophers' agreed to reject it. But whim or wit will not account for this original combination of genuine curiosity and full awareness of the hazardous nature of this 'science'. The conceits of the poet, the speculations of the thinker prove effective whenever they

mentioned, identified the angels with the Intelligences of Aristotle which governed the spheres but not human communities. In the Koran angels are messengers (XXII. 74), intercessors (XXXIII. 42), and every man may have two guardian angels (XII. 12, LXXXVI. 4, etc.), but there is no parallel to Donne's text. The Church Fathers, interpreting the Bible (Daniel 10: 13, 20; Revelation 1: 2, 2: 1, 12: 7), ascribed guardian angels to each church, nation, and even city (*Dictionnaire de Théologie Catholique*, t. I, c. 1215–16). St. Thomas placed 'the human multitude' under the care of archangels and principalities without expressly mentioning churches, nations, and cities (*Summa*, Ia, q. 113, art. 3), but the 'Index Tertius' of the Antwerp edition of the *Summa* in 1585 is more precise than the text, which shows that such distinctions were common: 'Angeli custodiunt particulares homines: archangeli provincias: principatus totam naturam humanam' ('Angelus', no. 329). Protestants, however, were usually diffident: see West, op. cit., pp. 49–50.

52 *De Augmentis*, II. xiii: *Philosophical Works*, pp. 442–7.

convey a truth, not about angels, but about the human mind or the human predicament.

To Henry Vaughan an angel never was a 'riddle', but a vision and a presence. The author of *Silex Scintillans* is never teased into (or out of) thought: he is filled with aesthetic delight by the 'beauteous files' or raised to mystic contemplation of another 'bright ring'.[53] Angels call to his soul in his dreams,[54] under the dark tent of night only rent 'by some Angels wing or voice' ('The Night'). Man, however, is now denied the diurnal apparitions enjoyed in the youth of the world, when 'he was sure to view them' in each bush and highway: he can only dream of his 'Angell-infancy'.[55]

This sharp contrast between Donne and Vaughan is noted first in order to show once more that the saintly Herbert is unexpectedly closer to the author of the *Songs and Sonnets*. A Latin poem, 'In Angelos', shows he was interested in the difference between 'the adult intellect of the Angels' and man's understanding. In *The Temple* he shunned scholastic subtlety yet a submerged theological significance lurks in some allusions. In 'Praise (III)' the use of *must* in 'Angels must have their joy' (line 21) implies that the faithful angels, 'converted' to God by the 'joy' of the beatific vision (whereas men are converted by grief), can no longer fall: 'Affliction (V)' makes the meaning clear (lines 13–14). Both 'Dulnesse' (lines 27–8) and 'The Sacrifice' (lines 182–3) suggest that angels are, like men, unable to love God or contemplate His face without the help of grace. Unlike the Swan of Usk the pastor of Bemerton does not seem to delight in the contemplation of angels or yearn for their presence on earth. Vaughan's 'Angell-infancy' conjured up an image of light and a 'nebula of emotion' (a phrase T. S. Eliot should have used to describe the poetry of Vaughan rather than Marvell's). When Herbert defines prayer as 'Angels age',

53 'Peace', 8 (cf. 'The Men of War', 21–2); 'Palm-Sunday', 22–3. In only two instances do angels appear in argument and the argument is neither theological nor complex: 'Dressing', 42; 'Repentance', 65–8.

54 'They are all gone', 25–6. His 'lifes kinde Angel' revives his inspiration and faith in 'The Agreement', 7–12.

55 'Corruption', 25–8; 'Religion', 1–8; 'Providence', 3. Angels came down on earth for the Nativity ('The Shepheards', 27) and the Resurrection ('Ascension-day', 25–6), and with Christ's Second Coming 'Angels here / Shall yet to man appear, / And familiarly confer / Beneath the Oke and Juniper' ('The Jews', 4–7).

only the idea of eviternal existence is conveyed.[56] The angelic world in *The Temple* is always a transcendent world of grace[57] whence music may call to man or manna flow.[58] Vaughan saw angels 'descending' (Son-dayes', line 15) and Traherne will exclaim, 'How like an Angel came I down' ('Wonder'). Herbert entertains no dream of angelic immanence in the world of nature, for his theme is God's immanence in the human heart. His angels do not move along Jacob's ladder from the spiritual world to the world of sense: they keep to their own world and 'Man ties them both alone' ('Mans medley', line 10).

When choosing scholastic angelology as a field of imagery Donne had been original. Poets who wished to vie in subtlety with the monarch of wit followed suit. But his persistent interest in the angelic mode of knowledge found an echo only in a minor Metaphysical. William Hammond shared Donne's craving for certainty and his awareness that the human mind cannot reach the substance 'Close couched under accidents', but he spoke of angelic knowledge in more Platonic terms: 'Spirits alone intuitive / Can to the heart of essence dive'.[59] Other poets either ignored the speculative approach or dallied with scholastic concepts for the sake of witty or even burlesque effects. The angel's body of condensed air could be turned into a decorative image, and Cleveland's 'Hecatomb' illustrates the debased use of a conceit which had conveyed the mysteriousness of love's incarnation in 'Aire and Angels':

> Suppose an Angel, darting through the air,
> Should there encounter a religious prayer
> Mounting to Heaven, that Intelligence
> Should for a Sunday-suit thy breath condense
> Into a body.[60]

In his epic poem the *Davideis* Cowley could be expected to approach angelology more seriously, and he did write learned 'notes' on the names of angels and their mode of apparition.[61]

56 'Prayer (I)', 1: see Hutchinson's note, p. 493.

57 'Sinne (I)', 12; 'The Temper (I)', 25.

58 'The Church-Porch', 388; 'The Sacrifice', 239.

59 'The World'; *Minor Poets of the Caroline Period*, ed. Saintsbury, ii. 508.

60 *Poems*, ed. B. Morris and E. Withington (Clarendon Press, Oxford, 1967), p. 50.

61 See *Davideis*, Bk. I n. 28; Bk. II nn. 25, 94, 95: pp. 273–4, 310, 321, in *Poems*, ed. Waller (Cambridge University Press, 1905).

But the poetic image and the scholastic notion were separated, which never happened with Donne. The commentary explains how Gabriel 'Bodies and cloathes himself with thickned ayr', but the Thomistic doctrine is used only to justify a witty description of the Angel as a comely youth who 'took for skin a cloud most soft and bright' and borrowed his blush 'from the morning beauties deepest red'. The pictorial approach is unlike Donne's and the lines anticipate Pope's Sylphs in the *Rape of the Lock* rather than Milton's angels in *Paradise Lost*.[62] Again, when 'Slow *Time* admires, and knows not what to call / The *Motion* [of the Angel], having no *Account* so *small*',[63] the poet's own 'admiration' is different from Donne's intellectual wonder and perplexity. Cowley's interest, as a poet at least, was not in the thought but in the literary adornment of thought. Hence his surprising confession: 'In this, and some like places, I would not have the Reader judge of my opinion by what I say'.[64] The opinions of Aquinas and the Schoolmen on the 'Figuration' of Spirits are reported, but 'they are beholding for this invention to the ancient Poets', Virgil and Homer, who made Apollo 'the best Artificer of *Vapours*'.[65] The modern poet must show that he is well-read but not credulous. Donne knew that some of the notions he played with were 'imperfect', but he did not invite disbelief unless irony were intended (as in his allusions to mermaids and mandrakes). His most elaborate conceits on angels often conveyed truths of human experience; Cowley's have no serious core of meaning. In *The Mistress*, the lyric poet can only emulate the witty impudence of Donne's Elegies: an 'Aire and Angels' was beyond his scope.[66]

When wit is divorced from thought a purely aesthetic approach proves more satisfying in poetry. Some of Marvell's allusions to angels are biblical, as expected in a Puritan, and fraught with historical meaning.[67] Others are unexpectedly

[62] *Davideis*, Bk. II: *Poems*, p. 304. Cf. *Rape of the Lock*, II. 59–68.

[63] *Davideis*, Bk. I: *Poems*, p. 252.

[64] *Davideis*, Bk. I n. 24: *Poems*, p. 272.

[65] *Davideis*, Bk. II n. 95: *Poems*, p. 321.

[66] See 'Verses lost upon a Wager', st. 3. 'My Heart discovered' is reminiscent of Donne, but not in the comparison of thoughts with Angels. The metaphors of stanza 5 in 'The Waiting-Maid', and stanza 2 in 'Thraldom' are literary hyperboles of little significance.

[67] England, the Garden of the World, is guarded 'With watry if not flaming Sword': 'Upon Appleton House', st. xlii. Cromwell, 'as the *Angel* of our

decorative in the Counter-Reformation style: 'I see the *Angels* in a Crown / On you the Lillies show'ring down.'[68] Marvell's vision, however, has something of the stillness of Pre-Raphaelite art; Crashaw's throbs with Baroque excitement. Golden-winged angels assemble in his poems with the swirling profusion of the heavenly hosts surrounding Christ or Mary in their Ascension.[69] In the poetry of Vaughan angels are isolated figures shining against a silent expanse of sky, or night, or greenery: with Crashaw they compose the background against which the contemplated object stands out—be it the Virgin, a saint, or a tear. In the very confrontation of the Seraph and St. Teresa the angel will lend his splendour to the saint.[70] Vaughan tends to merge the divine in nature; Crashaw, in humanity.

A more reflective approach might have been expected from Lord Herbert of Cherbury. The author of *De Veritate* acknowledged 'revelations' 'made with the medium of spirits which have been recognized in all ages as a special order of beings, invisible, impalpable, free of physical substance, endowed with rapid movement, and variously called angels, demons, intelligences and geniuses'.[71] But he refused to be disturbed by doubts 'concerning their nature', and resorted to angels only for conceited praise in two Platonic poems without the subtlety or irony of Donne.[72] For serious speculation we must turn to the Cambridge Platonists—notably Henry More and Cudworth—or to the author of *Paradise Lost*, whose conception of the angelic nature flowed from the same patristic and philosophic sources. But Milton and Donne were bound to 'handle' angels in different ways for several reasons: the opposition between the Scholastic system and a Puritan approach tinged with Platonism;

Commonweal, / Troubling the Waters, yearly mak'st them Heal': 'First Anniversary', 401–2.

68 'Upon Appleton House', st. xviii. This is the language of the Nun, but the image is also pictorial in 'The Loyall Scot', lines 45–50.

69 See 'On the Assumption', lines 23–5; 'A Hymne of the Nativity', st. 8; 'The Weeper', st. 6; 'The Teare', st. 6. The only metaphysical conceit is the assertion that 'A thousand Angells in one point can dwell' ('On a prayer booke', line 8), but this is a 'vulgar error' in angelology, condemned by Aquinas (*Summa*, Ia, q. 52, art. 3) and Scotus (Landry, *Scot*, pp. 274–5).

70 'The Flaming Heart': *Poems*, ed. L. C. Martin, pp. 324–5.

71 *De Veritate*, x: trans. M. H. Carré (Bristol, 1937), p. 309.

72 'Platonick Love', st. 4; 'The idea', lines 82–4: *Poems*, ed. Moore-Smith, pp. 71, 78.

the difference between narrative and lyric form, myth and conceit; last, but not least, the contrast between Milton's massive assurance, based on his interpretation of Scripture and the alleged evidence of 'right reason' (opportunely meeting his own heart's desire), and the intellectual indetermination and inconclusiveness displayed by Donne's 'riddling, perplexed, labyrinthicall soule'.[73]

With Thomas Traherne we move further away from Donne and from the Christian tradition. The 'Divine Philosopher' believed, no doubt, in angels and mentioned them among the 'Natures' studied by 'Natural Philosophy' (*Centuries*, III. 44). But 'to study Object for Ostentation, vain Knowledg or Curiosity is fruitless Impertinence though GOD Himself, and Angels, be the Object' (*Centuries*, III. 40). He had longed for a revelation, a book brought to him 'miraculously from Heaven' by 'som Angel' (*Centuries*, III. 27–8), but he found the secret of Felicity in his own mind, for his self-consciousness dictated his interpretation of the Bible.[74] His 'idealism'—despite the Platonic language—was related to new currents of thought which eventually enclosed the mind of man in the sphere of nature and made transcendence useless or illusory. Though unquestioned, the existence of angels is less important to Traherne than their metaphorical function: they are types of Adamic innocence. In 'a learned and a happy ignorance' the child 'like an angel . . . did see', and 'they that go Naked and Drink Water and liv upon Roots are like Adam, or Angels in Comparison of us'.[75]

By the end of the seventeenth century Reason will no longer be bound by Revelation and angels will cease to be objects of study for Natural Philosophy. Christians found it increasingly difficult to maintain a balance between the claims of rationality and the former curiosity about the invisible world of spirits. But even in an earlier age the scales had seldom been held evenly poised—never perhaps so evenly, though in quivering equilibrium, as they were for a time in the tense and restless mind of Donne.

73 Donne, *Sermons*, viii. 332.

74 As argued at length in my *Poètes métaphysiques anglais*, pp. 261–399.

75 'Eden', 1; *Centuries*, III. 12: *Centuries, Poems and Thanksgivings*, ed. Margoliouth (Clarendon Press, Oxford, 1958), ii. 117; i. 12.

Burton and Cardan

J. B. BAMBOROUGH

HENRY MORLEY, in what is still the principal biography of Cardan in English, says of him that

> He was the most successful scientific author of his time. . . . He was not only the most popular philosopher, but also the fashionable physician of the sixteenth century.[1]

This may be somewhat overstated, but there is no doubt of Cardan's contemporary fame, or his extraordinary range of interests. He was indeed a polymath, and wrote not only on many medical topics, but on Mathematics, Music, Moral and Natural Philosophy (Physics, Mechanics, and Optics), Politics, Natural History, Astronomy, and Astrology, as well as on such minor 'sciences' as Chiromancy, Oneiromancy, and Metoposcopy (which latter art he claimed to have perfected). The only major subjects about which he might have been expected to write, but did not, are Alchemy and Theology; it appears that he despised the former, and he very probably avoided the latter from prudential reasons—which did not prevent him from being accused of impiety, and, indeed, from being imprisoned on one occasion by the Inquisition.[2] Towards the end of his

[1] H. Morley, *The Life of Girolamo Cardano, of Milan, Physician* (Chapman and Hall, London, 1854), p. vii.

[2] Burton refers to Cardan's difficulties near the beginning of his subsection 'Causes of Heroical Love' (*The Anatomy of Melancholy*, Part III, Section II, Member ii, Subsection 1). The reference appears for the first time in the Third Edition (1628); in this edition Burton expanded his citation in the First and Second Editions of Cardan's commentary on Ptolemy (*Hieronymi Cardani Mediolanensis . . . in Cl. Ptolomaei Pelusiensis IIII De Astrorum Iudiciis, aut, ut vulgò vocant, Quadripartitae Constructionis, Libros Commentaria . . .*, Basle, 1554) by including extracts from Cardan's horoscope of himself, in which he speaks freely, for example, of his obsession with thoughts of sex. Burton indicates that it was for this frankness that Cardan was 'bitterly censured . . . by *Marinus Marsennus*, a malapert friar, and some others' (*Anatomy*, 3rd edn., p. 413). In fact Mersenne attacked Cardan for reporting the debate between the Christian, the Jew, and the Mohammedan in Bk. 11 of his *De Subtilitate*, and accused him of being the author of the notorious *De Tribus Impostoribus*. Cardan was also blamed for including a horoscope of

life Cardan boasted that he had published 138 books and had another 96 in manuscript: admittedly some of these 'books' are really chapters in longer works, but it is still a formidable output; some of it was never printed, but the Collected Works of 1663 are in ten Folio volumes, each of 700–800 pages, double column.[3] Burton might well have cited Cardan along with Aquinas and Tostato as an example of the furious industry of scholars.[4]

Of all this writing singularly little is of interest or importance today. Cardan is by no means totally forgotten, and continues to attract attention from biographers and historians of thought. But he is hardly a household name, and ironically the discoveries for which he is best known are probably not his at all. He made important contributions in mathematics, for example, but it has been maintained that the well-known 'Cardan's Rule'—for the solution of cubic equations in algebra of the type $x^3+ax = b$—should properly be called 'Del Ferro's formula', after the Bolognese Professor Scipione Del Ferro who first established it.[5] Similarly the invention of what are called 'Cardan joints', 'Cardan shafts', and 'Cardanic suspension'—familiar terms in the construction of the motor-car—has been attributed to others.[6]

Christ among his 'genitures', and other charges were made against him; see D. C. Allen, *Doubt's Boundless Sea* (Johns Hopkins Press, Baltimore, 1964), pp. 45–58. The exact reasons for Cardan's imprisonment in Bologna in 1570 remain obscure; see J. Eckman, *Jerome Cardan* (Supplements to the Bulletin of the History of Medicine, No. 7, Johns Hopkins Press, Baltimore, 1946), pp. 33–6.

[3] *Hieronymi Cardani Mediolanensis Philosophi ac Medici Celeberrimi Opera Omnia . . . Curâ Caroli Sponii Doctoris Medici Collegio Medd. Lugdunæorum Aggregati . . . Lugduni, Sumptibus Ioannis Antonii Huguetan, & Marci Antonii Ravaud, MDCLXIII* (hereafter cited as *Opera*). Cardan's list of his published and unpublished works is in Ch. 45 of his *De Vita Propria*, written in 1575 (the year before his death), but not published until 1643.

[4] In the subsection on 'Love of learning or overmuch Study' as a cause of Melancholy, *Anatomy*, I. II. iii. 15 (ed. A. R. Shilleto, George Bell & Sons, London, 1893, i. 351. Subsequent references to *Anatomy* by volume and page are to this edition).

[5] See the Foreword by Oystein Ore to the translation and edition by T. R. Witmer of Cardan's *Ars Magna Sive de Regulis Algebraicis*, first published Nuremberg, 1545 (*The Great Art, or The Rules of Algebra*, M.I.T. Press, Cambridge, Mass. and London, 1968, p. xii). It was the announcement by Cardan of this rule which led to his bitter controversy with the mathematician Niccolò Tartaglia of Brescia; see Witmer, ed. cit., pp. xvii–xxii, Morley, *Life*, Chs. 12 and 13, and Eckman, op. cit., pp. 59–66.

[6] See Eckman, op. cit., pp. 77–8. Cardan describes in Ch. 17 of *De Subtilitate* (*Opera*, iii. 612) the construction of a 'prince's chair' so suspended in gimbals that

Various medical discoveries have been credited to Cardan.[7] He gave, for example, the first clinical description of typhus (anticipating Fracastoro) in his first published work, *De Malo Recentiorum Medicorum Medendi Usu* (Venice, 1536), and he appears to have had some original ideas about the conveyance of infection by germs and the possibility of the transfusion of blood. The difficulty about such 'discoveries', in Cardan's as in other cases, is that it is one thing to adumbrate a theory or mention in passing a possible line of advance, and quite another to think an insight through and perform the necessary experimental work. Cardan was an exceptionally learned man, and, by his own account at least, a very successful practising physician, but he had little grasp of what were the growing-points in his profession: thus, although he knew Vesalius (and indeed cast Vesalius' horoscope),[8] he shows little knowledge of the new anatomy (compare Burton's apparent ignorance of Harvey's work on the circulation of the blood). Like Burton, Cardan knew very well what work had been done in the subjects in which he was interested, and what questions remained to be answered, but—like Burton again—he had no clear idea of the methods by which these answers were to be obtained (although to be sure he had more of what we should call 'the scientific mind' than Burton had). Sir Thomas Browne's judgement of him is not unfair:

> . . . a great Enquirer of Truth, but too greedy a Receiver of it. . . . Assuredly this learned man hath taken many things upon trust, and although examined some, hath let slip many others.[9]

To students of English literature he is of some marginal interest

it would remain upright no matter how rough the terrain over which it was carried, but he does not claim to have invented this. As for the universal joint, it has been suggested that Cardan may have derived this from the notebooks of Leonardo da Vinci, to which he may have had access (see K. D. Keele, 'Leonardo da Vinci's Influence on Renaissance Anatomy', *Medical History*, 8 (1964), 364).

7 See Eckman, op. cit., pp. 67–72.

8 Vesalius' geniture appears in *Hieronymi Cardani Medici Mediolanensis Libelli Quinque* (Nuremberg, 1547). Cardan's acquaintance with Vesalius may, however, have been only through the medium of correspondence: see Morley, *Life*, ii. 10–11 and G. Ongaro, 'Girolamo Cardano e Andrea Vesalio', *Rivista di Storia della Medicina*, 13 (1969), 51–61. In *De Vita Propria*, Ch. 39, Cardan says cryptically that 'various things' deterred him from the study of Anatomy (*Opera*, i. 31, col. 1).

9 *Pseudodoxia Epidemica*, Bk. 1, Ch. viii (*The Works of Sir Thomas Browne*, ed. G. Keynes, London, Faber & Gwyer, 1928, ii. 63).

in two quiet different contexts. It has been suggested that Shakespeare was familiar with his *De Consolatione*, in the English translation by Thomas Bedingfield,[10] and drew on it in *Hamlet*—indeed, it has been supposed that this is the book which Hamlet is reading at his entrance in Act II, scene ii, although how the audience is supposed to gather this is not clear. He appears again as a footnote to line 206 of Donne's 'First Anniversary' ('The Element of fire is quite put out'); in his autobiography Cardan notes that among his other achievements 'he removed fire from the number of the elements'.[11]

For Burton, however, Cardan was clearly a very important author. In the *Anatomy* he is quoted or referred to over 150 times—quite exceptional for a 'modern' authority, twice as many times as Burton refers directly to Aristotle, and more frequently, even, than he refers to St. Augustine.[12] It is difficult not to believe that Cardan held some especial significance for Burton. His two encyclopaedic works, *De Subtilitate* (first published 1550) and *De Rerum Varietate* (first published 1557), were certainly valuable sources, and Burton draws on them for a variety of subjects (in particular demonology: although he was sceptical about witchcraft, Cardan had much to say about demons, and Burton quotes, for example, his account of the conversation which his father Fazio Cardano had with seven devils 'in Greek apparel' in August 1491).[13] Burton makes use of Cardan, too, as a moral philosopher, quoting several times from his *De Sapientia* and *De Consolatione*. More than that, he actually cites *De Consolatione* as a precedent for *The Anatomy of Melancholy*. He believed, wrongly, that Cardan wrote it to comfort himself after his son's death, and, linking it with Cicero's supposed essay on the death of Tullia, quotes both works as justification for writing the *Anatomy* as a relief for his own melancholy mind.[14] In addition, he draws heavily on *De*

10 Thomas Bedingfield, *Cardanus Comforte* (1573; 1576). See H. Craig, 'Hamlet's Book', *Huntington Library Bulletin*, 6 (1934), 17–37.

11 *De Vita Propria*, Ch. 44 (*Opera*, i. 39, col. 2). The discussion of fire occurs in Bk. 2 of *De Subtilitate*.

12 I draw here upon the MS Index to Burton's references and quotations compiled by Mr J. M. Dodsworth of Royal Holloway College, with whom I am collaborating in a critical edition of *The Anatomy of Melancholy*.

13 *Anatomy*, I. II. i. 2 (i. 210). Burton somewhat expands Cardan's account of this incident, which is given in Bk. 19 of *De Subtilitate* (*Opera*, iii. 656, col. 1).

14 'Democritus to the Reader', *Anatomy*, i. 19; cf. ii. 147. In fact *De Consolatione*

Consolatione in his subsection on 'Discontents' (I. II. iii. 10), and still more in the 'Consolatory Digression containing the Remedies of all manner of Discontents' (II. III. i–viii) which has been called Burton's own '*De Consolatione*'.[15]

This use of Cardan may point to a more personal response on Burton's part. Perhaps he saw similarities between Cardan and himself. In 'Remedies against Discontents' he cites Cardan along with Erasmus, Melancthon, Budé, and Lipsius as a scholar who 'lived and died poor'. [16] Although Cardan claimed to have earned great rewards during his successful years of practice as a physician, he speaks freely of his great poverty up to the age of forty, and he seems to have been in distress in his old age. But whatever his circumstances, he never wavered in his devotion to the pursuit of knowledge, and this is a trait to which Burton would naturally respond. Commentators anxious to explain Burton's own melancholy, which led him to the writing of the *Anatomy*, usually stress the subsection (I. II. iii. 15) which contains the 'Digression on the Miseries of Scholars' and link it with the passages in which he writes of his own comparative lack of success in obtaining preferment; in one such passage he compares himself directly to Cardan as one who has failed to obtain patronage through his own negligence.[17] To some extent the 'Digression on the Miseries of Scholars' may be discounted as an exercise on a familiar contemporary theme, treated also, for example, in the 'Parnassus Plays' and *Histrio-mastix*; nor was Burton totally unsuccessful in gaining preferment. Nevertheless we need not doubt that he keenly felt the low estimation and poor reward afforded to scholars. Equally,

was published in 1542; the great tragedy in Cardan's life, the execution of his eldest son Gianbattista for the murder of his wife, did not take place until 1560. The work in which Cardan describes his grief and his efforts to save his son's life is his *De Utilitate ex Adversis Capienda*, begun in 1557 but not published until 1561. Burton may not have known this work at all, although there is a possible reference to it in *Anatomy*, i. 34 n. 2.

[15] See J. L. Lievsay, 'Robert Burton's *De Consolatione*', *South Atlantic Quarterly*, 55 (1956), 329–36; cf. R. L. Colie, *Paradoxia Epidemica* (Princeton University Press, Princeton, N.J., 1966), pp. 437 ff. There are references to or citations of *De Consolatione* on the following pages of vol. ii of the *Anatomy*: 145, 147 (three references), 148 (three references), 150, 152, 184, 196–7, 200 (two references), 202, 205, 223, and 228–9 (all within 'Remedies against Discontents').

[16] *Anatomy*, ii. 220.

[17] Ibid. i. 361–3; cf. i. 357 in which he cites Cardan as a poor scholar who had to grovel to 'respectless' (i.e. uncaring) patrons.

we should not ignore his fervent celebration of the pleasures of scholarship. 'Overmuch Study' may be a powerful cause of Melancholy, and both as a teacher and as a divine Burton warns against 'Curiosity', the insatiable seeking after knowledge in manners concerning which certainty may be unobtainable, not worth obtaining, or even perhaps presumptuous (God does not intend that we should know everything). At the same time he firmly maintains that 'amongst those exercises, or recreations of the mind within doors, there is none so general, so aptly to be applied to all sorts of men, so fit and proper to expell Idlessness and Melancholy, as that of *Study*',[18] and he continues with this theme for a dozen pages. There are several quotations from Cardan in this section, notably the passage beginning 'quid subtilius Arithmeticis inventionibus' (ii. 102), and on the following page the lines:

> *Arcana coeli, naturæ secreta, ordinem universi scire, majoris felicitatis et dulcedinis est, quam cogitatione quis assequi possit, aut mortalis sperare.*[19]

The joys of scholarship are a recurring theme in Cardan, perhaps most movingly stated in the Dedicatory Epistle to *De Rerum Varietate*, from which Burton took the quotations above:

> Tanta enim est sapientiæ dulcedo, tam gloriosa possessio, tam utilis exercitatio ejus, tam divinus amor fructus illius, tam secura quies in eius contemplatione, ut omnes homines hoc naturali desiderio teneantur.[20]

Burton, who rejoiced that he had been 'brought up a student in the most flourishing College of *Europe*',[21] and had continued there as a scholar for thirty years (indeed more), and who had as much as any man has ever had 'the scholarly passion for the acquisition of useless knowledge', could wholeheartedly echo

[18] Ibid., ii. 100.

[19] As so often with Burton, neither of these quotations is complete or accurate. They are based on passages from the *Epistola Nuncupatoria* addressed to Cardinal Madruccio and prefixed to *De Rerum Varietate*. This is not included in the 1663 *Opera*; in the first edition of *De Rerum Varietate* (Basle, 1557) the passage on p. 102 will be found on sig. $+4^{v}$, and that on p. 103 on sig. $+4^{r}$. Lines 15–16 on p. 104 ('*Ea suavitas . . . divelli*') are based on a sentence on sig. $+3^{r}$; lines 2–6 on p. 105 on a passage on sig. $+3^{v}$. There is a further reminiscence of the same Epistle (sig. $+2^{v}$) at the foot of p. 107 ('Cardan calls a Library the physick of the soul'). Lines 11–13 on p. 104 are, as Burton says, from § 3 of Cardan's *Hyperchen* (*Opera*, i. 284, col. 2).

[20] *De Rerum Varietate*, ed. cit., sig. $+2^{r}$; cf. *De Sapientia*, Bk. 2 (*Opera*, i. 525, col. 1).

[21] *Anatomy*, i. 13.

this: 'To most kind of men it is an extraordinary delight to study. For what a world of Books offers itself, in all subjects, arts, and sciences, to the sweet content and capacity of the Reader!'[22]

There is yet a further quality in Cardan which may have drawn Burton to him: he was enormously interested in himself. His *De Vita Propria* is his best-known work; it was praised by Goethe among others,[23] and has often been compared to the *Autobiography* of Benvenuto Cellini, his contemporary. Burton could not have read *De Vita Propria,* since it was not published until three years after his own death, but he refers several times to *De Libris Propriis* (first published in 1544), in which Cardan (following the example of Galen and Erasmus) lists and comments on his own writings and adds much autobiographical information, and to other places where Cardan speaks of himself. Cardan, in fact, could hardly refrain from bringing his own experiences and beliefs into his writings, and is sternly reproved by Morley for this:

> We should now very fairly turn from a writer who had the bad taste to obtrude himself in his own writings; but three hundred years ago, when modern literature was in its infancy, it had a right to prattle—the right age for talking properly was yet to come.[24]

Cardan has paid for his egocentricity. We know more about him than any other figure of his age: about trivial events in his life as well as major happenings; about his personal habits; his likes and dislikes (for example, his fondness for pet animals of all kinds); and about some of his most secret concerns. Unfortunately he also revealed himself as vain, credulous, and superstitious (as Burton noted).[25] His enemies—for example, Julius Caesar Scaliger—were able to fasten on his weaknesses in his lifetime; De Thou described his oddities of dress and manner in old age;[26] and finally Gabriel Naudé, who first

22 *Anatomy*. ii. 102.

23 See B. Caspari-Rosen and G. Rosen, 'Autobiography in Medicine', *Journal of the History of Medicine*, 1 (1947), 291–2.

24 *Life*, i. 288.

25 *Anatomy*, i. 239; cf. ibid. i. 418.

26 Under the year 1576 in Bk. LXII of *Historia Sui Temporis* (Geneva, 1626, iii. 136). De Thou was responsible for the story that Cardan starved himself to death to fulfil the prophecy he had made of the date of his own death in his horoscope; compare the story which Anthony à Wood says was current in Oxford that Burton

published *De Vita Propria* in 1643, added to it a 'judgement' of its author which represents Cardan as eccentric and scatter-brained, if not actually mad. Many efforts have been made to rehabilitate Cardan, but as late as 1971 an American writer was still able to call him 'that egomanical scalawag'.[27]

Yet the type of the vain and self-centred scholar is hardly unfamiliar, and perhaps we might today be readier than Morley was to acknowledge that egocentricity is not incompatible with great learning and rigorous thought. Burton may have recognized a kindred spirit: certainly he commends rather than condemns Cardan's frankness about himself ('methinks it is free, downright, plain and ingenuous').[28] His display of his own personality in the *Anatomy* has always been recognized, and like Cardan, he has suffered for it at the hands of critics. Accounts of him in the nineteenth and early twentieth centuries almost always followed the line indicated by Lamb in his famous description, 'that fantastic great old man',[29] and emphasized Burton's oddity and whimsicality to the point of ignoring his fundamental seriousness of purpose. More recently he has attracted the attention of critics fascinated by those complexities of irony and paradox which may be attributed to writers who to a greater or lesser extent conceal themselves behind a mask or 'persona', as Burton does in adopting the disguise of 'Democritus Junior'. Such approaches often seem to trivialize Burton quite as much as the most patronizing of Victorian allusions to his 'quaintness'. Indeed, they can be seriously misleading about the intent of the *Anatomy*. The 'paradoxical encomium', for example, was a favourite Renaissance rhetorical genre,[30] and Burton would have known many examples of it besides the most famous, Erasmus' *Praise of Folly*

'sent up his soul to heaven thro' a slip about his neck' in order similarly to validate his own forecast of his date of death (*Athenae Oxonienses*, ed. Bliss (1815), ii. 653). Perhaps this story was told of all astrologers.

27 C. F. Mullet, 'An Arte to make the Dumbe to Speake, the Deaf to Heare: a Seventeenth Century Goal', *Journal of the History of Medicine*, 26 (1971), 125.

28 *Anatomy*, iii. 65.

29 'Detached Thoughts on Books and Reading' (*The Works of Charles Lamb*, ed. E. V. Lucas, vol. ii (Methuen, London, 1912), 197–8).

30 See A. E. Malloch, 'The Techniques and Function of the Renaissance Paradox', *S.P.* 53 (1956), 191–203, and H. K. Miller, 'The Paradoxical Encomium with special reference to its vogue in England 1600–1800', *M.P.* 53 (1956), 145–78. For a consideration of the *Anatomy* as paradox, see R. L. Colie, op. cit., pp. 430 ff.

(Cardan, for instance, wrote in praise of the Gout). It does not follow that he intended the *Anatomy*, paradoxical though it may be at times, to be regarded in this light. His great work was both learned and humorous, but it was not a satire on learning, nor did he see himself as aggrandizing a trivial subject for comic effect. On the contrary, everything indicates that he saw Melancholy, despite its occasional absurd aspects, as a subject demanding the most serious study.

In a similar fashion, over-emphasis on 'role-playing' by Burton in the *Anatomy* may mislead the critic. It is true that having assumed the persona of Democritus Junior in his Satyrical Preface Burton proceeds at once not only to disturb the mask so as to reveal himself, but to explain to the reader why he adopted it in the first place, and it is true also that in 'Democritus to the Reader' he doubts whether any man can be wholly wise or any product of the human mind wholly sound. To go on from there to suggest that he 'undercuts' (a favourite word in this type of interpretation) every statement in the *Anatomy* so as to reach in it (in Professor S. E. Fish's words) 'a total unity of unreliability'[31] is to render it valueless. Professor L. Babb, in one of the best and most balanced studies of the *Anatomy of Melancholy*, has suggested that 'The choice of the pseudonym and the writing of the satyrical preface probably did not occur until the Anatomy of 1621 was near completion'. This may well be true, though direct evidence is lacking. What is certainly true is Professor Babb's further remark: 'Burton plays his role of Democritus Junior in the preface, not in the body of the book'.[32] In the Preface Burton is taking advantage of the wide spread of meaning attached to 'Melancholy' to produce an excursus on the well-worn theme, 'All men are (more or less) Mad', and in doing so adopts the appropriate stance; elsewhere—for example, when he writes his consolatory passages—he very properly speaks as a divine, in a quite different tone. Like Cardan, he is as likely to introduce his own experiences in one context as another.

If the comparison with Cardan may serve to remind us that egocentricity does not invalidate serious purpose, it may also

31 S. E. Fish, *Self-Consuming Artifacts* (University of California Press, Berkeley, Los Angeles and London, 1972), p. 330.

32 L. Babb, *Sanity in Bedlam* (Michigan State University Press, East Lansing, Mich., 1959), p. 15.

help to place Burton in the right context. Much attention has been paid in recent years to the tradition of 'Menippean Satire'. Burton has a place in this line: indeed Professor Northrop Frye speaks of the *Anatomy of Melancholy* as 'the greatest Menippean satire in English before Swift'.[33] Within this 'line' Burton has been chiefly associated with his immediate predecessors Erasmus, Montaigne, and Rabelais. With all three he certainly had something in common, but caution is necessary in speaking of their 'influence'. He certainly knew Erasmus' works well, and there are some seventy-five references to them in the *Anatomy*. Less than a quarter of these, however, are to the *Moriae Encomium* (most are to the *Adagia*), and of these only three occur in 'Democritus to the Reader', where one would expect the Erasmian model to be followed most closely. In composing his 'Satyrical Preface' Burton could and apparently did turn to other models such as J. J. Scaliger's *Confutatio Stultissimae Burdonis Fabulae* and J. V. Andreae's *Menippus sive Dialogorum Satyricorum Centuria*.[34] Professor Babb maintains that 'There is no very good reason to believe that Burton took anything from Erasmus beyond his acknowledged borrowings',[35] and goes on to suggest that their resemblances in tone and attitude may derive from their common reading of Lucian. Whether this view is correct or not, the resemblances are certainly there—for example, in their views on War. Burton's 'debt' to Montaigne and Rabelais is another matter.

Burton mentions Montaigne seven times. On the occasions when he does more than refer to a point made in one of the Essays, he partly quotes and partly paraphrases—in his usual manner—from Florio's translation.[36] It is a moot point whether in fact he knew enough French to be able to read the original; if he did not, then a statement such as that made by Professor Colie—that he was 'brought up on Montaigne'[37]—is not

33 N. Frye, *Anatomy of Criticism* (Princeton University Press, Princeton, N.J., 1957), p. 311.

34 There is a cluster of borrowings from both these works in the Satyrical Preface, *Anatomy*, i. 20–1.

35 Babb, op. cit., p. 52; see R. L. Colie, 'Some Notes on Burton's Erasmus', *Renaissance Quarterly*, 20 (1967), 335–41, for a contrary view.

36 Cf. *Anatomy*, ii. 147, lines 7–10, with Montaigne, *Essays*, trans. John Florio, (Dent, Everyman edn., London, 1910), ii. 58; *Anatomy*, iii. 240, lines 21–4, with Montaigne, ed. cit. ii. 182; and Ibid. iii. 314, lines 5–9, with Montaigne, ed. cit. ii. 458.

37 Colie, *Paradoxia Epidemica*, p. 450.

tenable: he would have been twenty-seven before Montaigne became available to him. It is a fact that he invariably quotes French authors such as Budé or Bodin from the Latin versions of their works, and there is no French to be found in the *Anatomy*. He did, however, own one French book, Jaques Ferrand's *De la Maladie d'Amour ou Melancholie Erotique*. On the three occasions when he mentions this book he emphasizes that it did not come into his hands until after the publication of the Third Edition of the *Anatomy* in 1628, and his copy, which is in Christ Church Library, bears his signature and the date '1629' on its title-page. It has been rebound, but is otherwise in what a bookseller would call 'mint condition', and is unmarked in any way. It is also noteworthy that the only specific reference that Burton makes to its contents is totally wrong;[38] unfortunately neither here nor elsewhere can misrepresentation of an author's views by Burton be taken as evidence that he had not read a work. It is very understandable that Burton should be anxious to disavow any knowledge of Ferrand's book before he wrote his own treatment of Love Melancholy,[39] because it inevitably covers much of the same ground and quotes many of the same sources. But it is not in fact possible to point to any clear evidence of indebtedness on

38 In the Fourth Edition of the *Anatomy* (1632) he interpolated into a statement in the subsection on 'Causes of Love-Melancholy', taken from the Italian physician Guianerius and concerning physical stimuli to amorousness, the phrase, '*Ferandus* a Frenchman in his Erotique Mel: to certain *atomi* in the seed' (p. 454). In fact Ferrand dismisses among the opinions concerning the causes of love 'fondées sur de faux principes, & pure chimeres' the opinion of Epicurus, as reported by Plutarch, that the images of desirable objects stimulate desire by a certain disposition of atoms which affects the seed (pp. 34–5). Ferrand himself takes the standard Galenic view that lust arises in the first instance from excessive blood which, 'blanchy par la chaleur naturelle' (p. 194), turns into seed, but that 'Manie Erotique' arises from the humour of melancholy made hot and dry by the adustion of choler, blood, or melancholy itself (pp. 52–3). Burton does not go into any detail about the physical causes of heroic melancholy, and his approach in the Third Partition is much more literary and anecdotal than medical.

39 In the Fifth Edition Burton inserted a parenthesis into the passage cited in the last note, after 'Mel:': (which† book first came into my hands after the third edition)'; the side-note reads, '†Printed at *Paris*, seven years after my first edition' (p. 444). In fact his edition of *De la Maladie d'Amour* (D. Moreau, Paris) was published in 1623 (there was an earlier version published in Toulouse in 1612 as *Traité de l'essence et guérison de l'amour*: presumably he did not know of this). 'Seven years after my first edition' must refer either to the date of the Third Edition of the *Anatomy*—i.e. 1628—or to the date at which he acquired his copy of Ferrand's book.

Burton's part in later editions of the *Anatomy*, and it may be that he did not use Ferrand because he could not.

If Burton could not read French he could nevertheless experience Montaigne through Florio; Rabelais he could not have read at all, since there was no Latin version, and the first English translation was not published until thirteen years after his death. Two of his references simply cite Rabelais as among 'modern' satirists: his third mention of 'that French Lucian' is fuller, but need not derive directly from the French text.[40] It is hard to prove a negative, but a statement such as 'Burton avait lu et relu [Rabelais] avant d'écrire son *Anatomy of melancholy*'[41] just does not seem to be true. In fact the two men seem very far apart in temperament; nor does the relationship seem all that close between Burton and Montaigne. They have indeed a number of attitudes and opinions in common: the difficulty in evaluating their similarities is the same as that of judging Burton's debt to Erasmus, or of distinguishing Cardan's possible influence on Shakespeare from that of Montaigne. So much concerning stock topics derives in all Renaissance writers from the same classical sources. In general terms Burton was interested in aspects of his own personality, as was Montaigne— and Cardan; but the kind of interest, and still more his type of personality, were quite different. A comparison, for example, of Montaigne's Essay 'Of the force of Imagination' (Bk I, Ch. 20) with Burton's subsection with the same title (*Anatomy*, I. II. iii. 2) illustrates this amply: so does a consideration of Montaigne's attitudes in his essays 'Of books' (Bk. 2, Ch. 10) and 'Of Pedantisme' (Bk. 1, Ch. 24), which are poles apart from the assumptions and values natural to scholars such as Burton and Cardan. Even if Burton could read Montaigne in the original, it does not seem right to term him 'a self-conscious disciple'[42] of Montaigne.

Questions of literary influence are notoriously difficult. In the case of a creative writer the merest hint from a predecessor may have profound significance, while conversely a writer may prove to have been quite ignorant of a work which critics

[40] *Anatomy*, i. 262. This passage refers to the comment in Bk. 1 of *Gargantua*, Ch. 41, that 'drunkenness is better for the body than physic, because there be more old drunkards than old Physicians'.

[41] Michaud, *Biographie universelle* (Paris and Leipzig, 1843), xxxv. 17.

[42] Colie, *Paradoxia Epidemica*, p. 436.

would naturally have assumed to have been vital in his development. With Burton, whose mind seems to have worked by accumulation rather than by inspiration, we may be on safer ground in assuming that frequency of overt reference implies relative importance. The consideration of the weight of demonstrable knowledge in him of Cardan on the one hand, and Erasmus, Montaigne, and Rabelais on the other, may serve to demonstrate a fairly obvious truth: that what seem to us to have been the pre-eminent authors of Burton's time, by whom he ought to have been influenced, may not have been at all those he himself regarded as of major importance or most worthy of emulation. To Burton, Cardan, with his great European reputation, may well have seemed a greater figure, at least in the spheres of knowledge of interest to himself, than any of the others. Nor was any 'line' or tradition which we may choose to pick out to day something of which Burton was necessarily conscious at all.

It is just possible that Burton owed something more to Cardan, in the area in which he claimed greatest originality, that of style. Burton stoutly maintains that while his material is mainly derivative and his subject one already handled by many others, 'the method only is mine own'.[43] Cardan, however, wrote a lengthy work on 'the contradictions of doctors', in which he set out to demonstrate the way in which medical authorities from Galen and Hippocrates onwards disagreed.[44] It is arranged as a consideration of a number of questions, some trivial ('Zinziber an flatuosum'), some very basic ('An finis ipsius medici sit sanitas'); some which naturally interested Burton and are referred to by him are those concerning the origins of the melancholy humour, e.g. 'Atra bilis an sanguinis fex'.[45] In presenting the debates Cardan sets out opinions and quotations at great length, with references, and may be seen as setting a precedent for Burton's lists of often contradictory authorities. The motives, indeed, are different. Cardan's declared purpose was to illustrate the confusions of medical writers, whereas Burton seems mainly content to set down all shades of opinion,

[43] *Anatomy*, i. 23.

[44] Burton also notes the inconsistency of the ancients, basing himself on Cardan (i. 85; ii. 241).

[45] *Contradicentium Medicorum Libri Duodecim*, Lib. 1, Tract. 3, contrad. 18 (*Opera*, vi. 356–8), referred to in *Anatomy*, i. 197; cf. i. 198.

often (though not always) without judging between them. The heaping-up of authorities, for that matter, is common practice in Renaissance works, though Burton and Cardan are exceptionally thorough. But Burton certainly acknowledges Cardan as a guide, and quotes Cardan's stylistic principle—'verba propter res, non res propter verba'[46]—as a precept he has had before him in composing the *Anatomy*. This may seem disingenuous to us, faced as we are by the undeniable verbal exuberance and cultivated singularity of the *Anatomy*, but possibly to a contemporary of Burton's, familiar (as we are not) with the intellectual framework and the range of knowledge deployed in it, the *Anatomy* may indeed have seemed much more matter of fact. The comparison with Cardan may serve to orientate us a little better in this respect. To talk of Cardan as a 'model' for Burton may be to press the evidence too far. Yet is does seem that he was something more to Burton than another authority to be referred to, and he may have a better right to be cited among Burton's intellectual ancestors than writers far more familiar to us today.

[46] *De Libris Propriis* (*Opera*, i. 123, col. 2); quoted in *Anatomy*, i. 30. Burton in the same passage (i. 31) expresses his fears that as many faults may be found in his work as Scaliger found in Cardan's *De Subtilitate*; this could be taken as further evidence of his sense of identification with Cardan.

The Growth of Plants
A Seventeenth-Century Metaphor

ELIZABETH MACKENZIE

WHEN Nehemiah Grew commented in 1672[1] on the backwardness of some aspects of botany, he was making more than a stock claim for the New Science. Botanists had indeed concentrated either on the compilation of Herbals or on problems of plant classification and paid virtually no attention to morphology. Of course a seventeenth-century gardener did not need Bacon—or Aristotle—to tell him that plants need warmth as well as moisture; but if he asked himself in Grew's phrase 'By what means is it that a plant, or any part of it comes to grow',[2] he would be hard put to it to find a modern answer before Grew's own *Anatomy of Vegetables* and his *The Idea of a Phytological History Propounded.* But it was a question that had been discussed for a very long time. The fullest treatise was the *De Vegetabilibus et Plantis* of the mid thirteenth century in which Albertus Magnus collected up Aristotelian material from the *De Plantis* (still thought to be genuine) and other works, notably the *Meteorologica,* and gave it a form which persisted in later discussions. He was popularly regarded as an authority as late as the end of the sixteenth century,[3] and Kenelm Digby is still relying on his material in a lecture of 1660 which he must have regarded as scientific. Before and after Albertus, Aristotelian material was involved with Christian, for example in commentaries on Genesis 1: 11, 12.

In the whole tradition of Christian writing, comparisons of the life of man with the life of tree or plant are commonplace, whether they see man's part in nature as source of comfort or despair. They derive their authority from many biblical texts and their patristic commentators, for example Job 14: 7–9 and

[1] *Anatomy of Vegetables* (1672), Preface.
[2] *The Idea of a Phytological History* (1673), p. 4.
[3] e.g. *Batman uppon Bartolome* (1582), vii. 270.

St. Gregory's *Moralia*.[4] Moralists make use of the comparison; man has an obligation to grow upwards; so Charron, 'Man is a divine plant, that flourisheth and growes up unto heaven',[5] or Joseph Mead, 'All things which grow upon the earth, turne their heads and faces upward, toward that, by whose influence they grow and are preserved. So should we unto him, in whom we live and move and have our being.'[6] Comparisons were encouraged by long-standing discussion of the nature of the soul, conveniently outlined by Burton.[7] The lowest faculty of the soul, the vegetal, was responsible for nourishment, growth, and reproduction, which are discussed in plant terms. Finally, some writers who were concerned with the transformation of the plant from root to flower, from darkness to light, may have remembered Homer's *moly*.[8] Something of the mystery of the processes of growth in the plant, remarked upon from the beginning, survives into overtly scientific description down to Grew himself.

Even to those not disposed to moralize, a plant or a tree growing speaks of process and of change. The achievement of maturity in flower or fruit is triumphant but it is also poignant: what blooms will fade, what ripens rots. It requires patience, at least, to accept the winter. 'Autumn having laid up the store, Winter following thereupon doth as it were lock the doors upon it.'[9] The consolation of 'time's covenant' is at its frailest and man identifies his fate with that of nature only to his discomfort.

vanisht man,
Like to a Lilly-lost, nere can
Nere can repullulate or bring
His dayes to see a second Spring.[10]

The ancient arguments for the beneficent, self-perpetuating changes of nature, its 'Eterne in Mutabilitie', much older than Christianity but admirably adapted to explain God's providential government of the world,[11] turn out to be insufficient

4 *Moralia in Job*, xiv. 7–9 (*P.L.* 75. 989 f.).

5 *Of Wisdome*, trans. Kennard [1606?], p. 8.

6 *Diatribe iv* (1652), p. 72.

7 *Anatomy of Melancholy*, I. I. ii. 5.

8 Cf. H. Rahner, *Greek Myths and Christian Mystery* (1963), pp. 179–222.

9 Grew, *Phytological History*, p. 106.

10 Herrick, 'His age, dedicated to M. John Wickes'.

11 Hakewill, *The Power and Providence of God* (1627), lays out the whole argument with the customary authorities.

to preserve the individual human being. To take charge of this, Tertullian[12] constructed an argument which became a model for subsequent discussions. He tries out the cycle of night and day and of the seasons as evidence of the resurrection, demonstrated in nature 'operibus eam praescripsit deus ante quam litteris'; then sees that it is in escaping from the cycle that the individual's future is secured and takes as his example the phoenix, 'animalis est res, et vitae obnoxia et morte'. But it was still possible to take a plant, to take the process of change from root to flower to signify the transformation of man himself: 'It is sown in corruption; it is raised in incorruption. . . . It is sown a natural body; it is raised a spiritual body.' An argument easier for the seventeenth century, which could read 1 Corinthians 15: 35–44 more literally than can modern man.

Herbert begins 'The Flower' with the winter behind him, but with its grief and cold sharply recalled. He begins the cycle of the plant's life with the root, as common sense and tradition would dictate. 'Men taking notice of what is outwardly visible, conceive a sensible priority in the root.'[13] Though morally it is the seed dormant in the ground that closes the circle from harvest to springtime—'that which thou sowest is not quickened, except it die'—St. Paul does not explain how the rotting seed turns into the prosperous root. Several attempts were made to do so in the seventeenth century, the most ambitious being Grew's, who, examining the root of his bean inside the seed, found 'a piece of work so fram'd and set together as to declare a design for the production of a plant',[14] taking up the idea of potentiality obviously associated with the seed, whether discussed as end or beginning of the process. The root naturally conditions the plant which grows from it. Cicero quotes the Stoics in a passage often referred to: 'in arborum autem et earum rerum quae gignuntur e terra radicibus inesse principatus putatur';[15] St. Gregory makes a more human application: 'Potest enim radix justi ipsa natura humanitatia intellegi, ex qua subsistit.'[16] Because it was clear that the plant took in

[12] *De Resurrectione Carnis*, ed. and trans. Evans (1960), pp. 32–4.
[13] Browne, *Garden of Cyrus*, ed. Martin (1964), iii. 147.
[14] *Anatomy of Vegetables*, p. 20.
[15] *De Natura Deorum*, II. xi.
[16] *In Job*, loc. cit.

nourishment through the root, 'The root of a plant is like the mouth of an animal,'[17] discussions of food and digestion persist in explanations of plant growth right down to Grew. It was indeed the only parallel between plants and animals on which early authorities agreed. There must be strength and bulk in the root, as Bacon puts it,[18] or the disintegration and death of the plant will follow. 'Quae videlicet radix senescit in terra cum natura carnis deficit in pulverem redacta. Cuius in pulvere truncus emoritur, quia exstinctum corpus a sua specie dissipatur.'[19] The activity of the root is even more mysterious than the subsequent growth from it; 'In occulte est radix, fructus videri possunt, radix videri non potest.'[20] 'Quite underground . . . dead to the world . . . unknown' is Herbert's 'mother root'; a good housekeeper, storing up nourishment for the plant, but not taking too much thought for the morrow lest 'Swelling through store' it becomes root-bound and forfeits paradise. As Eve, trusting in a providential nature, points out,[21] a larder was only necessary for the few things that are better eaten dry. But Herbert is talking not only of the Providence of God which, after the Fall, brings round the seasons, but of the instances of his Power which bring life and death unpredictably. For the plant, dew and rain and springtime naturally bring restoration; for man a more symbolic moisture is needed. His own poem 'Grace' provides a gloss, as do Job and St. Gregory:[22] 'Sed ad odorem aquae germinat, quia per adventum sancti Spiritus resurgit: Et faciet comam quasi cum primum plantatum est, quia ad illam speciem redit ad quam percipiendam creatus fuerat si in Paradiso positus peccare noluisset.'[23] Indeed, the return of spiritual health, which is the immediate subject of the poem, 'I once more smell the dew and rain, / And relish versing', must always seem to the poet somehow miraculous. Herbert's own efforts to attain the 'Paradise where no flower can wither' are abortive because in their pride they attempt to negate his transitoriness instead of accepting it.

[17] *De Plantis*, I. 3. 818a.
[18] *Sylva Sylvarum*, Century V. 410.
[19] *In Job*, loc. cit.
[20] Augustine, *In Psalmos*, LI. 7 (*P.L.* 36. 607).
[21] *Paradise Lost*, V. 322–5.
[22] Cf. L. Martz, *The Poetry of Meditation* (1954), p. 311.
[23] *In Job*, loc. cit.

Herbert handles the actual process of growth in an interesting way. He seems at first sight merely to indicate an upward movement followed by a decline. But this is like the 'young exhalation' of 'The Answer' which

> Scorns his first bed of dirt and means the sky;
> But cooling on the way, grows pursie and slow,
> And settling to a cloud, doth live and die
> In that dark state of tears.

Vaughan encourages one to believe that the parallel is no accident. As so often in his pondering, he brings to the surface things which in Herbert are only implied. Stanzas 2 and 3 of 'Disorder and Frailty' are very close to 'The Flower':

> I threaten heaven, and from my Cell
> Of Clay, and frailty break, and bud
> Touch'd by thy fire, and breath; Thy Bloud
> Too, is my Dew, and springing wel.
> But while I grow
> And stretch to thee, ayming at all
> Thy stars, and spangled hall,
> Each fly doth tast,
> Poyson, and blast
> My yielding leaves; sometimes a showr
> Beats them quite off, and in an hour
> Not one poor shoot
> But the bare root
> Hid under ground survives the fall.
> *Alas, frail weed!*
>
> Thus like some sleeping Exhalation
> (Which wak't by heat, and beams, makes up
> Unto that Comforter, the Sun,
> And sears and shines; But e'r we sup
> And walk two steps
> Cool'd by the dampe of night, descends . . .

And Grew still admits that the behaviour of exhalations may tell us something about plants.[24]

Exhalations, the vapours which rose naturally from the earth, seem to have become involved in theories of plant growth through the *Meteorologica*. They were of two kinds, cold and moist which went up as mist and came down as rain or dew—

[24] *An Idea of a Philosophical History of Plants* (2nd edn., 1682), p. 22.

remaining entirely within the cycle of sublunary nature—and hot and dry, often called smoky, which could go further up, were thought to engender meteors (wherever they were thought to be) and were often invoked in alchemical discussions. Vaughan is being precise, if witty, in 'The Showre' when he distinguishes between the mist which rises only to fall as rain and the fire of Love, 'the smoke and exhalations of the brest', which can have 'quick accesse' to God; with results that bring him again close to Herbert's 'The Flower'. It is scarcely possible to find any account of the world down to the end of the seventeenth century that does not discuss the exhalations. Félibien[25] praises Poussin for knowing all about them; indeed he painted one in 1658, in *The Landscape with Orion.* They provided the cycle of rising and falling waters that providentially, and aided by Psalm 104: 13, 14, made the grass grow, and are hence part of the whole providential argument. Because they explain the upward movement of moisture through heat, they provide an analogy for the upward movement of sap in the plant. The mythologizing of the process, in which the heavenly bodies feed on the exhalations, seems to depend on *Meteorologica*, II. 355a, though Aristotle in fact repudiates the suggestion. Perhaps the closest link with plants does not seem immediately to involve the exhalations. It is the discussion of concocting in Book IV. 'Ripening is a sort of concoction; for we call it ripening when there is a concoction of the nutriment in fruit . . . concoction is a sort of perfecting.'[26] This is a text which fascinates all the commentators—and it is the peculiarity of the *Meteorologica* that commentaries on it were still being written, and read, in the middle of the seventeenth century[27]—and from which derive two separate lines of discussion, the scientific and the alchemical, which are constantly entangling.

In his devotion to rooted natural objects, and his desire to inspirit the reader, Vaughan is inclined to attribute to plants and stones an aspiration which he knows to be unorthodox. In 'And do they so' he seizes on 'the earnest expectation of the creature' of Romans 8: 19 to refute the authorities: 'my volume

[25] *Entretiens sur les vies des peintres* (1705), iv. 126–7.

[26] *Meteorologica*, IV. 380a. Cf. Albertus Magnus, *De Vegetabilibus*, II. I. iii.

[27] e.g. Browne, *Garden of Cyrus* (1658), cites Cabeus's commentary of 1646. Ed. Martin, iii. 148 and n.

sed / They were all dull and dead, / They judg'd them senseless.' In 'The Tempest' the inbuilt movement of natural things teaches man to look upwards; the upward half of the exhalation cycle and the growth of trees and plants. He answers the question 'How do they cast off grossness?' by pointing first to the natural upward movement of the elements (except earth which, like man, will not be improved), then, by relating each part of the plant to its appropriate element, he shows how the plant naturally refines itself upwards.

> Plants in the root with Earth do most Comply,
> Their Leafs with water and humiditie,
> The Flowres to air draw neer, and subtiltie,
> And seeds a kindred fire have with the sky.[28]

Whereas Man 'yet hugs he stil his durt' and 'grows ne'r a flowr / To crown his temples'. In 'The Sap' the unhealthy, limp plant is unable to grow upwards and needs the assistance of divine moisture, as did Herbert's flower: the sap, cordial, or balm which will preserve and activate and raise up the spirits. It is to work together with 'the powerful, rare dew', the Comforter, already 'shut up' in the soul. Vaughan is here using an idea common in accounts of plant growth, that heat or moisture from outside joins the natural heat or moisture which the sap carries up the plant.[29] He is also, of course, drawing on the association of blood, sap, dew, balsam, elixir with the action of Grace, which has a long figurative history, biblical, patristic, and liturgical, behind it. It is a common image in Herbert and Vaughan, as it had been in Donne and Drummond. Outside specifically religious contexts, the life-giving function of the sap is also stressed. De Mornay uses it to parallel the action of the creative fire, 'joyning, knitting and uniting . . . by one common life';[30] the function is the same for the atomist; atoms in the plant are 'woven by the seminal or plastick Faculty'. Highmore, whose work Grew praised, sees the plant's juice or blood or quintessence as carrying to the appropriate part of the plant the 'seminal atoms' taken in through the root for the

[28] Cf. Cornelius Agrippa, *Three Books of Occult Philosophy*, I. vii (1533, p. xi; trans. J.F., 1651, p. 19).

[29] *De Vegetabilibus*, I. I. xiv; for an alchemical version cf. Senior, *Theatrum Chemicum V* (1622) p. 220; *Paradise Lost*, v. 609–12.

[30] *Trewness of the Christian Religion*, trans. Sidney and Golding (1587), p. 67.

purpose.[31] It is the upward movement of the sap, moisture rising through heat, that keeps the plant erect.

Whatever kind of life one believed the plant to have, it was generally agreed that heat and moisture were required in the digestion of its food. *De Plantis* had already established this; it was developed in *Meteorologica*, IV in the context of concocting and cooking and amplified by Albertus Magnus.[32] Comparisons with human digestive processes are common, because the vegetal faculty of the soul was responsible for them. So Burton[33] likens the liver in sensible creatures to the root or sap in plants, whose 'office is to turn the nutriment into the substance of the body nourished, which he performs by natural heat'. Some of the detailed processes of nourishment are paralleled in plants: Attraction, 'very necessary in plants, which suck up moisture by the root, as another mouth, into the sap, as a like stomach'; 'Digestion is performed by natural heat; for as the flame of a torch consumes oil, wax, tallow, so doth it alter and digest the nutritive matter'; Maturation is 'especially observed in the fruits of trees, which are then said to be ripe when the seeds are fit to be sown again'. Burton does not attempt to consider plants under Augmentation, the second operation of the vegetal faculty, which provides for growth in all dimensions, rather than a general upward movement. This aspect of growth was a worry to Grew, who could only suggest that plants grow in one direction because their parts grow lengthways rather than sideways.[34] Obviously a plant takes in the nourishment it needs for its growth; Highmore allows for a more discriminating taste: they 'make choice of that tincture that most delights their palates'.[35] As Burton points out, the natural concomitants of the vegetal faculty are life and death: 'To the preservation of life the natural heat is most requisite. . . . This heat is likewise in plants, as appears by their increasing, fructifying, etc. though not so easily perceived. In all bodies it must have radical moisture to preserve it, that it be not consumed.'[36]

[31] Charleton, *The Darkness of Atheism Dispelled* (1652), p. 122; Highmore, *The History of Generation* (1651), p. 47.

[32] *De Plantis*, II. 822a f.; *Meteorologica*, IV. 380a ff.; *De Vegetabilibus*, II. I. iii.

[33] *Anatomy of Melancholy*, I. I. ii. 5.

[34] *Anatomy of Vegetables*, p. 53 (= 51).

[35] *History of Generation*, p. 46.

[36] Loc. cit.

Grew's conclusions about plant growth are based on dissections and observations under the microscope more thorough than had ever been undertaken before, as one might hope in papers originally read before the Royal Society. He was able to detect the seminal root in his bean and, as we have seen, to trace through the process of growth from seed to root. 'The General Cause of the growth of a Bean, or other Seed is Fermentation', given that 'a moderate access of some moisture' is present. For Fermentation heat is necessary.[37] The sap is then filtered back into the bean, like beer into a barrel, and supplied with 'its proper seminalities or tinctures'[38] until it is 'wrought up and becomes (as they speak of that of an Animal) the vegetative Ros or Cambium'.[39] 'Cambium', as Burton tells us,[40] is the radical or innate humour comprehended in the body for its preservation and 'daily supplied by nourishment'. 'Ros' here, as in Burton, signifies another of the digesting liquids, though it could in ancient medicine mean the blood itself: hence some of its Eucharistic senses. Grew sees the fermentation as continuing up the plant, with gradual refinement of the sap, 'being well fermented both in the Root and its Ascent through the Trunk, and so its parts prepar'd to a further separation; the grosser ones are still deposited into the leaves; the more elaborate and essential only thus supplied to the Flower, Fruit, and seed, as their convenient Aliment'.[41] The sap in the fruit is in 'a laxe comparison, as the Wine; and that for the Seed a small part of the highest Spirit rectified from it'.[42] Grew also provides for the plant to take in air: 'All the more aetheriall and subtile parts of the air stream through the Root', ultimately finding their way into the scent of the flower.[43]

It is difficult, with so much terminology in common, to be sure sometimes what one is committed to. Clearly, when Bacon is instructing the gardener in 'comforting and exciting the spirits in the plant'[44] he is not advocating conversation with it but keeping it warm and moist. He is careful to point out that these 'Spirits or Pneumaticals' are in no sense souls but 'a

37 *Anatomy of Vegetables*, p. 19. 38 Ibid., pp. 21, 23. 39 Ibid., p. 53.
40 *Anatomy of Melancholy*, I. I. ii. 2. 41 *Anatomy of Plants*, p. 123.
42 Ibid., p. 165; cf. *De Vegetabilibus*, III. II. vii.
43 *Phytological History*, pp. 120, 136.
44 *Sylva Sylvarum*, Century V. 405.

Natural Body rarefied', responsible in their ceaseless activity for the nourishing and preservative functions.[45] There are problems also where terms are used which can bear an alchemical sense: fermentation, sublimation, tincture, elaborate (something produced by art), balsam. In the last case, this form of the word seems to have come back into English about 1600 under the influence of Paracelsus; but this does not help us to decide how to read it. Though he was probably the most powerful influence on sixteenth- and seventeenth-century alchemical writing, he was also widely regarded as a Modern, a man of the New Science. Most writers seem able to manipulate ancient explanations of plant growth without embarrassment, though certainly aware that they were still being used in figurative contexts. But Robert Sharrock, Fellow of New College, whose book Grew praises, is concerned in the most practical way with the propagation of plants, and determined to avoid 'Behemenical, Paracelsian and such phrases as many Alchemists use . . . like rhetorical tropes they create darkness'.[46] Whatever his terminology, Grew himself did draw a line somewhere. When he looks to those few men in England who have concerned themselves with the anatomy of plants he does not mention Kenelm Digby, whose lecture on the vegetation of plants was read before the Royal Society some twelve years before his own papers. It is inconceivable that, as a Fellow, he should not have known it. In any case, Highmore's book is in large part a refutation of Chapter 23. 7 of Digby's *Generation of Creatures*, 1644, from which *A Discourse of the Vegetation of Plants* was developed. Unlike Hooke, Highmore, and Sharrock, there is little evidence in Digby's work that he had turned from the theory to examine an actual plant. And, though this is a difficult line for a modern reader to draw, what remains metaphorical in Grew seems to be intended literally in Digby. He therefore provides a useful bridge between scientific and alchemical plants.

Much of Digby's explanation is very close to Grew's. Once growth has begun, 'that new digested and spiritual juice is continually sublimed up into that round green tender part,

45 *Sylva Sylvarum*, Century I. 98; cf. *Anatomy of Melancholy*, I. i. ii. 2.

46 *History of the Propagation and Improvement of Vegetables* (1660), p. 3. There is a very obscure plant in Boehme's *Signatura Rerum*, trans. Ellistone (1651), viii. 67–9.

which was sprung up out of the Earth into the Air; and that we may now call the stalk'.[47] When, by the action of heat, branches grow out of the main stem, the plant 'partakes herself to works of less rumbustuous force and, refining still more by gentle sublimations and depurations the juyce she hath brought up thus high, she continually makes it cast off the grosser parts'; these are 'subtil in respect of the grosser juyce they are sublimed from and that remains below in the body and trunk of the plant; and gross in respect of the ardent spirit and balsamick oil that is rectified from them'.[48] One might not suspect his account of the return of spring, with the Sun, the great Archeus, 'beginning to dilate and sublime up to the superficies of the Earth, that volatile and balsamick salt which his remoteness during the winter had suffered to be shrunk up altogether'.[49] But when he suggests that 'a tincture extracted out of the whole plant' is 'at last dried up into a kind of Magistery; full of fire and salt', he is speaking unmistakably as an Alchemist. He openly explains the efficacy of 'well digested Dew' in making the plant prosper by 'the Spagyrick Art'.[50] However, he seems not to have been a very clever 'empiric alchemist'. Athanasius Kircher told him he had succeeded in the Palingenesis experiment which could produce 'out of the Ashes, the idea of a Flower'—Digby only produced a nettle.[51]

The ripening and perfecting text of *Meteorologica*, IV certainly encouraged alchemical imagery in a botanical direction, as did the assurance of Albertus, himself believed to be an alchemist, that stones grow like plants,[52] and the dictum attributed to Hermes Trismegistus, 'Est enim sicut arbor, unius rami et folia et flores et fructus sunt ex ea'.[53] We are not here concerned with the depiction of the 'philosophical tree', which shows the branches and stages of the art on the pattern of the many schematic trees of the Middle Ages and later,[54] or the more naturalistic version of Myllius with the sun and moon

[47] *A Discourse of the Vegetation of Plants* (1661), p. 22.

[48] Ibid., p. 27. [49] Ibid., pp. 8–9. [50] Ibid., p. 60.

[51] Ibid., pp. 74–5. Cf. Browne, *Religio Medici*, i. 48, ed. Martin, p. 46.

[52] *De Vegetabilibus*, I. I. xiv.

[53] *Theatrum Chemicum V* (1622), 'Senioris Zadith, filii Hamuelis Tabula Chemica', pp. 245–6.

[54] e.g. S. Norton, *Mercurius Redivivus* (1630), frontispiece, pp. 5, 6: branches of the tree, pp. 11, 15, 18 and his *Catholicon Physicorum* (1630), pp. 5, 11, 14.

hung up in it.[55] It was the growth of plant or tree, a process of refinement brought about through heat, which provided the alchemist with a perfect analogy and even perhaps with something that might help the alchemical process to take place. As Maier says, 'Chemia est omnino parallela agriculturae . . . sub allegoria absolutissima.'[56] The stone itself germinates: 'Lapis niger, vilis, et foetens et dicitur Origo Mundi, et oritur sicut germinantia.'[57] Nothing can grow without the alchemical secret; it is the root without which no seed can sprout and no rose coming into flower unfold its petals.[58] The green colour which occurs in the early stages of the alchemical work also links it to the plants;[59] so does the liquor which nourishes the stone, as it does all live things.[60] The end of the work reaches up to heaven.[61] Reading Senior, particularly, it is difficult to remember that an alchemical and not a botanical process is being described. The alchemists also used the exhalations as a model, 'unde etiam Spagiriti is suis operationibus circulatione nominarunt qua imitantur hanc naturae circulationem'.[62]

It is difficult to see how far the claims of the philosophical alchemists really go. At least, their detractors felt, the divine alchemy of nature was doing the job much better. Hence the famous gibe, sometimes attributed to Cardano, that the Lord brought everything out of nothing and the alchemists nothing out of everything.[63] La Primaudaye administers a stock rebuke in terms of ordinary natural change:

> We shall consider how the Almightie creator of heaven and earth causeth so many fruits to grow . . . through the distillations of raine and through the heate of the Sunne, we holde in great admiration this worthy naturall Alchimie. . . . For all this world is to him as a fornace, and a limbeck wherein he maketh so many goodly and profitable distillations. . . . The earth is this fornace, and all the

[55] *Philosophia Reformata* (1622), p. 316.

[56] *Atalanta Fugiens* (1618), p. 34.

[57] Thomas Vaughan, *Lumen de Lumine* (1651), p. 32.

[58] *Atalanta Fugiens*, p. 118.

[59] Ibid., p. 159.

[60] T. Norton, *Ordinal of Alchemy*, ed. Reidy (*E.E.T.S.*, 1975), lines 2291–2. Ashmole printed the *Ordinal* in *Theatrum Chemicum Britannicum* (1651).

[61] *Theatrum Chemicum I* (1602), Dorn, 'Congeries Paracelsiae', p. 583.

[62] Cabeus, *In Quattor Libros Meteorologicum Aristotelis Commentarii* (1646), i. 256. Cf. i. 113, where the two exhalations are identified with the alchemists' Sulphur, Salt, and Mercury.

[63] Cf. Mersenne, *Questiones in Genesim* (1623), col. 1483.

plants and trees so many limbecks . . . this is a marvellous and very rare Limbecke, wherein God converteth water into wine. . . . For all the excellent liquors and fruits, which we draw out of these plants . . . are principally caused by the heate of the sunne and by the watering of rain from heaven, which by this meanes seemeth to change nature. . . . And yet this sunne, by means of whome, as by a fire, God performeth so many sundry and admirable conversions and distillations, hath not his face smeared with coles, to kindle and maintain his fire, nor yet his faire eye soiled therewith, or with any smoake. So then I hold them very wise who profit in the contemplation of this Alchimie and employ their time and cunning therein as husbandmen doe who till the earth, attending in good hope after their travell.[64]

Drummond speaks in the context of the alchemist's endeavour to bring about the final perfection of all things:

Can the Spagericke by his Arte restore for a space to the dry and withered Rose the natural Purple and Blush: And cannot the Almightie raise and refine the Body of Man, after never so many alterations in the Earth? Reason himself finds it more possible for infinite powers to cast out from itself a finite world, and restore anything in it, though decayed and dissolved to what it was first; than for Man a finit peece of reasonable misery to change the form of matter made to his hand.[65]

But there was an argument that saw it as proper, even as obligatory, for man to use Art to complete what nature had begun: and by Art we are to understand any process which changes the nature of its raw material: iron into tools; corn into bread; stone into buildings; and the art of the alchemist. The argument was encouraged immediately, perhaps, by Paracelsus,[66] but became a commonplace, providing a moral, because natural, place for man's activities.[67] Vigenère is an interesting alchemical example.[68] 'Fire is the operatour here below, in the workes of Art, as the Sunne and Celestial fire

64 *The French Academie*, trans. T.B.C. (1618), iii. 50, 754–5.

65 Drummond of Hawthornden, *Poems and Prose*, ed. Macdonald (1976), p. 171.

66 e.g. *Astronomia Magna*, I. iii (*Opera Omnia*, 1658, ii. 540).

67 e.g. Charron, *Of Wisdome*, p. 61; [Du Vair], *True Way to Vertue and Happiness*, trans. Court (1623), pp. 65–8; Browne, *Religio Medici*, i. 16; Hooke, *Micrographia*, Preface, sig. a.

68 Blaise de Vigenaire, *An Excellent Treatise of Fire and Salt*, trans. Stephens (1649). *Theatrum Chemicum VI* (1661) has a Latin version which claims to be translated from a French original.

in them of that nature, and in the intelligible, the holy Spirit.'[69] The 'speculative understandings' of the alchemists imitated the slow action of the sun and extracted from inferior elements an incorruptible substance, 'a model and pattern of that, whereto the whole universe should at last bee reduced: from hence we here draw from Soot a representation and image of the works of nature, upon vapours and exhalations'.[70] He too uses the image of the plant, combined with the flame of the torch which Burton had used in the same way to explain the digestion, to show the process of nourishment and refinement which is the action of fire: 'The branch that drawes its juice or sap, by the root, is the same as the weik, where the fire is maintained by the liquor it drawes unto it . . . the branches and the boughes, clad with leaves, the flowers and fruits . . . are the white flame when all comes to be reduced.'[71] The Latin has 'sunt flamma alba ad quam omnia aspirant', which seems to combine flower and flame. The sun is responsible for 'primitive' digesting and baking, 'as we may see in what the earth produceth, but for that the naturall heat doth not bring them wholly for our use, to the last and perfect degree of maturity, fire for the most part supplyes its wants and defaults; for the regard of the concocting of what we eat, for we hardly therby make our profit being raw, there where it is baked in the fire, it becomes of more facil digestion, and less corruptible . . . at last it doth gather together in a new composure the pure homogenialities; which composure then consisteth of soul, body and spirit, from now forward inseparable and incorruptible . . . which may be seen in glasse, which is an image of the Philosophicall Stone'.[72]

The most fascinating of all the plants is Milton's (*Paradise Lost*, v. 479 ff.), the culmination of a passage beginning at line 308 with the unexpected arrival of Raphael to luncheon. Eve's supplies are hanging on the trees about her; though she takes trouble to prepare the food, she does not need to cook it to make it digestible, and she offers fresh grape-juice not fermented wine. Before the fall, the arts which make natural things fit for man's use are not needed. But Adam is doubtful about their suitability for a spiritual visitor. In setting his mind at rest Raphael, still in the context of nourishment, gives Adam his

[69] Blaise de Vigenaire, op. cit. p. 37. [70] Ibid., p. 52. [71] Ibid., p. 12.
[72] Ibid., pp. 67–8.

first lesson about the universe and his place in it, beginning with the nature of angels. Here Milton cuts through a long and complicated argument about their faculties and their relationship to the heavenly bodies, which was still of interest to Kepler,[73] and attributes to them most carefully all the lower faculties of sense, particularly those that concern the taking in and digestion of food, since his whole argument is designed to show how each part of the universe naturally makes its contribution to the sustaining and transforming of the whole. He would agree with Henry More that the 'Defination of a Spirit is, the power of altering the Matter'.[74] In fact it is in terms of nourishment and transformation that More goes on here to describe the spirits: 'A seminal form is a created spirit organising duly-prepared matter into life and vegetation'; man is 'A created spirit indued with Sense and Reason, and a power of organising terrestrial Matter into humane shape by vital union therewith'; an angel is 'A created spirit indued with Reason, Sensation, and a power of being vitally united with and actuating of a Body of Aire or Aether onely'.[75] To illustrate that 'whatever was created, needs / To be sustained and fed', Milton takes the cycle of the elements, then the exhalations and their feeding of the heavenly bodies. This, as we have seen, goes back to the *Meteorologica*; it was also given wide currency through Cicero's *De Natura Deorum*, where it is presented as part of the Stoic argument for the reasonable government of the world, together with discussions of growing plants, digestion, and the nature of the heavenly bodies. Cicero reports Cleanthes as saying, 'eum sol igneus sit, Oceanique alatur umoribus quia nullus ignis sine pastu alique posset permanere'.[76] Pliny maintained that the moon and the stars eat likewise.[77] Hakewill looks back to both these passages in an argument for the interdependence of heaven and earth.[78] Where Pliny had suggested that the moon sucked up dirt from the earth with her moisture, Milton, strictly within the terms of his metaphor, attributes her spotty complexion to a sluggish digestion: she would lack the

73 Cf. H. Wolfson, 'Souls of the Spheres', *Dumbarton Oaks Papers*, 16 (1962), 65–93.

74 *Immortality of the Soul* (1659), I. vii. 6 (*Philosophical Writings*, 1662, p. 33).

75 Ibid. I. viii. 3, 5, 8.

76 *De Natura Deorum*, II. xv.

77 *Naturalis Historia*, II. vi.

78 *Power and Providence*, p. 91.

necessary heat. Appropriately, the angels normally eat those heavenly substances which after the fall, as we have seen, descend as life-giving moisture to man or plant.[79] Presumably with this food there was no waste. Eating earthly food, Milton's angels function like plants; and how plants function was of course discussed.[80] Even the substance they do not require is vaporized or it could not be transpired; it is transubstantiated by concoctive heat.

It is with the idea of food still in his mind that Adam questions Raphael about the chain of creatures. As his answer he is given the image of the plant:

> So from the root
> Springs lighter the green stalk, from thence the leaves
> More aerie, last the bright consummate floure
> Spirits odorous breathes: flours and their fruit
> Man's nourishment, by gradual scale sublim'd
> To vital Spirits aspire

to stand at once for the created universe and Adam's function in it. Working naturally, 'Improv'd by tract of time', Adam might by eating the plants imitate their own alchemy; concoct and hence bring nature to perfection. Perhaps it was for her own future rather than for man's that, after the apple had been eaten, nature 'sighed that all was lost': as Hakewill sadly remarks, there is no article for the restoration of the creatures.[81] Milton is carefully unspecific about the colour of his flower, though, as for the alchemists, it is bright and it is the end of the process: 'fient ambae albae resplendentes, habentes lucem et splendorem, deinde colorat anima'.[82] It was often red, 'the flower of the sun / The perfect ruby which we call elixir', according to Epicure Mammon. Vigenère argues for the superiority of white over red in the Christian faith and makes gold the equivalent of red and white together.[83] The colours of alchemy are the most confused of all; the only agreement is that the beginning is black. This is particularly clear for the plant metaphor where the transformation of the black root of *moly* to white or gold flower provided a pattern, as Maier points

79 Cf. *Commentarii Collegii Conimbricensis Societatis Jesu in Libros Meteorum Aristotelis* (1593), VII. xi. 73–4.

80 *De Vegetabilibus*, III. II. vii.

81 *Power and Providence*, p. 448.

82 Senior, *Theatrum Chemicum V*, p. 220.

83 *Fire and Salt*, pp. 13, 87.

out.[84] The flower which is achieved is an unfading flower, 'the Rose that cannot wither', transcending 'the scheme of generation'. Perhaps one need look for no further authority than Dante:

> Nel giallo della rosa sempiterna,
> Che si dilata ed ingrada e redole
> odor di lode al sol che sempre verna.[85]

The transubstantiation by digestive heat which Raphael foretells is much more gentle than the action of that other fire in which, at the end of the world, nature was to be consumed. Of this also eating metaphors were used. Donne, after imagining the new earth 'where all their grasse is corne, and all their corne, Manna; where all their glebe, all their clods of earth are gold', describes the marriage supper of the Lamb, 'where, not onely all the rarities of the whole world, but the whole world it selfe shall be serv'd in; The whole world shall bee brought to that fire, and serv'd at that Table.'[86] He was fascinated by 'Origens extreme error': 'He thought that at last, after infinite revolutions, (as all other substances should be) even the Devill himself should be (as it were) sucked and swallowed into God, and there should remaine nothing at last (as there was nothing at first), but onely God.'[87] Though expressed in less heretical form than Origen's, the idea of the compacting together of all the phenomena of nature at the end of the world was common; vitrification, it is often called.[88] But there is also the hope, only half expressed, that what has shut up as into a seed may somehow open up again, as was provided for in nature: 'In every particle of this compacted dust, the nature of the whole plant resides perfectly and entirely.'[89] Henry More uses the seed to explain the relationship of time and eternity: 'The seed of a plant hath all the whole tree, branches, leaves and fruit at once, in one point after a manner closed up, but potentially. Eternity hath all the world in an indivisible indistant way at

[84] *Septimana Philosophica* (1620), p. 126, quoted by Rahner, *Greek Myths*, p. 219.

[85] *Paradiso*, xxx. 124 ff.

[86] *Sermons*, ed. Potter and Simpson, viii. 83.

[87] Ibid. vii. 217; cf. i. 164 and iii. 115–16. I am grateful to Miss Juliet Palmer for tracing these references.

[88] e.g. Browne, *Religio Medici*, i. 50; Marvell, 'Upon Appleton House', st. LXXXVI; *Fire and Salt*, p. 68.

[89] Digby, *Vegetation of Plants*, p. 43.

once, and that actually.'[90] He is able to preserve in eternity the liveliness of nature without its drawbacks: 'Vigour of life is root, stock, branch and all; / Nought here increaseth, nought here hath its fall.'[91] It is Browne who suggests that after all man might have some means of saving nature, 'for man subsisting, who is, and will truly appeare a Microcosme, the world cannot bee said to be destroyed. For the eyes of God, and perhaps also of our glorified selves, shall as really behold and contemplate the world in its Epitome or contracted essence, as now it doth at large and in its dilated substance. In the seed of a Plant to the eyes of God, and to the understanding of man, there exists though in an invisible way, the perfect leaves, flowers and fruit thereof: (for things that are in *posse* to the sense, are actually existent to the understanding). Thus God beholds all things, who contemplates as fully his workes in their Epitome, as in their full volume, and beheld as amply the whole world in that little compendium of the sixth day, as in the scattered and dilated pieces of those five before.'[92] If man is no longer a plant to transform, he may at least be the seed to preserve.

[90] *Philosophical Poems* (1647), Notes upon 'Psychozoia', p. 336.
[91] Ibid., 'Psychozoia', st. 14, p. 4.
[92] *Religio Medici*, i. 50.

George Wither and John Milton

CHRISTOPHER HILL

GEORGE WITHER was born in 1588, John Milton in 1608. Wither published all his best poetry before he was thirty-seven. He continued to write incessantly for the remaining forty-two years of his life. Milton published his first book of verse at the age of thirty-seven, and already had a few prose pamphlets to his credit. He too wrote far more in bulk thereafter, much of it in Latin, all of it of incomparably higher quality than Wither's later writings.

Wither's sad deterioration is usually attributed to his vision of himself as an inspired prophet with a message for the English people. 'God opened my mouth', he declared in 1641, 'and compelled me, beyond my natural abilities, to speak.'[1] But Milton's view of his relation to his Muse in *Paradise Lost* is not essentially different. I want very briefly to draw attention to the many points of similarity between the political careers and the political and religious ideas of the two poets. This will do nothing to explain the greatness of Milton: but if we see how much he had in common with even the later Wither, it may help us to understand that he was no unique and lonely genius.

Wither and Milton were both self-consciously Spenserians. Milton was introduced as an imitator of Spenser in 1645; he himself told Dryden that Spenser was 'his original'. Spenser was associated with the radical political wing in government circles, with Leicester, Walsingham, Ralegh. The Spenserian succession—Sidney, Daniel, the Fletchers, John Davies, Drayton, Browne, Wither, Milton—was also a political succession.[2] Many of these poets followed Spenser's example in using the conventions of pastoral poetry to make political

[1] G. Wither, *Hallelujah*, ed. E. Farr (1857), p. xxiv; cf. pp. xxxi, 384–6; *Vox Pacifica* (1645), pp. 10–12, 32 ff.; *Epistolium-Vagum-Prosa-Metricum* (1659), p. 28; *Parallelogrammaton* (1662), p. 30; *Ecchoes from the Sixth Trumpet* (1666), p. 98. (Whenever possible I quote Wither from the Spenser Society reprints, but cite the page number of the original edition where this is given.)

[2] See my *Milton and the English Revolution* (1977), pp. 19, 50, 59–64.

criticisms without drawing the attention of the censor. One thinks of *Britannia's Pastorals* by Wither's friend Browne, of Wither's own *Shepheards Hunting* and *Philarete*, of *Lycidas*. After the collapse of the censorship in 1640 the vogue dies out. Wither was patronized by Southampton and the third Earl of Pembroke, who succeeded to the political attitudes and patronage of Leicester and Walsingham. Wither regularly dedicated his most controversial poems to Pembroke, who apparently came to Wither's rescue when he was in prison in 1615.[3] On Pembroke's death Wither applied to the fourth Earl.

Wither went to Oxford, Milton to Cambridge. Both left 'somewhat discontented'. But Wither, being a gentleman, proceeded to an Inn of Chancery, whilst Milton—aiming then at a clerical career—returned to Cambridge. However, both retained a considerable contempt for the university curriculum and for dons.[4] Wither, like Milton, was no respecter of rank unaccompanied by virtue. From his earliest satires he attacked court luxury, extravagance, and corruption, purchase of offices and peerages, bribery, monopolies. Similar themes underlie Milton's pamphlets of the early 1640s, and are emphasized in *The Ready and Easy Way to Establish a Free Commonwealth* of 1660.

But it was the international situation which really alarmed Wither from the 1620s, as it did Milton: the failure to support England's natural Protestant allies on the Continent from Habsburg attack, the sense that Protestantism was not yet secure in England. Both poets very early took up a patriotic anti-Spanish stance, which comes out in the poems which each wrote for the Fifth of November. Hence, whilst both strongly favoured toleration of all Protestants, they did not extend this to those whom they regarded as a Spanish fifth column in England or in Ireland. Both shared the Puritan desire to purge the English Church of popish remnants, and consequently abhorred the Laudian regime: Wither indeed had earlier shown considerable scepticism about bishops. This extended for both to a passionate anti-clericalism, a hatred of ambitious clergymen, of simony and the patronage system, of the state church,

[3] I owe this point to Margot Heinemann. For Pembroke's role as patron of opposition writers see her 'Middleton's *A Game at Chess*: Parliamentary Puritans and Opposition Drama', in *English Literary Renaissance*, 5 (1975), 232–50.

[4] Wither, *Juvenilia*, i. 2–5, 175–82; ii. 319–20.

its tithes, its courts, its excommunications, its fees, its superstitious ceremonies and uneconomic observation of saints' days. The censorship, Wither thought, brought 'authors, yea the whole commonwealth and all the liberal sciences into bondage'; under it, Milton agreed, 'no free and splendid wit' could flourish.[5]

Wither's quarrel with the Stationers' Company played a similar role in his development to the furore over Milton's divorce pamphlets. Wither wrote no *Areopagitica*: but long before Milton he had acquired a strong and lasting hatred of censorship as an insult to human dignity.[6] The effects of the censorship on him can be simply shown. Between 1612 and 1628 he published sixteen works in sixteen years, the last of them—*Brittans Remembrancer*—printed by himself because he could not find a publisher. Between 1641 (when the censorship collapsed) and 1666 he published fifty-six works in twenty-five years. In the intervening thirteen years, the Laudian years, he published only two translations—*The Psalmes of David* (in the Netherlands, since he could find no English publisher) and Nemesius's *The Nature of Man*—together with the politically innocuous *Emblemes* (1635). A consistent feature of the thinking of both poets was a reasoned defence of the rights of the individual conscience, a rejection of implicit faith, of reliance on the judgement of others, and of the use of force in religious affairs.

> 'Tis not the cutting off of one man's ears
> Will stop the voice that everybody hears,

wrote Wither after the restoration.[7] Persecution, both came to think, was antichristian. Like Milton in *Lycidas*, Wither in 1632 hoped to see God inflicting 'that vengeance which is prepared for impenitent persecutors'.[8]

Wither disliked the 'blind mouths' of the clergy as much as Milton did: 'mute as a rich clergyman' was Wither's phrase.

5 *Milton and the English Revolution*, pp. 19, 154.

6 Wither, *Juvenilia*, iii. 630–3; *The Schollers Purgatory* (?1624), *passim; Brittans Remembrancer* (1628), sig. B2, p. 287. F. S. Siebert, *Freedom of the Press in England, 1476–1776* (Illinois University Press, 1952), p. 132. *The Schollers Purgatory* may have been published abroad.

7 Wither, *A Proclamation in the Name of the King of Kings* (1662), p. 68.

8 *The Psalmes of David* (The Netherlands, 1632), p. 180; cf. *Juvenilia*, i. 93; *Hallelujah*, pp. 76–7; *Vox Pacifica* (1645), p. 141; *Prosopopaeia Britannica* (1648),

To be thy shepherds wolves are stolen in . . .
Men use religion as a stalking-horse
To catch preferment . . .[9]

In his comment on Psalm 68 Wither prayed that 'heretics, hirelings and contentious persons may be reproved and reformed or cut off'. The Miltonic 'hirelings' comes between two words which could give no offence to the hierarchy.[10] Both Wither and Milton disliked the Laudian campaign against lecturers: Wither made the point by visualizing Jesus first expelling merchants from his church and then himself lecturing there.[11] 'As if we could not pray', he had complained in 1628, 'until our preaching we had sent away.'[12]

Like Milton, Wither thought that the clergy and bishops (whom Charles I 'out of the dunghill had promoted') were largely responsible for the civil war. In 1628 he predicted, with remarkable accuracy, how the clergy would take the lead in polarizing society:

If ever in thy fields (as God forbid)
The blood of thine own children shall be shed
By civil discord, they shall blow the flame. . . .

One part of these will for preferment strive
By lifting up the King's prerogative
Above itself. They shall persuade him to
Much more than law or conscience bids him do
And say, God warrants it.

In reaction, others will preach

Rebellion to the people, and shall strain
The Word of God sedition to maintain.[13]

This sort of erastian anti-clericalism explains how Wither could have been a friend of Selden's, and of Milton's crony, Marchamont Nedham. It is very close to Milton's position in the mid forties.

pp. 90, 95–6, and *passim*; *Westrow Revived* (1653), p. 10; *Speculum Speculativum* (1660), pp. 125–6; *Parallelogrammaton* (1662), pp. 100–1.

9 *Juvenilia*, ii. 436; *Brittans Remembrancer*, pp. 244–5; cf. p. 191.

10 *The Psalmes of David*, ii. 141.

11 *The Hymnes and Songs of the Church* (1623). I quote from the edition of E. Farr (1856), p. 194.

12 *Brittans Remembrancer*, p. 247; cf. pp. 244–55, *passim*.

13 Ibid., pp. 262–3.

Wither shared Milton's horror of idolatry. Both in consequence approved of iconoclasm.[14] Both rejected set forms of worship (as idolatry) and indeed any state church at all. As early as 1645 Wither spoke for 'union without uniformity'.

> God in no need stands
> Either of churches, tithes or rents on lands

he declared eight years later.[15]

Wither deliberately cultivated a plain style in writing. It was a style at which Milton aimed only after the defeat of the Revolution. The reliance of both was on the middling sort: virtue more than compensated for humble birth. Wither favoured the sturdy independence of the 'freeborn', whom he contrasted with servants. Like Milton, Wither believed in human equality, but associated it with a mobile society. 'Indiscreet and fond compassion' for the poor could be a vice.[16] When Wither like Milton in 1660 advocated 'the just division of waste commons', he seems to have regarded this as a means of getting rid of poor squatters.[17] Both had to recognize after the civil war that 'the rabble' might be in favour of monarchy.[18]

Unlike Milton, Major Wither took an active part in the civil war fighting. But like Milton he originally accepted the leadership of the 'Presbyterians' in the interests of unity, though as early as 1642 he seems to have been described as an Independent.[19] He soon became a supporter of the win-the-war party. His extremism is shown by his suggestion that the estates of royalist gentlemen should be confiscated, so that they should becomes peasants—'a degree to which honest men are born;

[14] *Brittans Remembrancer*, pp. 133–4; *Parallelogrammaton*, pp. 111, 117; *Salt upon Salt* (1659), pp. 24–5; Milton, *Eikonoklastes*, *passim*.

[15] *Vox Pacifica*, p. 145; *Westrow Revived*, p. 56; *Parallelogrammaton*, pp. 109, 117, 125; *Three Private Meditations* (1666), pp. 46–8.

[16] *Juvenilia*, i. 19–20, 131, 265–6; ii. 436–8, 478–9; iii. 625–30, 691–2, 719–29, 733–4, 776–7; *Hymnes and Songs*, p. 231; *Brittans Remembrancer*, pp. 10–11, 117, cf. p. 248; *Hallelujah*, p. xxviii. Cf. Milton, *Complete Prose Works* (Yale edn.), iv. 271.

[17] Wither, *Fides-Anglicana* (1660), pp. 52–4; cf. Milton, *Works* (Columbia edn.), xviii. 6–7.

[18] Wither, *Prosopopaeia Britannica* (1648), pp. 47–8; *Epistolium-Vagum-Prosa-Metricum* (1659), p. 20; Milton, *Complete Prose Works*, iv. 635.

[19] Wither, *Reasons humbly offered in justification of an order granted to Major George Wither* (1642), p. 4.

and too good for them, some of them being made lords and knights for attempting to enslave freemen'.[20]

In 1643 Wither claimed sovereignty for Parliament ('in whose commands the King's are best obeyed'). The doctrine that the King can do no wrong means that his ministers can be called to account. But a new note is coming in. 'The people first did make both laws and kings'—a Leveller (and Miltonic) rather than Parliamentarian maxim.[21] In 1645 this was made rather more specific:

> There is on earth a greater thing
> Than an unrighteous Parliament or King.

By 1646 he was calling ominously for a purge of Parliament.[22]

In the late 1640s Wither became no less disillusioned with Parliament than was Milton at the time of writing *The Character of the Long Parliament.* Both experienced delays and perversion of justice by Parliamentary committees. The Revolution turned out to be

> A good play spoiled
> And by unworthy actors foiled.[23]

In October or November 1648 Wither called for a fundamental overhaul of the Parliamentarian apparatus, and argued simultaneously against the enforced religious uniformity insisted on by the Presbyterian clergy. Like Milton in *The Tenure of Kings and Magistrates* shortly later, Wither urged before the event the trial and execution of justice upon the King.[24]

For Wither, as for Milton, Pride's Purge of Parliament in December 1648, the trial and condemnation of Charles I, the abolition of the House of Lords, and the proclamation of the republic seemed to offer new hope. In August 1649 he expressed unqualified jubilation at the victory of Parliament's troops in

20 Wither, *The Speech Without Doore* (1644), p. 5; *The Two Incomparable Generalissimos of the World* (1644), single sheet.

21 Wither, *Campo-Musae* (1643), pp. 8, 10–11, 33, 44–6, 49–50, 63–4; cf. *Tuba Pacifica* (1664), p. 20.

22 *Vox Pacifica*, p. 213; *Opobalsamum Anglicanum* (1646), p. 9.

23 Wither, *Amygdala Britannica* (1647), p. 9.

24 *Prosopopaeia Britannica, passim.*

Ireland.[25] In 1650–1 he composed hymns to celebrate the anniversary of Charles's execution:

> This is the day whereon our yoke
> Of Norman bondage first was broke
> And England from her chains made free.[26]

Parliament recognized the debt due to Wither and gave him a job as commissioner for sale of the King's goods.

Like Milton, Wither accepted office under the Protectorate of Oliver Cromwell. In 1657 he published a poem in which he declared that:

> We look for such a government as shall
> Make a way for Christ. . . .
> His Highness hath made progress in a path
> As far toward it as any hath
> Since Christ ascended.[27]

The hyperbole is exceeded only by Milton's extraordinary statement that the events of the English Revolution were 'the most heroic and exemplary achievements since the foundation of the world'—not excepting apparently the life and death of Christ. By his own account at least Wither was on terms of some intimacy with Cromwell, though he proved less able to influence him politically than he had hoped.[28] But, also like Milton, Wither did not shrink from warning the rulers of England of their failure to live up to the ideals of the Good Old Cause. Such warnings go back to 1645, when Wither spoke of the 'avarice and ambition' of military men, words which were often repeated by Milton later.[29]

Again like Milton, Wither disapproved of the offer of the crown to Cromwell in 1657. He was particularly critical of Cromwell's (and Charles II's) foreign policy of alliances with

[25] Wither, *Carmen Eucharisticon* (1649), *passim*.

[26] Wither, *Three Grains of Spirituall Frankincense* (1651), p. 9. For Wither's acceptance of the radical theory of the Norman Yoke see further *Campo-Musae*, p. 47, and *Speculum Speculativum* (1660), p. 58. For Milton see my *Milton and the English Revolution*, p. 100.

[27] Wither, *A Suddain Flash* (1657), p. 16.

[28] Milton, *Complete Prose Works*, iv. 549; Wither, *A Cordial Confection*, in W. M. Clyde, *The Struggle for the Freedom of the Press from Caxton to Cromwell* (Oxford University Press, 1934), pp. 338–42.

[29] Wither, *Vox Pacifica*, p. 196; *Prosopopaeia Britannica*, pp. 58–71; *Westrow Revived*, pp. 70–2, *Vaticinium Causuale* (1655), pp. 8, 14–16.

papist powers; we may compare the Son of God's rejection of alliances in *Paradise Regained*, Book III. For Wither, like Milton, had seen the English Revolution as an opportunity for reversing Charles I's pro-papist policy and replacing it with a Protestant crusade. Both thought the Pope was Antichrist, and both believed that the end of the world and the destruction of Antichrist were approaching. Christ was 'shortly-expected King', whose kingdom 'is now at hand', foreboding 'hasty ruin and a destruction to all tyrants'.[30] Wither proclaimed in 1632 that the 'Second Coming . . . now draweth nigh'; 'the worst age is come'.[31] Like Milton later, Wither thought of the English as the chosen people; this must have affected both poets' political attitudes when the Revolution came. In 1643 Wither referred to the royalists as 'bands and . . . confederates of Antichrist'; 'his last great battery Antichrist now rears', he wrote in 1645.[32] 1666 seemed to him the likely date of the end of the world and the Second Coming; this belief was no doubt reinforced by the manifest triumph of the Beast in 1660. Like Milton again, however, Wither rejected Fifth Monarchist attempts to expedite Christ's coming by political violence.[33]

In August 1659 Wither clearly saw that the restoration of monarchy was imminent, but he continued, even later than Milton, to proclaim his adherence to 'that which is not called amiss the Good Old Cause'. Wither still asserted that:

> the cause we had
> Was very good, though we ourselves are bad.[34]

He shared all Milton's horror at the betrayal of the Revolution by the English people, which had led God to desert what both believed to be his cause. Milton's phrase 'choosing them a captain back for Egypt' has often been praised: Wither anticipated it in 1659:

30 Milton, *Complete Prose Works*, i. 706–7; iii. 210, 256, 316, 536, 598–9. Milton held these views in 1649 no less than in 1641, Wither in 1612 no less than in 1662 (*Prince Henries Obsequies*, 1612; *Parallelogrammaton*, pp. 48–58).

31 *The Psalmes of David*, ii. 184, 145; cf. *Campo-Musae*, pp. 25, 66, 68; *Westrow Revived*, pp. 54–5; *Parallelogrammaton*, pp. 98, 123, 137.

32 *Brittans Remembrancer*, pp. 18, 22, 24; *Campo-Musae*, p. 64; *Vox Pacifica*, p. 68.

33 *A Suddain Flash*, p. 16; *Epistolium-Vagum*, p. 25.

34 *Furor-Poeticus* (1660), pp. 19–20; cf. *Vox Vulgi* (1661), p. 17. I quote from the reprint of 1880, ed. W. D. Macray.

They now rebelliously a captain choose
To lead them back to bondage, like the Jews.[35]

The people had been influenced by a mistaken short-run idea of their own interests, by the 'vain and groundless apprehension that nothing but kingship can restore trade', not by any regard for Charles II.[36]

Like Milton, though rather earlier, Wither apparently moved from Calvinism to an undenominational Arminian position. As early as 1638 he rejected the absolute decrees.[37] In 1636 he insisted on free will. Without it 'we neither husband the gifts of nature (which is God's common grace) nor endeavour as we ought to do according to that ability which we have received'. At the Fall 'we lost indeed our light but not our eyes'. Christ would reprobate 'those only who rejected' the light, 'not because they saw it not but because they loved it not'. All men 'received . . . that common grace . . . so far forth as might have enabled them to become Sons of God'.[38] Nemesius, as translated by Wither, anticipated *Areopagitica*: 'either man should have been made void of reason, or else being indued with reason and exercised in action, he must have in him free will'. God gave him choice, as he gave it to the angels. So man can ultimately attain

to a state that's better
Than what he lost

—a Paradise within him, happier far. Like Milton in *Areopagitica*, Wither thought that knowledge can help us to recover from the consequences of the Fall. In 1662 he proclaimed free will and universal redemption.[39]

Wither early rejected a fugitive and cloistered virtue: those who withdraw into 'an heremetical solitariness . . . wrong their country and their friends', and are 'weak, . . . slothful and unjust'.

35 *Epistolium-Vagum*, pp. 24–5; *Speculum Speculativum* (1660), pp. 42–3, 69–75; Milton, *Works* (Columbia edn.), vi. 149.

36 *Speculum Speculativum*, pp. 81–3.

37 *Brittans Remembrancer*, pp. 39–40, 52–9, 249–52; cf. *The Psalmes of David*, ii. 168, 303–4.

38 Nemesius, *The Nature of Man*, Englished by George Wither (1636), sig. A3–5. William Haller noted the importance of this passage (*Liberty and Reformation in the Puritan Revolution*, Columbia University Press, 1955, p. 177).

39 Nemesius, op. cit., pp. 568–9; Wither, *Vaticinia Poetica* (1666), p. 27; *Parallelogrammaton*, pp. 61–5; cf. *Juvenilia*, i. 263–4; Milton, *Complete Prose Works*, ii. 366–7.

Give me the man that with a quaking arm
Walks with a stedfast mind through greatest harm;
And though his flesh doth tremble, makes it stand
To execute what Reason doth command.[40]

This is of course conventional Puritanism: trust in God *and* keep your powder dry. But it gives a courage in adversity that looks forward to Abdiel.

Do as you please; my way to me is known,
And I will walk it, though I walk alone.[41]

Like Milton in *Paradise Lost*, Wither saw it as his task to rally the defeated remnant of God's servants, to save them from despair. They must not repine at God's will as revealed in history. At Naseby, Wither had declared in 1649, God had shown himself on the side of Parliament.[42] Now the restoration of monarchy has come as God's punishment for the English people, who had failed to take advantage of the opportunities which he had offered them. Men get the government they deserve[43]; everything that happens is in accordance with God's will:

And he that would, and he that would not too,
Shall help effect what God intends to do. . . .

Yea they who pull down and they who erect
Shall in the close concur in one effect.[44]

Christopher Clobery saw in the events of 1659 fulfilment of the predictions of *Brittans Remembrancer*: referring to 'these nations', he took the Miltonic point that 'their fall is wilful'.[45] In prison after the restoration, Wither's faith was strengthened against 'atheistical arguments and objections of carnal men . . . by looking back as far as the creation'. He learnt that the restoration was 'a trial . . . of . . . obedience to God's commands', both for Charles II and for God's people. God 'will provide

40 *Juvenilia*, i. 281; *Brittans Remembrancer*, p. 62, cf. pp. 286–7.

41 *Campo-Musae*, pp. 64–5; cf. *Brittans Remembrancer*, pp. 13, 44, 54, 59–72, 78, 82, 98–9; *Opobalsamum Anglicanum*, p. 6.

42 *Carmen Eucharisticon* (1649).

43 *Epistolium-Vagum*, pp. 16, 19–23, 29; *Vox Vulgi*, pp. 25, 35.

44 Wither, *The Dark Lantern*, pp. 18–19.

45 J. M. French, 'Thorn-Dury's Notes on Wither', *Huntington Library Quarterly*, 22 (1959–60), pp. 386–8. A glance at *Brittans Remembrancer*, pp. 245–52, will show how right Clobery was. Cf. *Juvenilia*, i. 49–52.

deliverers', but in his own time.[46] Yet Wither died before the publication of *Paradise Lost*. The analogies derive from the historical context.

In this light Wither's attitude towards the sects is interesting. In *The Schollers Purgatory* (*c*. 1624) he tells us that he was much wooed by the sectaries. In 1628 he mentioned Familists and Brownists without the ritually expected horror, just as Milton was to do in 1641. As early as 1623 Wither made the classic Familist distinction between 'the history' and 'the mystery', and he referred more than once to 'the Everlasting Gospel', a phrase used mainly by radical sectaries. In 1661 he exposed the humbug of blaming everything on to 'fanatics'.[47] His attitude towards the Quakers resembles Milton's. Wither anticipated them in mocking at exaggerated social compliments, and took up the point again, explicitly in defence of the Quakers, in 1661.[48] He virtually aligned himself with Quakers as despised 'messengers of God', and spoke with admiration of their courage and of their opposition to oaths. 'They are our Levellers new named', he wrote—a point normally made by the Quakers' enemies.[49]

Wither disliked lawyers, the delays and venality of the law, and the mumbo-jumbo of law French ('this Norman gibberish', Milton called it). He linked the traditional enemies of the radicals, lawyers, and priests.[50] Like Milton and most of the radicals, Wither exalted reason above precedent, experience above authority; again he expressed these points relatively early. But, again like Milton, he was prepared to plead precedent against both King and Parliament when it suited him.[51]

Like Milton, Wither had not much use for the Fathers of the Church, preferring to follow his own reason and conscience. Both thought that many disputed theological matters concerned things indifferent, and became increasingly concerned

[46] *Parallelogrammaton*, pp. 46, 68–70, 74; cf. pp. 28, 38, 45.

[47] *Brittans Remembrancer*, p. 247; cf. p. 50; *Hymnes and Songs*, p. liii; *Vox Vulgi*, p. 19; Milton, *Complete Prose Works*, i. 783–8, ii. 178.

[48] *Hymnes and Songs*, p. xxxvii; *The Prisoners Plea* (1661), p. 27.

[49] *Speculum Speculativum*, pp. 51–2; *Parallelogrammaton*, pp. 43–4, 88–93; *Vaticinia Poetica*, pp. 10–12.

[50] *Juvenilia*, i. 198–200; *Brittans Remembrancer*, pp. 30, 107, 129, 186–9; *Speculum Speculativum*, p. 67.

[51] *Juvenilia*, iii. 679–80, 700; *Brittans Remembrancer*, pp. 234–6; *Vox Vulgi*, pp. 14, 30; *Parallelogrammaton*, p. 101.

as such squabbles fragmented the unity of the radicals.[52] Both accepted astrology, with reservations, but both objected to idle curiosity, to prying 'into those secrets God meant should be hidden'—for instance what God was doing before he created the world.[53]

Like Milton, Wither though that hell was a state of mind.[54] Milton's heresies do not appear in Wither's writings, but then we should not know about Milton's real beliefs if the unpublishable *De Doctrina Christiana* had not survived. The translation of Nemesius, and especially Wither's Preface, was one of the sources on which Richard Overton drew for his *Mans Mortalitie* of 1643. But Nemesius merely reports Hebrew views on the close union of body and soul, and that 'man was made from the beginning neither wholly mortal neither wholly immortal'. Wither appears to reject the mortalism which Milton adopted.[55] There is likewise no evidence that Wither was anything but orthodox on the Trinity, though he emphasized the triumph of Christ's manhood at the resurrection. He recorded, without comment, that some rejected the historical Jesus Christ who died at Jerusalem.[56] He laid especial emphasis, as Milton did, on the *liberty* to which Sons of God might attain. For him, as for Milton, 'the Lord's anointed' meant the elect rather than kings.[57] But in all this there is nothing as positive as the anti-Trinitarianism to which Milton in private committed himself.

Wither perhaps approaches Milton's antinomianism. He was no strict Sabbatarian. 'Bodily labours and exercises' might be used on Sundays 'wheresoever (without respect to sensual or covetous ends) a rectified conscience shall persuade us that the honour of God, the charity we owe to our neighbours or an unfeigned necessity requires them to be done'. This is exactly Milton's position in the *De Doctrina Christiana*.[58] Neither poet

52 *Juvenilia*, iii. 679; *Carmen Expostularium* (1647), *passim; Ecchoes from the Sixth Trumpet*, p. 19. Cf. *Milton and the English Revolution*, pp. 199, 212, 369.

53 *Brittans Remembrancer*, p. 47; *Juvenilia*, i. 300–1. Cf. Milton, *Complete Prose Works*, i. 293, 319–20; *Paradise Lost*, VIII. 188–97, *Paradise Regained*, Bk. IV.

54 Wither, *Meditations upon the Lords Prayer* (1665), p. 96.

55 Nemesius, op. cit., pp. 23–6, 82–93; cf. pp. 242–3; *Westrow Revived*, p. 37.

56 *Hymnes and Songs*, pp. 206–7; *Hallelujah*, pp. 244–6; *Ecchoes from the Sixth Trumpet*, p. 121.

57 *The Psalmes of David*, ii. 246; Preface to Nemesius, op. cit., sig. A5; *Fides-Anglicana*, p. 22.

58 *Hymnes and Songs*, p. 216; *Emblemes*, II. 15, IV. 26; *Parallelogrammaton*,

was a killjoy Puritan. The creatures exist in order to be enjoyed.[59] Like Milton in 1645, Wither thought amorous poems more suitable for youthful years; both continued to enjoy a rude story, a sexual innuendo. Wither wrote, but did not publish, a mildly naughty epithalamium.[60] Both smoked, both appear to have been betting men.[61] For Wither as for Milton hypocrisy was the worst of crimes.[62]

Wither shared Milton's high ideal of love in marriage, and rejected marriage for money and enforced virginity. Both insisted that children should choose their marriage partners, but Wither shared the contemptuous (and biblical) view that

> The woman for the man was made
> And not the man for her,[63]

which Milton expressed as 'He for God only, she for God in him'; both, however, had more appreciation of the woman's point of view than most of their contemporaries. Wither's references to his own 'dear Betty' are touchingly affectionate and appreciative. But Wither had no occasion to discuss divorce. When he wrote, 'Nor rob I her of aught which she can miss', he was referring to a stolen kiss. When Milton apparently echoed the words, he was referring to male adultery.[64]

Wither, 'the English Juvenal', was a favourite with Milton's headmaster Alexander Gil, who probably made his pupils translate him into Latin. Influences are tricky things to establish, and I should not like to claim as much as some of Wither's editors. Circe occurs in *Brittans Remembrancer*, Sabrina

pp. 49–56; Milton, *Complete Prose Works*, vi. 353–4, 537–41, 639–40, 708–14.

59 *Hallelujah*, p. 45.

60 *Juvenilia*, i. 236–42, 258–62; Milton, *Prolusion VI*, *Defensio Secunda*, *passim*; French, 'Thorn-Dury's Notes on Wither', pp. 383–5.

61 Wither, *An Improvement of Imprisonment* (1661), pp. 98–100. Contrast the diatribe against tobacco in *Juvenilia*, i. 222–4—written perhaps with an eye on James I. For betting see *Juvenilia*, iii. 751; *Brittans Remembrancer*, p. 4; *Milton and the English Revolution*, p. 59.

62 *Brittans Remembrancer*, p. 19; *Campo-Musae*, p. 66; *Westrow Revived*, p. 8 ('Hypocrisy / Is worse than error'); *Furor-Poeticus*, p. 43; *Vox Vulgi*, p. 17; *Paradise Lost*, III. 682–5, IV. 121–2, 744–7.

63 *Juvenilia*, ii. 480–3; *Hallelujah*, pp. 309–19; *Parallelogrammaton*, p. 34.

64 *An Improvement of Imprisonment* (1661), pp. 81–8, 92–5, 105–7, 120; *A Memorandum to London* (1665), p. 72; *Juvenilia*, iii. 920; Milton, *Complete Prose Works*, ii. 674.

in one of Wither's epithalamia. More interesting perhaps are parallels, uses of the same imagery. They may serve to remind us how unoriginal Milton was. Wither, for instance, often refers to Sons of Belial, and echoes, 'Licence they mean when they cry liberty' more than once. The North was false for Wither in 1642 and 1660, as it was for Milton in 1648 and 1667, no doubt for political as well as biblical reasons.[65] In 1659 Wither observed that Samson (like Wither himself) could only 'be roused up to execute God's vengeance upon the enemies of his country' after he had suffered personal injury.[66] Professor Kermode suggested that the train of thought which led to the versification of *Samson Agonistes* derived from Wither's discussion of Hebrew poetry in *A Preparation to the Psalter* (1619).[67]

A few miscellaneous coincidences. Wither, like Milton, seems to have had difficulties with his father over his choice of a poetic career: the epigram in which he explained himself foreshadows Milton's *Ad Patrem*.[68] Both Wither and Milton were devoted to music.[69] They shared a sturdy linguistic patriotism. Wither argued that the phrase Roman Catholic was 'an absurd term, contradictory to itself'; Milton improved the joke, referring to 'the Pope's bull', 'a particular universal'.[70] Wither admired Robert Gell, who probably married Milton to his third wife; Wither quoted Gell's views on the Second Coming.[71]

In *Brittans Remembrancer* Wither wrote:

> If thou forbear
> What now thy conscience bids thee to declare
> Thy foolish hope shall fail thee.

This passage may have been in Milton's mind when he wrote his famous words: 'When time was, thou couldst not find a syllable of all that thou hadst read or studied to utter on her

[65] *Campo-Musae*, p. 52; *Furor-Poeticus*, p. 24.

[66] *Epistolium-Vagum*, pp. 23, 27.

[67] F. Kermode, '*Samson Agonistes* and Hebrew Prosody', *Durham University Journal*, New Series 14 (1952), pp. 59–63.

[68] *Juvenilia*, ii. 361–3.

[69] *Emblemes*, II. 3. We have Percy Scholes's authority for Wither's keen interest in and competent knowledge of music (*The Puritans and Music*, Oxford University Press, London, 1934, p. 156). Scholes referred especially to *A Preparation to the Psalter*.

[70] *Juvenilia*, i. 22; *Parallelogrammaton*, p. 105; *Three Private Meditations* (1665), p. 46; Milton, *Works* (Columbia edn.), vi. 167.

[71] *Ecchoes from the Sixth Trumpet*, pp. 8–9.

behalf'.[72] Like Milton and many more of his contemporaries, Wither looked to later ages for the justification he had not found in his own day. *Brittans Remembrancer* was dedicated 'to posterity and to these times (if they please)'. In *Campo-Musae* he appealed to 'better times to come'.[73] In 1661, like Milton, he felt that had become an exile in his own country.[74]

One conclusion to draw from the foregoing might be that the historical method cannot help us to grasp the differences between a Wither and a Milton; the similarities are so great that we have to fall back on individual genius to explain the differences. But I think we can do a little better than that. It could be argued that it was Milton's good fortune that he was just reaching the height of his poetic powers when he actively participated in 'the most heroic and exemplary achievements since the foundation of the world'. So far from the writings of his left hand being a waste of time, it was the hopes, the illusions, of the English Revolution, culminating in the traumatic defeat of God's cause, that transformed the intended Arthuriad into *Paradise Lost*, *Paradise Regained*, and *Samson Agonistes*. For Wither the equivalent experience was the plague of 1625; *Brittans Remembrancer* aspired to be his *Paradise Lost*, justifying God's ways to men. There are powerful passages in the poem, but the event—or rather Wither's reaction to the event—would not carry the burden which he laid on it. The plague shocked and horrified Wither, but his personal involvement extended no further than to a self-righteous satisfaction that he had not fled from the City as other men did. His main concern was to use the tragedy to denounce the sins of others in a wholly traditional manner. Even when Wither recalls Marvell's 'double heart', his expression of it is flat:

> But, oh my God! though grovelling I appear
> Upon the ground, and have a rooting here,
> Which hauls me downward, yet in my desire
> To that which is above me I aspire.[75]

Milton, on the other hand, was totally involved in the Revolution, and felt a share in the guilt of the English people

[72] *Brittans Remembrancer*, p. 7; Milton, *Complete Prose Works*, i. 804.

[73] *Campo-Musae*, pp. 2, 48; cf. Milton, *Works* (Columbia edn.), vi. 100.

[74] *An Improvement of Imprisonment*, p. 101; Milton, *Works* (Columbia edn.), xii. 113–15.

[75] *Emblemes*, IV. I.

which had led God to desert his own cause. Milton's whole position, after twenty years of effort and self-sacrifice, was in ruins and had to be reconstructed, rethought, and refelt. Wither too experienced disillusionment and defeat, he too was arrested, imprisoned, and suffered financial loss at the restoration, and he too admitted his own share in 'our national demerits'.[76] But Wither had his glib explanation ready-made: sin, which Wither had been denouncing for forty years. Milton arrived at a theologically similar conclusion, but after travelling through hell and heaven to find it.

76 *Furor-Poeticus*, pp. 19–20; *Vox Vulgi*, p. 17.

Lycidas, Daphnis, and Gallus

J. MARTIN EVANS

Of all Milton's English poems, *Lycidas* is perhaps the most specifically imitative. It invokes, that is to say, not only a long-established generic tradition but two particular components of that tradition: Theocritus' first *Idyl* and Virgil's tenth *Eclogue*. As generations of editors from Thomas Newton to A. S. P. Woodhouse have pointed out, the address to the nymphs in *Lycidas* echoes the question with which the formal lament begins in both the earlier works:

> Where were ye Nymphs when the remorseless deep
> Clos'd o'er the head of your lov'd Lycidas?
> For neither were ye playing on the steep,
> Where your old Bards, the famous Druids, lie,
> Nor on the shaggy top of Mona high,
> Nor yet where Deva spreads her wizard stream.
> (*Lycidas*, 50–5)

Where were you when Daphnis pined away, where were you, O Nymphs? Were you in the lovely vales of Peneus, or of Pindus? You surely did not haunt the mighty stream of Anapus or the steep of Aetna or the sacred water of Acis. (*Idyl*, I. 66–9)

What groves, what glens possessed you, Naiad maidens, when Gallus was languishing with an unworthy love? It was not the mountain ridge of Parnassus or of Pindus that delayed you, nor even Aonian Aganippe. (*Eclogue*, X. 9–12)[1]

No less obviously, Triton, Hippotades, Cam, and Saint Peter have their counterparts in Hermes, the shepherds, Priapus, and Cypris, who visit the dying Daphnis in the *Idyl*, and Menalcas, Apollo, Silvanus, and Pan, who try to console Gallus in the *Eclogue*.

[1] I quote throughout from the translations of the first *Idyl* and the tenth *Eclogue* in Thomas P. Harrison, *The Pastoral Elegy* (Austin, 1939), and from the text of Milton's works in Merritt Y. Hughes, *John Milton Complete Poems and Major Prose* (New York, 1957).

So much is well known. Indeed, it is almost too well known, for these parallels have become so familiar that they are often taken for granted and their implications left unexamined. For example, when J. H. Hanford comes to discuss the relationship between the above-quoted passages in his classic essay on the pastoral elegy, he pauses only to assess the seventeenth-century poet's relative indebtedness to his two classical models. Milton's lines, he concludes, 'are directly reminiscent of the Greek rather than the Latin poet'.[2] I would like to suggest, however, that the whole point of the allusion lies in the *doubleness* of its reference. During the previous four verse paragraphs we have caught numerous individual echoes; now, for the space of six lines, we can hear two voices accompanying Milton's in a continuous descant, and our critical energies are more profitably occupied by the task of exploring the implications of that phenomenon than with worrying about which of the two additional voices sounds the louder.

The phenomenon itself, of course, stems from a simple fact of literary history which most of the poem's original audience would have learned at school: Virgil's tenth *Eclogue* is an imitation of Theocritus' first *Idyl*. Moreover, the features which distinguish it as an imitation are precisely those which Milton reproduces, namely the address to the nymphs and the procession of visitors. Like Plato's painted bed in the *Republic*, *Lycidas* may be defined as an imitation of an imitation. In which case Hanford's literary book-keeping is not merely beside the point. It is positively misleading, for if Milton chose to allude to those very elements which the Greek and the Latin poems have in common with each other, one can hardly escape the conclusion that he wanted us to recall both works simultaneously.

As soon as we attempt to do so, however, we encounter a major problem. Despite the verbal and structural similarities between the first *Idyl* and the tenth *Eclogue*, their respective heroes are polar opposites. To begin with the *Idyl*, most recent studies follow G. E. Gebauer in seeing Daphnis as a second Hippolytus who 'had vowed to resist love. Aphrodite was affronted and angered by such audacious arrogance and

[2] 'The Pastoral Elegy and Milton's *Lycidas*', reprinted in C. A. Patrides, *Milton's Lycidas, The Tradition and the Poem* (New York, 1961), p. 32.

inspired in him an overpowering passion. Rather than gratify it and thereby break his vow, Daphnis chose to languish and die.'[3] Following the example of the Greek tragedians, Theocritus dramatizes only the climactic sequence of events, the hero's final decision and subsequent death. The earlier part of the story is gradually reconstructed by the speeches of the minor characters who come, like Samson's visitors, either to divert him from his purpose or to deride him for persisting in it. Each successive encounter sheds fresh light upon the nature of his predicament until, by the time he delivers his parting words, it is fully illuminated. Thus Hermes' opening question establishes no more than the cause of Daphnis' sickness: 'Who makes thee suffer thus? With whom, my good lad, art thou so much in love?' (lines 77–8). Taken on its own, this could well suggest that the lovelorn shepherd was dying of unrequited passion,[4] but Priapus' ensuing rebuke reveals that the situation is more complicated than we might have suspected: 'Wretched Daphnis, why dost thou pine away? The maiden is roaming among all the springs, all the groves . . . searching for thee. Thou art too poor a lover and art a helpless creature' (lines 82–5). Clearly Daphnis could indulge his feelings if he wished to, so some further consideration, as yet unspecified, must be holding him back. The jeers of Cypris, who arrives on the scene shortly afterwards, disclose what it is: 'Surely thou didst boast, Daphnis, that thou wouldst throw Love for a fall; but hast thou not rather thyself been thrown by irresistible Love?' (lines 97–8). He has evidently taken a vow of chastity, and in revenge Cypris has made him fall in love with the maiden to whom Priapus referred earlier. Only now that his dilemma has been adequately defined does the hero break his silence by announcing his intention to die rather than yield to the power of Cypris. He may be 'dragged down to Hades by Love' (line 130) but even there he promises to 'bring grievous pain to Love' (line 103).

All this, it should be added, represents a radical departure from the more common version of the myth attributed to the

[3] I quote from the summary of Gebauer's thesis which R. M. Ogilvie provides during the course of his vigorous attempt to refute it in his article 'The Song of Thyrsis', *J.H.S.* 82 (1962), 107.

[4] In Virgil's *Eclogue*, x. 21 the shepherds put a similar question to a lover who really is in this predicament.

two Sicilian poets Timaeus and Stesichorus, according to which Daphnis was 'the child of a Nymph, who exposed him under a laurel bush from which he took his name. He became a herdsman and was loved by a Nymph, to whom he vowed eternal fidelity. A princess made him drunk and seduced him, whereupon he was blinded.'[5] Nevertheless both A. S. F. Gow in his authoritative edition and Gilbert Lawall in his full-length critical study of the *Idyls* agree with Gebauer that Theocritus completely transformed the traditional version of the story to serve his own purposes. In Lawall's words:

The nymph of the myth is simply replaced by nature herself. In the myth the nymph made Daphnis swear not to love a woman, but he was finally seduced and punished. Theocritus' Daphnis is made of sterner stuff; a true tragic hero, he resists all temptation and so pines away to his death. By retaining his chastity, he remains faithful to nature, wild animals, woods, and streams.[6]

By no stretch of the imagination could the same claim be made for the famous soldier, statesman, and poet, Cornelius Gallus, whose unhappy love affair with Lycoris is the immediate subject of Virgil's tenth *Eclogue*. He is unambiguously and unrepentantly dedicated to sexual passion, and he dies not because he refuses to indulge his feelings but because he cannot; his mistress has left him for another man. Rejecting all the conventional consolations of pastoral, he continues to love her in spite of her infidelity, and with his last words affirms the sovereignty of Eros: 'Love is victor over all. Let me too yield to Love' (line 69). The contrast between the Roman warrior and the Greek shepherd could scarcely be more extreme. Daphnis conquered love; Gallus willingly surrenders to it. As a result, although the processional figures in the *Eclogue* once again reveal the nature of the hero's dilemma, the sentiments they express during the course of their disclosures are far removed from those of their Theocritean predecessors. Whereas Daphnis' visitors came to tempt or to mock him, Gallus' are concerned only to comfort or to admonish him. Priapus, for example, urged Daphnis to pursue his beloved; Apollo urges Gallus to

[5] I quote from the summary of the traditional version of the myth in A. S. F. Gow, *Theocritus* (Cambridge, 1952), ii. 1.

[6] Gilbert Lawall, *Theocritus' Coan Pastorals* (Harvard, 1967), p. 25. Cf. Gow, p. 2.

forget her: 'Gallus, why art thou so mad? Thy beloved Lycoris has followed another amid snows and rough camps' (lines 22–3). Cypris exulted over the misery of an adversary. Pan advises a fellow-lover to stop grieving: 'Will there be no end of this? . . . Love cares not for such deeds; cruel Love is not sated with tears nor the grasses with streams nor the bees with clover nor the goats with leaves' (lines 28–30). The theme of the *Idyl* was heroic chastity. The theme of the *Eclogue* is the irresistible power of love.

What, then, are we to make of Lycidas' relationship to the heroes of these two very different poems? Before we can even begin to answer this question, we must first answer a prior one. How were the first *Idyl* and the tenth *Eclogue* interpreted in the sixteenth and early seventeenth centuries? Davis P. Harding and others have taught us that the 'Renaissance Ovid' was by no means identical with either the classical or the modern one,[7] and there is no reason to suppose that the same might not be true of the Renaissance Theocritus and the Renaissance Virgil. Certainly the pastoral works of both were the subject of intense scholarly scrutiny during the hundred or so years preceding the composition of *Lycidas*. The *Idyls* were annotated in considerable detail by such influential humanists as Joseph Scaliger, Isaac Casaubon, Daniel Heinsius,[8] Fredericus Lamotius,[9] and Joannes Meursius.[10] And in order to make them available to a wider audience, Theocritus' works were frequently translated into Latin. By the time Heinsius published his comprehensive collection of Greek bucolic poetry in 1604 no less than six partial or complete Latin versions were already in existence.[11]

7 See, for example: Davis P. Harding, *Milton and the Renaissance Ovid* (Urbana, 1946); Don Cameron Allen, *Mysteriously Meant* (Baltimore, 1970).

8 The annotations of all three are reprinted in Daniel Heinsius, *Theocriti, Moschi, Bionis, Simii quae extant: cum Graecis in Theocritum Scholiis & Indice copiose . . . Accedunt Iosephi Scaligeri, Isaaci Casauboni, & eiusdem Danielis Heinsii Notae & Lectiones* (Heidelberg, 1604).

9 *Theocriti Idyllium Primum Annotationibus Frederici Lamotii illustratum* (Paris, 1552).

10 *Ioannis Meursi ad Theocriti Syracusani Poetae Idyllia Spicilegium* (London, 1597).

11 *Seriatim*: *Theocritus scripsit Philethicus Latihum* [sic] *fecit Bucolicum Carmen Res Acta Syracusis* (Rome, *c.*1480); *Theocriti Syracusani eidyllia trigintasex, Latino carmine reddita, Helio Eobano Hesso interprete* (Basle, 1531); *Theocriti Syracusani Opera Latine a Ioanne Trimanino ad verbum diligentissime expressa, locis unde Virgilius sumpsit, indicatis* (Venice, 1539); *Theocriti Syracusani poetae Clarissimi idyllia trigintasex, recens e graeco in latinum, ad verbum translata, Andrea Divo Iustinopolitano interprete* (Basle, 1554);

Virgil's *Eclogues* were even more exhaustively analysed. Antonio Mancinelli, Jodocus Badius Ascensius,[12] Joannes Pierius Valerianus, Juan Luis Vives, Helius Eobanus Hessus, Richardus Gorraeus, Philip Melanchthon, Stephanus Riccius Peter Ramus, and Thomas Farnaby[13] (who, by an odd coincidence, was Edward King's teacher)[14] all produced elaborate commentaries, while the annotations of the two best-known earlier scholiasts, Servius and Probus, were reprinted throughout the period. In addition, Abraham Fleming,[15] John Brinsley, William Lisle, and John Bidle[16] translated the *Eclogues* into English, often with extensive marginal notes. Brinsley's painstakingly literal version, 'written chiefly for the good of schools',[17] is particularly useful as an indication of the way in which the young Milton may have first encountered the poem. It is with these interpretations of both the first *Idyl* and the tenth *Eclogue* that any discussion of the relationship between *Lycidas* and its models must begin.

Moschi, Bionis, Theocriti, Elegantissimorum poetarum idyllia aliquot, ab Henrico Stephano Latina facta (Venice, 1555); Hieronymus Commelinus, *Theocriti Syracusii Idyllia & Epigrammata* (Heidelberg, 1596).

12 I quote both Mancinelli and Ascensius from the following edition: *P. Virgilii Maronis Opera . . . cum xi acerrimi iudicii virorum commentariis* (Venice, 1544).

13 *Seriatim*: Available in *Opera Vergiliana* (n.p., 1528); *Io Lodovico Vivis in Bucolica Vergilii Interpretatio, Potissimum Allegorica* (Milan, 1539); *Publii Vergilii Maronis Mantuani Opera* (includes 'Eclogae decem, cum Annotationibus et castigatione Helii Hessi et al.') (London, 1535); *P. Virgilii Maronis Bucolica Cum Commentariis Richardi Gorraei Parisiensis* (Venice, 1554); *Argumenta seu Dispositiones Rhetoricae in Eclogas Virgilii Authore Philip Melanchthon* (n.p., 1568); *Paraphrases, Ecphrases, succintae questiones, & brevia Scholia Textus in easdem Eclogas Authore M. Stephano Riccio* (n.p., 1568) (printed together with the preceding item); *P. Virgilii Maronis Bucolica P. Rami Professoris Regii, praelectionibus exposita* (4th edn., Frankfurt, 1582); *Publii Virgilii Maronis Bucolica, Georgica Aeneis, Notis admarginalibus illustrata a Thoma Farnabio* (London, 1634).

14 Thomas Warton in his *Poems upon Several Occasions* (London, 1791) warns us not to confuse King's schoolmaster with the 'celebrated rhetorician' (p. 37) but the *DNB* does not distinguish between them.

15 In fact, Fleming made two attempts, the first in fourteener couplets (1575), the second, from which I quote, in unrhymed fourteeners: *The Bucolicks of Publius Virgilius Maro . . . All newly translated into English verse by A*[*braham*] *F*[*leming*] (London, 1589).

16 *Seriatim*: *Virgil's Eclogues . . . Translated Grammatically* (London, 1620); *Virgil's Eclogues Translated into English by W. L. Gent* (London, 1628); *Virgil's Bucolicks Englished* (London, 1634).

17 Fleming also claimed that his 1575 translation was made 'for the benefit of young learners of the latine tongue'.

One of the first and most interesting facts they reveal is that the differences between the Greek and the Latin poems which I have just discussed appear to have escaped the Renaissance commentators entirely. Melanchthon, Fleming, Brinsley, and Farnaby all emphasized Virgil's debt to Theocritus without so much as a hint that he may have modified his predecessor's meaning in any way. Fleming, for instance, declared in the preface to his translation of the tenth *Eclogue*: 'Touching the argument, it is all in a maner taken out of *Thirsis*, that is, the first Idyll of *Theocritus*, who handleth the like matter in all points in his *Daphnis*.'[18] Nor was this view confined to the interpreters of Virgil. In his lecture on Theocritus' first *Idyl* Heinsius claimed that 'Virgil translated the most ancient, and to this extent the most original, material of bucolic song [in his poem] to Gallus: the whole of this eclogue . . . is a kind of imitation of the misfortunes of Daphnis'.[19] So closely were the two poems associated with each other, indeed, that they seem to have virtually coalesced in the minds of many sixteenth-century readers. The most striking evidence of this process is provided by Hessus, who incorporated whole lines from the tenth *Eclogue* into his Latin translation of the first *Idyl*, notably in his rendering of Thyrsis' address to the nymphs:

> Quae nemora, aut qui vos saltus habuere puellae
> Naiades, indigno quum Daphnis amore periret?
> Pulchra ne vos tenuisse putem Peneia Tempe?
> Num iuga Thessalici Phoebo gratissima Pindi?[20]

And when Virgil's *Eclogue* was in turn translated into Greek by Heinsius, Scaliger, and Daniel Alsworth, several of Theocritus' most striking phrases were conscripted into service to Gallus.[21] The first *Idyl* and the tenth *Eclogue* have become almost indistinguishable from each other.

[18] Op. cit., p. 29. Cf.: Melanchthon, sig. G7: 'It is written in imitation of Theocritus' first Idyl concerning Daphnis'; Brinsley, p. 93: 'All this argument is almost taken out of *Thyrsis* of *Theocritus*, where he prosecutes the like love of *Daphnis*'; Farnaby, p. 28: 'Almost all the argument is taken from the Thyrsis of Theocritus, where he relates the similar love of Daphnis.'

[19] 'Scholae Theocriticae' in Heinsius, p. 302. I am indebted to Professor A. G. Rigg throughout for his help in translating the commentators' Latin.

[20] Op. cit., sig. a8v. The borrowing establishes Daphnis' love as *indignus*.

[21] The translations of Heinsius and Scaliger are contained in the former's reissue of Commelinus' *Theocriti Syracusii Idyllia* (Heidelberg, 1603), pp. 128–31. Daniel

Needless to say, this conflation could not have taken place without a radical transformation in the character of one or other of their respective protagonists. Bearing in mind the chronological priority of the *Idyl*, we might have expected the dissimilarities noted above to have been resolved in favour of Daphnis, but in fact it was Gallus who proved to be the dominant partner. Two factors seem to have been responsible for his victory. First, there was the retrospective influence of the tenth *Eclogue* on the interpretation of the first *Idyl*. In a critical reversal of the mimetic process of composition, the Greek original was read in the light of the Latin imitation rather than vice versa, and the chaste pastoral prototype was refashioned in the image of his concupiscent elegiac descendant. Instead of producing the Theocritean Gallus we might have anticipated, the commentators of the sixteenth and seventeenth centuries thus created a distinctly Virgilian Daphnis, animated by the same all-consuming passion that had brought Lycoris' lover to his death. Second, there was the prospective influence, so to speak, of Timaeus and Stesichorus' version of the myth. For thanks to such references to it as Ovid's in Book IV of the *Metamorphoses*, the notion that Daphnis was an unfaithful lover was still very much alive in the Renaissance. For example, John Rider explained in his etymological dictionary that Daphnis was

> a young man of Sicily who compacted with a Nymph whom he loved that whether of them soever should violate their faith, which they had plighted to one another, should lose both their eyes: Daphnis, forgetting his promise, fell in love with another; the gods that were called to witness in the oath, did punish the breach of it by making him blinde.[22]

In combination these two pressures (the retrospective and the prospective) were irresistible, and Theocritus' defiant virgin reverted to his original amorous persona.

The interpretative consequences of these developments are clearly reflected in the commentaries of Lamotius and Heinsius on the first *Idyl*. Both simply took it for granted that Theocritus had followed the traditional form of the Daphnis myth in his treatment of it. As Heinsius wrote:

Alsworth's was published in his *Imitatio Theocritea Qua Virgilii Eclogae, ita Doricis versibus exprimuntur* (Rome, 1594).

22 *Dictionarium Etymologicum Proprium Nominum* (London, 1648), p. 257.

Timaeus, the authority on Sicilian matters, calls this nymph Echenais, with whom Daphnis had made an agreement or resolution that he would undergo the penalty threatened by the fates if he broke faith by falling in love with someone else. . . . Parts of the speeches are assigned to this nymph in the idyl, as will be clear by the emendation of a single word.[23]

The word in question occurs during the course of Priapus' address to the dying shepherd:

Wretched Daphnis, why dost thou pine away? The maiden is roaming among all the springs, all the groves . . . searching for thee. Thou art too poor a lover and art a helpless creature. (*Idyl* I. 82–5)

The Greek verb rendered here by 'searching' is *zateusa*. This, Heinsius ingenuously insisted, made nonsense, for there was no reason that he could see why a maiden who had just been betrayed by her lover should still be searching for him. In place of *zateusa* he therefore proposed another Doric word, *zatōsa*, that is, 'speaking' or 'reproaching'. Everything thereafter, he concluded, was spoken not by Priapus, as all earlier editors had assumed, but by the nymph herself:

All this speech belongs to the nymph Echenais, who is castigating Daphnis for his promiscuity and unstable raging. By the loves of Theocritus, I swear that there is no passage that has been less understood by the scholiasts and their successors. . . . The Greek scholiast did not see how to resolve these problems, namely how she whom Daphnis had offended could be said to seek him when she ought rather to flee from him. . . . He thinks the whole speech belongs to Priapus who is consoling Daphnis, when in fact it belongs to the indignant girl whom he has betrayed and offended by his inconstancy.[24]

On the basis of this crucial emendation he then went on to summarize the lines I quoted above as follows: 'The girl is borne through springs and all the groves and *complains* [*conqueritur*] thus: "Assuredly Daphnis you are too fickle in love

[23] Op. cit., p. 302. Cf. Lamotius, p. 12: 'Suidas says he [Daphnis] was blinded because he had intercourse with another woman when he was drunk.'

[24] Op. cit., p. 303. The hapless '*Graecus interpres*' is a constant target of Heinsius' editorial barbs.

and too impetuous." '[25] So what in the original text had been a light-hearted piece of encouragement directed to a steadfast virgin became a deeply felt rebuke delivered by a wronged mistress. Theocritus' innocent shepherd on his way to martyrdom has turned into an unfaithful lover about to pay the just penalty of his transgression.

Virgil's tenth *Eclogue* was treated no less moralistically by the translators and annotators of the period. Servius had remarked in his commentary on the poem that 'in Gallus is exhibited the impatience of shameful love [*inpatientia turpis amoris*]'.[26] This theme was taken up and developed with evident relish by such Renaissance scholars as Melanchthon, Ramus, Riccius, Farnaby, and Brinsley. Although few of them went quite so far as Fleming, who subtitled his translation of the poem 'the mad love of Cornelius Gallus',[27] they all agreed that Virgil's amorous friend was at the very least 'fond' as another translator put it.[28] According to Brinsley, for instance, his love for the 'harlot' Lycoris was 'out of measure',[29] and as such it could bring only anguish and degradation in its train. The

[25] Op. cit. p. 304. It was this interpretation of the passage which Heinsius incorporated into the Latin translation of the first Idyl which he made for the 1603 reissue of Commelinus' text:

> Puella
> Per varios fontes pedibus per devia fertur . . .
> Multa movens: in amore levis nimiumque vagaris . . .
> (82–5)

But a year later, fearing perhaps that this was not clear or emphatic enough, he revised the translation of line 85 for the 1604 edition to read 'Vocibus his: Levis ah Daphni es, nimiumque vagaris . . .'. The translations of Trimaninus, Divus, and the anonymous translator all render *zateusa* by *quaerens* (seeking), while Hessus prefers *requirens* (searching). It is worth noting also that Heinsius translates *duseros* in line 85 as *levis* or 'fickle' rather than the more common 'poor at loving', thereby anticipating R. M. Ogilvie's point in 'The Song of Thyrsis', loc. cit.

[26] *In Vergilii Bucolica et Georgica Commentarii*, ed. G. Thilo (Lipsiae, 1887), p. 118. Cf. Riccius, sig. M7: 'Gallus died through the impatience of love [*inpatientia amoris*].'

[27] Op. cit., p. 29. Cf. Riccius, who throughout his *Brevia et erudita scholia* insists that Gallus was *insanis* (pp. 7^{v}, 8^{v}, 9^{v}), and Hessus, who explains in his comment on lines 31 ff. that 'Fingit Gallum respondentem, ut magis ob oculos ponat hominis insaniam' (p. 14^{v}).

[28] John Bidle, sig. C2^{v}: 'Scorcht with Idalian Flames, fond Gallus is / Enamour'd on the Strumpet Cytheris.' Cf. Melanchthon, sig. G8: '*stulti amatoris imago*'.

[29] Op. cit. The phrase is Brinsley's addition to Servius' note. Compare Brinsley: '. . . who whenas he out of measure affected an harlot called Cytheris . . .' (p. 92) and Servius: 'hic autem Gallus amavit Cytheridem meretricem . . .' (p. 118).

apparently aimless and disconnected series of fantasies Gallus describes in lines 50–69 revealed, in Riccius' words, the 'inconstancy of love [*amoris inconstantiam*]',[30] while the work as a whole affirmed the melancholy truth that

there is no strength so great, no force of mind so powerful, even in the greatest of men, which cannot be ennervated and dissipated by the enticements of love, no vigour so great that it cannot grow languid, cannot be dominated and subjugated by the sweetness of love, which in appearance seems pleasant, delightful and gracious when in reality it is nothing but pure poison [*merum fel*].[31]

But human nature was not entirely at the mercy of Venus and her son. There was, the Renaissance commentators maintained, an external force which could give mankind the strength to resist, namely the agency invoked by Gallus himself at the height of his frenzy:

I will go, and those verses which I composed in the Chalcidian measure I will now attune to the pipe of the Sicilian shepherd. I am determined to choose suffering in the woods among the dens of wild beasts and to carve the tale of my love in the young trees. (*Eclogue* x. 50–4)

In these lines, claimed Brinsley (translating Ramus), 'Gallus propounds unto himselfe the remedies which he wil use for the curing of his love, by contrary studies. As first by giving his minde to the studie of Poetrie.' Unfortunately, however, he was already too far gone for this classic *remedium amoris* to have any effect. Just twelve lines later, Brinsley went on to note, 'the Poet suddenly disliking the former remedies, setteth out the inconstancie of love, and that no remedies can cure it, neither the pleasures of the woods, nor the study of Poetrie, no nor any musicke, nor yet any toyles can asswage the rage thereof'.[32] The time for Gallus to have sought the aid of poetry was when he felt the first stirrings of passion.

Which was just the point of Virgil's opening address to the nymphs as the Renaissance commentators interpreted it. As

30 The phrase runs like a refrain through Riccius' *Brevia et erudita scholia*. It connects Gallus with Daphnis, of whom Heinsius writes, 'Obiicitur Daphnidi amoris inconstantia' (p. 303).

31 Op. cit., sig. M7. Gorraeus agrees, but also approves (p. 154).

32 Op. cit., p. 98. Cf. Ramus, p. 166. Brinsley evidently knew Ramus' commentary well and did not hesitate to borrow interpretations from it. Cf. sig. A4.

Servius had originally observed,[33] the locations from which the nymphs were absent while Gallus was pining away were all associated with poetic inspiration. Parnassus and Pindus were both consecrated to Apollo and the Muses while Aganippe's literary connections were too well known to deserve comment. The Naiades, it followed, were no other than the Muses, and Virgil's questions to them contained an implicit rebuke to the only power he knew which could have saved his friend from his fate: 'He seems to say this', Servius remarked, 'because, if the Muses had been present with [Gallus], that is, if he had given [himself] the task of writing songs, he would not have fallen into such amatory difficulties [*tantas amoris angustias*].'[34] In a characteristically detailed note on the same passage, Ascensius explained to his Renaissance readers the assumption underlying Servius' interpretation. 'The presence of the Muses can restrain love,' he pointed out, 'because, as the divine poet teaches in Book II of the *Aeneid*, the chaste goddesses have no dealings with Venus, whence Aeneas could not see them until Venus went away.' The Naiades were 'the goddesses of the fountains, that is, the Muses who preside over the fountains; for according to Varro the Muses and the Nymphs are the same, maidens, that is, chaste and flourishing in perpetual virginity (whence, as Catullus said, the poet ought himself to be chaste) . . .'.[35] By the time Brinsley produced his annotated translation of the *Eclogues* in 1620 this view of the episode was commonplace: 'He accuseth the Muses that they were so carelesse of Gallus', he wrote, 'to let him so to leave his studies and to perish in such unbeseeming love.'[36] Like the fourth book of the *Aeneid*, then, the tenth *Eclogue* was read in the Renaissance as an example of the distracting power of love:

So love disturbs many from their mind and sanity, and drives them

33 Servius, p. 120. Cf. Lisle, p. 184, Brinsley, p. 95.

34 Servius, p. 120. Riccius repeats this phrase word for word without acknowledgement in his *Brevia et erudita scholia*, p. 5^{v}.

35 Op. cit., p. 49. See also: J. M. Steadman, 'Chaste Muse and *Casta Juventus*: Milton, Minturno, and Scaliger on Inspiration and the Poet's Character', *Italica*, 40 (1963), 28–34.

36 Op. cit., p. 95. Cf. Riccius, p. 5^{v}, Ramus, op. cit., p. 161. In his *Erotemata in Decimam Eclogam*, sig. V^{v} Riccius draws the same moral but substitutes philosophy for poetry: 'By saying this without doubt he intended to signify only that love, the most powerful of emotions, can be, if not removed, at least assuaged, by excellent precepts drawn from the recondite and hidden points of philosophy.'

either to say or to do something against the decorum of their persons. For love is a violent fire with which as long as the mind burns, it can restrain itself only with difficulty from breaking bounds. So in this *Eclogue* is set forth the picture of a foolish lover [*stulti amatoris imago*] so that by looking at this picture we may learn to avoid all the occasions and enticements by which this fire is wont to be aroused.[37]

Omnia vincit Amor was a warning, not an affirmation.

For commentators like Vives and his English translator Lisle this was all far too literalistic. 'The matter itselfe and subject of this worke', they declared, 'doth plainly witnesse in sundry places, that it is not simply, but figuratively spoken, under a shadow: which makes me admire the more at *Servius Honoratus*, who will in this booke admit of no Allegories.'[38] The dig at Servius was doubly unfair, for not only *did* he admit of allegories, both in theory and in practice,[39] but he unwittingly provided Vives with the raw material for his figurative interpretation of the tenth *Eclogue* by identifying its subject as follows:

Cornelius Gallus, the first governor of Egypt . . . was originally a friend of Caeser Augustus; later, when he had come under suspicion of conspiring against Caesar, he was killed.[40]

In Vives' *Interpretatio in Bucolica Vergilii, Potissimum Allegorica* (1539) this brief biographical sketch was transformed into the 'Argument' of the entire poem:

Cornelius Gallus, (a man of most exquisite and dextrous witt, and an admirable Poet, after hee had been preferd to Augustus and rais'd by him to the government of Ægypt), was accus'd to Caeser, to have conspir'd, and to have attempted something contrary to his mind; for grief of which accusation, hee killed himselfe: This his death Virgil deplores under the title of Love.[41]

37 Melanchthon, sig. G8.

38 I quote from Lisle's translation, p. 11. Cf. Fleming's letter of dedication to his 1589 translation: 'The matter or drift of the poet is meere allegoricall, and carrieth another meaning than the litterall interpretation seemeth to afford' (sig. A2^{v}).

39 See, for instance, his comment on line 17 of Virgil's *Eclogue*, x: 'Allegorically this says: nor should you be ashamed to write pastoral poems' (p. 121).

40 Ed. cit., p. 118.

41 Lisle, p. 175, translating Vives, p. 34. Cf. Fleming's 'Argument': 'How this Gallus was an excellent poet, and so familiar with Caesar, and likewise so favoured of him, that he gave and bestowed upon him the government of Ægypt. Howbeit

Political rather than erotic entanglements were thus responsible for Gallus' downfall, and Virgil's real purpose in writing the elegy was to vindicate a brilliant young statesman whose career had been cut short by the slanderous accusations of his rivals and the gullibility of his emperor. The latter, cast somewhat disconcertingly as Lycoris,[42] had adopted Mark Antony as his new favourite, leaving the hapless governor of Egypt to meditate on the perils of high office.

According to this reading of the poem, then, the address to the nymphs was a rebuke to the Muses not for letting Gallus fall in love but for allowing him to be ensnared by affairs of state:

> These were the places of *Gallus* his retrait amongst the Muses, and to the study of sweete Poesie: wherein if hee had still retir'd himselfe . . . and had not aspired to the great Imployments, and Business of state, which caus'd his ruin, hee had still liv'd.[43]

Unfortunately, like his literal counterpart in Brinsley's commentary, he learned his lesson too late. 'I wish now', he lamented in Vives' paraphrase of lines 35–6, 'that I had continued my study, amongst my Books, and held mee to my private life, then I had proved learned like others; at least I might have had the happiness, to have been always in the company of Schollers and learned men.'[44] The love which had brought about his downfall, the love which Pan insisted could never be 'reconciled, or satisfied, with teares, and repentance'

afterwards growing in suspicion of conspiracie or treason against Caesar, he was slaine at his commandment' (p. 29). The disagreement as to whether Gallus 'killed himselfe' as Lisle believed or 'was slaine' as Fleming asserts seems to depend on whether the writer in question interprets Servius' *occisus est* as a passive or a reflexive verb. Melanchthon compromises by claiming that Gallus was ordered to kill himself (sig. G6^{r}).

42 Melanchthon, on the contrary, appears to cast Gallus as Lycoris and Caesar as Gallus: 'I think that secretly the discord which had arisen between Antony and Augustus is being lamented. For Gallus was very close to both' (sig. G6^{r}).

43 Lisle, p. 184, translating Vives, p. 34. Cf. Riccius, *Ecphrasis*: 'For I have no doubt that if Gallus had persevered in the study of poetry he would not have desired the friendship of the powerful to such an extent nor undertaken those affairs which brought him to his death' (sig. M8^{v}).

44 Lisle, pp. 187–8, translating Vives, p. 35^{v}. Cf. Melanchthon: 'This signifies that a private life is sweeter than the administration of the Republic' (sig. G6^{v}); Riccius: 'Would that I had stayed in studies of letters and in private life, or had been erudite . . .' (sig. N^{r}).

was the 'love of rule and dominion'.[45] *Omnia vincit amor* was still a warning, but it was a warning against the thirst for power—hence Riccius' rendering of this famous phrase in his *Ecphrasis Allegorica in Decimam Eclogam*: 'For nothing will be able to assuage this desire of Augustus's for ruling.'[46] As Melanchthon put it in one of his comparatively rare excursions into allegory, the hero of the tenth *Eclogue* was a 'memorable example of the kind of fortune one gets at court [*memorabile exemplum aulicae fortunae*]'.[47]

Seen in this context, as I believe it should be, *Lycidas* begins to look rather less conventional than most critics have taken it to be. Far from being just another pastoral hero who died young, Edward King emerges as the exact antithesis of Daphnis and Gallus, or, more precisely, of the Renaissance Daphnis and Gallus. Unlike both, he had remained chaste all his life, thereby earning the right, reserved for those who 'were not defiled with women', of participating at the marriage of the Lamb.[48] His only mistress was his Muse. Unlike Daphnis, moreover, he did not betray her. Even though she had proved to be as 'thankless' as the cruel and fair lady of the courtly tradition, he resisted the consolations of the nymphs. Amaryllis and Neaera were never able to make him break his vow 'to scorn delights, and live laborious days'. Unlike Gallus, on the other hand, he did not abandon his studies in order to pursue a political career. Nor was he even suspected of disloyalty to the master he *had* chosen to serve. The bark was 'perfidious', not Lycidas; he had 'meditated' his Maker no less 'strictly' than his Muse.

We might well conclude, then, that Daphnis and Gallus function in this poem in much the same way that Achilles and Ulysses function in *Paradise Lost*: as counterfigures, whose pagan imperfections define the Christian virtue of Milton's hero. But I believe that there may be rather more to the matter than that. For there is one final difference between Edward King and his

45 Lisle, p. 187, translating Vives, p. 35^{v}.

46 Op. cit., sig. N^{v}.

47 Op. cit., sig. G6^{r}. Only the first of Melanchthon's *Argumenta* treats the poem in allegorical terms. The remaining five are rigorously literal.

48 Revelation 14, 19. Not until he wrote the *Apology for Smectymnuus* in 1642 did Milton assume that St. John's words referred only to fornication, on the grounds that 'marriage must not be called a defilement'. In the *Epitaphium Damonis*, for example, Diodati is permitted to participate in 'the immortal marriage' of the Lamb because he 'did not taste the delight of the marriage bed' (lines 212 ff.).

two classical predecessors which totally transforms the significance of all the rest: his death was an accident. It simply could not be attributed, as theirs had been, to some fatal error on his part. He had neither sported in the shade nor striven in the field. On the contrary, he had obeyed all the rules which the protagonists of the *Idyl* and the *Eclogue* had broken, yet he had still been cut off 'ere his prime'. Hence the bitterness of Milton's criticism of his own version of the address to the nymphs: 'Ay me, I fondly dream! / Had ye been there—for what could that have done?' Hence, too, the ensuing allusion to Orpheus' solitary period of abstinence after the death of Eurydice. If a life of austere dedication to poetry was no guarantee of survival, if the 'blind Fury' was as powerful and remorseless as Venus and Caesar Augustus, then what *was* the point of sexual and political self-denial, what *did* it 'boot' to 'tend the homely slighted Shepherd's trade'? The contrasts we have noted between Daphnis and Gallus on the one hand and Edward King on the other could hardly have afforded Milton much comfort, then. They may have demonstrated King's superiority over his predecessors, but they must also have called into question the very standards by which that superiority was measured.

The literary context within which Milton lamented the death of his fellow student, I would like therefore to suggest, may have served to focus his anxieties not about the possibility of suffering the same fate himself, as Tillyard has proposed, but rather about the validity of the 'fugitive and cloistered virtue' advocated by the commentators on Theocritus and Virgil, and thus about the validity of the kind of life he himself had been leading since he had come down from Cambridge in 1632. Should this suggestion be accepted, the erotic elements in the poem—Venus' myrtle in the opening line, the rathe primrose which in an earlier draft died 'unwedded', suffering the pangs of 'uninjoyed love',[49] the myth of Alpheus and Arethusa—need no longer be dismissed, as they often have been, as extraneous or inappropriate. And the 'fresh Woods and Pastures new' of the last line, in addition to standing for Italy, or the broad expanses

[49] Cf. the reference in the *Elegia prima* to the *puer infelix* who 'must leave his joys untasted and is torn away from his love to perish lamentably' (lines 41–2). Milton seems to have been particularly sensitive to the pathos of 'uninjoyed love'.

of the epic, may symbolize the world of sexual and political engagement which lay beyond the confines of Horton. What I am suggesting, in short, is that *Lycidas* should be read *against* the tradition of the pastoral elegy, that it was written *contra* Theocritus' first *Idyl* and Virgil's tenth *Eclogue* as the Renaissance understood them. Five years later, at all events, Milton was doing precisely what the commentators on the two classical poems had insisted a poet should not be doing: embroiling himself in the dust and heat of politics and marriage.

Milton's Admirer, Du Moulin of Nîmes

E. E. DUNCAN-JONES

. . . he had need
All circumspection, and we now no less
Choice in our suffrage: for on whom we send
The weight of all and our last hope relies.

Paradise Lost, Book II.

IN his letter of 21 April 1659 to Jean Labadie, minister of the Protestant church of Orange in Languedoc, Milton sends cordial thanks to Labadie's friend Du Moulin of Nîmes who has procured him 'the goodwill of many good men in those parts by his kind words and most friendly commendation of me'. ('Maximam interim habeo gratiam Molinaeo vestro Nemausensi qui suis de me sermonibus et amicissima praedicatione, tot per ea loca bonorum virorum me in gratiam immisit.') Admitting that his writings—he refers to those against Salmasius—have brought him considerable reputation far and wide, whether because he did not shrink from the contest with so famous an adversary, or because of the interest of the subject, or because of the style of his composition, Milton turns to the reflection that 'the only real fame I have is the good opinion held of me by good men'. ('Sic tamen existimio me tantundem dumtaxat habere famae quantum habeo existimationis apud bonos.') Milton seems here to be speaking of something other than literary fame. As regards Du Moulin the implication seems to be that he is pre-eminently a good man and in a position to promote Milton's fame from more than knowledge of his writings.

Who was this paragon? From Masson onwards commentators have been communicative about Jean Labadie, the celebrated founder of a sect, but of his friend Du Moulin of Nîmes there is no convincing identification that I have seen; one of the candidates proposed was already dead when Milton wrote and none has any particular connection with Nîmes.

Yet there was in 1659 a Du Moulin most likely to have been a friend of the Protestant minister of Orange and also of Milton, who, in a sense uniquely, deserved the epithet 'Nemausensis', one whose services to the Protestants of that town no longer ago than January 1658 had made him celebrated certainly in Languedoc and probably in London, at any rate amongst those concerned, as Milton was, with the affairs of 'the foreign protestancy'. Seven years after Milton had written the letter mentioning Du Moulin, Philip Skippon, son of the Major-General, was travelling in France with his tutor John Ray and other English gentlemen. 'At night we arrived at the pomme rouge at Nismes and there found Monsieur du Moulin of Aberdeen who shew'd us a large testimony under the hands of the ministers, deacons and elders of the protestants in Nismes, signifying his kindness to them in O. Cromwell's time.'[1] The most eloquent account of the services rendered by Du Moulin to the Protestants of Nîmes in Cromwell's time is Clarendon's, written in exile at nearby Montpellier in 1671. To illustrate the truth that Cromwell's 'greatness at home' was only 'a shadow of the glory he had abroad' Clarendon gives two instances. The first is Cromwell's successful interposition with the Duke of Savoy after the slaughter kept famous by Milton's sonnet; the second, now generally forgotten, though it seemed to Clarendon 'yet greater and more incredible', concerns a 'sedition' at Nîmes in December 1657; and in this story Du Moulin, for whom Clarendon's term is 'one Moulins a Scotchman', plays an essential part. The trouble occurred during the election of magistrates. The accounts that I have seen differ. According to C. H. Firth,[2] it was not religious in origin, though the Protestants took part in it. All agree that it was serious, blood had been shed, and there was no doubt that Louis XIV would take the opportunity of putting down the Protestants, who in Nîmes outnumbered the Catholics. 'The Court', says Clarendon, 'was glad of the occasion, and resolved that this provocation . . . should warrant all kind of severity in that city . . . and a part of the army was forthwith ordered to march towards Nismes, to see this executed with the utmost rigour.

'Those of the religion in the town were quickly sensible into what condition they had brought themselves; and sent with

[1] 'An Account of a Journey through Part of the Low Countries, Germany, Italy and France by Philip Skippon Esquire', in A. and J. Churchill, *Collection of Voyages and Travels* (1734), vi. 724.

[2] *Last Years of the Protectorate*, ii. 20.

all possible submission to the magistrates to excuse themselves, and to impute what had been done to the rashness of particular men, who had no order for what they did. The magistrates answered, that they were glad they were sensible of their miscarriage; but they could say nothing upon the subject till the king's pleasure should be known; to whom they had sent a full relation of all that had passed. The other very well knew what the king's pleasure would be, and forthwith sent an express, one Moulins a Scotchman, who had lived many years in that place and in Montpelier, to Cromwell, to desire his protection and interposition. The express made so much haste, and found so good a reception the first hour he came, that Cromwell, after he had received the whole account, bade him refresh himself after so long a journey, and he would take such care of his business, that by the time he came to Paris he should find it despatched; and that night, sent away another messenger to his ambassador Lockhart; who, by the time Moulins came thither, had so far prevailed with the cardinal, that orders were sent to stop the troops which were upon their march towards Nismes; and within few days after, Moulins returned with a full pardon and amnesty from the king, under the great seal of France, so fully confirmed with all circumstances, that there was never farther mention made of it, but all things passed as if there had never been any such thing. So that nobody can wonder that his memory remains still in those parts and with those people in great veneration.'[3]

The earliest account of this episode is that given by Philip Skippon in his journal. Having the story from Du Moulin himself he of course can say more about the part played by the messenger sent to England. After describing the plight of the Huguenots of Nîmes in mid winter 1657–8 and their preparation for armed resistance to Mazarin's troops Skippon says, 'But some more considerate persons . . . at last resolved to send Dr. Moulins then at Nismes, into England, and acquaint the protector with it, and to desire his intercession with the court of France; so Dr Moulins immediately and privately rode away to Lyons in bitter snowy weather, and in eight days arrived in England, having first waited upon Lord Lockhart, the English ambassador, in Paris . . .

[3] *History of the Rebellion*, xv. 153–4.

'Dr. Moulins stay'd but a very short time at London, and then returned with secretary Thurlo's letter to the English ambassador and cardinal Mazarin; the postscript of the letter was written with the protector's own hand; the words were to this effect; As you shew kindness to the protestants so you have me your friend or your foe.

'Dr. Moulins upon his arrival at Paris, delivered the letter to the ambassador. Within a short time he attended on the ambassador to the cardinal's who read the letter, and then had some private conference with Lockhart; and then Moulins was called in, who heard the cardinal's promise to the ambassador, the protestants at Nismes should not be meddled with, and added Mr. Ambassador, you know France is not in a condition to deny England anything. Accordingly orders were sent express to stop the troops which were marching against Nismes, and within a day's march of the place when they received the order.'[4] The 'bitter snowy weather' in which Du Moulin (or Dr Moulins as he had become by 1666) made his hurried journey is stressed in Skippon's narrative. The scientific curiosity that he shared with his travelling companions John Ray and Martin Lister no doubt makes him record Du Moulin's communication of the strange effect of frostbite on the post-boy, and how it was cured. From this and other hints it is likely that Du Moulin had become a doctor of medicine. The weather that he had to struggle against was phenomenal. Evelyn records that in England it was 'the severest winter that man alive had known'.

Du Moulin's visit to England clearly took him into the company of Cromwell and Thurloe: probably also into that of Milton who as Latin secretary would have been called on to write the letter to Mazarin, unless the task was deputed to Marvell, then also working with Thurloe.

The arrival of the emissary post-haste from Nîmes, with the lives and property of many Protestants depending on the speed and success of his mission, must have made some stir amongst those like Milton and Marvell who spent much of their official time working for the well-being of Protestants abroad. In April of the same year, 1658, Marvell was furthering the attempts of one Kretschmer to collect money for twenty Protestant families

[4] Churchill, *Voyages and Travels*, vi. 733.

driven out of Bohemia.[5] (Kretschmer made his demands more acceptable by presenting them together with a printed paper of anagrams, a move which though discouraged by Samuel Hartlib, in fact delighted 'his highness and the whole court'. Were the anagrams that Marvell is said to have composed[6] also for the Protector's delectation?)

A little-regarded work, Gregorio Leti's Italian life of Cromwell, gives more details about Du Moulin. Before the events at Nîmes he must already have had dealings with at least the fringes of Cromwell's court and was quite possibly already known to Milton. Du Moulin had come to France as governor to Cromwell's sister's son, Nathaniel Desborough. In 1656, the year when Marvell took Cromwell's young ward William Dutton to the Protestant town of Saumur, Du Moulin took Cromwell's nephew, eldest son of 'the Lord Desborough', to the Protestant town of Nîmes. Du Moulin's tutorship gave him the chance to render a signal service to foreign Protestants, carrying through an action that might have made a subject for Dumas, had he known of it and had Protestant sympathies. If Marvell did anything comparable, the traces of it have not been found. All we know of his time at Saumur is that he showed about his copy of Milton's *Defensio Secunda* and that he impressed a disreputable Royalist remotely related to his pupil as infinitely cunning. If some political action of Marvell's underlies James Scudamore's description of him as 'a notable English Italo-Machavillian' rather than, as seems likely, an unsuccessful attempt of Scudamore's to borrow money from young Dutton, his wife's third cousin, foiled by a prudent tutor, we do not know what it was.

Gregorio Leti's[7] life of Cromwell, *Historia et memorie recondite alla vita di Oliviero Cromvele*, 2 vols., was published at Amsterdam in 1692, translated into French by J. le Pelletier, Amsterdam 1694, and German, Hamburg 1710. I have used the French, following the Italian at doubtful points.

5 *Works of the Honourable Robert Boyle* (1744), v. 274.

6 Samuel Parker, *A Reproof to the Rehearsal Transpos'd* (1673), p. 269: 'your juvenile Essays of Ballads, Poesies, Anagrams . . .'.

7 Leti, who was born in Milan in 1630 and died in Amsterdam in 1701, was a convert to Protestantism and a most prolific author. He spent many years in Switzerland and some in England, and was at one time historiographer to Charles II.

Leti is not thought a reliable author. Some things in his life of Cromwell, such as the tales of Cromwell's amour with Akaka Lambert and his being pistolled by Lucrezia Greinvil, lover of the beautiful Lord Francis Villiers, hardly bear the stamp of truth. But I see no reason to doubt his account of Du Moulin, nor his claim to have known Du Moulin well while they were at Geneva in 1661. What he says of Du Moulin's suitability for the dangerous enterprise of 1657–8 is of particular interest.

'There was at that time at Nismes' (I translate) 'a certain du Moulin, born in Scotland of a French father, a good Protestant; but his mother was Scottish, and one of the most zealous Puritans in all that kingdom: so they took great pains to bring up their son in the love and knowledge of the purest Calvinism. Having lost his parents while he was still young, and not having wherewithal to live on, as soon as he was twenty-six he resolved to seek employment. As he had long had a great wish to see France he was glad to accept the position of governor to a young nephew of the Protector's.' In the Italian Leti calls Du Moulin's pupil 'il nipote di sorella di Cromvel', 'Cromwell's nephew by the sister's side'. The surname of the youth Leti does not give, but there is no doubt that the eldest son of Cromwell's sister Jane and Major-General Desborough was at this time in France for his education, which was to prepare him to undertake foreign embassies.

'With this young man he went over to France in the month of March 1656. After they had travelled about they went to Nismes, resolved to spend a whole year there . . .

'The Protestants could not have found any one better suited to extricate them from their great danger. They were overjoyed to have found a man so fertile in devices' (the Italian has *intrigante*) 'as Du Moulin, one who combined great ability and knowledge with great prudence and judgement, a man in whom they had always found a great inclination to render service to the Protestant cause. He had indeed all the qualities to be wished for in the governor of a nephew of Cromwell's and that might ensure the success of the important transaction they were to entrust him with. I speak', says Leti, 'as having seen and known him well at Geneva (1660) where I often had occasion to converse with him during the months he spent there on the way back from a second journey in Italy with a young lord Saniam [St. John?].

'It was Du Moulin who first advised the Protestants of Nîmes to have recourse to Cromwell in their trouble. Cromwell alone had the power to avert the storm that menaced them. . . . The difficulty was how to inform Cromwell of the state of their affairs. To write to him would have been highly dangerous as would the sending of deputies. The zealous Du Moulin undertook the mission. . . . The better to conceal the object of his journey, as he did not lack resourcefulness, he pretended to be in dispute with his Merchant, who was a Protestant and one of the most important in Nismes, about some letter of exchange. He brought the matter before the judge, created a great stir and feigned great anger against the Merchant. He pretended that as he had not sufficient proofs to win his case he needed to go to London to make inquiries from some merchants there. So leaving behind him at Nismes the young lord to whom he was governor and travelling post, he made with all speed for London.

'The Protector who wanted nothing more than the chance to show his zeal towards the Protestants had no reluctance to receive the emissary whom the Protestants of Nismes had sent to him, as secretly as they could for fear of incurring the penalties laid down against those who asked help from foreign powers. The Protector sent him away as secretly as possible and charged him to assure those who had sent him that he was well-inclined to take their part and to protect them. As the matter was delicate for the Protestants and there were grounds to fear that in declaring himself too openly for them he might bring greater misfortunes on their head Cromwell thought it well to use great and powerful means which having no visible connection with his principal purpose were all the more likely to make it succeed.'[8]

Leti then gives the text of a Latin letter from Cromwell to Mazarin to be taken to him by one of Cromwell's most trusted 'Secretaires du Cabinet'. The name of this personage is given as Doste (Gualter Frost?). The letter is merely to introduce the bearer and to cover the message in Cromwell's own hand. 'I have just learnt of the revolt of the inhabitants of Nismes. I recommend to your Eminence the interests of the Protestants.'

[8] *La Vie d'Olivier Cromwel*, pp. 377–9.

The letter to Mazarin may be that which enclosed the Protector's message. Leti certainly at one time had access to English State documents and his life of Cromwell is peppered with Latin letters to heads of State. But if so the date is wrong, a year too early, December 1656.

Du Moulin's exploit of 1657–8 may have had a distant sequel. Leti mentions that when in the 1660s Du Moulin left Switzerland for France he was sent to the Bastille and kept there for nine months, for three of which he was incommunicado. Skippon was with him in Paris when the arrest was made. They were on the point of returning to England. 'After dinner, and just as . . . Dr. Moulins, Mr. Lister and myself were going out of our lodging . . . one of the French king's officers, a Captain de Guet, asked for monsieur Moulins . . . hurried him away in a sedan to the bastile. . . . Mr. Lister and myself staid a little longer in Paris: in which time we could not learn anything concerning the imprisonment of Dr. Moulins; only guesses were made that his chief crime was, he had lived too long among the French protestants in Languedoc; and that the French king suspected he might discover the present inclinations of that party after his arrival in England, he being very intimate with some of good quality that were discontented with the present manage of affairs in France.' It is at this point that Skippon tells the story of Nîmes and Cromwell in 1658.

From the Bastille Du Moulin sent a note to their lodging asking for some linen. 'Mr. Lister returned by the messenger a little billet which only condoled his misfortune, but the captain of the guard at the Bastile tore it in pieces. All this while we heard no crime laid to his charge. He was kept a prisoner at the king's charge and well dieted.

'After the city of London was burnt, the French king sent a courtier to Moulins, to acquaint him he should make any province in France his prison if he would give security of a great sum, which he said he was not able to give. . . . At last the king sent for him, and told him he had done him no wrong, and then bid him be gone out of France within a fortnight.' 'This relation', says Skippon, 'I had from Dr. Moulins after his coming into England.'

Leti mentions that some believed that Du Moulin had been imprisoned at the request of the English ambassador for having plotted against the Stuarts. If his Du Moulin is the same as the 'Monsieur du Moulin of Vevay' who in 1664 had saved the regicide Ludlow from three assassins and raised the town of Lausanne against them[9] the hostility of the English ambassador might be explained. It may also be significant that during the months of 1666 when Du Moulin was in the Bastille his former pupil Desborough was in the Tower: an agent of Arlington's, he was suspected of playing a double game in Holland.[10]

After Du Moulin's return to England nothing is certainly known of him. But there is a clue now to his Christian name, and to his first university: he would hardly have been made governor to Cromwell's nephew without academic credentials. I incline to adopt the suggestion of Charles Raven that the Dr Moulins whom Ray and Skippon, both of Trinity, Cambridge, met and travelled with in 1666 is the 'James Molins M.A. of Aberdeen' incorporated at Trinity in 1667.[11] There were several surgeons of this name practising in England under Charles II. One of them may be Milton's Molinaeus Nemausensis, the man who made 'Alone the dreadful voyage' and whose praises pleased Milton.

[9] E. Ludlow, *Memoirs*, ed. Firth, pp. 367–8.

[10] *DNB*.

[11] *John Ray Naturalist* (2nd edn., 1950), p. 137.

The End of the Big Names: Milton's Epic Catalogues

BARBARA EVERETT

> Argument is carried on oftener and more firmly by name than by notation.
>
> (*A Fuller Institution of the Art of Logic*, Columbia Milton, xi. 225)

> If . . . any name whatever can be so pleasing to God, why has he exhibited himself to us in the gospel without any proper name at all?
>
> (*Christian Doctrine*, Columbia Milton, xiv. 295)

WHEN a good poet writes adversely of another, his object may be not the other man's work but what Bacon might have called an *idol* of it. Ben Jonson's 'Would he had blotted a thousand', and 'For not keeping of accent he deserved hanging' do not sound like serious criticism of Shakespeare and Donne; they are loaded sentences aimed at current misconceptions of what the two men's genius really consisted in. The other Johnson's 'dull in a new way' and 'easy, vulgar and therefore disgusting' appear to take as their target an illusion in the reader more than the malpractice of the writer. What Gray and Milton had written would stay written; but readers' minds can always be cleared of cant. No writer seems more strongly to provoke others into this attempt to destroy *idols* (or more to create the idols) than does Milton—an interesting fact, in view of his career. And equally interesting is the fact that F. R. Leavis chose the word 'dislodgement' to describe Milton's case as he saw it, nearly fifty years ago now: for dislodgement is a thing that happens to idols. Leavis took as his point of reference certain of T. S. Eliot's poems, together with the occasional word that Eliot had let fall critically concerning Milton's 'magniloquence'. A few years later, in 1936, Eliot himself wrote the essay later reprinted as *Milton I*. It is often assumed that this is an attack to which the later *Milton II* provides a treacherous or reassuring counterpart of defence; but *Milton I* does something more useful than attack. Taking pains to advise the reader that criticism is neither 'iconoclasm' nor 'hoodlumism', the writer defines a current *idol* and does what he can about demolishing it. He does so through that style of all-but-formal irony which bring Eliot's criticism closest to his own later verse. For in this essay he considers the nature of Milton's greatness while stating explicitly (and always assuming implicitly) that it is at least as important for poetry to be *good* as it is for it to be *great*. Milton becomes the case of the 'great poet', all too attractive to a reader whose love of a good poem is replaced by the need for a great poem; who hungers for the *classic* in a bad sense, for the established, the authoritative. For such a reader, Milton is a mind whose funtion it is to emit large, oracular, and handy public statements.

Near the end of his essay Eliot displays the brilliant knack he had of nailing his theses to particular local points. He brings up the question of Milton's name-dropping: usually practised to gain 'the effect of magnificence', but now and again (Eliot suggests) so intemperate, so grotesque as to bring to the fore a real weakness in Milton's art. He quotes, as example, from that long catalogue in Book XI of *Paradise Lost,* which lists all the places revealed to Adam in his vision of future time, from

> Cambalu, seat of Cathaian khan,
> And Samarchand by Oxus, Temir's throne,
> To Pachin of Sinaean kings, and thence
> To Agra and Lahor of great mogul . . .

and all the way round the 'hemisphere of earth', ending with *El Dorado*. The list is long, the names impassive, the action static. We assume, says Eliot, that Milton really did want what we clearly want him to want: to be a very great, a very important public poet, a mouthpiece of philosophical and theological statement—a man, as we say, of weight. Therefore everything in his work that does not succeed in these aims, or even appear to attempt them, must be the equivalent to nonsense—mere style, mere 'music'. The conclusion that Eliot comes to is that *Cambalu* and the rest, being evidently not weighty, must be the alternative: 'mere levity . . . not serious poetry, not poetry fully occupied about its business, but rather a solemn game.'

Eliot's distinctive gift as a critic was economy of means in achieving largeness of ends: turning rapidly—however obliquely—to the most important issues and surrounding them with question-marks. For on to the smaller question of Milton's 'great names' he is here focusing, and wholly justifiably, the whole larger question of the poet's Grand Style: what he did with it, what we make of it. And meanwhile under this argument there are all the time moving even larger issues. By lightly and provocatively questioning the Grand Style as a self-justifying value, Eliot is also asking: Should we think a writer *good* because he is *great*? And (in any case) should we think a writer *great* because he is *grand*? And (in any case) should we call Milton *grand* because he merely names grand names? He raises the possibility that Milton is culpable of having first enforced these divisions of 'great' and 'good', 'meaning' and 'music'; and culpable too because a passage like the Book XI catalogue encourages us to connive with the poet in confusing a high-falutin meaninglessness with poetry.

Any reader who appreciates Milton's verse should be able to answer Eliot: to say why he finds this Book XI catalogue *good*, without having recourse to the word 'music', or its equivalent. And yet, despite the apparent increase in the sophisticated analysis of poetic language since Eliot published his essay, Milton's roll-calls still seem to induce a lapse of thought. In 1977 A. L. Rowse's *Milton the Puritan*, for instance, stated firmly:

> Really, it is a baroque poem, gorgeous in its magnificence when it chooses to be. . . . There . . . follows a roll-call of reverberating names, a regular feature contributing crystal and chalcedony and chrysoprase to the poetry. (If one may have such baroque splendour in verse, why not in church? But Milton was visually defective here, inhibited by his Puritanism).

There is curiously little distance between this and a work that one can take as characteristic of the whole late-Victorian approach to Miltonic style, Mackail's seventy-year-old (and not insensitive) *Springs of Helicon*, which lamented that old age, fatigue, and disillusionment should so have malformed the writing of Book X of *Paradise Lost*, and much after it: 'This is not the organ-music that we knew. What's become of all the gold? Has the golden oil ceased to flow into the lamp now that night is so deep? . . .' Mackail's tone was compassionate. Rowse perhaps does rather worse in imputing to the poet's whole career what must be either stupidity or dishonesty—Milton was 'inhibited by his Puritanism'. Rowse is using the word 'Puritanism' here in its common sense of 'hatred of the arts'—a usage that cannot be wisely applied to a man as signally aesthetic as Milton shows himself to be; but the error, and the illogic (or worse) imputed to Milton are both entailed by thinking of poetic style as semi-precious lumps of applied adornment. Similarly, Mackail's regret that *Paradise Regained* shows something like a stylistic death of the spirit depends on the assumption that the earlier writing was 'organ-music'—it was lovely, it was public, and it worked by starts and stops.

Eliot's grave allusions to Milton's *music* are a deference to and a provocation of that part of our mind and of the poet's audience at large that looks to his work for this kind of too-easy pleasure. The poet who on another occasion referred ironically to his own verse as 'a mug's game' (and who in Section III of *East Coker* was to imitate Milton at his darkest and most unworldly) called the Book XI catalogue a 'solemn game'. The challenge was clearly for someone to describe it better. But it is less clear that anyone has ever answered the challenge on Eliot's own terms, and made poetic *sense* of Milton's long, cold rigmarole. Eliot's point was taken up, only a few years after he wrote, by Sir Maurice Bowra's study of the literary epic, *From Virgil to Milton*. This stated that the Book XI catalogue could not possibly be a solemn game because Milton was there practising a formal device of epic: he was in this particular case indebted to the vision of the future in the tenth book of Camoens's *Lusiads*. But Bowra's scholarly point is less potent as a critical argument; for it is open to anyone to answer that an epic device is only an even solemner game. The argument hardly advances beyond a more sedate form of Rowse's 'It's-naughty-but-it's-nice' aestheticism. This distinction may seem in itself a mere game of words and terms. But it has to be remembered that Milton's epic was written at just that moment in time when mock-heroic was emerging as the new form: and some very nice literary points were turning on the fact that differences could be greater than resemblances. Milton's *Cambalu* passage has an individual quality that makes it quite different from the vision of the future in Camoens. It differs, probably, from most other epic catalogues; and certainly enough from (say) Homer's Catalogue of the Ships to have almost, though not quite, an ironic relationship with it. This personal quality, this differentiating predominance of what it is necessary to call style (though it is also dangerous to isolate that quality of style from substance)—this is so positive a factor as to undermine the idea that there can be a general style which we call 'epic form', and which can explain Milton's poetry.

Bowra turns, having dealt with Eliot, to examine another epic device, the simile: in particular, Milton's Book I comparison of fallen angels to autumn leaves in Vallombrosa. In doing so, he throws some incidental light on the use the poet makes of these 'great names'; for the cluster of names here both resembles and differs from the Book XI catalogue. Bowra finds in the image a *topos* which he traces back, very interestingly, through Marlowe and Tasso and Dante and Virgil to Bacchylides, a Greek poet of the fifth century BC, who imagined:

> the ghosts
> Of unlucky men by Cocytus' streams
> Like leaves that the wind flutters
> On Ida's glittering headlands
> Where the flocks graze.

Bowra concludes: Milton's 'Vallombrosa is exact as Bacchylides' Ida and has the immediacy of Greek poetry.' Again, the search for a classic ideal is clouding the difference between two poets. It is relevant, I think, that Bowra quotes of Milton only two and a half lines, which may seem to bring the later image closer to the lucidity of the far-distant Greek source; but the truncation radically alters Milton's image:

> His legions, angel forms, who lay entranced
> Thick as autumnal leaves that strew the brooks
> In Vallombrosa, where the Etrurian shades
> High overarched embower; or scattered sedge
> Afloat, when with fierce winds Orion armed
> Hath vexed the Red Sea coast, whose waves o'erthrew
> Busiris and his Memphian chivalry . . .

It is often difficult to tell where to start or finish a quotation from *Paradise Lost*, where every phrase, sentence, and paragraph can seem to intertwine within a great mesh of currents of energy that hold the whole poem from beginning to end. It is because *Vallombrosa* has its place on that great mesh or map of energy that it is *not* 'exact and immediate' and *not* like the Ida of Bacchylides—or any other place, in or out of any other poem. *Vallombrosa* is not a place, but an aspect of its own brilliant context, a shadowy meeting-place for legions, angels, leaves, winds, waves, and chivalry, for Hell and Heaven and the whole of Milton's poem. In this sense the name is what it declares, an actual 'Valley of Shadows'; and it is this aesthetic self-consciousness, perhaps, which most measures the distance between Milton and his Greek predecessor.

If such formalist descriptions as 'epic device' give only a limited insight into what Milton does with names, the same must be said of any scholarly treatment of the poem's substance which separates that from form. The forty-odd years since Eliot wrote his essay have seen a great expansion in theological and philosophical, and more recently historical and political, work on Milton: an interest reflected also in the concern for relevance to be found in the glosses of a good modern edition, or in the discussion of particular stylistic points. A critic will attempt to relate this or that epic simile with some grammatical firmness to this or that vehicle, or will display the local appropriateness of a given great name. This is a gain in clarity, common sense, and information. But the method often meets suggestive difficulties. It may be impossible to be convinced that (say) 'Jacob's ladder' or 'the careful ploughman' really does refer decidedly to this *or* that poetic actor, *or* would make better sense or better poetry if it did refer so decidedly. A similar problem arises when the names are considered as cases of the informational. In his Longman's edition of *Paradise Lost*, a splendid mine of information in its own right, Alastair Fowler tackles *Fontarabbia* and is driven very close to admitting that strictly speaking it almost doesn't exist:

> . . . all who since, baptized or infidel,
> Jousted in Aspramont or Montalban,
> Damasco or Marocco or Trebisond,

Or whom Biserta sent from Afric shore
When Charlemagne with all his peerage fell
By Fontarabbia . . .

The problems of *Fontarabbia* Professor Fowler sets out in a note which tells us that Fuenterrabbia was forty miles distant from Roncesvalles, where Roland fell; that though one Spanish author, Mariana, put the defeat of the French at Fuenterrabbia itself, '*There was no version in which Charlemagne fell*'; and wonders whether Milton may be contrasting the greater Charles with his own later monarch, who went to Fuenterrabbia in 1659 to engage in some ignoble diplomacy. This speculation of Fowler's provides a genuinely fascinating context for *Fontarabbia*; but it is a context which (like all scholarly contexts) defines the field of Milton's poem as shadow does light. That field can only be crossed by going to Fontarabbia through Milton's own directions. The meaning of the name is not in history or geography or other nations' myths or other men's poems; but in the repetitions and iterations and monotony of splendour. The lines have their climax in the dying fall of Charlemagne, followed by the greatness and the smallness of mockingly alliterated Fontarabbia: a good name for the romantic place, recalled with tenderness and harsh irony, where a battle was not fought for a king who did not die there. The context is the arrogant, dreaming mind of Satan, as he desperately calls up his legions to send them against a God bound to defeat them: a heroic gesture—as the names are beautiful—but with a heroism that always moves on the rapid current of the godly poem towards its proper end, the expulsion from Innocence. Thus, the echoing high polysyllables, Aspramont and Montalban (the dark mountain and the bright mountain), baptized or infidel, by recurrence converge to the purity and monotony of trumpet-blast, a note that by its emptiness holds enormous power of connotation: all courage, all romance, all arrogance, all delusion—the pastness of the dead past recalled in a voice of brass: *Fontarabbia*.

These effects are not best called 'musical': for the reason that we do not praise the B Minor Mass or *Così fan tutte* by calling them 'very musical'. Verbal art resembles music only in the purity with which it isolates and concentrates to obtain meaning, not in its absence of any meaning; and the music and the meaning of Milton's verse should only separate themselves out if we choose to define either term in a manner perversely contradictory of the other. That the will to affect the opinion of others ('meaning') and the need to enjoy private aesthetic pleasures ('music') are both of them intensely strong in Milton's mind, and perhaps so self-defining as to exist, each in some dislocation from the other—this is the possibility that Eliot raises; and it is clear that Milton does provoke in readers reactions that seem to be alternatives, to comment on the context *or* to enjoy the 'gorgeousness' *or* to do both, alternately. It can only be said in answer, if we consider the 'great names', that the Fontarabbia passage manifests an intense awareness of the possibilities of language that places Milton among the greatest verbal artists; but it is an awareness that goes well beyond the Tennysonian. It is perhaps an aftermath of the Victorian disease of mind that makes us call artists like Milton and Marvell 'Puritan', meaning 'haters of the arts', because they disbelieved in rule by bishop, and then makes us find them self-contradictory: when in fact their principles infuse and shape their art. Milton's *Vallombrosa* and *Fontarabbia* have an extreme beauty of form and association: each is like Othello's image of the world, 'one entire and perfect chrysolite'. But (like that same image) they carry with them always the distinctness of detachment: their elegant consistency is a self-judging quality. It is to the point that, though always described as of a Tennysonian musicality, occurring as a random and inevitable stylism, these great names in fact come in quite local clusters. To put the matter as briefly as possible, they come densely in the First Book, then with less frequency in the Second, Third, and Fourth; they disappear until the Ninth, when they return to describe the charms of the serpent; then disappear again until their 'positively last appearance' in the great catalogue of the Eleventh Book, where they reveal the fallen world to Adam. Where they occur, they have marked literary effect. Their *absence* from God's speech at the beginning of Book III, and from the Eden of Book IV, has an effect of an almost audible and visible simplification, even of purification; they re-enter only with Satan's re-entry into these books; and it is under the aegis of Satan's surveying consciousness that they colour our developing reaction to Paradise with that profounder, sadder, and therefore more penetrating complexity of nostalgia and doubt which 'Not that fair field / Of Enna . . .' and the rest so classically voices.

If we look briefly outside *Paradise Lost* there appears the same effect of artistic purposiveness in the use of these great names. Milton's first public poem in English, the 'Vacation Exercise', introduces

> kings and queens and heroes old
> Such as the wise Demodocus once told
> In solemn songs at King Alcinous' feast,
> While sad Ulysses' soul and all the rest
> Are held with his melodious harmony
> In willing chains and sweet captivity . . .

The traditional heroic art which the names attend seems to involve the hypnotic capacity to enslave: a 'sweet captivity'. If we turn to Milton's last works, *Samson Agonistes* has Dalila thinking with some complacency of becoming one of the 'famousest of women'; in *Paradise Regained*, the great names primarily grace the devil's temptations, though they also describe the disciples' bewilderment when they have lost Christ: so that they could be said finally to constitute that whole established 'public' culture, whose power to authorize Christ formally denies.

Though there is clearly artistic consciousness here, it is not necessary to ascribe to Milton some kind of special symbolic cleverness over names; for what is perceptible in his art is to some degree generic throughout the seventeenth century, which was a period that saw a great wearing-out—or casting-aside—of the great names. A moment's reflection on the functions of the Proper Name will not be irrelevant, particularly since Milton himself considers the topic theologically and philosophically in his prose writings. A name's virtue is its specificity. Like Dryden's style in Eliot's definition of it, it may not suggest much but 'it states immensely'. When an age or an individual loses the sense of distinction between proper names and common nouns, and personifies too much—like the late Augustans, say, or W. H. Auden—there is always a consequent sense of being culturally lost. But the reverse process can happen too, and any proper name may be appropriated into use as a common noun, or its specific knowledge may be borrowed for uncommon purposes. This is what is happening when Milton replaces Fuenterabbia by *Fontarabbia*, or when he removes *Vallombrosa* into a context that dissolves it into its valley and its shadows ('Shades/High overarched embower . . .'). Milton's use of names continually converts the denotative into the connotative. This might seem evidence of his egoism, that digests everything into the great private dream of his epic style, that 'sweet captivity'. If it is so, then all civilization shows traces of such egoism, continually converting names into History, and History into Myth. But in the course of time myths wear out or their uses grow corrupt; great names are found to be too far from any meaning they once had, or ought to have; the power retained by name or myth will seem tyrannical, irrational. The process is beautifully summarized in Shelley's sonnet 'Ozymandias'—the big name, the broken statue, the empty threat, the wide desert: 'My name is Ozymandias . . . Nothing beside remains.' During the seventeenth century a comparable process of thought produced the Civil Wars; in his *First Defence* Milton angrily orders his audience to stop thinking about 'the State of Grammar—of Words, to wit' and start thinking about the State of England; forget the name of King 'and for the future know that words are subordinate to things'. In more literary terms one could say that the decade which saw Charles capable of endowing one Captain Smith with the medieval order of 'Banneret' for retrieving his captured standard at Edgehill also saw Milton giving up his project of writing an *Arthuriad*. The name had died on him. A few decades later, Augustanism invents derisive games with names—'This *Flecknoe* found'; and even more cruelly, Pope will reduce names to noise—'Noise and Norton, brangling and Breval'.

It is not surprising that Milton, who lived through the major power-struggles of his time, should show in his verse continual reflection concerning the meaning and value of the 'great names', what one might call the 'words of power'. Few poets have displayed a more direct instinct to inherit the great names of their culture, its powers and its traditions; or a more rational and principled decision to reject them. Something of the changes and developments in Milton's style throughout his career seems to depend on this inheritance and this rejection: from—one could say—the appropriative heroics at their most magnificent in the early books of *Paradise Lost* to the potent abstentions of the closing books, most mysteriously beautiful in *Paradise Regained.* It is within this process of development that one should perhaps see the oddities of the Book XI catalogue of names in *Paradise Lost.* For the qualities which made Eliot find in it something like 'levity . . . a solemn game' surely do exist there, and need explaining: a coolness, a dryness, an impassivity; almost, one could say, a striking tone of tonelessness. The passage has a quality of unaccidental absence: absence of glamour, absence of energy, absence of commitment of any kind. And yet it is not 'bad': while we read it, it means a great deal. All these attributes, I think, derive in part from its context, and from its mixture of similarity and dissimilarity to the great names that occur earlier in *Paradise Lost.* To these it bears that relationship of near-irony always emerging in Milton's use of epic devices. The poetic use of names in Book I and after needs therefore to be momentarily recalled.

The invocation of Book I of *Paradise Lost* contains a scattering of lucid and quiet 'holy names'. But the real 'great names' begin where the action of the poem begins, after the colloquy of Satan and Beelzebub. After their speeches the vision of the poem moves backward in an almost cinematic panning to reveal the arch-fiend objectively, replacing the sympathetic inwardness of near-monologue with the cold externality of the physical. Seen thus Satan looms in a great cluster, indeed a sardonic overplus of nouns and epithets of scale, *long*, *large*, *many a rood*, *huge*, *monstrous*, *hugest*; and this gigantism flowers effortlessly into an excrescence of great names—

> As whom the fables name of monstrous size,
> Titanian, or Earth-born, that warred on Jove,
> Briareos and Typhon, whom the den
> By ancient Tarsus held, or that sea-beast
> Leviathan . . .

The virtue of the poem's insistent style—idiosyncratic from the beginning—is to create an isolating medium of the 'aesthetic' within which, in fact, ethical and even political points make their effect instantly. It could be said that, within the first two hundred lines of the poem, the great names form a code which converts the holy into the great, and the great into the big: from God to Leviathan in two easy lessons. *Scale* is the devil's spirit, a shining linguistic 'bad eminence'. This impression derives not merely from vocabulary, but from rhythm and syntax as well. For the big names enter to a significant rhythm, a paratactic sprawl towards simile: and that simile is the vexing story of the whale. Just as the poem's first great names are those of mere size, the giants on the earth (as its last great names are,

> whose great city Geryon's sons
> Call El Dorado

—the replacement of Paradise, a Golden City, named by a giant's sons)—so does its first great epic simile involve a whale, and concern delusion and bewilderment: it is the grotesque *size* of the whale, its 'unnatural' nature, which tricks and may destroy the unwary sailor. It is not insignificant, either, that the exact grammatical function of the simile creates dispute among commentators. For there begins here that splendidly energetic, large and licentious movement that characterizes the style of Milton's Hell—never precisely random, but always tending towards randomness. So original is the movement, so elusive the decorum that divides 'narrator' from 'actor' and 'actor' from 'poem' that these entities continually interpenetrate. Within that all-dominating Grand Style of the poem the meditative and yet heightened statements of commentary are scarcely distinguishable from the proud rhetoric of fallen angels. Thus, the great names do not merely succeed the description of the 'head uplift above the waves', they positively appear to emanate from it. To put the matter loosely: so closely does the aggrandizing fantasy of the images approach the nobly sick consciousness of Satan, it appears a form of it; the great names are 'Satan's dream'.

While we read, it is always possible to feel the opposite of that impression of sickness: to feel that the names introduce a disturbing but wonderfully refreshing breath of the real world elsewhere, as the whale-simile brings in a deeply touching memory of the absurd but living littleness of the real, the natural. But it is presumably this very response, this precise hunger for the 'real', which tugs Satan irresistibly towards the fourth book, to find created Paradise: to offer, 'Hell shall unfold / To entertain you two, her widest gates'. Just as the import of the whale-simile is that things are not remotely what they seem, so the great names, which seem to interrupt Hell with the real, can also seem a means whereby Hell reaches out and dissolves history and geography into the shadows of Satan's imagination. For the most imaginatively dazzling aspect of Milton's Hell is its voracious instability, instability that often undermines through the delusion of great names:

> His ponderous shield . . .
> Hung on his shoulders like the moon, whose orb
> Through optic glass the Tuscan artist views
> At evening from the top of Fesole . . .
> His spear, to equal which the tallest pine
> Hewn on Norwegian hills, to be the mast
> On some great ammiral, were but a wand . . .

The immense shield diminishes into the distant moon which shines close to the eye in Galileo's glass before retracting into Hell to join the spear, which extends to a pine which is hewn into a mast which is really a wand. Milton knows all the games of relativity which the Augustan Swift will later on play in *Gulliver's Travels*: no wonder Satan's steps are 'uneasy'. Tuscany and Norway, which seem to promise the security of the known —they are proper names—are appropriated into epithets and used for mere name-dropping, little more than footholds in the vertigo of 'greatness'. The poet does something similarly astonishing in the beautiful narrative of Mulciber's fortunate fall, accompanying him rhythmically on a shining descent through space and time—then dropping backwards out of it into a quite different dimension of truth:

> like a falling star
> On Lemnos, the Aegean isle: thus they relate,
> Erring.

The softness of the names is soporific, and the bald word *Erring* wakes us.

Mulciber is the architect of Pandaemonium, the palace of sound or the 'State of Grammar', and the remarkable description of its raising is in effect oddly close to the poet's own use of great names, the 'words of power':

> Anon out of the earth a fabric huge
> Rose like an exhalation, with the sound
> Of dulcet symphonies and voices sweet,
> Built like a temple . . .

Something with the apparent solidity of the world itself—physical, material, *real*—goes up like a meteor and dissolves into breath ('exhalation' includes these meanings); though built like a temple and accompanied by sweet sound, all it has is a spooky simulation of the holy. At the heart of its raising is a dreamy evocation of names that call up all the bad grandeur of history:

> Not Babilon,
> Nor great Alcairo such magnificence . . .

The description of Pandaemonium could be said to be somewhere between intoxication and nightmare. In this, it summarizes the first two books of *Paradise Lost*; and the great names have a vital part to play in this.

All the more striking is the contrast when Book III takes us out and up, through rapidly thinning names, to a nameless empyrean where God sits and speaks. The book's invocation shows something not unlike a negative way, a state where 'the bird / Sings darkling', and the true seer is blind. There is perhaps faintly adumbrated here that divine negation which emerges as a governing principle through Milton's later work, whereby goodness is '*not* to have sinn'd, *not* to have disobey'd', and to be '*un*wearied, *un*obnoxious to be pain'd': a denial of the world felt as intensely dramatic, from a mind so naturally physical. There is something of this divine negation in the first appearance of God. His first long speech has had few admirers. What appears here is not, perhaps, Milton's God but Milton's poem's God: for whom morality is a matter of what can be done with words. Eliot himself had something to say about Heaven's unfurnished apartments; but it is also true that this very emptiness, relatively, of God's mind has a distinctly healthful and astringent effect when it immediately succeeds the overcrowded, dizzying, and name-dropping consciousness of Milton's Hell:

> So will fall
> He and his faithless progeny: whose fault?
> Whose but his own?

Milton's God is not much worse than logical. His long and icy speech may be thought legalistic, and is so; but it is the pride of English common law to be independent of persons, including kings and other big names. By comparison with the fierce lawlessness of Hell, legalism takes on the white light of justice.

It is also, and very obviously, true, however, that that rich lawlessness has already undermined—and makes us feel that it has—our capacity to respond with full feeling to mere justice, in a failure that foreshadows the complex experience of fall. Milton scarcely meant his Heaven to be disappointing: but his inability to communicate it, or Paradise either, except through fallen language (*not* this, *not* that) is a motif of the poem. The sense of loss, by contrast, of the *price* of experience, is intrinsic to the pattern, as to the meaning, of his poem, and gives it its title. The whole epic is a lapse towards that grey, luminous daylight of the real into which Adam and Eve step in its last lines; the poem is, on its tragic side—and its origins are with tragedy—an enormous elegy. In a poem that depends as massively as does Milton's on sequentiality, on what becomes of things in time, Heaven is the reality that survives Satan's intoxicating illusions. This relation of the Third to the First and Second Books has some light to throw on the relation of the Book XI catalogue to what comes before it. Intrinsic to the great names of the first books of the poem, there is a perpetual excitement, a hope and promise of experience. By the end, this has been transmuted into disillusioning fact. Something of the blank hardness of the Book XI catalogue derives from the presence in this part of the poem of the sense of reality, conjunct with the sense of loss. Even the great world as yet undiscovered, the cities as yet unfounded, and the history as yet unwritten, are lost: fallen from the beginning. And we feel this all the more as we hear, in the great names, the unexpressive irony of the trumpet-calls, still sounding:

> His eye might there command wherever stood
> City of old and modern fame, the seat
> Of mightiest empire, from the destined walls
> Of Cambalu, seat of Cathaian khan,
> Or Samarchand by Oxus, Temir's throne,
> To Pachin of Sinaean kings . . .

The limits of Adam's vision here, while Michael shows him in dream and as from a high mountain all the world there is, lie at *El Dorado*: the illusory Golden City of the future, which will replace Eden, the innocence of the past. For it is at the end of this sequence of the poem that we have the extraordinary, painful, and yet magnificent vision of Paradise itself wrecking, going

> Down the great river to the opening gulf

to become only a bare island out at sea, echoing with the inarticulate cries of animals and birds.

The wreck of Paradise comes as the climax of that vision of History which is given to Adam. The landscape before him transmutes into a sequence, static but greyly luminous, of moments of time: the world as site of fratricide, as sick-bay, as battlefield, as ocean. These scenes from Old Testament history have a curious characteristic which the Longman's editor has pointed out: they entirely lack proper names—even Cain and Abel are nameless. This partly intensifies their timelessness. History, though a sequence of moments, is also something in perpetuity; civilization is no more and no less than the consciousness of falling, and the world is a landscape whose future is always frozen under the grey dawn of its past. But the absence of names has another effect. The vision from the mountain was all names, nothing but names—the scenes on the plain below are nameless; the two sequences take on a relationship, as of an antithetical pairing. The catalogue becomes almost the index to a book, and *explains* what follows; and Michael's role as Presenter increases this suggestion that the catalogue is explanatory prelude. As a result, Adam's objective scanning changes its nature and becomes a root act of conquest by knowledge—'His eye might there command'. Even the contemplative life is not free of the sins of the active. From this primal act of possession, however unwilled and dream-like, this instinct for what the catalogue names as 'glory', 'command', 'fame', there descend directly those horrors of fratricide, disease, and warfare that drown the world.

Adam's dream in effect revives Satan's dream; and it does so through the continuity of the great names. They are assisted by the peculiar time-scheme of the poem, that circling and spiralling timelessness-within-time which results from Milton's having subordinated his materials to an epic structure (and a grand style) in an act of possessive discipline like Adam's: so that we have the continual sensation of being *in mediis rebus.* In a way, nothing has happened since the beginning of the enormous poem: and the very bareness of the format of this late catalogue makes lines like

> Mombaza, and Quiloa, and Melind . . .

seem to be saying, 'Not again!' to be answered—

> (Morocco and Algiers and Tremisen)—

'again and again'. The difference lies in that bareness of format, that 'solemn game', whose very abstentions and withdrawals are signs of knowledge, of consciousness. At the end of the list, Michael tells Adam, 'Now ope thine eyes', but the names are open-eyed already. Being so, they have lost their power either to seduce or threaten. All the same, Adam's degree of guilt makes sense of the Quaker Ellwood's protest to Milton that he had shown in this poem only *Paradise lost*, not *Paradise found.* Only in his last poem does Milton conclude his struggle with the inherited powers of history, and outstand—as does his Christ—the end of the great names.

‘Full of Doubt I Stand’
The Final Implications of *Paradise Lost*

G. A. WILKES

‘*Paradise Lost* does not profoundly trouble, profoundly satisfy us, in the manner of great tragedy,’ wrote A. J. A. Waldock in 1947, ‘it cannot, because of that embedded ambiguity at the heart of it.’[1] This was the conclusion Waldock drew from Milton’s management of the fall, where the sympathy which the poem compels us to feel for Adam’s choice is fatally at odds with the thesis the poem is urging, so that in the upshot man’s ways are justified against God’s ways. The answer to Waldock that remains for me most persuasive consists in relating the episodes of the temptation and fall of man to the grand theme of *Paradise Lost*, the operation of Providence in bringing forth good from evil—which is at the same time to replace the structure which Addison, Waldock, and others have extracted from the twelve books of the poem, and called *Paradise Lost*, with the poem Milton actually wrote.[2] Waldock’s charges have also been answered indirectly by the critical movement away from regarding *Paradise Lost* simply in terms of ‘linear narrative’. Scholars like Isabel MacCaffrey and Jackson Cope have taught us to see it as also a ‘complex metaphor’,[3] a structure working through prolepsis, cross-reference, and parallelism so that not only the fall of the angels but the fall of man also has taken place before the narrative begins, in a cyclic pattern already on the way to redemption.

[1] *Paradise Lost and its Critics* (Cambridge University Press, Cambridge, 1947), p. 145.

[2] See G. A. Wilkes, *The Thesis of Paradise Lost* (Melbourne University Press, Melbourne, 1961).

[3] See Isabel Gamble MacCaffrey, *Paradise Lost as ‘Myth’* (Harvard University Press, Cambridge, Mass., 1959); Jackson I. Cope, *The Metaphoric Structure of Paradise Lost* (Johns Hopkins Press, Baltimore, 1962); Joseph H. Summers, *The Muse’s Method* (Harvard University Press, Cambridge, Mass., 1962); Michael Wilding, *Milton’s Paradise Lost* (Sydney University Press, Sydney, 1969).

Yet a misgiving remains. In a poem on this scale the major difficulty for the critic is to respond to it as a totality, to hold it all in the consciousness at once, and convey its import. While the 'metaphoric' or 'cyclic' view of *Paradise Lost* helps us to experience it as a unity, the interpretation it encourages is the one which Marjorie Nicolson reached by another route: '*Paradise Lost* . . . is not a tragedy but a divine comedy.'[4] So it is, in a sense, but does this really equate with our total experience of it? As a 'linear narrative', the poem shows Providence operating ineluctably to make the fall productive of the greater good of the incarnation and the redemption, making Satan advance its purposes while he believes he is subverting them, bringing

> Infinite goodness, grace and mercy shewn
> On Man by him seduc't, but on himself
> Treble confusion, wrauth and vengeance pourd.[5]

Again this is demonstrable from the text, but to what extent does it confirm our imaginative experience of *Paradise Lost*? The misgiving that remains, whichever standpoint we adopt, is that the positive movement of the poem—Providence working its counter-stroke, the fall becoming fortunate—is simply too theoretical, and leaves a fainter impression. The loss of paradise is powerfully brought home to us; the process of redemption and restoration may seem by contrast a mechanical victory. Words like 'scheme', pattern', and 'machinery' come naturally to mind, 'as though' (as J. B. Broadbent has put it) 'the cosmos were a factory'.[6] Has Milton criticism in recent years demolished the supports of Waldock's argument, only to confirm his conclusion—that '*Paradise Lost* does not profoundly trouble, profoundly satisfy us, in the manner of great tragedy'?

Acknowledging the difficulty, Professor Kermode has also proposed a brisk solution to it. These problems arise from regarding the redemptive scheme as central to the intention of *Paradise Lost*. 'There is, of course, such an intention or "scheme"; the mistake is to suppose that it is paramount. It is in fact

4 Marjorie Hope Nicolson, *John Milton* (Thames and Hudson, 1964), p. 322.

5 *Paradise Lost*, I. 218–20, in volume i of the *Poetical Works*, ed. Helen Darbishire (Clarendon Press, Oxford, 1952). All subsequent references are to this edition.

6 J. B. Broadbent, *Some Graver Subject* (Chatto and Windus, 1960), p. 283.

subsidiary.'[7] Professor Kermode's exposition of 'the less explicable theme of joy and woe' would command assent by its characteristic perceptiveness, only for the qualm that it seems again to offer a replacement of the poem Milton wrote—an improvement on it, perhaps, but a replacement none the less. *Paradise Lost* asserts unequivocally that the Providence of God envelops the evil in its path and works towards the day when 'over wrauth Grace shall abound' (XII. 478). This intention is paramount, and the question remains whether there is something amiss in Milton's execution of it in the events following the fall.

The critical defence of the later books, persuasive as it has been, is not especially apposite. The fall, in Milton's presentation, has been found to have both the dramatic interplay of Elizabethan tragedy and the psychological subtlety of a post-Jamesian novel. The transition to what follows is not now regarded with the same consternation as Addison felt at the minor change between Books XI and XII:

> To give my Opinion freely, I think that the exhibiting Part of the History of Mankind in Vision, and part in Narrative, is as if an History Painter should put in Colours one half of his Subject, and write down the remaining part of it. If *Milton's* Poem flags any-where, it is in this Narration, where in some places the Author has been so attentive to his Divinity, that he has neglected his Poetry.[8]

While an occasional limpness in the verse may not be denied, the more pictorial, discursive, and homiletic books have yet been shown to have their subtleties, just as the faltering process by which Adam and Eve move from recrimination to repentance sustains a psychological interest, if in a lower key. The 'weaker' impression made by the later books might then be ascribed to the constraints of a more intimate, domestic psychology, or else be seen as a casualty of the change in taste which has subjugated all other modes to the dramatic. Yet the 'weaker' impression lingers, and there is one defence of it still to be made. It is that what we interpret as 'weaker' is quite purposeful, and a key to the more disturbing vision that *Paradise Lost* is meant to offer.

7 Frank Kermode, *The Living Milton* (Routledge and Kegan Paul, 1960), p. 102.

8 'The Spectator', No. 369, in *The Spectator*, ed. David F. Bond (5 vols., Clarendon Press, 1965), iii. 386.

It is supremely difficult, as I have said, to grasp the final implications of a poem of this scale and complexity. But in the later books, as Providence pursues its invincible course, two other realities are gradually borne in upon us. The first is almost too obvious to need stating. Certainly the new Eden promised it to be superior to the Eden that has been lost, raising man (in the language of the *De Doctrina Christiana*) 'to a far more excellent state of grace and glory than that from which he had fallen' (I. xiv). But the realization of this paradise is outside the scheme of the poem. It is a promise, an assurance of an event that is far off, 'till fire purge all things new' (XI. 900). This holds whether *Paradise Lost* is seen as linear narrative or complex metaphor. If the action is circular, then the circle has not yet turned to the point at which the world is redeemed and Satan is finally defeated. This is an implication of the metaphoric structure, but not an actuality. It is a paramount concern of the poem to stress what the culmination of the process is to be, but it is far from Milton's intention to conclude, as Dante's *Paradiso* does conclude, with that blinding vision.

It is the fallen world that remains before us, its history refracted in the experience of fallen man. To him Michael describes the contest of 'supernal Grace' with 'sinfulness of Men' (XI. 360), until in the fulfilment of the Messianic prophecy, the second Adam comes to undo the sin of the first. The doctrine of the redemption is presented theologically in Michael's exposition of it, and dramatically in Adam's response:

> O goodness infinite, goodness immense!
> That all this good of evil shall produce,
> And evil turn to good; more wonderful
> Then that which by creation first brought forth
> Light out of darkness! full of doubt I stand,
> Whether I should repent me now of sin
> By mee done and occasiond, or rejoyce
> Much more, that much more good thereof shall spring,
> To God more glory, and more good will to Men
> From God, and over wrauth Grace shall abound.
>
> (XII. 469–78)

As Professor Martz demurs, 'can a hundred lines of hopeful

doctrine outweigh six hundred lines of visionary woe?'[9] The point is worth pursuing, except that the more telling aspect of Adam's response demands comment. For him—and therefore for the reader guided by his responses—the ultimate bliss is never envisaged as other than ultimate. Indeed the recurrent images in which it is presented—conflagration, military triumph, imperial figures on thrones of glory, miraculous renewal—seem to emphasize its remoteness, its impersonality. Unavoidably so, perhaps: and yet Adam never responds to the vision of bliss as Dante does at the end of the *Paradiso*, as almost a participant. The moment when the fallen Adam accepts Christ as his redeemer, and becomes the first Christian, offers an opportunity to render the doctrine in more human terms, but in fact this moment is not signalized in the poem, and some theological expertise may be needed to discern it.[10]

The remoteness of the second Eden does not seem to me another intractable feature of his material which Milton failed to subdue, but a reality which he is concerned to impress upon us. What he does see as relevant to fallen man has been austerely prescribed by God in Book III:

> To prayer, repentance, and obedience due,
> Though but endevord with sincere intent,
> Mine eare shall not be slow, mine eye not shut.
> And I will place within them as a guide
> My Umpire *Conscience*, whom if they will hear,
> Light after light well us'd they shall attain,
> And to the end persisting, safe arrive. (III. 191–7)

To this end the Comforter is sent in Book XII, and this is the purport of Michael's final advice to Adam:

> onely add
> Deeds to thy knowledge answerable, add Faith,
> Add Vertue, Patience, Temperance, add Love,
> By name to come calld Charitie, the soul
> Of all the rest: then wilt thou not be loath
> To leave this Paradise, but shalt possess
> A paradise within thee, happier farr. (XII. 581–7)

[9] Louis L. Martz, *The Paradise Within* (Yale University Press, New Haven and London, 1964), p. 163.

[10] See C. A. Patrides, *Milton and the Christian Tradition* (Clarendon Press, Oxford, 1966), p. 127.

This daunting series of injunctions gives the paradise within a certain remoteness too. The immediate recourse of fallen man is to 'prayer, observance, discipline, thought and action', and the Eliot contemplating that possibility in *Four Quartets* is close to Milton's vision: 'For us, there is only the trying'.[11] It would be a misreading to assume that Milton has somehow lost his grip on the redemptive pattern which Providence has ordained. The truth is that the poem is delineating the distinctive way in which it figures in Milton's mind.

I may define its uncompromising quality more exactly by describing the second major impression which the later books convey. It is true—and nothing in *Paradise Lost* impugns this—that 'supernal Grace' will be finally victorious, and that mankind in the interim has the individual solace of the 'paradise within'. But at the same time as Books X to XII are showing the reclamation of Adam and Eve by prevenient Grace, and tracing the larger process by which the promised seed will all restore, this account of the undoing of the effects of the fall is remorselessly demonstrating another truth: that the fall itself is irreversible. The moving forward leaves the garden ever father behind, and presents it in ever more unattainable terms. Just as the opal towers and sapphire battlements glimpsed by Satan on his journey through chaos showed how achingly remote was now his 'native Seat' (II. 1050), so the beauty and fecundity of Eden become more intense in retrospect, as we look back on Books IV and V from the bleakness of Books XI and XII, from the standpoint of the fallen world. Eve's response to the loveliness of the garden is more acute because she knows it is now forfeit:

> Must I thus leave thee Paradise? thus leave
> Thee Native Soile, these happie Walks and Shades,
> Fit haunt of Gods? where I had hope to spend,
> Quiet though sad, the respit of that day
> That must be mortal to us both. O flours,
> That never will in other Climat grow,
> My early visitation, and my last
> At Eev'n, which I bred up with tender hand
> From the first op'ning bud, and gave ye Names,
> Who now shall reare ye to the Sun, or ranke

[11] The quotations are from *The Dry Salvages* and *East Coker*.

Your Tribes, and water from th'ambrosial Fount?
Thee lastly nuptial Bowre, by mee adornd
With what to sight or smell was sweet; from thee
How shall I part, and whither wander down
Into a lower World, to this obscure
And wilde, how shall we breathe in other Aire
Less pure, accustomd to immortal Fruits?
(xi. 269–85)

This movingly human plaint, for the flowers that 'never will in other Climat grow', shows the aspect in which the fall is irrevocable. The Eden that Adam and Eve have lost will be replaced by something else, which is better. But it can never be replaced by itself: that perfection they can never have again.

There is an unflinching quality in *Paradise Lost* that relates it to that other great work of its century, *King Lear*. There is a refusal to repose in easy solutions, to allow things to seem as other than they are. Adam finds, as Lear found, that choices once made cannot be cancelled; that errors may be forgiven, but the original situation cannot then be recovered unimpaired. If the theology of *Paradise Lost* is translated into human experience, these are among the truths it enforces. Because its teaching is presented in the form of 'myth', Milton's God becomes the figure who seems to legislate in this way, and there is a testimony to the central grimness of the poem in the desire of critics for a cosier God than Milton has provided. The grimness remains, as it remains in *King Lear*, from a refusal to evade the realities of life as we know it, from an insistence on confronting the facts.

If *Paradise Lost* does not profoundly trouble us, in the manner of great tragedy, then we have not attended to what it is saying. This is not to subtract from the paramouncy of the theme of good being produced from evil, but it is to define it more exactly. The 'World restor'd' is promised, but deferred; a state of greater felicity, it will not give the first Eden back again; the 'paradise within' will be the reward of no fugitive and cloistered virtue. 'Then wilt thou not be loath To leave this Paradise', Michael claims, but this is a moment that never comes. The last events of the poem are the banishment and the mounting of the fiery guard, as

They looking back, all th' Eastern side beheld
Of Paradise, so late thir happie seat,

and the concluding lines catch exquisitely the mingled resolution and wistfulness of the human pair. While the world lies before them, with Providence their guide, the 'wandring steps and slow' mark their lingering departure, and the image 'hand in hand',[12] acknowledging the responsibility of the future, is retrospective too. When Satan had first seen Adam and Eve in Book IV, then

> hand in hand they passd, the lovliest pair
> That ever since in loves imbraces met,
>
> (IV. 321–2)

and when in Book IX Eve had prevailed on Adam to let her garden alone, then

> from her Husbands hand her hand
> Soft she withdrew, and like a Wood-Nymph light . . .
> Betook her to the Groves.
>
> (IX. 385–8)

In their exile they join their hands again, and while 'restore' may be the last word spoken in the poem, the last epithet is 'solitarie':

> Som natural tears they dropd, but wip'd them soon;
> The World was all before them, where to choose
> Thir place of rest, and Providence thir guide:
> They hand in hand with wandring steps and slow,
> Through *Eden* took thir solitarie way.

[12] This has of course been noticed before, but not quite in the configuration I suggest.

Dryden's Sigismonda

EMRYS JONES

DRYDEN often aspired to the heroic; he seldom achieved it. Or if he did achieve it, the result was perhaps not exactly what he intended—it was likely to be mixed with other elements, not quite mock-heroic but not fully heroic either. An undoubted success in this vein takes the form of a story from the *Decameron* which, by a fine inspiration, Dryden adapted for *Fables Ancient and Modern* at the end of his career. All three of his Boccaccio adaptations were successful, but 'Sigismonda and Guiscardo' drew from him a peculiarly strong and rich response. It keeps closely to the lines of Boccaccio's story, yet it is more than a translation: it reads as a fully Drydenian poem, quite as revealing of its author as many of his more obviously original works. I want to suggest that, in order to account for Dryden's achievement here, we need to bring together two strains of his literary personality which are too often thought of in isolation: an aspiration to the noble and magnanimous on the one hand, and on the other a frank, and to many readers disconcerting, delight in coarseness and indecency. Without the presence of the second 'low' strain, he could not (or so I shall argue) have so securely brought off his splendid performance in the higher style.

But first I had better recall the outlines of the story as told by Boccaccio. It follows a familiar pattern. Tancredi, Prince of Salerno, loves his daughter with a dangerous possessiveness. She, Ghismonda, is as strong-willed as himself and, early widowed, decides to take a lover from among her father's court. She selects the low-born Guiscardo, and they meet repeatedly in secret. One day Tancredi, who has free access to his daughter's bedchamber, enters alone and falls asleep behind a curtain near her bed. He wakes suddenly and, to his horror, finds himself compelled to witness a love scene. He keeps silent, but decides on revenge. Next day he confronts his daughter with his knowledge of her lover. Seeing that

Guiscardo is to die, she scorns evasion and defends herself in a long, forcefully argued, and completely impenitent speech. Her father's revenge follows promptly. He sends her a gold chalice containing her lover's heart. Ghismonda's self-control, however, never wavers. She carries out her own formal ceremony of mourning: she fills the chalice with tears, silently shed; drinks poison; and calmly awaits death. Tancredi arrives just in time to receive her final stern reproach together with her command that she and Guiscardo should be honourably buried together.

The story was, it seems, one of the most popular of Boccaccio's tales until at least the early nineteenth century.[1] It belongs to the 'wilful love punished' formula, like Boccaccio's tale of Isabella, which Keats adapted, and like the story of the Duchess of Malfi. But in Boccaccio's telling the story of Sigismonda, as Dryden called her, has some special features which probably made a strong appeal to him and helped to decide his choice of subject.

The first is the means whereby Guiscardo gains access to Sigismonda. She is at first perplexed as to how they can arrange to meet in secret. But inspired by love (or Love, as Boccaccio has it), she remembers what her father himself once told her—that there was a secret subterranean passage through the hill on which the palace stood; it led to a staircase which connected to her own apartment. Its far end issued in the bottom of a shaft, whose upper entry was hidden by briars and thorns. It was through this difficult passage that Guiscardo, instructed by Sigismonda, was to force his way. He duly provides himself with a rope-ladder to descend the shaft and puts on a suit of leather to protect himself against the thorns.

The oddly circumstantial nature of this description gives the narrative at this point a special degree of heightening and pressure. What enforces the attention is the physicality of Guiscardo's ordeal, if it can be called that. And the ordeal is given precise definition by the tough leather suit he wears whenever he is making a rendezvous with his mistress.[2]

[1] H. G. Wright, *Boccaccio in England from Chaucer to Tennyson* (1957), pp. 265–77, 318–36, 407–14.

[2] For a detailed interpretation, see Guido Almansi, *The Writer as Liar. Narrative Technique in the 'Decameron'* (1975), pp. 133–57.

The second feature which distinguishes the tale is the way Sigismonda receives the news that her father has discovered her secret and is determined to punish both her lover and herself. She responds in the form of an exceptionally long, logically ordered, lucid, and forceful speech—an oration, in fact—in which point by point she replies to all her father's accusations and, more than that, goes beyond them to justify her conduct, making no concessions of any kind. It is a frankly rhetorical set-piece, powerfully rational in its marshalling of arguments, but moving in its fearlessness and magnanimity. It made an obvious appeal to Dryden, the expert in versified argument.

The third feature arises out of the second. It is, quite simply, the character of Sigismonda. Unlike the corresponding figure in the stories of Isabella and the Duchess of Malfi, Sigismonda does not merely helplessly suffer. On the contrary, she takes the initiative in the early stages of the love affair (in this at least, like the Duchess of Malfi), and in face of her father's fury is masculinely defiant. (It is Tancredi, in Boccaccio's version, who breaks down and weeps like a child.) But though strong-willed, she is far from unalloyed strength and self-sufficiency. The most telling of the arguments with which she justifies her taking a lover is an appeal to her human susceptibility and frailty: 'You are made of flesh and blood, Tancredi, and it should have been obvious to you that the daughter you fathered was also made of flesh and blood, and not of stone and iron. Although you are now an old man, you should have remembered, indeed you should still remember, the nature and power of the laws of youth.' She reiterates the point: 'As I have said, since you were the person who fathered me, I am made of flesh and blood like yourself. Moreover, I am still a young woman. And for both of these reasons, I am full of amorous longings, intensified beyond belief by my marriage, which enabled me to discover the marvellous joy that comes from their fulfilment. As I was incapable of resisting these forces, I made up my mind, being a woman in the prime of life, to follow the path along which they were leading, and I fell in love.'[3] Sigismonda may be sexually susceptible and to that extent weak, but the weakness is itself sanctioned by Nature. As Guiscardo had put it a little

[3] English quotations from *The Decameron*, trans. G. H. McWilliam (Harmondsworth, 1972), p. 337.

earlier, when captured and brought bound before Tancredi: 'Neither you nor I can resist the power of Love.' Boccaccio's powerful endorsement of this appeal to Nature was one with which Dryden could feel a deep sympathy.

Dryden introduced several changes to Boccaccio's story. Guiscardo's social rank was so low ('a young valet of her father's . . . of exceedingly humble birth') as to call attention to Sigismonda's rashness in choosing him. Dryden makes him 'of gentle blood', though 'far below her high estate', once a page to Tancred and now his squire. The change to some extent weakens the force of Tancred's social arguments against him, though also, no doubt, for Dryden's readers, increases sympathy for the lovers. His second chief change was to have the lovers marry before consummating their love. Something of Boccaccio's radical boldness was sacrificed, but again with a gain in sympathy for the lovers, and especially for Sigismonda. In making this change, however, Dryden added a long passage which constitutes his chief departure from Boccaccio and is important for the way it modifies the character of the whole poem. As it is also crucial to my argument, I shall return to it.

These narrative changes were far-reaching enough, but in converting a prose tale into a poem in heroic couplets Dryden reshaped, reorchestrated, and fundamentally reimagined it so that finally every detail was transformed. While keeping close to the fourteenth-century narrative, he also modernized it, giving it a collocation of qualities which makes it at once recognizable as a poem of the late seventeenth century. In a word he 'regularized' it; he imbued it with the proportions and rhythms consonant with the aesthetic assumptions of his time. In Dryden's version, everything is bolder than in Boccaccio, and bolder in a more 'regular' way; the diction more sonorous, the rhetorical figuration more squarely given to antithesis and balance. Dryden's entire stylistic system is more histrionically rhetorical than Boccaccio's, more external, more of a performance. We *watch* the performers going through their motions and emotions, with their postures and gestures dictated by those current baroque principles whereby outward signs dynamically enact inner states. So, halfway through the poem, Sigsmionda faces her father: 'with dry Eyes, and with an open

Look / She met his Glance midway.'[4] The eye-contact has more dramatic impact than the corresponding place in Boccaccio. So too at the end, she 'clos'd her Sight, / And quiet, sought the Covert of the Night'. And even during her father's last visit she 'sternly' repels him: 'excluding Day, her Eyes / Kept firmly seal'd'—a detail not in Boccaccio. Lying on her death-bed, the world and light itself shut out, she recalls a posture familiar in baroque statuary (for example Bernini's Blessed Lodovica Albertoni, stretched flat on her pillows), and the calm in which she dies is an animated baroque calm, achieved only by the strenuous exertion of will.

At the same time, certain of Boccaccio's effects were beyond Dryden's range. Boccaccio's Tancredi bottles up his horror and rage while forced to witness the scene on his daughter's bed. When the lovers have finally left, he too takes his exit—not through the door, however, but by climbing out through the window and down into the garden. The action, so eccentric in a man of his age and rank, declares his inner turmoil; but it makes its point too abruptly and obliquely for Dryden to be able to make use of it in his psychologically more conventional system.

The regularizing expectations of Dryden's time found their most forceful expression in the Augustan heroic couplet which, more than anyone else, he himself had established as the verse norm. Its effect is particularly obtrusive in narrative poetry, where its insistent point-making almost competes with the more irregular claims of the narrative. In 'Sigismonda and Guiscardo', therefore, we are given simultaneously the pleasure of narrative and the pleasure of intensely pointed verse rhetoric; the larger gratifications of the story and the immediate stimulus of the couplet. The opening paragraph shows this dual effect very clearly:

While *Norman Tancred* in Salerno reign'd,
The title of a Gracious Prince he gain'd;
Till turn'd a Tyrant in his latter Days,
He lost the Lustre of his former Praise;
And from the bright Meridian where he stood,
Descending, dipp'd his Hands in Lovers Blood.

[4] Dryden quotations from *The Poems and Fables of John Dryden*, ed. James Kinsley (Oxford, 1958).

We absorb the personal details but are also made to imagine a kind of regular arc: Tancred, like the sun, reaches his 'bright Meridian' before setting in blood. Insistently, throughout the poem, the couplet rhetoric encourages this regularizing expectation. In so modernizing Boccaccio, Dryden no doubt felt (as he did with Chaucer) that he was endowing him with a more finished, because more regular, form, rounding out his expressions and so perfecting them.

Dryden's desire for regular form shows not only in his couplets and verse paragraphs but in the larger organization of the poem. His story of Sigismonda makes an extremely satisfying aesthetic impression. When we look for the source of our satisfaction, we find, I think, that the tale falls into two perfectly balanced parts. The division is not overtly insisted on, but seems to occur naturally as a result of what happens in the narrative. The first part tells of the happy secret love of Sigismonda and Guiscardo; the second part tells of their death. But an analysis in those terms would not in itself bring out what Dryden saw in their story; it would fail to specify how he imagined it and why he was excited and moved by it. To do that, we need to recall the precise contents of each of the two parts.

In the first, we are told how Sigismonda, a young widow, seeks a lover and finds him; how she discovers a way by which they can meet in secret (the overgrown shaft, the underground passage); and how they love each other insatiably. In the second, Tancred puts an end to their happiness, and Sigismonda justifies herself in her resoundingly rational oration. Later, on receiving the gift of Guiscardo's heart, she ceremoniously mourns him and, without wavering, arranges her own death. We can put it more summarily as follows: in the first part she succumbs to the needs of her body; in the second she meets the demands of her mind. It is in such terms as these—first physical, then mental or spiritual—that Dryden seems to have conceived his subject.

This dualistic conception helps to explain a feature of the poem which readers in the past have often disliked—Dryden's unabashed insistence on the physical aspect of the lovers' relationship. Sigismonda especially is shown to be a creature of almost gross appetitiveness. But in the central transitional couplet of the poem, a hinge-moment when she sees in a flash that her happiness is over, she changes at once from a woman of uninhibited sensuality to one of Heroic Mind. No longer sexually motivated, she is now sublimely rational, caring nothing for the body's pleasures or pains. The transitional couplet is this:

> The *Heroine* assum'd the Woman's Place,
> Confirm'd her Mind, and fortifi'd her Face . . .
> (376–7)

—which comes almost exactly half-way in this poem of 757 lines.[5] (Apart from names, '*Heroine*' is the only italicized word in the poem.) Her great speech of self-justification follows at once:

> *Tancred*, I neither am dispos'd to make
> Request for Life, nor offer'd Life to take:
> Much less deny the Deed; but least of all
> Beneath pretended Justice weakly fall.
> My Words to sacred Truth shall be confin'd,
> My Deeds shall show the Greatness of my Mind . . .

The impression she now makes is one of overwhelming mental power and spiritual nobility; and the phrase she has just used is pointedly repeated when she has finished speaking, no other phrase in the poem receiving emphasis in this way:

> She said: Nor did her Father fail to find
> In all she spoke, the Greatness of her Mind.

Her new tone of formidable exaltation is maintained to the end, at its most superbly elevated at the moment when she receives the gold cup:

> Or not amaz'd, or hiding her Surprize,
> She sternly on the Bearer fix'd her Eyes:
> Then thus: Tell *Tancred*, on his Daughter's part,
> The Gold, though precious, equals not the Heart:
> But he did well to give his Best; and I,
> Who wish'd a worthier Urn, forgive his Poverty.

In this large structural body–mind antithesis, Dryden follows Boccaccio, except that Boccaccio is altogether less explicit.

[5] The poem can be further subdivided into four parts, with Sigismonda's speech constituting the third part. The first two parts are almost equal in number of lines (194, 195); the third part (Sigismonda's speech) is 192 lines; the remainder of the poem falls short, with 176 lines.

Boccaccio's description of the concealed shaft and passage are certainly erotically suggestive, as Guido Almansi has argued; and Dryden undoubtedly understood Boccaccio's symbolism (as lines 181–4 show). But Boccaccio does not press the other half of the antithesis—he does not insist, as Dryden does, on the greatness of Ghismonda's mind. Indeed it is possible that Boccaccio did not consciously intend any such contrast. He is certainly less explicit than Dryden on the physical aspect of his heroine's love, and describes it briefly in general terms: 'After giving each other a rapturous greeting, they made their way into her chamber, where they spent a goodly portion of the day in transports of bliss.' In place of this sentence, as we have seen, Dryden substituted a much longer passage, which is so different in style from the rest of the poem that it needs special consideration. Since his lovers are to be married before they retire, Dryden supplies a priest:

> The conscious Priest, who was suborn'd before,
> Stood ready posted at the Postern-door;
> The Maids in distant Rooms were sent to rest,
> And nothing wanted but th'invited Guest.
> He came, and knocking thrice, without delay,
> The longing Lady heard, and turn'd the Key;
> At once invaded him with all her Charms,
> And the first Step he made, was in her Arms:
> The Leathern Out-side, boistrous as it was,
> Gave way, and bent beneath her strict Embrace:
> On either Side the Kisses flew so thick,
> That neither he nor she had Breath to speak.
> The holy Man, amaz'd at what he saw,
> Made haste to sanctifie the Bliss by Law;
> And mutter'd fast the Matrimony o're,
> For fear committed Sin should get before.
> His Work perform'd, he left the Pair alone,
> Because he knew he could not go too soon;
> His Presence odious, when his Task was done.
> What Thoughts he had, beseems not me to say;
> Though some surmise he went to fast and pray,
> And needed both, to drive the tempting Thoughts away.

And the next paragraph begins: 'The Foe once gone, they took their full Delight.'

This passage is not quite the leering intrusion which a whole tradition of criticism has made of it. Although Wordsworth admired the poem as a whole and thought it 'noble', he was clear that it had 'very gross defects': 'I think Dryden has much injured the story by the marriage, and degraded Sigismonda's character by it. He has . . . degraded her still more, by making her love absolute sensuality and appetite, (Dryden had no other notion of the passion).'[6] A century later, Mark Van Doren, though uncensorious, substantially agreed: 'we see a secret bride and groom somewhat brutally enjoy each other.'[7] And in his admirably forthright attack on Dryden as a poet, C. S. Lewis singled out this poem and this passage for his most contemptuous treatment: 'I will not quote the pitiful lines in which Dryden winks and titters to his readers over these time-honoured salacities.'[8]

The first thing to be said about this passage is that it is not an indefensibly inartistic digression, a mere lapse into Restoration crudity, but an essential part of Dryden's conception of his subject. Its function is to dramatize Sigismonda's passionate physical nature, and so help to establish the body–mind antithesis on which the whole poem turns. Without it, the poem would have been lacking in structural equilibrium, a quality for which Dryden—with his sense of aesthetic regularity, which is at one with a sense of realism—was striving throughout.

But this passage is not, anyway, a drop into poor writing, to be deplored and passed over as quickly as possible. It is quite as well written as any part of the poem. Its erotic effects are especially nervous and acute, for Dryden lightened his style so as to catch the quick movements of a lover's sensations and feelings:

> He came, and knocking thrice, without delay,
> The longing lady heard, and turn'd the Key . . .

The syntactical solecism ('knocking thrice . . . The longing lady heard') is boldly carried off—she almost performs the action for him, pushing him from his place as subject of the sentence

6 Letter to Scott, 7 Nov. 1805; quoted in *Dryden: The Critical Heritage*, ed. James Kinsley and Helen Kinsley (1971), p. 324.

7 *The Poetry of John Dryden* (New York, 1920; 1946 edn.), p. 229.

8 'Shelley, Dryden, and Mr. Eliot', in *Rehabilitations and Other Essays* (1939); and in *Selected Literary Essays*, ed. Walter Hooper (Cambridge, 1969), p. 192.

('longing' chiming with 'knocking', as if in eager anticipation). Then Sigismonda

> At once invaded him with all her Charms,
> And the first Step he made, was in her Arms . . .

Lewis derisively compared Dryden's 'lascivious widow' with Sterne's Widow Wadman; but an apter comparison would be with Ovid's water-nymph Salmacis, whose sensuality is of the same order as Sigismonda's:

> And now she fasten on him, as he swims,
> And holds him close, and wraps about his limbs.[9]

The difference is that, unlike Hermaphroditus, Guiscardo is not in the least unwilling. Nor does the couplet that comes later—

> On either Side the Kisses flew so thick,
> That neither he nor she had Breath to speak

—show (as Lewis thought) that 'even Dryden's skill in language deserts him'. This is a studied stylistic lowering, comic certainly, in suggesting that there are certain activities which words are ill-suited to cope with, but hardly evidence of loss of control.

Dryden's imaginative involvement in this wedding episode is shown throughout by the way he pays it the tribute of humour. The priest, first 'suborn'd', and then made by his lingering presence an involuntary 'Foe', may be Dryden's concession to the proprieties, and an ambiguous one, but he is a sharply caught presence. (He may have contributed something to Keats's 'holy man', the beadsman, in his own erotic romance *The Eve of St. Agnes*; and in fact Dryden's two triplets and final Alexandrine give the verse here a stanzaic effect reminiscent of the Spenserian stanza.) The whole passage is of course noticeably freer in style than the rest of the poem: more informal and colloquial, no longer heroic. Only here is the impersonal narrative voice suspended, as when Dryden with an assumed coyness makes a reference to himself ('What Thoughts he had, beseems not me to say'), while the mysterious persons referred to in the next line ('. . . some surmise he went to fast and pray') are outside the narrative situation altogether, invented on the spot to effect a bridge between the medieval romance and the poem's present readers, contemporaries

9 *Ovid's Metamorphoses by Several Hands* (1717), i. 129.

whether willingly or not of the Revd Jeremy Collier. At this moment of intimacy and privacy the poet glances at his readers who, like Sigismonda, like the priest even, like the poet himself, are all equally subject to Love's laws which are also Nature's: 'Neither you nor I can resist the power of Love.'

Sigismonda passes, then, from an unashamed sensuality, realistically and therefore (for Dryden) comically conceived, to an austere and lofty nobility of soul, a prompt withdrawal from the world. And it was, it seems, the coexistence of these two extreme states which satisfied Dryden's desire for equilibrium and for a kind of comprehensiveness. Only by showing her as a creature of imperious appetite—what Rachel Trickett calls 'a peculiarly mundane passion'[10]—could he give full imaginative credence to her subsequent exaltation. Dryden was surely right to obey his intuition. His dualistic treatment, unsparing though it is, makes his heroine not less but more believable than a simpler, more decorous one would have done; its discontinuities challenge the reader, putting heavier imaginative demands on him. The conclusive reply to C. S. Lewis here ('Dryden will presently try to make sublime this same woman') must be a pragmatic one: he did not merely try to make her sublime—he succeeded.

The incongruity of spirit in a world of bodies is a recurring theme in Dryden's poems and plays. At innumerable points there is a sense of strain, an uneasiness, in the way the physical and the spiritual realms are envisaged as fitting together. The critic who has done most towards analysing the characteristic Drydenian tonality here is D. W. Jefferson. In the course of his excellent discussion of Dryden's imagery, he remarks that one of his 'favourite *motifs* . . . is a comic conception of the human species, of the processes appertaining to its creation and procreation, and of the relation between soul and body'. And he adds: 'Matter was, for Dryden, a stimulating idea.'[11]

Dryden's treatment of Sigismonda should be seen as one further variant on this essential Drydenian theme. Readers have often noticed that his panegyrics—poems in which lofty value judgements find a natural place—may have precarious moments in which they threaten to topple over into absurdity.

[10] *The Honest Muse* (Oxford, 1967), p. 70.

[11] 'Aspects of Dryden's Imagery', *Essays in Criticism*, 4 (1954), 25.

But instead of reproving his inability to maintain 'decorum' and keep a straight face, we should perhaps rather accept it as a sign of the genuine and unofficial authenticity of his writing impulse. In *All for Love* (to take an opposing example), his failure to achieve his own personal seriousness is betrayed by the fact that the risible dimension is hardly ever admitted to the play—neither Antony nor Cleopatra is exposed (not deliberately, at any rate) to laughter or a more quizzical philosophical contemplation. Sigismonda's heroism, on the other hand, is unflinchingly located in the anarchic farcicality of the body's appetites. Unlike the sentimentalized, unphysical Cleopatra of *All for Love*, she can be thought of as having the bulk, the all-too-human rotundity of an opera singer destined for the more taxing heroic roles. But the girth of such a singer will have a mixed effect—it may give her not only a comic vulnerability but an involuntary pathos, the spirit-voice so improbably triumphing over the obstructively heavy body. Such a prima donna, in different terms, is Sigismonda, forceful, formidable, with splendid tone and stamina, but after all, as Dryden himself insists, not only a 'Heroine' but a 'Woman'.

As a poet, we may say finally, Dryden might be amused but he was also moved and excited by certain manifestations of human weakness. He was especially stirred by the idea of human beings of heroic stamp brought low by some common, not to say banal, frailty or failure. This might take the form of sexual enthralment, folly or stupidity, or a mere weakness for strong drink. It was out of this region of feeling that he created the great figures of the satires—Mac Flecknoe, Og, Doeg, and the rest—and the heroic weaklings of the plays, as well as Alexander drunk at his feast and the gods of his Homer translation drunk at theirs. It was from a similar region that his finest passage of religious poetry came—the personal confession in *The Hind and the Panther* (III. 281–97)—where the worldly weakness and pride are Dryden's own. Something of this very private feeling, or fellow-feeling, for human weakness can be found in 'Sigismonda and Guiscardo'. Not that the poem is finally anything but what it has always seemed to be—a ripely assured adaptation of a famous Italian tale. But it is also, like all the best things in the second and richer half of Dryden's career, a highly personal performance.

A Select List of the Published Writings of Dame Helen Gardner
DBE, MA, DLitt, FBA, FRSL[1]

COMPILED BY HELEN PETERS

1933

Walter Hilton and the Authorship of the *Cloud of Unknowing*', *RES*, ix. 129–47.

1936

'The Text of *The Scale of Perfection*', *Medium Ævum*, v. 11–30.
'Walter Hilton and the Mystical Tradition in England', *Essays and Studies*, xxii. 102–27.

1938

'Lawful Espials', *MLR*, xxxiii. 345–55.

1942

'The Second Part of *Tamberlaine the Great*', *MLR*, xxxvii. 18–24.
'The Recent Poetry of T. S. Eliot', *New Writing and Daylight*, Summer 1942, 84–96. Translated into French with additions in *Gants du Ciel* (Montreal, 1944), 91–109.

1944

'John Donne: A Note on Elegie V, "His Picture" ', *MLR*, xxxix. 333–7.

1946

'Notes on Donne's Verse Letters', *MLR*, xli. 318–21.

[1] This list omits scripts of discussions broadcast on BBC Third Programme and 'The Critics' during the period 1954 to 1963 together with a few other radio broadcasts. It omits, as well, readings given in St. Paul's Cathedral, 1972 and at the Mermaid Theatre, 1972–4. Reviews in the *Birmingham Post*, 1937–46 are also omitted. Finally, reprints, as opposed to revised or expanded works, are omitted.

1947

'*Four Quartets*: A Commentary', *Penguin New Writing*, ed. John Lehmann, xxix. 123–47; reprinted in *T. S. Eliot: A Study of his Writings by Several Hands*, ed. B. Rajan (Dennis Dobson, London, 1947), 57–77 and in *Critiques and Essays in Criticism 1920–1948*, ed. R. Stallman (Ronald Press, New York, 1949), 181–97: an expansion of the earlier essay.

'François Mauriac: *A Woman of the Pharisees*', *Penguin New Writing*, ed. John Lehmann, xxxi. 93–104.

Review of *The Cloud of Unknowing and the Book of Privy Counselling*, ed. Phyllis Hodgson, *Medium Ævum*, xvi. 36–42.

1948

Review of H. S. Bennett, *Chaucer and the Fifteenth Century*, *Cambridge Review*, 1 May.

'Milton's Satan and the Theme of Damnation in Elizabethan Tragedy', *English Studies*, *Essays and Studies*, NS i. 46–66.

1949

'Lord Byron', *Time and Tide*, 19 February.

Review of H. Fluchère, *Shakespeare, Dramaturge Elizabethain*, signed H. L. G., *Oxford Magazine*, 5 May.

'A Crux in Donne', letter to *TLS*, 10 June.

THE ART OF T. S. ELIOT (Cresset Press, London; Dutton, New York; Faber and Faber, London, 1968). Translated into French by Claude Guillot (Seghers, Paris, 1975).

1950

'The Cocktail Party', *Time and Tide*, 25 March.

'Byron Himself', ibid. 13 May.

'Memoirs of Percy Simpson' (unsigned), prefixed to *A List of the Published Writings of Percy Simpson* (Clarendon Press, Oxford).

1952

Memoir of Eleanor Rooke, signed H. G., *Oxford Magazine*, 21 February.

'Spatial Thinking', review of G. Wilson Knight, *Lord Byron: Christian Virtues*, *New Statesman and Nation*, 29 November.

JOHN DONNE: THE DIVINE POEMS, ed. (Clarendon Press, Oxford).

1953

'Donne's "Divine Poems" ', letter to *TLS*, 30 January.

'The Art of Preaching', review of *The Sermons of John Donne*, eds. G. R. Potter and Evelyn Simpson, *New Statesman and Nation*, 7 November.

'The Unchristened Heart', review of Donat O'Donnell, *Maria Cross*, *New Statesman and Nation*, 26 December.

1954

'The Confidential Clerk', 'Books in General', *New Statesman and Nation*, 20 March.

'Learning and Gusto', review of C. S. Lewis, *English Literature in the Sixteenth Century*, *New Statesman and Nation*, 30 October.

1955

Review of Dorothy Everett, *Essays in Middle English Literature*, signed H. G., *Oxford Magazine*, 17 November.

'The Noble Moor', *Proceedings of the British Academy*, xli. 189–205.

1956

'Milton's First Illustrator', *Essays and Studies*, NS ix. 27–38.

THE LIMITS OF LITERARY CRITICISM: REFLECTIONS ON THE INTERPRETATION OF POETRY AND SCRIPTURE, Riddell Memorial Lectures, printed for the University of Durham (Oxford University Press, London).

'Poetic Tradition in Donne', letter with J. B. Leishman to *TLS*, 11 May.

'Donne and the Church', letter to *TLS*, 25 May.

Review of M. M. Ross, *Poetry and Dogma*, *RES*, NS vii. 437–9.

1957

Review of Louis L. Martz, *The Poetry of Meditation*, *RES*, NS viii. 194–200.

'Another Note on Donne: "Since she whome I lov'd" ', *MLR*, lii. 564–5.

THE METAPHYSICAL POETS (Penguin Poets; 2nd edn. 1966; 3rd edn. 1972. Oxford University Press, London 1961; 2nd edn. 1967; 3rd edn. 1972).

'Shakespearean Critics', review of James Winney, *The Frame of Order*, Kenneth Muir, *Shakespeare's Sources*, M. M. Mahood, *Shakespeare's Word Play*, Margaret Webster, *Shakespeare Today*, *London Magazine*, December, 73–8.

1958

Review of E. M. W. Tillyard, *The Metaphysicals and Milton* and K. Svendsen, *Milton and Science*, *Oxford Magazine*, 30 January.

'Symbolic Equations', review of A. C. Wilson, *W. B. Yeats and Tradition*, *New Statesman and Nation*, 1 February; with subsequent correspondence, 15 February and 8 March.

'The World of C. P. Snow', 'Books in General', ibid. 29 March.

'Don Juan', review of T. G. Steffan and W. W. Pratt, Variorum Edition, *London Magazine*, July, 58–65.

Review of Austin Warren, *Richard Crashaw: A Study in Baroque Sensibility*, 2nd edn., *RES*, NS ix. 344–5.

'The Aged Eagle Spreads his Wings', interview with T. S. Eliot on his seventieth birthday, *Sunday Times*, 21 September.

Review of *The Songs and Sonets of John Donne*, ed. T. Redpath, *RES*, NS ix. 451–2.

Review of Geoffrey Keynes, Kt., *A Bibliography of Dr. John Donne*, 3rd edn., *Book Collector*, vii. 432–5.

1959

THE SONNETS OF WILLIAM ALABASTER, ed. with G. M. Story (Clarendon Press, Oxford).

Review of Grover Smith, *T. S. Eliot's Poetry and Plays: A Study in Sources and Meaning*, *RES*, NS x. 101–3.

'What the Poet Wrote', review of Fredson Bowers, *Textual and Literary Criticism*, *New Statesman and Nation*, 18 April.

'As You Like It', *More Talking of Shakespeare*, ed. John Garrett (Longman's, London), 17–32.

THE BUSINESS OF CRITICISM: THE PROFESSION OF A CRITIC, lectures delivered at the University of London (1953) and THE LIMITS OF LITERARY CRITICISM, Riddell Memorial Lectures (1956), (Clarendon Press, Oxford).

'The Academic Study of English Literature', *Critical Quarterly*, i. 106–15.

'The Argument about "The Ecstasy" ', ELIZABETHAN AND JACOBEAN STUDIES, presented to F. P. Wilson, ed. with Herbert Davis (Clarendon Press, Oxford), 279–306.

1960

'Latin at Oxford', *Encounter*, xiv. 64–5.

'The Case for Compulsory Latin', *American Oxonian*, xlvii. 1–5.

'Donne MSS. for the Bodleian', *TLS*, 11 March.

Review of George Williamson, *Seventeenth-Century Contexts*, *Listener*, 8 September.

Review of C. S. Lewis, *Studies in Words*, *Listener*, 22 September.

Article on John Donne, signed Hn. G. *Encyclopaedia Britannica.*

Review of R. E. L. Strider, *Robert Greville, Lord Brooke*, *MLR*, lv. 268.

Review of Staffan Bergsten, *Time and Eternity: A Study in the Structure and Symbolism of T. S. Eliot's Four Quartets*, *Studia Neophilologica*, xxxii. 368–71.

1961

Edwin Muir, W. D. Thomas Memorial Lecture, University College of Swansea (1960), (University of Wales Press, Cardiff).

Review of W. K. Wimsatt and Cleanth Brooks, *Literary Criticism: A Short History*, *RES*, NS xii. 220–4.

Introduction to *The Poems of George Herbert* (World's Classics, 109, 2nd edn., Oxford University Press, London).

'Empson's Milton', review of William Empson, *Milton's God*, *Listener*, 5 October.

Review of D. C. Allen, *Image and Meaning: Metaphoric Traditions in Renaissance Poetry*, *JEGP*, lx. 576–81.

1962

Article on John Donne, *Concise Encyclopaedia of English and American Poetry*, eds. S. Spender and D. Hall (Hutchinson, London), 81–6.

Essays on 'The Good Morrow', 'A Valediction: forbidding Mourning', and 'The Sunne Rising' for British Council *Notes on Literature*, no. 17.

TWENTIETH CENTURY VIEWS: JOHN DONNE; A COLLECTION OF CRITICAL ESSAYS, ed. (Prentice Hall, Englewood Cliffs, New Jersey).

Review of T. S. Eliot, *George Herbert*, *Listener*, 27 December.

1963

Obituary of Percy Simpson, signed H. G., *Oxford Magazine*, 7 February.

Obituary of F. P. Wilson, *The Times*, 30 May.

'Ideal Elizabethans', review of John Buxton, *Elizabethan Taste*, *Manchester Guardian*, 2 August.

Obituary of Evelyn Simpson, *The Times*, 12 September.

Article on T. S. Eliot, signed Hn. G., *Encyclopaedia Britannica*.

'In Praise of Milton', review of Christopher Ricks, *Milton's Grand Style* and Anne D. Ferry, *Milton's Epic Verse*, *Listener*, 10 October.

'Two Ministers', *Spectator*, 13 December.

1964

Review of Kenneth Muir, *Life and Letters of Sir Thomas Wyatt*, *Listener*, 2 April.

'Shakespeare in the Age of Eliot', *TLS*, 23 April.

'Hotson's Choice', review of Leslie Hotson, *Mr. W.H.*, *Listener*, 28 May.

Review of John Sparrow, *Independent Essays*, *RES*, NS xv. 229–31.

Review of C. S. Lewis, *The Discarded Image*, *Listener*, 16 July.

Review of W. R. Mueller, *John Donne Preacher*, *RES*, NS xv. 341.

Review of *John Donne: The Anniversaries*, ed. Frank Manley, *JEGP*, lxiii. 780–4.

1965

Reply to Hugh Sykes Davies, *Review of English Literature*, vi, no. 1. 108–10.

'Johnson on Shakespeare', *New Rambler*, xvii, June, 2–12.

JOHN DONNE: THE ELEGIES AND THE SONGS AND SONNETS, ed. (Clarendon Press, Oxford).

Obituary of R. C. Bald, *The Times*, 26 August.

'Donne's Platane Tree', letter to *TLS*, 26 August.

Review of Morris Weitz, *Hamlet and the Philosophy of Literary Criticism*, *Shakespeare Quarterly*, xvi. 262–3.

A READING OF PARADISE LOST, The Alexander Lectures, University of Toronto (1962) (Clarendon Press, Oxford).

'Clive Staples Lewis', obituary, *Proceedings of the British Academy*, li. 417–28.

1966

'The Comedies of T. S. Eliot', a lecture delivered to the Royal Society of Literature (1965), *Sewanee Review*, lxxiv. 153–75 and in *Essays by Diverse Hands*, NS xxxiv. 55–73.

T. S. Eliot and the English Poetic Tradition, Byron Foundation Lecture, no. 36 (1965), University of Nottingham.

'The Titles of Donne's Poems', *Friendship's Garland, Essays presented to Mario Praz*, ed. Vittorio Gabrieli (Edizioni di Storia e Letteratura, Rome), 2 vols. i. 189–207.

'John Donne', reply to William Empson, *Critical Quarterly*, viii. 374–7.

1967

JOHN DONNE: SELECTED PROSE, selected by Evelyn Simpson, ed. with Timothy Healy (Clarendon Press, Oxford).

King Lear, John Coffin Memorial Lecture, University of London (1966), printed for the University of London (Athlone Press, London).

'Ill Donne: Well Donne', letter to *TLS*, 8 June.

'Herbert John Davis', obituary, signed H. G., *Oxford Magazine*, 16 June.

'On Editing Donne', letter to *TLS*, 24 August.

Literary Studies, Inaugural Lecture at the University of Oxford (Clarendon Press, Oxford).

Review of J. B. Leishman, *The Art of Marvell's Poetry*, *RES*, NS xviii. 464–6.

1968

' "Othello": A Retrospect, 1900–67', *Shakespeare Survey*, xxi. 1–11.

'The Landscapes of Eliot's Poetry', Robert Spence Watson Lecture, Newcastle Literary and Philosophical Society (1966), *Critical Quarterly*, x. 313–30.

'Herbert John Davis', obituary, *Proceedings of the British Academy*, liv. 289–99.

1969

F. P. WILSON: SHAKESPEAREAN AND OTHER STUDIES, ed. (Clarendon Press, Oxford).

'T. S. Eliot: Explorer of Moral Distress', Reassessment 9, *New Statesman*, 28 November.

Letter to *Critical Quarterly*, xi. 375.

1970

'The Professorship of Poetry', letter to *Oxford Magazine*, 6 February.

'All the Facts', review of R. C. Bald, *John Donne: A Life*, *New Statesman*, 13 March.

F. P. WILSON: SHAKESPEARE AND THE NEW BIBLIOGRAPHY, revised and ed. (Clarendon Press, Oxford).

' "The Dream of the Rood", an Exercise in Verse-Translation', *Essays and Poems presented to Lord David Cecil*, ed. W. W. Robson (Constable, London), 18–36.

'Johnson *Improvisatore*', Presidential Address to the Johnson Society, Lichfield, *Transactions of the Johnson Society*, 34–47.

1971

RELIGION AND LITERATURE: RELIGION AND TRAGEDY, T. S. Eliot Memorial Lectures, Canterbury (1968), and RELIGIOUS POETRY, Ewing Lectures, California (1966) (Faber and Faber, London; Oxford University Press, New York).

'Altered in Fulfilment', review of *The Waste Land: A Facsimile and Transcript*, ed. Valerie Eliot, and Robert Sencourt, *T. S. Eliot: A Memoir*, *New Statesman*, 12 November.

'T. S. Eliot', *Harvard English Studies*, 2, *Twentieth-Century Literature in Retrospect*, 27–44.

1972

'Donne's Verse-letter', letter to *TLS*, 21 January.

'The Waste Land', letter to *TLS*, 4 February.

THE FABER BOOK OF RELIGIOUS VERSE, ed. (Faber and Faber, London; Oxford University Press, New York).

'Donne the Preacher', *A City Tribute to John Donne* (Grosvenor Press, Portsmouth).

THE NEW OXFORD BOOK OF ENGLISH VERSE, 1250–1950, ed. (Clarendon Press, Oxford; Oxford University Press, New York).

The Waste Land: 1972, Adamson Lecture (Manchester University Press).

'The "Metempsychosis" of John Donne', *TLS*, 29 December.

John Donne's holograph of 'A Letter to the Lady Carey and Mrs Essex Riche', published with a facsimile by Scolar Mansell in conjunction with the Bodleian Library, Oxford.

Poems in the Making, the first Gwilym Jones Memorial Lecture, University of Southampton.

1973

' "The Waste Land": Paris 1922', *Eliot in His Time*, ed. A. W. Litz (Princeton University Press, Princeton, New Jersey), 67–94.

1974

'Milton's "Talent" ', Letter to *TLS*, 1 February.

Entry on John Donne, *The Oxford Dictionary of the Christian Church*, 2nd edn., eds. F. L. Cross and E. A. Livingstone (Oxford University Press, London), 419–20.

1975

'The Great Cloud of Witnesses', the University Sermon preached in the University Church of St. Mary the Virgin, Oxford (16 June 1974), *Christian*, ii. 201–8.

'The Novels of Joyce Cary', *Essays and Studies*, NS xxviii. 76–93.

'Through Fair and Foul', letter to *TLS*, 25 July.

1976

Preface to *Joyce Cary: Selected Essays*, ed. A. G. Bishop (Michael Joseph, London).

'James Coutts Maxwell', *Notes and Queries*, NS xxiii. 194–5.

1978

'Dr. Leavis and Mr. Eliot', *The Times*, 7 January.

THE COMPOSITION OF 'FOUR QUARTETS' (Faber and Faber, London; Oxford University Press, New York).

JOHN DONNE: THE DIVINE POEMS, ed., 2nd revised edn. (Clarendon Press, Oxford).

'Tragic Mysteries', *Shakespeare: Pattern of Excelling Nature*, eds. David Bevington and Jay L. Halio, International Shakespeare Association Conference, Washington (1976) (University of Delaware Press, Cranbury, N.J.), 88–94.

1979

'Dean Donne's Monument in St. Paul's', *Evidence in Literary Scholarship: Essays in Memory of James Marshall Osborn*, eds. René Wellek and Alvaro Ribeiro (Clarendon Press, Oxford), 29–44.

Index

Abondio, Antonio, 2
Addison, Joseph, 271, 273
Aeschylus, 117–18, 121, 123
Alabaster, William, 294
Albertus Magnus, 194, 201, 204
Alfonso II (of Este), 6
Allen, D. C., 295
Allott, Robert, 50
Almansi, Guido, 286
Alsworth, Daniel, 234
Andreae, J. V., 189
Anna Karenina, 13
Apollonius of Rhodes, 5
Appius and Virginia, 135
Aquinas, St. Thomas, 161–2, 164–7 170–1, 181
Ariosto, Lodovico, 42
Aristophanes, 36, 54
Aristotle, 33, 35, 38, 161–2, 183, 194, 199
Arlington, Earl of (Henry Bennet), 253
Arne, Thomas, 42
Ascensius, Jodocus Badius, 232
Auden, W. H., 262
Augustine, St., 161, 183

Babb, L., 188
Bacchylides, 258–9
Bacon, Francis, 21, 52, 165, 167, 174, 193, 197, 254
Bald, R. C., 295, 297
Barbarino, Bartolomeo, 41
Barton, Anne, 83
Battenhouse, Roy W., 17, 18
Bedford, Lucy, Countess of, 54
Bedingfield, Thomas, 183
Bellini, Giovanni, 6
Bembo, Pietro, 36
Bennett, H. S., 292
Bergsten, Staffan, 294
Bernard, St., 163
Bernini, Giovanni, 283
Bidle, John, 233
Blake, William, 13; *Songs of Innocence and Experience*, 12
Blissett, W. F., 75
Boccaccio, Giovanni, 279–80, 282–5
Bodin, Jean, 190
Borges, Jorge Luis, 12
Botticelli, Sandro, 10
Bowers, Fredson, 294
Bowra, Sir Maurice, 257–8
Boyle, Elizabeth, 53
Bradley, A. C., 18, 74, 77–8, 87–8
Brinsley, John, 233–4, 237–9, 241
Broadbent, J. B., 272
Brooke, Nicholas, 74, 76
Brooks, Cleanth, 294
Browne, Sir Thomas, 169, 182, 211
Browne, William, 42, 212–13
Browning, Robert, 6
Buckingham, Duke of (George Villiers), 21
Budé, Guillaume, 184, 190
Bullough, Geoffrey, 111–12
Burton, Robert, 179–93, 195, 201–2, 207
Buxton, John, 295
Byron, George Gordon, sixth Baron, 292–3

Calvin, Jean, 165, 173
Calzabigi, Ranieri, 36
Camoens, Luis de, 257–8
Campi, Bernardino, 9
Campion, Thomas, 42, 97, 112
Cardano, Girolamo (Cardan), 179–94, 205
Cary, Joyce, 298
Casaubon, Issac, 232
Cavalieri, Emilio del, 41
Cecil, Lord David, 297
Cellini, Benvenuto, 186
Chapman, George, 48, 50
Charles I, 8, 105, 215, 217, 263
Charles II, 218, 219, 253
Charron, Pierre, 195
Chaucer, Geoffrey, 284
Chekhov, Anton, 13, 24
Chester, Robert, 44–5, 47–8, 52, 55
Cicero, 183, 196, 208

Clarendon, Earl of (Edward Hyde), 246
Cleveland, John, 176
Clobery, Christopher, 221
Colie, R. L., 189
Collier, Jeremy, 289
Cope, Jackson, 271
Corbett family, 51
Cortegiano, Il, 10, 53
Coulson, C. A., 140
Cowley, Abraham, 176–7
Crane, Ralph, 65
Crashaw, Richard, 178, 293
Cromwell, Oliver, 21, 24, 218, 246–7, 250-1
Cudworth, Ralph, 167, 178

Daniel, Samuel, 48, 97, 105, 212
Dante, 210, 258, 274–5
Da Ponte, Lorenzo, 42
Davenant, Sir William, 42
Davies, Hugh Sykes, 295
Davies, John, 212
Davis, Herbert, 294, 296
Dekker, Thomas, 41, 97, 101, 107
Del Ferro, Scipione, 181
Derby, Countess of (Alice Stanley), 143
Derby, fourth Earl of (Henry Stanley), 44
Derby, fifth Earl of (Ferdinando Stanley), 46
Derby, sixth Earl of (William Stanley), 46
Desborough, Nathaniel, 249–50, 253
Desmond, Earl of (James Fitzgerald), 46
Dessen, Alan, 16, 17
Devereux, Penelope, 27
Digby, Sir Kenelm, 194, 203
Dolce, Lodovico, 10
Donne, John, 52, 141–50, 151–63, 164–79, 183, 200, 210, 254, 291–8
Dossi, Dosso, 6
Dover Wilson, J., 63
Drayton, Michael, 135, 212
Drummond, William, 200
Drury, Elizabeth, 158
Dryden, John, 262, 279–90
du Bellay, Guillaume, 36
Duchess of Malfi, The, 26, 37, 42, 280–1
Duns Scotus, Joannes, 169–70, 171
Dutton, William, 249

Egerton, John (first Earl of Bridgewater), 144–5
Egerton, Sir Thomas (Baron Ellesmere) 141–4
Egerton, Sir Thomas (the younger), 141–50
Eliot, T. S., 33–5, 175, 254–7, 259, 261–2, 264, 267, 276, 291–2, 294–8
Elizabeth I, 47, 55, 99, 107, 143, 160
Ellwood, Thomas, 270
Empson, William, 295, 296
England's Helicon, 54
Erasmus, Desiderius, 184, 187, 189, 191–2
Essex, Earl of (Robert Devereux), 24, 55, 142
Eugene Onegin, 13
Euripides, 36, 43, 122
Evelyn, John, 248
Everett, Barbara, 74
Everett, Dorothy, 293

Farnaby, Thomas, 233–4, 237
Farnham, Willard, 17
Félibien, André, 199
Ferdinand I, 9
Ferrard, Jaques, 190
Ferry, Ann D., 295
Filosseno, Marcello, 36, 40
Firth, C. H., 246
Fish, S. E., 188
Fleming, Abraham, 233–4, 237
Fletcher, Giles, 212
Fletcher, John, 15
Fletcher, Phineas, 212
Florio, John, 189, 191
Fluchère, H., 292
Ford, John, 14, 15, 17, 18; *Broken Heart*, 19, 26, 27, 28; *Perkin Warbeck*, 19; *'Tis Pity She's a Whore*, 19
Fowler, Alastair, 251–9
Fracastoro, Girolamo, 181
Frye, Northrop, 189

Gabrieli, Vittorio, 296
Galen, 192
Galileo Galilei, 18, 266
Gallus, Cornelius, 231, 235, 237–9, 241–2
Gardner, Dame Helen, 1, 18, 23, 34*n*., 147, 157–8, 161
Gauradas, 36
Gebauer, G. E., 228, 231

Gell, Robert, 225
Gil, Alexander, 224
Godshalk, W. L., 15
Goethe, Johann Wolfgang von, 186
Gonzaga, Federigo, 9
Goodere (Goodyer), Sir Henry, 148, 155–6
Gorraeus, Richardus, 233
Gosson, Stephen, 30
Gow, A. S. F., 231
Gray, Thomas, 254
Greene, Robert, 114–16, 118–19
Greg, Sir Walter, 56
Gregory, St., 196–7
Greville, Fulke, 4
Grew, Nehemiah, 194–6, 198, 200–3
Grierson, Sir Herbert, 141, 146–7
Groto, Luigi, 38
Guarini, Giovanni Battista, 36–7

Hakewill, George, 208–9
Halsall, Dorothy, 46
Hammond, William, 176
Hanford, J. H., 229
Harding, Davis P., 232
Hardy, Thomas, 35, 43
Harrison, G. B., 27
Hartlib, Samuel, 249
Harvey, William, 182
Havelock, Eric A., 31
Hay, Lord, 96, 112–13
Hazlitt, William, 15, 31
Heinsius, Daniel, 232, 234–5
Heliodorus (of Emesa), 6
Henri III, 3
Henry VII, 98–9, 107
Henry, Prince (son of James I), 105, 113
Herbert, Edward (Lord Herbert of Cherbury), 41, 154–5, 178
Herbert, George, 175–6, 196–8, 200, 294–5
Herbert, Mary, Countess of Pembroke, 4, 7
Hermes Trismegistus, 204
Herodotus, 50
Hessus, Helius Eobanus, 233–4
Heywood, Thomas, 169
Highmore, Nathaniel, 200–201
Hill, Christopher, 21
Hilliard, Nicholas, 4
Hilton, Walter, 291–2
Hippocrates, 192
Histriomastix, 184
Hobbes, Thomas, 23, 24
Holinshed, Raphael, 111
Holland, Philemon, 9, 51
Homer, 33, 38, 177, 195, 258
Hooke, Robert, 203
Hooker, Richard, 52
Hotson, Leslie, 295
Hunter, George K., 55

Jaggard, Isaac, 56
James I, 94, 97–100, 104, 110, 112, 149, 160
Jefferson, D. W., 289
Johnson, Samuel, 32, 76, 254, 295, 297
Jones, Inigo, 97, 112
Jonson, Benjamin, 1, 16, 17, 41–2, 46, 48, 50, 52, 65, 97, 100, 103, 105, 106, 118, 149, 254
Jorgenson, Paul, 87
Jusserand, J. J., 2

Keats, John, 280, 288
Kepler, Johann, 208
Kermode, Frank, 225, 272–3
Keynes, Sir Geoffrey, 294
King, Edward, 242–3
Kircher, Athanasius, 204
Kittredge, J. L., 64
Knight, G. Wilson, 292
Knights, L. C., 78
Kocher, Paul H., 23

Labadie, Jean, 245
Lamb, Charles, 187
Lambert, Akaka, 250
Lamotius, Fredericus, 232, 235
Languet, Hubert, 1, 2, 3, 4, 10
La Primaudaye, Pierre de, 205
Lawall, Gilbert, 131
Lawes, Henry, 42
Leavis, F. R., 254, 298
Lee, Desmond, 31
Lehmann, John, 292
Leicester, Earl of (Robert Dudley), 9, 212–13
Leishman, J. B., 293, 296
Leslie, Nancy T., 20
Leti, Gregorio, 249–52
Levey, Michael, 2, 8, 11
Levy, F. J., 2
Lewis, C. S., 287–8, 293–4, 295, 296
Lipsius, Justus, 184

Lisle, William, 233
Lister, Martin, 248, 252
Litz, A. W., 297
Louis XIV, 246
Lucian, 189
Ludlow, Edmund, 253

MacCaffrey, Isabel, 271
Machaut, Guillaume de, 34
Machiavelli, Niccolo di Bernardo dei, 20, 22
Mackail, J. W., 256–7
Mahood, M. M., 293
Maier, Michael, 204, 209
Malone, Edmond, 63
Mancinelli, Antonio, 233
Marks, Carol, 74
Marlowe, Christopher, 1, 14, 15, 20, 23, 31, 258; *Dr Faustus*, 16, 25; *Tamburlaine*, 17, 20, 21, 22, 24, 31, 291
Marriot, John, 145–6
Marston, John, 48, 50, 52
Martz, Louis, 274–5, 293
Marvell, Andrew, 12, 13, 175, 177, 226, 248–9, 296
Mary Stuart, 34
Masson, David, 245
Mauriac, François, 292
Maximilian II, 2, 5, 6
Maxwell, J. C., 298
Marazin, Jules, 247, 251–2
Mead, Joseph, 195
Medawar, P. B., 17
Melanchthon, Philip, 184, 234–4, 237, 242
Meursius, Joannes, 232
Middleton, Thomas, 14, 97; *Women Beware Women*, 15
Milton, John, 13, 22, 42, 165, 168–9, 177–8, 212–27, 228–44, 245–53, 254–70, 271–8, 292, 295, 298; *Ad Patrem*, 225; *At a Vacation Exercise*, 262; *Comus*, 134; *De Doctrina Christiana*, 223, 274; *Defensio Prima*, 263; *Defensio Secunda*, 249; *L'Allegro*, 12; *Lycidas*, 228–44; *Il Penseroso*, 12; *Paradise Lost*, 12, 207–8, 226, 254–70, 271–8, 296; *Paradise Regained*, 218, 226, 257, 264; *Samson Agonistes*, 225, 226, 262
Moby Dick, 25
Montaigne, Michel Eyquem de, 189, 191–2
More, Ann, 143
More, Sir George, 143
More, Henry, 178, 208, 210
Morley, Henry, 179, 186–7
Mornay, Philippe de, 200
Mozart, Wolfgang Amadeus, 42
Mueller, W. R., 295
Muir, Edwin, 294
Muir, Kenneth, 293, 295
Mulryne, J. R., 15
Munday, Anthony, 97
Murdoch, Iris, 31
Mylius, J. Daniel, 317

Naudé, Gabriel, 186
Nedham, Marchamont, 215
Nemesius, 220, 223
Nero (emperor), 9
Newton, Thomas, 228
Nice Wanton, The, 138
Nicolson, Marjorie, 272

O'Donnell, Donat, 292
Oedipus Rex, 25
Origen, 210
Osborn, J. M., 2
Overton, Richard, 223
Ovid, 235, 288; *Metamorphoses*, 36, 37, 235

Paracelsus, 203, 206
Parnassus Plays, The, 184
Parry, Robert, 46
Passionate Pilgrim, The, 54
Pearse, Nancy Cotton, 15
Peele, George, 41
Pembroke, third Earl of (William Herbert), 47, 213
Petrarch, 38
Philip II, 3, 5, 6
Plato, 12, 27, 28, 29, 30, 31, 229; *The Republic*, 14, 28
Pliny (the Elder), 51, 208
Plutarch, 114
Poirier, Michel, 22
Poliziano, Angelo, 35, 36, 37, 38, 39–40
Pope, Alexander, 177, 263
Popper, K. R., 31
Poussin, Nicolas, 199
Prodromos, Theodore, 36
Puttenham, George, 35, 38

Quadrio, Francesco Saviero, 35
Quintilian, Marcus Fabius, 35

Rabelais, François, 189, 191–2
Rajan, B., 292
Ralegh, Sir Walter, 212
Ramus, Peter, 233, 237–8
Raven, Charles, 253
Ray, John, 246, 248
Riccius, Stephanus, 233, 237, 242
Ricks, Christopher, 295
Rider, John, 235
Robson, W. W., 297
Ronsard, Pierre de, 36
Rooke, Eleanor, 292
Rosenburg, John D., 75, 76
Ross, M. M., 293
Rowse, A. L., 256–7
Rudolf II (emperor), 7
Rugoff, M. A., 151

Sadeler, Aegidius, 9
Salingar, L. G., 15
Salkeld, John, 167, 173
Salmasius (Claude de Saumaise), 245
Salusbury, Ferdinando, 46
Salusbury, Jane, 45
Salusbury, Sir John, 44, 46–8, 55
Salusbury, Lady (*née* Ursula Stanley), 44–6, 48, 55
Salusbury, Thomas, 44, 47–8
Sannazzaro, Jacopo, 6, 10
Scaliger, Joseph Justus, 189, 232, 234
Scaliger, Julius Caesar, 35, 186
Schleiner, Winfried, 162
Scrope, Jane, 51
Scudamore, James, 249
Selden, John, 215
Sencourt, Robert, 297
Serafino dell' Aquila, 36, 40
Servius, Marius Honoratus, 233, 237, 239–40
Settle, Elkanah, 42
Shadwell, Thomas, 42
Shakespeare, William, 1, 30, 31, 32, 33, 132–40, 191, 254, 292–3, 294–7, *All's Well that Ends Well*, 56–73, 135, 136; *Antony and Cleopatra*, 132, 153; *Cymbeline*, 94–113; *Hamlet*, 52, 132, 183, 296; *Henry IV*, 16; *Henry V*, 136; *2 Henry VI*, 134; *Henry VIII*, 104; *King John*, 134, 136; *King Lear*, 27, 28, 31, 74–93, 106, 133–4, 138–9, 277, 296; *Love's Labour's Lost*, 54, 136; *Macbeth*, 25, 111; *Measure for Measure*, 135, 138; *Merchant of Venice*, 136; *Othello*, 16, 132, 134, 293, 296; *Phoenix and Turtle*, 44–55; *Richard II*, 24; *Richard III*, 133, 136, 137; *Timon of Athens*, 5, 133, 135; *Troilus and Cressida*, 136; *Twelfth Night*, 133; *Venus and Adonis* 11, 37; *Winter's Tale*, 113, 114–31, 135, 137, 138
Sharrock, Robert, 203
Shelley, P. B., 29, 263
Sidney, Sir Philip, 1–11, 55, 212; *Arcadia*, 1, 2, 4, 5, 11, 40–1; *Astrophel and Stella*, 54–5; *Defence of Leicester*, 9; *Defence of Poetry*, 1, 7
Simonides, 118
Simpson, Evelyn, 295
Simpson, Percy, 292, 295
Skelton, John, 51
Skippon, Philip, 246–8, 252–3
Smith, Gregory, 30
Smith, Grover, 294
Snow, C. P., 293
Sophocles, 118
Sparrow, John, 295
Spenser, Edmund, 1, 47, 49, 53, 165, 212; *Faerie Queene*, 47, 49; *Fowre Hymnes*, 10
Spingarn, Joel, 30
Spranger, Bartholomaeus, 7
Stallman, R., 292
Stampfer, J., 75
Stavig, Mark, 15, 18, 19, 25
Stendhal (Henri Marie Beyle), 26
Sterne, Laurence, 288
Stesichorus, 231, 235
Stilbes, 36
Stoppio, Niccolò, 3
Strider, R. E. L., 294
Suetonius, 9
Surrey, Robert, Earl of, 36, 38, 40
Swift, Jonathan, 189, 266

Tasso, Torquato, 258
Tertullian, 196
Theocritus, 228–44
Thoms, W. J., 7
Thou, Jacques-Auguste de, 186
Three Ladies of London, The, 138
Thurloe, John, 248
Tillyard, E. M. W., 118, 243, 293
Timaeus, 231, 235
Tintoretto (Jacopo Robusti), 2, 3, 5
Titian (Tiziano Vecelli), 1–11
Tostato, Alonso, 181

Tourneur, Cyril, 15; *Atheist's Tragedy*, 18
Traherne, Thomas, 169, 176, 179
Trickett, Rachel, 289
Tyrone, Earl of (Hugh O'Neill), 142
Tzetzes, John, 36

Valerianus, Joannes Pierius, 233
Van Doren, Mark, 287
Van Laan, Thomas, 75
Vasari, Giorgio, 3
Vaughan, Henry, 165, 175–6, 178, 198–200
Veronese, Paolo, 2, 3, 5, 8
Vesalius, Andreas, 182
Vespasian, 9
Vignère, Blaise de, 206
Virgil, 12, 177, 228–44, 258
Vives, Juan Luis, 233, 240–1

Waith, Eugene M., 13
Waldock, A. J. A., 271–2
Waldron, F. G., 146
Walsingham, Sir Frances, 212–13
Walton, Izaak, 141
Walton, J. K., 74
Warren, Austin, 293
Webster, Margaret, 293
Weitz, Morris, 296
Wethey, Harold E., 3, 5, 7–10
Williamson, George, 294
Wilson, A. C., 293
Wilson, F. P., 294–7
Wimsatt, W. K., 294
Winney, James, 293
Wither, George, 212–27
Woodhouse, A. S. P., 228
Woodward, Rowland, 149
Wordsworth, William, 287
Wotton, Edward, 2
Wyatt, Sir Thomas, 36, 38, 39–40, 295
Wynn, Blanch, 46

Yeats, W. B., 29, 293

Relationship between literary and painting
& music & heraldry
on Bibliography / textual crit.

Good piece on Dance & Cons

Juxtaposition — Ellrodt & Carey
pieces